Books by
LOUISE HALL THARP

A Sounding Trumpet
*Julia Ward Howe and the Battle Hymn
of the Republic*

Champlain: Northwest Voyager

Company of Adventurers
The Story of the Hudson's Bay Company

The Peabody Sisters of Salem

Until Victory
Horace Mann and Mary Peabody

UNTIL VICTORY

Horace Mann

When Mary Peabody Mann finished her biography of her husband she decided not to include a picture of Horace Mann because none did him justice. Then Sophia Hawthorne drew a pencil sketch of Mann from memory and with the help of daguerreotypes. This Mary sent to John Sartain, English-born pioneer illustrator of American periodicals. He "engraved . . . in mezzo-tint . . . my sister's drawing of my husband," Mary said. "It is exquisitely done."

Until Victory

HORACE MANN and MARY PEABODY

by

LOUISE HALL THARP

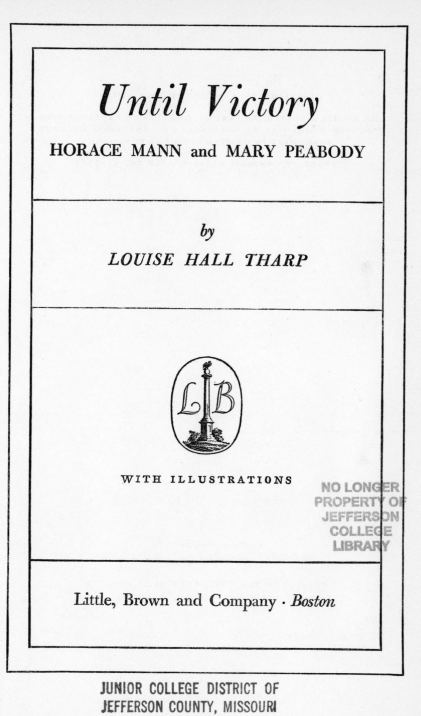

WITH ILLUSTRATIONS

Little, Brown and Company · *Boston*

Published simultaneously
in Canada by McClelland and Stewart Limited

PRINTED IN THE UNITED STATES OF AMERICA
BY THE HADDON CRAFTSMEN, SCRANTON, PA.

To Horace Mann
third of the name

. . . neither painter nor biographer
can carry out his task satisfactorily
unless he be admitted behind the scenes.

— ALEXANDER SMITH

Be ashamed to die until you have won some victory
for humanity.

— HORACE MANN
*Commencement Address,
Antioch College, 1859*

Contents

xii   *Contents*

Illustrations

UNTIL VICTORY

CHAPTER ONE

Mr. Mann of Dedham

THE weather was "severely cold" even for Boston. Fresh-fallen snow lay across the Common, while on Beacon Hill, "on a spot of ground in Boston commonly called the governor's pasture," the Bulfinch State House carried new and additional moldings and cornices of pure white — an arctic order.

Emerging from the Exchange Coffee House on Congress Street, on this seventh day of January, 1829, a tall young man buttoned his greatcoat [1] against the cold and climbed Cornhill with confident strides. Upon the steps of the capitol he paused, standing very straight [2] — a habit of his. There was "not enough snow for good sleighing," the *Boston Patriot and Mercantile Advertiser* had said, "but a few sleighs are out." And now the young man caught the sound — joyful as children's laughter — bright as his own hopes — the sound of sleighbells! His strongly marked features were so expressive of his inner thoughts that "radiant" described him.

"Who is he?" people asked, turning to look at him again.

"Just a country lawyer — not well known in Boston," would have been the reply from some of the senators now pushing their way into the State House to escape the cold. But five hundred and one representatives were also convening for the short session of the legislature this morning and all five hundred could have told who this particular one of their number was. It was Mr. Mann of Dedham.

The solemn tones of the clocks beginning to strike the hour of ten caused Horace Mann to turn quickly, cross the capitol rotunda and mount the stairs, two at a time. On the second floor in the north corner, the representatives were crowding into their small but elegant assembly room. And now those who had failed to notice the outside world, all freshly re-created by the snow, were forced to observe much that was new and changed within. During the winter recess, carpenters had been at work.

Gone was the gallery which had cut the light from the north windows. The speaker's desk (with the snuffbox still upon it, however) had been shifted from the north to the south end of the room, and the members' chairs — new and more comfortable ones — had been turned accordingly. No longer could petitioners and visitors crowd between the speaker and the representatives. A new gallery was provided for them over the entrance doors, beneath the fine barrel vault with its patriotic arabesques of Federal blue and white. All well and good. There were nods of approval.

But the gilded codfish which hung by wires from the ceiling had also swung around. This symbol of Boston's prosperity no longer faced the sea from whence he came. Now the codfish was headed upstream! [3] There was laughter as it was observed that the codfish was a wise old fellow. He was looking for the Merrimack, where the Appleton and Lowell mills were the new source of wealth for the Commonwealth of Massachusetts. Among the representatives favoring the shipping interests, however, and using the great names of Forbes and Perkins to conjure with, the laughter was a trifle forced.

Making his way to his reoriented seat, Horace Mann knew from experience that certain of his colleagues would never change their point of view, no matter how often it pleased the state to shift their chairs. A surprising number of the representatives were orthodox ministers, for example — determined to keep the church under the control of the state as in old Puritan days. Horace Mann had already come into conflict with these. He believed ardently in the rights of the individual and his maiden speech had been in defense of "religious liberty."

At least two hundred of the representatives styled themselves "farmers." The golden codfish might change his course but the farmers kept a course of their own, sturdily independent. They were somewhat the foe of both factory and shipping and some of them could still remember tales their fathers told of the fight for freedom at Bunker Hill and Lexington. With these men Horace Mann rarely quarreled. His own father had been a patriot farmer from Franklin, Massachusetts.

But there was a new element in the legislature in this year of change. "Mechanics" they called themselves when, in the next election, forty-four of them won seats. They were Jackson democrats and, in the opinion of many New Englanders, they would change course with every shift of the political wind. The State House codfish would have been a better symbol for them (or at least for their leaders) had it been a weathervane.

Friend and admirer of John Quincy Adams, Mann had come to the legislature as a National Republican. He joined enthusiastically in the legislative vote of confidence in President Adams when Adams was accused of making a deal with Clay. The recent Jackson victory caused little rejoicing in Massachusetts, since it was of course President Adams' home state. "Jackson clubs" were beginning to spring up, however, among the immigrants and day laborers who were building a greater Boston at scandalously low wages. Yet these were the very people the National Republicans were pledged to help.

Which way would Horace Mann turn in these days of change? He was one of the youngest members of the House of Representatives and he had been elected in 1827 — only two years previously. Probably no one bothered to ask him where he stood in 1829 when the codfish changed its course. But one thing was certain: Horace Mann would stand firm against a dangerous new force for which a new word had been coined, "mobocracy." It was the word "justice" that was most often on Horace Mann's lips, and justice he would do to the best of his ability.

On February 26, 1829, the *Boston Patriot* carried the text of an order in the House. "Ordered that Messers Mann of Dedham, Lord of Lancaster and Denny of Leicester be a committee to examine the practicability and expediency of erecting or procuring at the expense of the Commonwealth, an asylum for the safeguarding of lunatics and persons furiously mad. . . ."

"Unassisted and against great odds," Mann had brought about this first move — had laid the groundwork for his first great victory for humanity. There had already been many conferences, so that Speaker Calhoun knew what to expect when he gave Horace Mann the floor that February day. And with the formality that was the fashion, Mann began. "In 1816, it was made the duty of the Supreme Court to

commit the insane person to prison, there to be kept until his enlargement would be deemed compatible with the safety of the citizens or
until some friend or relative should procure his release by becoming
responsible for all damage which he, in his insanity, might commit . . ."

Most of Mann's hearers nodded and looked well satisfied. This was
the law and a good one. But now Mann presented them with a new
idea. "The insane among us have been visited with a heavier doom
than any criminal. They have suffered as no criminal was ever condemned to suffer! The construction of their cells often deprives
them of light and air. With fire they cannot be trusted. Madness
strips them of their clothing. . . ."

Mr. Mann paused and looked down at a sheaf of papers which he
held in his hand. He had been visiting jails and almhouses in country
towns wherever insane people were imprisoned according to the law.
The sights he had seen, the sounds he heard and the stench he often
endured — all were past description. In case his hearers disbelieved
him, he had taken notes and he had here the proof.[4] There was the
woman, imprisoned for six years and found lying on straw, chained
to the wall under a broken window through which the snow blew
in. A man had been chained and manacled in that same cell for
twenty-one years. Prisoners were fed like dogs, their cells rarely if
ever cleaned, and in some cases the insane were kept in cages where
they could neither stand nor even sit upright.

Horace Mann could paint a scene. Representatives might stare
at the vaulted ceiling or they might look out of the tall windows and
try to calculate their next year's chances of re-election — but a striking sentence would catch them unaware and they would be listening
again and shivering as Mann made them feel the coldness of a prison
cell.

"Until recently, insanity has been deemed incurable," Horace
Mann said. He "cast no reflection upon the keepers of our jails,
houses of correction and poorhouses, as humane men . . . but . . .
a physician and a man of science" could often heal the mentally ill.
And again, here was an entirely new idea to Mann's listeners, for
psychology was still an unopened book and Mann was a generation
ahead of his time as he went on to say that "an alienated mind should
be touched only by a skillful hand," and that "great experience and
knowledge are necessary to trace the causes which first sent it

devious, into the wilds of insanity; to counteract the disturbing forces, to restore it to harmonious action."

Mann's early life had taught him the lesson of frugality and he would no more have advocated the wasting of state funds than he would have thrown away his own hard-earned dollars. He now brought figures to bear to show that if only half the number of the insane now in jail could be cured, the citizens would save more than the cost of a hospital.

Members of the House of Representatives could not help being impressed. Those who thought only in terms of votes must have remembered that the imprisoned insane cast no ballot — but they were moved in spite of themselves. The orthodox ministers were the most sincerely perplexed. They believed, as their forefathers had done, that madness was a divine punishment. This talk of care and cure in a hospital was therefore flying in the face of Providence. But Christ, the great physician, had cured minds "gone devious." Perhaps, in this year of change, here was a new idea they could safely entertain. All were not convinced, of course. There were the graybeards that called Horace Mann "boyish" in his enthusiasm. But the "order" passed and Mann's project was under way.

This session of the legislature ended on the fourth of March. Home hastened the ministers to catch up with their parish calls, and the farmers hurried home to plow their fields. Horace Mann went back to Dedham, where he had recently hung out his shingle and where he now argued as many cases in court as he possibly could before the next session should begin — on the next to last Wednesday in May.

On May 30, "This day closes the festival week of Massachusetts," said the *Boston Patriot* with something like a sigh of relief. Barrels of good New England rum had been set out under the trees on all the village greens during election week. Candidates for office gave free drinks by the dipperful to all comers — only hoping that their constituents could remember who gave the most rum when the voting began.

Dedham, the Norfolk County seat, was famous for the lusty good times both townspeople and farmers enjoyed on election day. But Horace Mann had recently become interested in the new Temperance Society — meaning exactly that, temperance but not total abstinence. He announced that he would not "treat" but would give

the price of a barrel of rum to charity. The opposition rejoiced.
But the voters drank their rum and then voted for Mr. Mann anyway!

Now came the seventeen-day organization session, in the course of
which Mann was appointed to the "Joint Standing Committee on
Railroads and Canals." The graybeards could call him "boyish"
again, for great was his enthusiasm for that daring new innovation,
the railroad!

But now the legislature adjourned for the summer and Mann had
by no means forgotten his asylum project. During the summer
months, he read what few books were available on the problem of
mental illness. He wrote to doctors known to have had experience in
treatment of the insane and he visited private asylums and hospitals.
In July, he engaged a seat on the Providence stage from Alden's
Hotel in Dedham. His ultimate destination was Hartford, where he
planned to visit the Hartford Retreat, founded in 1824; one of the
few and one of the finest hospitals for the mentally ill in the country.
Great and good things were being said of Dr. Samuel Woodward,
who, with Dr. Eli Todd, headed this hospital. And Horace Mann
was looking for exactly the right doctor to direct a hospital for the
destitute insane of Massachusetts — a project as yet merely on paper.

A stopover in Providence would be natural enough. From Providence, a boat carried passengers along the coast and up the Connecticut to Hartford. There was also a stage line reaching Hartford over-
land from Providence. The road was about as rough as the Atlantic
in a coastwise storm but the traveler had at least a choice of routes.
Moreover, Mr. Mann was finding it necessary to stop over in Providence quite frequently of late. His friends were joking him about it.

There was a look of joyous anticipation in Mann's eyes as he
waited for the stage to be made ready. Surely a lawyer, bent on a
charitable mission, should look more solemn! He saw to the stowing
of his portmanteau with especial care — for it contained his best
clothes: the gleaming silk waistcoat, "white pantaloons." Mr. Mann's
leghorn hat was set at a jaunty angle as he climbed into his seat
aboard the lumbering coach. Surely these were curious preparations
on the part of a man going to visit an insane asylum!

Mann settled himself in his corner of the coach and now his eyes
took on a faraway look. He seemed to be rehearsing something to
himself — a speech perhaps? When a stranger spoke to him he started

in surprise. And if a friend had questioned him, Horace Mann could hardly have denied that he was thinking of a call he planned to make at the Reverend Asa Messer's house in Providence.

Asa Messer had been president of Brown when Mann was an undergraduate. Messer was now a successful businessman, a successful farmer, and soon to be candidate for state governor. Always friendly to Horace Mann, Messer had watched his young student's career with interest, offering much sage advice. But this time Horace Mann hoped that Dr. Messer would be away from home.

It was too much to hope for, but he would have liked to find Mary Messer, oldest of the Messer children, away somewhere with her mother, and Caroline, younger and prettier than Mary, out chaise-riding with one of her various admirers. Mann knew from experience that it was far more likely that Caroline would have preempted the parlor for her callers. And as for Mary, she seemed to have but one concern and that was her younger sister, Charlotte. It was remarkable how Mary could help her mother, direct the several servants, attend to her father's visitors — and still keep an eye on Charlotte so that no one could get a word alone with the girl!

Except of course that Charlotte had a mind of her own. If she felt like it, she could contrive to find a private corner of the garden in which to talk to a tall young lawyer from Dedham who, after all, came a long way to see her. Inevitably she laughed at him and teased him about his solemn duties in the Massachusetts legislature. She seemed to know a good deal about his law cases — which was flattering. But Horace Mann could never tell whether Charlotte was any more interested in him than in a dozen other students and former students of her father's.

Charlotte! "Little Gypsy," they called her at home. She was eighteen now, lovely to look at, with great dark eyes that seemed to speak her thoughts — sometimes grave, more often gay. Charlotte loved people. She had hosts of young friends and she delighted in dancing parties, picnics and sleigh rides. But she was forever overtaxing her strength and falling ill. She was forever certain that she would be well again next day or at least the day after — until at last her coughs and fevers subsided. So much spirit in so frail a body aroused in Horace Mann a passion of protective longing. He was sure that if he could drive everyone else away from Charlotte and take care of her himself she would be well and strong.

She must do this and she must not do that, Horace told her. And she rewarded him with bursts of laughter. When Charlotte laughed the sun seemed to come out — even if it were raining.

When it was, exactly, that Horace Mann realized that he loved Charlotte Messer and wanted to marry her, he never knew. Looking back, he felt sure that he loved her the first moment he beheld her — but she had been a child then and he an almost penniless student at Brown. It made no difference when, exactly, he fell in love — he wanted to marry Charlotte now and he had earned a right to ask for her.

Alone in his hotel room on the night of July 8, 1829, Horace Mann took pen in hand. It was a solemn moment and solemnly he wrote: [5]

> Miss CHARLOTTE MESSER:
>   In obedience to feelings whose utterance I can no longer repress, I take the liberty of this mode to request permission to visit you hereafter in the character of an *avowed*, as I have hitherto done, in that of a *secret admirer*.

He paused and his lawyer's mind must have risen within him and said, *Now you've done it. There'll be no going back on this*. But a commitment was what he wanted and the lawyer in him wrote:

"Although the expression of this desire requires, in the cold formality of a letter, but few words, it springs from feelings, whose fervor and intensity, cannot be infused into language; nor can a life of devotion to your happiness exhaust their energies."

Horace Mann was not satisfied. Somehow all the Fourth of July orations he had written, all the speeches in the House of Representatives and all the addresses to the jury had been easier to write than this. He tried again.

"Did I feel much less, I could say more, but the means have no adequacy for the end, for it is only on the broad canvas of a life, that the proportions and coloring of my esteem for you can be painted."

By now, he had torn up half a dozen drafts and yet he could not feel sure that this was the letter that would win him his Charlotte.

She was not a judge nor yet a jury. How inadequate he felt! Better face the possibility of defeat.

> With sentiments of regard for you, which will survive even the wreck of hope, and flourish in my heart, though all else were desolate, I shall always remain, as I have been, ever since I knew the beauties and excellencies of your nature, your more than friend,
>
> HORACE MANN

For one dreadful moment it must have occurred to Horace to wonder if Charlotte would laugh. She so often lightened his mood when he was too solemn. But here was a matter in which one could hardly be serious enough. He sighed and added a postscript.

"An answer will find me at the hotel opposite to the market."

But Miss Charlotte Messer sent no reply.

CHAPTER TWO

Wrentham Road

THERE were those who might have said that Horace Mann, son of a farmer from the village of Franklin, Massachusetts, aimed high when he proposed to marry the daughter of Asa Messer, former president of Brown University. But Messer himself had been a farmer's son, a clerk in a wholesale grocery at the age of thirteen — and a scholar through sheer perseverance and love of learning. Mann was secure in the knowledge that his own family was as good as anyone's, his own ability better than average and his prospects bright. Later generations might look into Mann family lineage. Horace Mann remembered vaguely that there was a certain Samuel Man, "first minister of Wrentham," of whom his family was proud — that sufficed him.

The Mann family records[1] remained buried in the very early archives of the small area west and south of Boston which was still Horace Mann's own particular province. To Cambridge, Massachusetts, came one William Man of Kent, England — so say cousins and contemporaries of Mann's children. Some members of the family thought that William Man of Kent was the son of Charles Man of Halton Bradock, in Kent, knighted in 1625 by Charles I. If so, William's only son, the Reverend Samuel, never heard of it.

"October 25, 1699, my house was burned and all records," wrote Samuel Man. "If memory doeth serve, my father William came from the other England and was the youngest of eleven children." William was born "about the year 1607," his son thought. Samuel was an only child born in Cambridge, Massachusetts, July 6, 1647. He was orphaned at fifteen — but his father left him more than enough to pay for his education and he graduated from Harvard in 1665.

Up the winding, slow-flowing Charles River and along the equally winding Neponset lay natural meadows, lush with "fowl grass." This grass "was brought into a spacious meadow on the Neponset River by wild fowl," wrote Dr. Nathaniel Ames, an early settler. Whether the grass or the ducks came first, the Indians soon followed and these meadows had long been the prized hunting ground of the Wampanoags. The meadows were now, by means of various purchases only half understood by the Indians, the property of a group of English settlers holding their title from the General Court in Boston. Dedham, they called the town which they were building. Three thousand acres of land belonged to the proprietors in shares, according to the wealth of each. "Cow-Common Rights," these shares were called, and they carried the obligation to pay for additional territory if acquired but also the right to share in the profits from the sale to individuals of lands within the grant.

Dedham had been settled ten years when Samuel Man graduated from Harvard. It was still a village of logs and thatch for the most part but they had a meetinghouse, a school. They needed a schoolmaster and Samuel needed a job. The town fathers were impressed with Samuel's education and the books he owned; they hired him in 1667. But it was probably not the first and most certainly not the last time that a teacher was underpaid, for in 1672 he was getting a salary of 8 pounds 10 shillings a year — in Indian corn at 3 shillings the bushel! Mr. Man added to his income by preaching at Wollonopaug.

In 1673, the handful of pioneers about fifteen miles south of Dedham at Wollonopaug achieved two things. They changed the unpronounceable name of their town to Wrentham and they persuaded their parent town of Dedham to allow them to become an independent parish. "Not being willing to live like heathen, though they dwelt in the wilderness," they asked Samuel Man to become their minister.

Only one person in Dedham was considered "more learned" than Mr. Man, so the settlers knew they must make him a handsome offer. They granted him a house lot out of public lands, "so much as shall arise upon ten cow-commons," and also "libertie to choose half his portion of the meadow, the rest to take as other men," which was by lot. He was to have fifty pounds in money to build his house. Since the finest house in Dedham was valued at only twenty pounds, this was glory and honor. As in Dedham, the Wrentham settlers owned Cow-Common shares in proportion to their wealth and each Wrentham settler agreed to pay one shilling and sixpence per share toward the minister's salary.

There were but sixteen families in Wrentham, however, and although they laid claim to natural meadowland there was vastly more unbroken forest land all around them. It took courage to accept this call, but Samuel Man set out along the Wrentham road.

"Trodden paths," they called the early roads, and this Wrentham road was hardly more than that. Trees had been cut down to allow an ox wagon to pass — the stumps left in for the ox wagon to jolt over. This was a countryside notable for dense swamps where wolves and wildcats lurked long after they had been exterminated in other sections. Where the road crossed the swamps, logs had been laid so that the straining oxen could just barely pull a loaded wagon without miring down. Many hours of hard labor had gone into the building of the Wrentham road and Samuel Man was glad to see such evidence of industry on the part of his future parishioners, for he was bringing his bride, Esther Ware of Dedham, to share his new home, his hopes and fears. They were married May 13, 1673, and Esther's father was wealthy in land. Her dowry of iron kettles and hand-woven linens was piled in the wain along with her husband's precious books. Hebrew, Greek and "Lattine" books he had and there were certain of them that Esther loved. In view of her husband's bequest to her upon his death, it seems probable that Esther Ware could read a little Latin — with the help of the Reverend Samuel, who had been a schoolteacher. Samuel Man taught only "male children" in the Dedham school, but perhaps he privately instructed a girl in "English. Writeing. Grammar. and Arithmeticke."

All went well in Wrentham. Willing hands helped to build the minister's house and there was great rejoicing when a little daughter was born to him on April 7, 1674. Springtime never seemed more full of hope and promise. On August 8, 1675, their first son was born and named Samuel, for his father.

But in the autumn came news of Indian warfare. "King Phillip, Chief of the Wompanoags," had formed an alliance among the tribes, and the English captives from the settlements along the

Connecticut River began their terrible march to Canada. News of the Deerfield massacre hardly penetrated as far as Wrentham. It was understood that the colonists had recruited a force that would soon punish the Indians. Some of the more venturesome young men wanted to leave Wrentham and join the expedition but this seemed foolish when there was so much work for strong young men to do right at home in the new settlement.

During the late summer and early autumn, pestilence struck in the form of smallpox and the young minister tried to comfort the bereaved and help them to bless the name of the Lord who gave and also took their little children. Indians were seen in the village but it was understood that they were only friendly Narragansetts come to trade a beaver skin or two for some corn. The Indians were careful to keep away from the two houses in town where the smallpox had been.

And then on the morning of March 30, 1676, the Reverend Mr. Samuel Man rose early as was his custom. He walked out into his dooryard before he called his little household together for morning prayers. Due north and hardly eight miles away a column of smoke was rising into the clear cold air. It could only be Medfield — burning! [2]

Quickly the settlers gathered, white-faced, gun in hand. A conference took place — probably in the minister's house, for he was the temporal as well as the spiritual leader of his people. It was decided that Wrentham could not be defended. The only thing to do was to seek sanctuary in the parent town of Dedham.

Samuel Man and his wife Esther bundled their children against the chill. Their little daughter Mary was not quite two years old but must learn that New England children never cry. Little Samuel was only six months old and his mother held him close. Her next child, Nathaniel, would be born in Dedham, not Wrentham after all. The Reverend Samuel put on his armor — as did the other settlers, who still wore the heavy breastplate and helmet of Cromwell's day.

Back along the Wrentham road journeyed Samuel Man, and this time how endless was the way! Early spring was in the air and as the sun rose higher the frost came out of the ground and the road grew muddy. Where it entered the swamp, the crosswise logs could hardly be seen. Halfway to Dedham and a scant four miles northeast lay what had once been Medfield; and the smell of smoke carries

far and lingers long in woodland country. The settlers marched close
with matchlocks ready while their minister prayed to Almighty
God to save them.

"Through the prevailing goodness of God and their seasonable
withdrawal, no lives were cut off by the heathen," and the Wrentham
settlers reached Dedham in safety. Their homes in the settlement they
had left behind were burned with the exception of the two houses
where the smallpox had been — so the Wrentham people knew that
their supposedly friendly Indians had turned traitor and joined
King Philip.

The Reverend Mr. Samuel Man taught school again in Dedham.
He accepted a call to Milton but when the Wrentham settlers returned and rebuilt their town their beloved minister returned to
them and to the pleasant acres they had given him to be his own
forever. Like his grandfather, Samuel Man had eleven children.
They were "husbandmen" most of them, and well did he provide
for them by giving them land during his lifetime and in his will.

The century had turned and it was 1719 when the Reverend Mr.
Samuel Man died at the age of seventy-two. To his wife Esther he
left, along with considerable other property, " 'Mr. Gurnall's Christian armor,' a book so-called." Also "Books, Hebrew, Greek or
Lattine." The books were of course among the most valuable of his
possessions. Perhaps he gave them to Esther for this reason but it
would almost seem as though Esther, even after bearing eleven children, was still fond of reading!

Sixth child of the Reverend Samuel was Thomas Man. He was
twenty-seven when his father died. Like his father, he decided to
cast his lot with a new community and so he set out upon a new
road with his wife and two little daughters. This road was as rough
as the old Wrentham road had been and it led into unbroken wilderness but the distance from Wrentham was only four miles before
the site of the new township was reached. "Man's Plain" they called
the fine level acres along this road where Thomas and his family
settled down.

The new settlement had grave difficulties in becoming an independent township. At first they were only allowed to have a school,
and Theodore Man, brother of Thomas, was the first schoolmaster.
The Wrentham church was loath to lose the church tax due from

those members now living four miles to the west but they consented to a part-time preacher. The second of these was Hezekiah Man, nephew of Thomas. When at last the little settlement became "Wrentham West Precinct," Thomas Man donated an acre of land for a site for their church.

Nathan, only son of Thomas, inherited the homestead on Man's Plain upon his father's death in 1756. He had seven children and it was to his second son, Thomas, that he left the land. Nathan was still living when the Revolution swept over the colonies — and when Wrentham West Precinct made it clear to the General Court in Boston just how they felt about the British.

"RESOLVED, That it is the opinion of this town that the act of the British Parliament in assuming the power of legislation for the colonies . . . for the express purpose of raising revenue without their consent . . . depriving people in the Cols. of their right to trial by Jury and such-like innovations . . . reduce us to a state of abject slavery," they said — in town meeting in January 1773. Forty-eight heads of families had applied for the Precinct charter in 1773. Doubtless the number had increased but whether the town were large or small, Wrentham Precinct never hesitated to speak up! Thomas Man, son of Nathan, was among those signing this petition.

By January 4, 1775, Deacon Thomas Man was a member of a committee "to secure 2 companies of minute men," to be equipped at town expense "with a good fire-arm, bayonet, pouch, knapsack and thirty rounds of cartridge." The muster rolls of Wrentham West Precinct have disappeared, so there is no record of Deacon Thomas Man's having joined himself. In any case, a patriot farmer was as important to the colonies as a fighter.

The year was 1786 and Thomas Mann, now spelling his name with two *n*'s, journeyed all of ten miles to find himself a bride — Rebecca Stanley of Attleboro. Thomas brought her to "Mann's Plain" and the old homestead, but not to "Wrentham West Precinct." In 1778 the name of the town had been changed to Franklin.

Horace Mann, third son of Thomas and Rebecca, was born in Franklin, Massachusetts, May 4, 1796. He never remembered hearing his father speak of the first Thomas who had cleared the land and built the house where he was born. But he received the impression that somewhere in the distant past there was an ancestor whose memory the family kept alive. "First minister of Wrentham," they called him, and there was a tradition that he taught his children the art of a happy marriage. Somewhere among the family papers there was an ancient letter, falling apart now though never handled except with reverent care. Copied, preserved, handed down in the family, it exists today.

"To my children about to be married," wrote the Reverend Samuel Man: "It seldom happens that praying husbands and praying wives do not live in some measure as they ought to do, while such as are neglectful on this account are very apt to carry it ill toward one another; therefore let me intreat you not engage in the cares of the day, without first praying in the morning for the guidance and protection of God that he would make you ready and willing . . . whether to give good counsel to such as ask it, or attendance upon the sick at a neighbor's house, or a call for the right of hospitality at home . . . and when the cares and labors of the day are over, do not forget to call your family together to seek the protection of your heavenly father through the night, and be assured, if it is the main desire of your hearts to serve God by keeping his commandments, he will send a band of angels to defend you while sleeping, and will prove a more effectual guard in time of danger and alarm than battalions of soldiers."

The Reverend Samuel Man knew whereof he spoke, and from this wilderness prophet was Horace Mann descended.

CHAPTER THREE

King of Terrors

HORACE MANN'S childhood, as he remembered it, consisted of two things: work and churchgoing. Work began at dawn and lasted till sundown. The cornfield, the hayfield, the barnyard and the kitchen garden — this was the unceasing round of tasks endlessly repeated and never done. Winter brought a change, to be sure: wood chopping and snow shoveling were then the equally futile, equally endless chores. Impatient, mercurial in temperament, young Horace found no pleasure in the slow growing of crops, and when a sudden frost destroyed them he had no meekness in his make-up with which to accept the blow and say, "God's will be done."

Not but what he knew about the will of God. The Mann family kept the Puritan Sabbath, banking their fires on Saturday night at sundown and preparing cold food, to be taken with them to church on Sunday and eaten at noon under the pines on the common in summer. In winter they ate at one of the "noon houses" built alongside the horse sheds on Thomas Man's acre. Then back into church they filed for another session with their sins.

The old hay-thatched church on Man's acre was gone now. Nine more acres had been purchased of villagers less generous than Thomas Man, and a new meetinghouse was completed in 1791. Pews close to the steps of the pulpit were reserved for the minister's family and he filled them well. The remaining fifty-five pews, with ten in the gallery, were auctioned off to the highest bidder, to belong to him and his family, his heirs and assigns forever. The money so raised helped defray the cost of the church, and Thomas Mann, bidding as high as his means would allow, received half of pew Number 32.

The imprint of the Franklin church and of its minister, the Reverend Dr. Nathanael Emmons, remained in Horace Mann's mind forever. He remembered one bleak Sunday in December in 1808 when he was twelve years old. Young men and boys sat in the "southwest elbow of the gallery," and he climbed the steep stairs, his feet on the narrow treads knocking against the risers with a hollow sound. Just ahead went his oldest brother, Thomas Stanley, known in the family as Stanley. He was twenty, red-haired, handsome and happy-go-lucky — casting an eye over the girls seated demurely in their fathers' pews below. Next came Stephen, aged sixteen. He slid along the bench with a cheerful grin and a sly, friendly kick at a neighbor's boy as he made way for his brother Horace to sit beside him.

Horace looked down at his family's half of pew Number 32. His father sat on the aisle, tall and excessively thin; he had his Sunday look, one of pleasant anticipation. Next came sister Rebecca, twenty-one years old, not married yet and not even keeping company but right now keeping an eye on her little sister Lydia, who was ten and plenty old enough to sit still. At the end of the half-pew sat the mother of the family, Rebecca Stanley Mann, plump-cheeked, serious, her nearsighted eyes looking anxious behind their iron-rimmed spectacles.

Young Horace sighed. He too felt serious and anxious, but also deep inside him he was pleasantly excited as he watched for the appearance of the minister. And now the new church bell rang out its final summons. Its solemn tones from the tower so close above the gallery sent a shiver of anticipation through Horace Mann's bones.

There was a pause. Then a short, tense little man entered and climbed into the high box-pulpit.[1] On each side of the window behind the pulpit was a wooden peg. On one the minister hung his three-cornered hat, and on the other his blue-black cloak. His bald head shone in the cold light from the window behind him. He turned and surveyed his flock with a penetrating look as though beholding more evil than good in all of them.

The subject of the sermon was "The Unknown of Death"[2] and the text was from the Book of Job, the thirty-eighth chapter and the seventeenth verse. "Have the gates of death been opened unto thee? Or hast thou seen the doors of the shadow of death?"

Birthplace of Horace Mann, Franklin, Massachusetts
This fairly grim picture by an unknown artist is more
honest than some later prettified versions.

Photograph by Stanley G. Chilson

The Reverend Nathanael Emmons

This striking portrait hangs in a downstairs room in the
Ray Library, Franklin, Mass. There are apologists for
Emmons who say that he was really gentle and mild.

Young Horace shuddered. He had known it would be something like this. He listened with fear and admiration, not missing a word. "We know not when we shall be called to pass out of this world into the other. Though God has determined the months and days and even the moments of everyone's life . . . yet no man knows what a day or a moment may bring forth. . . . Man knoweth not the time; as the fishes are taken in an evil net, as the birds are caught in the snare, so are the sons of man snared in an evil time." The Reverend Dr. Emmons had a high, penetrating voice. You could not escape it if you would, and he had a vivid style which evoked a series of dreadful pictures in Horace Mann's wonderfully vivid imagination.

Nathanael Emmons was meticulous and exacting. His daily life of study and contemplation never varied and the floor under his study table was worn thin by the hourly pressure from his faithful feet. His wood fire must be laid just so, no speck of ash upon his hearth. And his sermons never varied. Selecting a text from Job, one of his favorites, or from one of the more terrifying prophets of doom, he would set up a field of speculation and then solve his own riddle under a series of headings — demolishing the views of other theologians as he went along.

Young Horace learned under heading Number 5 that "spirits after they leave the body . . . exist from death to the resurrection. It is not very probable that they exist . . . without being clothed with some material vehicle." Horace saw ghostly shapes flitting through his mind. "The angels are represented as having faces . . ." and Horace felt better. But "the angels have faces which they cover . . ." and all was ghostly again.

After headings and subheadings had been expounded there came the "improvement." The congregation had been paying close attention — so compelling were their minister's word pictures, so sharp and penetrating his voice — but now they all sat still straighter and a light sigh went over them like wind over a field of grain. The Reverend Dr. Emmons, for twenty-seven years their pastor, would now speak personally of their several sins, of which, although he rarely left his study, he seemed to know all too much. "Learn the misery of departed sinners gone to light and despair," he said, glancing about with that all-seeing eye of his. "Learn the duty of mourners which is unconditioned submission — God has taken his pleasure and they know not what it is." And summing it all up, "If mankind know so little about death before it comes; then it is not strange that it should be the king of terrors."

On the way home, young Horace was astonished to see his father smiling and nodding his head in approval. "A fine sermon," he was saying. "A fine sermon, indeed." His father seemed particularly pleased.

Six months went by and it was June. The corn was doing well and it looked as though there would be a good hay crop. The kitchen garden which Horace, being the youngest son, took care of almost singlehanded, was a living tribute to his care, with its weedless rows of fernlike carrot tops, of tiny beets almost ready for thinning — the culls to be eaten as greens. Only once or twice had a hill of beans lost a promising sprout, cut down by Horace's too impatient hoe. All would have been well with the Mann family, save that the head of it, Thomas Mann, was failing in health and strength.

They had taken Father's cough for granted. He always seemed to catch a cold in the autumn which lasted all winter and sometimes all through spring. This year the warm weather had not seemed to cure it. He was weakened with heavy sweats at night, and during the spring planting he had handed over the plow to Stanley and gone exhausted to the house — a thing unheard-of. Now came the dread, the well-known sign: he was spitting blood. No need to wait for more than one hemorrhage. On June 9, 1809, he made his will.

"In the name of God, Amen — I Thomas Mann of Franklin in the County of Norfolk and Commonwealth of Massachusetts — yeoman . . ." Thomas Mann took first care of his wife, Rebecca. Son Stanley would surely marry before long. Who knew what sort of wife he would bring home to the old homestead? A widow must have rights of her own — and dignity. "I give unto my wife Rebecca Mann the use of my chaise and a horse to use at pleasure." Her greatest pleasure would be going to church. She was to have "the improvement of my half of number thirty-two pew in Franklin meeting house and the horse stable near the same." Rebecca was also to have "the east room below in my dwelling house and the chamber above the same, my east Bedroom below and equal liberty with my son Thomas S. Mann in my back kitchen, cellars and garret." Rebecca was to have her widow's third of all the property, but besides that son Thomas must "bring in annually to her, Ten bushels of Indian corn, and to procure for her a sufficiency of fire-wood fitted for the fire and brought into the house, so long as she shall remain my Widow. And I exclusively give to her my silver watch, one cow, all my household furniture and indoor moveables."

The will was finished at last, with careful provisions for each child, with Thomas Stanley in charge of carrying out everything. There were days now when Thomas Mann lay quietly in his bed; when between attacks of coughing he smiled and joked and told them that now his will was made he'd outlive them all. But on June 20 he called them together. He spoke to Stanley about the tavern — a pleasant place on a winter's night — a cool glass of ale no harm on a summer's day. But the tavern was dangerous and a man could go there too often. Stanley was to take care of his mother. Stephen was to study. He was the brilliant one. And Horace? He was to work hard, take care of his mother and his sisters — help his brothers. Horace heard all the words of advice to himself and to the others and took them all to heart whether they applied to him or not. He was barely thirteen years old. How intensely he admired his father, who was so brave and calm even in the face of death! Death — "the king of terrors."

The lawyer came back again to read the will. Horace heard his own name: ". . . to my son Horace I give and devise one fourth part of all my lands and territory not hitherto disposed of."

Sister Rebecca had a legacy of three hundred dollars to be paid her by her brother Stanley one year after their father's death. Lydia would receive "two hundred and thirty-three dollars to be upon interest when she shall arrive at the age of fifteen" and to be paid her when she was twenty-one. To Stephen went one hundred and thirty-five dollars on similar terms. He was "entitled to his earnings" after he was seventeen. It was expected that Stephen would use his money for schooling.

Horace watched the lawyer, sitting there reading the will in such solemn tones. It was a dramatic scene and the lawyer made the most of it. What a fine thing to be so important a person as a lawyer! It would be better than owning a fourth part of Mann's Plain (and a third of his mother's share after her death). A farm represented not drama but drudgery.

These half-formed thoughts Horace Mann kept to himself until, in later years, he wrote with bitterness of his childhood and the heavy labor on the farm. He kept to himself his passion for books and his secret imaginings about them. He read every volume dealing with history in the Franklin library. This was not such an impossible feat as might be supposed, since the Franklin library consisted of 116 volumes, forty of them being sermons or works on theology.

When Wrentham West Precinct became a town, in 1778, Benjamin Franklin had just secured the treaty with France. Twenty-eight American towns promptly honored the national hero by naming themselves Franklin.[3] But Wrentham West Precinct was the first (so the story goes) and Benjamin Franklin gave his first namesake a present. It is said that he offered a bell for the meetinghouse but on learning how serious were the townspeople he decided they would prefer "sense to sound." In any case, Franklin wrote to the Reverend Richard Price of London "to make a choice of proper books to commence a library for the use of the Inhabitants of Franklin."

In 1802 Thomas Mann was treasurer of the library and so continued through 1806. He had very little treasure to keep track of but his children learned early of the treasure to be found in books. *Gordon's Tacitus*, in five volumes, young Horace Mann made particularly his own. He became a Roman of the Romans, conducting military campaigns against the weeds in the corn — making farming endurable because of the secret world of his imagination. Oratory he listened to every Sunday and was at liberty to practice, if he pleased, when sent to the pasture for the cows at night. Later, he deplored his early reading, feeling that no child should be allowed to admire military heroes — yet the Roman imprint never quite left his mind.

"I never had more than ten weeks of schooling in a year till I was sixteen," Horace Mann wrote. Even those ten weeks at the district school at Plains Corner cost money because the children must provide their own books. Horace braided straw for money to buy textbooks.

Franklin provided a peculiar opportunity for farm families to make a little much-needed cash — an opportunity which began soon after Horace was born and lasted only about a generation. The straw-braiding industry was started in Providence, in 1798, by a twelve-year-old girl, Betsy Metcalf. Late in life, she told her own story. "My father, Joel Metcalf, brought home some oat straw which he had just mowed. I cut the straw with my scizzors and split it with my thumb nail. I had seen an imported bonnet but I never saw a piece of braid, and could not tell the number of straws. I commenced the common braid with six straws and smoothed it with a junk bottle, and made part of a bonnet, but found it did not look like the imported ones. I added another straw and then that was right. . . . Soon after, I learned Sally Richmond, a near neighbor, to braid all kinds. She went on a visit to Wrentham and learned them there."

In 1809 a two-wheeled cart came over from Wrentham regularly. The driver would stop at each farmhouse door, deliver fine oat straw, and pick up finished braid. By 1812 straw bonnets were being made in Franklin, and each day in winter, once the chores were done, straw braiding began; families braided straw on summer evenings out under the trees in the dooryard on all the farms. It was no wonder that Horace Mann remembered a childhood of unremitting labor. It was no wonder that he remembered that reading for pleasure was considered sinful idleness. His impatient fingers were never skillful like his sisters' slower hands, and schoolbooks were hard earned and much respected. They were shared by all the family, and Horace taught his younger sister Lydia to spell — following her about the house and drilling her while she baked and while she swept the floor. It was wonderful what patience Horace had in this endeavor, Lydia thought — when he could hardly endure to braid straw for half an hour.

It was the summer of 1810 and somehow the fatherless family had managed to get along. In some ways life was easier, for with Stanley in charge of the farm the two younger boys found their rare half days of freedom coming a little more frequently. Once in a while Stephen, now seventeen, would slip off through the woods to Uncas Pond and come back cool and shining, with his hair plastered close to his head. Sometimes Horace went along with Stephen, but a boy of fourteen was not particularly welcome among the seventeen-year-olds. They could all swim, more or less — having now and then succeeded in thrashing their way ashore when they accidentally stepped off into deep water. Once or twice when Sunday came Stephen was not in church, nor were certain of his friends.

The Reverend Dr. Nathanael Emmons preached powerfully on the subject of keeping the Sabbath. "It has always been found that those who profane the Sabbath are incurably vicious," he said. "Well-instructed and well-governed children and youth rarely become notorious Sabbath-breakers." The faithful flock listened meekly and the widow Mann grew red with embarrassment, for she knew without turning around to look that her second son was not in the balcony. She had words with him but Stephen only laughed and said he was not a "notorious Sabbath-breaker." He had kept the Sabbath all winter.

On Sunday, July 22, 1810, Stephen Mann was not in church. A boy his own age, white-faced and terrified, brought the dreadful news. They had gone swimming in Uncas Pond. Stephen was drowned.[4]

Stephen the joyous one! He was so full of life, so sure of his happy future — it did not seem possible that death could claim him. Horace had loved and admired Stephen as only a younger brother can do. Added to grief was the almost unbearable public disgrace.

The Reverend Dr. Emmons, famous theologian and leader of "New Light" orthodoxy though he was, nevertheless overlooked many passages in his New Testament. He brought no help to the widow and the fatherless, no comfort to them that mourned. Clear in his conscience, Dr. Emmons believed that here was his God-given opportunity to save the souls of other young men and boys in his parish — provided he could bring the lesson of Stephen's death before them with sufficient power. Not but what all of them were fore-ordained either to heaven or hell, and even the faintest hope of heaven would have been a form of self-love. But they must be willing to "be damned for the glory of God," and to do this they must cease their sinful ways.

The young people were all in church this time. Dr. Emmons described "the terrible Last Judgment" and "the lake which burneth with fire and brimstone." He left no doubt as to the future eternal fate of Stephen Mann. In the stunned silence which followed the minister's final words, Horace heard his mother moan.

Ever since he could remember, Horace had been troubled with terrifying dreams. Now the theme was always Stephen. Sometimes he was trying to save Stephen, sometimes he was drowning with him — but always there was the dreadful vision of God the Judge, seeing and enjoying the torment of Stephen. Horace woke and lay

rigid with clenched fists, staring into the darkness, struggling not
to cry out. If this was the justice of God, then he hated God! And the
Reverend Dr. Emmons had obviously been created in God's image.
These were terrifying thoughts for a boy of fourteen.

Horace was much too young to understand Nathanael Emmons.
Emmons too had suffered from visions of the burning lake — as he
wrote years later in his autobiography. A thunderstorm had given
him such "an awful sense of God's displeasure and of going into a
miserable eternity" that he had lain sleepless all night. Nathanael
Emmons was also acquainted with grief. His first wife, whom he
dearly loved, "fell into a decline, which terminated in a proper consumption," and hers was "a great and heavy loss." She left two
little boys whom Nathanael Emmons "loved to excess, they were so
tender, kind," so like their mother. About two months after their
mother died, the children came down with dysentery. Their father
was alone, but for "a hired man and a maid." Five days later, his
older little boy "expired in extreme agonies, about one o'clock at
night." The younger child, a baby hardly a year old, "would go to
no one but myself," he remembered. This baby was "just alive and
there was a bare possibility of his recovery." But he lived hardly half
a day longer than his brother. "My heart rose in all its strength
against the government of God," Emmons confessed.

Emmons searched his soul to see why God had punished him. He
had "presumptuously indulged in high hopes" — the children "became his idols" and he had "loved them to excess," so this was the
"correcting hand of Providence." Horace Mann, at fourteen, could
not possibly understand this grim old Puritan. To "submit" was not
in his nature. But Sunday after Sunday Horace learned the power of
the spoken word; he learned the use of imagery so that in later years
he too could paint pictures in other men's minds. He learned the
power and effectiveness of Bible language.

CHAPTER FOUR
Tuition Twenty Dollars

STEPHEN, the brilliant one, was gone now, and for the first time it struck the Mann family that Horace was rather studious. Sister Lydia never conceded for a moment that Horace had Stephen's promise, but he did have patience — at least where books were concerned and in the matter of spelling lessons. When Horace was fourteen, Franklin citizens in town meeting moved "to see if the town will provide some suitable person to instruct youths in the Greek and Latin languages." Here was the first and only chance Horace had ever had of preparing for college and it was agreed that he could be spared from the farm when the new school opened. Horace privately resolved to be first in line at the door. Then, in May of that year, the smallpox appeared in Franklin and the little community voted "to grant to Dr. Nathaniel Miller the sum of fifty dollars for his inoculating the inhabitants with the Hine pox matter." The grammar school would have to wait, and young Horace Mann's chance for college had gone glimmering.

To be sure, the Reverend Dr. Emmons took promising pupils and prepared them for college, Brown University preferably — or Rhode Island College as it was called until 1804 — where they were least likely to imbibe heresies. But in Horace Mann's heart there burned a fierce personal pride which kept his head erect and his ambitions strong but secret. His widowed mother might give her grief-stricken acquiescence to the words from the pulpit — "Sabbath-breaker . . . notoriously vicious" — but Horace would never ask the Reverend Dr. Emmons for a favor, even if he could have paid the fee for tutoring.

Mann went to the village school [1] — a tall boy among the little children in the ungraded room. Undismayed, he wrote essays, poetry and drama. "The Country Justice, A Satirical Play,[2] by Horace Mann of Franklin," he headed his manuscript, and "January 18, 1811" was the date — the playwright not yet fifteen.

"Judge Meanwell" was the butt of Horace's humor and "Lawyer Ellery" was his hero. Ladies were conspicuously absent from the cast and the plot dealt with a damage suit concerning some "tarnation hogs" and a "tater field" — a suit remarkably similar to Mann's first law cases! But playwright Mann's best shafts of humor were reserved for the Judge in his capacity as representative.

Judge Meanwell had been attending state legislature and "laying taxes on new laws," as Horace had him say. And, "they just past an act to keep dogs from running mad."

Sounding astonishingly like the Horace Mann of future years, "Lawyer Ellery" talked of "justice and equality" and referred the Judge to the Constitution.

"I never read the Constitution in my life," Horace made the Judge reply. "I had a deal of private business to attend to when they were reprobating that subject; but I came in jest before they put it to the vote, they most all voted for it, and so I thought I might too. . . ." It would seem as though young Horace had already journeyed as far as Boston and had attended a session of the legislature — so well did he satirize it at the age of fourteen!

Hero "Lawyer Ellery" was made to speak in a most elegant style. No Malaprop he — and the Judge was easily worsted, exclaiming with heat, "I can tell you, you're a fool Sir; and Quacibus Lawyernus est pestimus omnorum foolorum." Young Horace had missed his chance to go to grammar school but he had picked up enough Latin to make fun of it. It is easy to see, on reading this really remarkable play, that Horace Mann had decided to become a lawyer — if miracles could happen!

In March 1815 a curious personality crossed Horace Mann's path and the miracle was on its way. This person was "Master Barrett," [3] itinerant teacher. Whence he came or where he went remains a mystery, but he was a genius of sorts with a phenomenal memory. He could recite Greek and Latin by the hour without referring to text and he knew the Latin grammar by heart with all its rules and exceptions. A garbled recitation seemed to give him physical pain, and students remembered that "it was grateful to hear him repeat it all over to himself, in the most soothing, motherly voice, as though he would heal its wounds and dislocated parts. Sometimes he would croon off . . . page after page of an author, winding up each paragraph with such an inarticulate chuckle of delight, as only a very fat man like him could give."

It was said that Master Barrett knew nothing beyond Latin and Greek and could not so much as tell time; that he went on periodic drunken sprees — the reason for his traveling from place to place. That is as may be. Barrett charged no more than the Manns could afford and Horace was allowed to study with him. Horace had already read so much in translation that he almost knew the classics by heart himself — in English. Now the familiar passages acquired a fresh and vigorous life as he read them in the language in which they were written. His ardent mind sprang to the task of learning and he surprised even the exacting Barrett.

Horace bought a fine notebook of heavy, high-quality paper with leather-backed, block-printed binding. "The Property of Horace Mann, Wrentham, Feb. 3, 1816," he wrote on the flyleaf, and this notebook he filled with problems in geometry. The pages had beautifully ornamented headings, and the figures, drawn in ink, looked like copperplate engravings. If Master Barrett knew no mathematics, then Mann had found someone to help him just the same. "I never went to an academy in my life," [4] Mann wrote, years later. He prepared himself for college nevertheless.

According to the terms of Thomas Mann's will, Horace was entitled to a share in Stephen's legacy, now that Stephen was dead. After the other surviving children had been paid, Horace would receive about one hundred and twenty dollars when he came of age — or "at need." Tuition at Brown University was twenty dollars a term. Horace needed some of his money now and brother Stanley willingly promised to advance it. [5]

Stanley had little use for book learning himself but he was proud of Horace. He was in Bellingham on March 15, 1815, when he wrote — dispensing with punctuation for the most part:

BROTHER HORACE

As I shall not have an opportunity to see you at present I have some things I wish you to see to in my absence. I want you to sell that Hay & attend to the grazing [?] of the cattle. . . .

Brother I am anxious for your welfare and that of my Friends. I want to give some advice to you now in positive love I wish to see you engaged in your studies, but am told that you are too much so . . . diligence is ever to be commended but not in the extreme, your health should be your greatest care. look after yourself, Mr. Fisher, should he acquire the greatest Fame it will never compensate for the loss of his health. I wish you to think of these things, Brother H & so should you live as you may wish you had. . . .

Horace was pleased with the letter but the warning went unheeded. He went right on trying to outdo Alexander Metcalf Fisher, Franklin's mathematical genius, pupil of Dr. Emmons, who had graduated from Yale two years previously at the age of nineteen. Fisher had been appointed Tutor at Yale but his health had broken and he had just come home to his father's farm. Horace knew in his secret heart that he was the equal of Fisher but, held back by poverty, he was only on the threshold of his college career — and in May he would be twenty! So Mann studied harder still — believing in later life that "emulation" was the worst thing in the world for a student and that he broke his own health at this time.

It was in September 1816 that Horace Mann set out for Providence. He looked curiously at his fellow passengers in the stage — evidently college bound. Most of them were not over fifteen and Horace felt an old man at twenty, angry with the fate that misspent his youth in the hayfield. Intense by nature, he determined with still greater intensity to make up for lost time. He began reciting lines from Virgil. How well he knew them — and yet he could imagine forgetting them all, flunking his entrance examination, and being sent home in disgrace. It would be humiliating for himself and his whole family. It would be the farm forever.

In spite of his anxious frame of mind, Horace's heart lifted at the sight of Providence. It was still a town but to his country boy's eyes it seemed a city, crowded close along the river with its hill behind it, green with gardens, fields and pasture land. The river was full of masts of sailing ships and Horace was for the first time aware of the smell of the sea. As the coach rumbled along, he glimpsed a warehouse, caught the whiff of molasses and hides; he saw bales of cotton that had come by sailing vessel from the South.

Only one street led directly from the river to the top of the hill and, knowing nothing as yet of Providence family names, Horace wondered why the street was called Angell.[6] (He was to marry into the Angell family, first settlers with Roger Williams.) He climbed the steep ascent and reached an open field. This was the college campus. A large brick building, puritanical in its plainness, yet well-proportioned and pleasing to look at, faced the campus. This was University Hall, and it *was* the university. The only other buildings on the campus were President Asa Messer's house and barn.

Horace knew that he must face both an oral and a written examination conducted by President Messer personally. "Upon examination of the President and Tutors [the candidate] must read accurately, construe and parse Tully and the Greek Testament, and Virgil; and shall be able to write true Latin in prose; and hath learned the rules of Prosody and Vulgar Arithmetic; and shall bring suitable testimony of a blameless life and conversation."

It was all so much easier than Horace expected that he forgot his nervousness and began to enjoy himself thoroughly. The questions ranged further than he expected — into Horace which he had read for the sake of his name, and Xenophon which he loved for its story of military adventure. As for his "blameless life," Horace doubtless had letters with him from friends of his family, but written for all to read was the look of holy joy upon his face as he spouted Greek and Latin. There was the generous honesty of his wide, sensitive mouth, smiling now with pleasure in this most "blameless conversation."

When the examination was finished, Horace handed over twenty dollars and his receipt was signed by President Messer in person. "Brown University Sept. 25, 1816 Rec'd of Horace Mann twenty dollars for admission to our Sophomore Class," it said. Here was joyful news. A legacy of one hundred and thirty dollars would probably pay for a college degree since Horace had a chance to get one in three years. There would be other charges of course. Meals at Commons cost $1.89 a week with "Steward's services" at $2.21 for the term and "sweeping" at $1.17.

Gladly would Horace have attended to sweeping himself, had the term referred to ordinary tidiness in his room. But his room was heated by a fireplace as were all the others, and the university *Laws and Rules* had something to say: "Every chimney in the college shall be swept once every year, at the expense of the occupants, and it shall be the duty of the Steward to see this done at such times as the President shall direct, and the Steward shall charge the expense in the quarter bills."

During his junior and senior years at Brown, Horace Mann's room was Number 30, University Hall, and Ira M. Barton was his roommate. Ira was a solemn young man of about Horace's age, coming from Oxford, Massachusetts. He later became a judge, and when asked for reminiscences of his famous roommate his memory proved remarkably pious. "The dissipations of neither the college nor the city had any attractions for us," Ira wrote. "During the two years of our college life I recollect not a single act of impropriety on his part." Fortunately, Horace's letters to his sister Lydia show that he was by no means as painfully proper as Ira remembered. In 1817 Horace wrote that two members of his class had been "rusticated" and one expelled, "from which I derive some hope for myself, as after a shower has passed over, we do not look for another so soon," Mann said.

Term time, in Mann's day, was arranged so that there was an eight-week vacation beginning the last Wednesday in December. Many students taught school during these weeks, and in later life Horace Mann spoke of having done the same. The second term began in February and lasted into late July. During June and July 1817 Horace was in Providence, writing home of great goings-on. President Monroe was making a tour of New England, with Providence a stopover; visits to Brown University and the Pawtucket mills, with their "first frame upon the Arkwright plan," on his agenda.

The President was expected on Monday afternoon, June 30, and the town fathers prepared a welcome. Militia would turn out and escort the President from General Carrington's Wharf to Chappolin's Hotel. There would be bell ringers in the churches, ready to begin "a merry peal" (as a Providence paper, the *Patriot and Columbian Phenix*, put it) as soon as the signal gun from the river announced the President's approach. Bonfires were laid at intervals along the principal streets for an evening "illumination." But during the morning of June 30 it rained heavily and the President was delayed. "Troops and citizens" who had "assembled to greet him" waited dismally at the wharf till nine at night when the "Steam-Boat *Fire-Fly*" finally appeared, "escorted by three U. S. vessels." Off went the "salutes of artillery" and the "merry peal of bells" — but the wood was wet and the bonfires refused to burn. Those that could be gotten going sputtered and burned out well before the President passed, and the best the paper could say was that the streets were "partially illuminated"!

The press was remarkably honest. "In compliment to the President, the edifice of Brown University was brilliantly illuminated"! It was indeed, since the boys had waited till the rain was over and since they had a habit of burning everything inflammable that they could lay their hands on — their own well house and President Messer's front fence being no exceptions. By the Fourth of July the students were not exactly at peace with the town or with their faculty. When the "Order of Procession" for the Fourth of July parade was published, the students found that the city fathers had assigned them to the next to the last place in procession. Just ahead of them would march "Associations of Mechanics and Manufacturers" while behind came "Strangers and Citizens." It was intolerable! There was talk of breaking up the parade — which might be fun. But wiser counsels prevailed, and the students "voted to celebrate by themselves and sent a committee to the President requesting permission to go into the Chapel to hear Orations."

Reasonable as this request seems to be, it was denied. Prexy was in a bad mood. Horace Mann wrote all about it in a letter home to Lydia. "However, they [the students] determined to go in & hazard the consequences, 'peacably if they could, forcibly if they must.' It was then expected that the door must be burst in but in the morning this inscription was found upon it, written in Greek, 'And the door shall be opened unto you' which was all done in its proper time (and which, by the way, I think to be of great verification of scripture)."

Ira Barton,[7] in later years, thought that it was Horace Mann who was instigator of the plot to unlock the door and that it was he who led the students into the chapel because he was the chosen orator and did not want to miss the chance to shine before his classmates. Horace may well have thought up the scheme and he may have led the boys, for he wrote home with all the gusto of a successful conspirator and strategist. But "Mr. Allen orated," he told Lydia, and it was not until 1818 that Mann got his turn at a chapel oration — speaking on freedom of the press, "freedom from the double-thonged scourge of Civil and religious persecution."

Foremost in Mann's mind and the delight of his heart was oratory. He had loved it ever since *Gordon's Tacitus* had captured his imagination — all five volumes of it in the Franklin library. He lived in an age when pulpit oratory was the chief source of public entertainment and patriotic oratory attracted great crowds on numerous annual occasions. To be sure, there were courses that interested Mann — there was astronomy which opened his eyes to the universe and to which he referred often throughout his entire lifetime. He had no use for literature, however — the novel in particular. "Perhaps few kinds of amusement are more prejudicial to the attainment of solid sciences, or productive of more permanent injury to the mind than the excessive perusal of that species of fictitious history embraced in novels and romances," he wrote in one of his college essays. Horace left the novel without a leg to stand on, but he tried to be fair. There was some excuse for fiction in prehistoric times, he said — but "none now, since history can be read!" With his capacity for concentration, Mann stood high in all his classes yet found time to devote to his first and only love — oratory.

At Brown there were two clubs for students, the Philermenians and the United Brothers — with oratory as their reason for being. On February 22, 1817, the United Brothers [8] voted to invite Horace Mann to join them and a month later he "took his seat," according to the minutes of the society. From that time on, the minutes were full of Mann and his doings. Fellow members became lifelong friends.

Dues were three dollars the freshman year, two-fifty the sophomore and junior years, and seniors paid a dollar. Mann owed only the two-fifty, therefore, but this was a sum not lightly to be tossed away and he soon arranged matters. On June 21, 1817, the Brothers "voted to compromise with Mr. Mann for his room as Society room during the present quarter for $2.50."

Six members were chosen in alphabetical order from the membership list to debate at each meeting — three for the affirmative and three for the negative. During 1817, Horace Mann took the affirmative on the question, "Is it politic for the Republic of the United States to establish military schools?" and the affirmative won. It would now be Mann's turn to take the negative when his name came up again. Mann's side won again when he and his friends upheld the negative, "Can a republic make war more effectively than a monarchy?"

During his senior year, Mann was secretary of the United Brothers, then "vice-president and Lecturer" and finally president. He was appointed marshal to lead the Brothers in solemn procession down the steep hill to the First Baptist Meeting House — the Taunton Band supplying the music not to "exceed thirty dollars." It was an unforgettable senior year but, like all good things, it ended too soon. On July 13, 1819, Horace Mann was orator at the final Examination Dinner of the Senior Class. This was the highest class honor and he approached it with exaltation — declaiming that education was "like the ladder beheld in the vision of the Patriarch," and that it should "reach from earth to heaven."

On the bottom rung of Jacob's ladder and a long way from heaven was Horace Mann when he entered the law office of the Honorable J. J. Fiske of Wrentham! Mann knew what he meant to do. He would "read law" when there were no briefs to copy, for this was the way that many a young law clerk rose in the world under the benevolent eye of a fine lawyer, interested in seeing the boys in his office admitted to the bar. But patience was never one of Horace Mann's virtues. Before a year was out, it seemed to him that he would remain forever "Student at Law, Wrentham," as his college friends addressed his letters.

On January 1, 1820, Asa Messer, President of Brown, so addressed a letter which began:

SIR

As we now need a Tutor, I wish to enquire whether you are willing to become one? And if so how long you would be willing to remain one? I request you to send me, as soon as you can, answer to these questions; and hoping that they may be such as will secure you an appointment, I remain very respectfully your friend. . . . P.S. The Salary this year will be at the rate of $375.00 a year; and it will commence at the commencement of Service.

Horace Mann accepted, promising to stay two years. He also added a postscript: "I have presumed that the consideration mentioned is to be exclusive of board." Mann was right.

But was this really the next rung in the ladder? Mann had doubts, withdrew his acceptance — was urged, and accepted again. By August 1820 he was installed at Brown, "at the head of forty freshmen," as he wrote his sister Lydia. ". . . The appellation is no irony, I assure you," he went on. "They come to college with heads erect and hearts elate, thinking no doubt that everyone beholds them with awe and envies their elevation. To step at once on so lofty an eminence is more than most heads can bear without dizziness."

Among the more dizzy of Horace Mann's students was a boy named Samuel Gridley Howe. Gay, companionable, handsome to an astonishing degree, Sam was interested in almost everything except his studies. One morning Prexy's poor old white horse was found at the top of the three long flights of stairs at University Hall — and it was Sam Howe who put her there. Sam was rusticated several times but somehow managed to graduate and go to Harvard Medical School, where his studies for the first time intrigued him. Even so, the grim adventure of stealing a corpse from a graveyard for laboratory study was the Medical School experience Sam best remembered.

When there were disturbances in Mann's classes (and it happened more than once) Sam Howe was more than likely to be at the bottom of them. But Sam was never ill-natured and Horace Mann afterwards remembered that somehow he had never managed to be very angry with the boy. In later years, Dr. Samuel Gridley Howe would become one of Mann's dearest and most intimate friends.

There were other students much more troublesome and lacking in that fundamental good will that made Howe lovable. There was Sumner Lincoln Fairfield, for example, a young poet but a misfit in college, who satirized his professors and from whose caustic pen neither President Messer nor Horace Mann escaped. The tall, heavy-set Asa Messer, with his knee breeches of the fashion of a previous generation, his cane with which he cut at the roadside weeds as he strode along, was a "queer figure" even to his friends. Said Fairfield, "He is a strong-built man, unequally formed, with drumstick legs, broad chest, John-Bull neck, slouching shoulders, high cheek-bones, little grey rabbit eyes, full moon face and square bald

head. He moves like an automaton. He speaks like a growly bear.
. . . He cannot but tyrannize . . . his avarice is great . . . he oc-
cupies the Presidential Chair as a bear would a throne."

Horace Mann came out considerably better at Fairfield's hands —
but not altogether scatheless. Mann was "a tall elegant gentleman
who atones for his classical defects by the suavity of his manners
and the kindness of his disposition."

As to the "elegance" — there could be no doubt about it. Mann was
wearing a new blue cloth coat with six gilt buttons, these days. He
had taken steps in the direction of intellectual elegance as well, having paid three dollars "for instruction in the french language," according to a receipt signed by "Andrew Louis."

During his student days, Mann had been a frequent caller at President Messer's house. He found Messer no tyrant at all but friendly,
even fatherly in his attitude. Great and glorious were the discussions,
particularly upon theological subjects. Soon a storm would break
that would drive Asa Messer from Brown — because he chose to
address a group of Unitarian young people upon a Sunday afternoon!
Horace Mann could not help but admire such a person.

At President Messer's house there was good talk and there was
also music and perhaps even a little dancing of a sedate and proper
sort! Dr. Messer's three daughters were fond of giving parties, with
Mary, twenty-one years old, a little too eager to direct the efforts
of everyone, including a tall young Tutor named Mann who proved
difficult. Caroline was fifteen, but pretty and popular. The youngest
daughter was only twelve when Horace Mann was Tutor. She was
a bewitching little girl with big dark eyes and her name was Charlotte. They said that Horace Mann liked Charlotte best. When his
two years were up and Mann came to the Messer house to say good-
by — they said that Charlotte cried.

CHAPTER FIVE

Flute and Flageolet

IN his letter to Horace Mann, President Messer capitalized the title of "Tutor." He was fond of capitals, to be sure, but he also hoped that Mann might see the offer as an opening to a career. A "Tutor" could become a Professor (surely with a capital letter) and a Professor could be College President — such had been Messer's own career. But Mann, at the age of twenty-five, was not at all attracted to the teaching profession. His "ladder . . . of the Patriarch" was still the law, which led "upward from earth to heaven" — or from Providence to Litchfield, Connecticut. By the spring of 1821, Horace was writing to friends who were already studying at Litchfield,[1] first American law school. On March 4, 1821, William Ennis, a Brown classmate from Newport, replied:

"I came to Litchfield with a hatred for the study of the law & nothing but the necessity to which all men are subject could have induced me to give it a moment's attention. But since my residence here, it has acquired a far different aspect. What before was a mass of perplexity and confusion (& Judge Gould be thanked for it) has been rendered as plain and simple as its nature will permit. I had devoted a year to the law, with how great application I leave you to imagine, previously to my arrival here. But I was a far greater proficient in the science after one month's attendance on the lectures than I had been while in Hazard's office. There are now 17 students in this institution. In summer, the number varies from 20 to 30."

Ennis now put down the items of greatest importance to Mann. "I pay $3.50 for my board and washing," he said, "$100.00 for a course of lectures . . . as to contingencies, it depends upon yourself how great a sum will be necessary. The young men in the office are generally close applicants, & some, whose funds are abundant, make but little use of them."

Litchfield Law School was founded in 1784 by Judge Tapping Reeve, a graduate of the College of New Jersey (Princeton). He had been an ardent supporter of the Revolution, going about Connecticut enlisting men to join Washington's army. After the war he was an equally ardent Federalist and was indicted for libel because of his fiery denunciations of Jefferson. It was said that Jefferson himself requested that charges be dismissed, and Reeve settled down to practice law in Litchfield.

According to custom in Massachusetts at that time, a man must "read" for three years, in some law office, before being admitted to the bar; he might be admitted within two years if he were a college graduate. Tapping Reeve had been a teacher and at one time a tutor at Princeton, so he found it impossible to have young men reading law in his office without trying to help them to learn law. There were few American lawbooks — Judge Reeve had yet to write them.

It was not long before Judge Reeve had more young men applying to read law in his office than he could possibly use. His law practice was poor right after the Revolution. It occurred to him, therefore, to open a law school. The students always referred to their school as "the Office" — a souvenir of the days when it was exactly that.

Reeve had remarkable personal magnetism. Lyman Beecher, who knew him well, remembered "soft dark eyes of rare beauty and a beaming expression of intelligence and benevolence." He was also so absent-minded that stories of his queer doings were always current. He was said to have held his horse's bridle, walked down the street with it and tied it to a hitching post without noticing that the horse had slipped the bridle and gone home. Amusing and charming all this might be, but Reeve needed a man who could organize and direct his school with efficiency. He found just the person in James Gould, one of his own student graduates.

In 1821, Judge Reeve was seventy-seven. His voice had failed so that he spoke in a whisper. His beautiful and beloved wife, Sally Burr, sister of Aaron Burr, had long since died, and Judge Reeve sat alone in his colonial mansion. His son and only child died and neighbors were scandalized when he married his housekeeper. It was said that he sought the solace of brandy more often than was wise, these days.

With the cruelty of youth, William Ennis reported: "The retirement of Judge Reeve will be very beneficial to the interests of the establishment. He had become superannuated and is incapable of speaking articulately and very little advantage resulted from attending his lectures. . . . Great persuasion was required to induce him to surrender the sole management of the office to [Judge] Gould. The latter has the reputuation of having improved the defects in the plan of his predecessor. He is a man distinguished for the urbanity of his manners and the interesting and perspicacious manner in which he explains the dry and complex principles of the law."

The letter went on at considerable length, but by now Horace Mann knew that Litchfield Law School was what he wanted. He went over his accounts. Expenses, May through September 1821, had been $57.59. He had done pretty well but was in need of clothing, so he ordered "one cloak and vest compleat" for which he paid $15.50. He would sell all his furnishings in his tutor's room at Brown: "3 window blinds" ought to bring eleven dollars, and "5 chairs" would be $7.50; "1 rocking chair, $2.50." The shovel and tongs for the fireplace he sold for a dollar and a half — he sold everything all the way down to "1 water pail .25 cents." It was harder to part with a set of Homer but he needed the $4.50 it would bring. Four wineglasses were reminiscent of good times but in Litchfield his landlady would doubtless furnish some.

Welcome Burgess, who graduated from Brown the year after Horace Mann, was now at Litchfield and wrote advice. "Buy nothing in town," he said. "Owing to the excitement of a Religious Revival which is at present scarifying the town, they cheat ten times worse than usual."

W. A. Burgess, the letter was signed, the name "Welcome" being rather a burden for so gay and irrepressible a young man. Welcome was five years younger than Horace, a native of Providence, and after leaving Litchfield he practiced law in Taunton — then died when he was only twenty-seven. He packed a good deal of living into his brief years and his letter to Horace was full of humor which he well knew would be appreciated. "Litchfield is in fact the place to make a lawyer," his letter went. "Everything is legal and subordinate to the study of the law. Law is the *prevailing fashion*. The minister will pray for you as the law directs. The Merchant will cheat you as the law directs. The Student will get drunk according to the present Letter of the Statute in such case made and provided. There is not a Girl in town who has not read enough law to understand and in some cases to practice the doctrine of *entails* & *inheritance,* consequent therefrom." This was not a letter that Horace would send on to his sister Lydia!

Mann went home to Franklin in 1821 and in February 1822, he set out due west for his new adventure.[2] Lydia went with him as far as Mendon, ten miles from home. There had been a heavy snowstorm but it was bright and clear the morning they started. "Hill and plain and ice-encircled tree cast back a myriad images of the rising sun," Horace recalled. He felt elated. This was the way such a momentous day should break and he felt that the omens were good. Then Lydia left him and there proved to be an hour's wait before the stage arrived, and Mann's spirits dropped. Now he felt "an air of sadness . . . a gloom that seemed to speak of past misfortune or dwell on apprehensions for things to come."

Horace was lonesome for his favorite sister Lydia, that was all. In 1815, his sister Rebecca had married Calvin Pennell, a man from Colrain, Massachusetts, in the northwest of the state. She had two children, Calvin and Rebecca. Mann's brother Stanley married the following year. His wife was Eliza Scott of Cumberland, Rhode Island, and they and their three children lived in the old homestead at Mann's Plain. Lydia, handsome and with much of her brother Horace's charm, was nevertheless single though approaching twenty-four — an advanced age in those days of early marriages. She was and ever would be Horace's dear companion and he set to work to write her of his journey.

"I never was robbed nor murdered nor attacked, nor have I ever met even with that vulgar occurrence of up-setting," he told her, warning her not to expect melodrama — but willing at the same time to get as much drama as he could out of his adventures.

"We soon passed out of Mass." — and this was Mann's first journey beyond his own state, except for his trip to Providence, Rhode Island. "I knew the moment we crossed the line for the cigar which one of my fellow travellers was smoking all at once burnt 'blue' and sent forth a most villainous stench."

The travelers spent the night at an inn at Ashford and started out again before dawn. They crossed the Connecticut River on the ice and apparently without the slightest misgivings as to whether the ice was thick enough to carry a coach and all its passengers. The roads were deeply rutted and frozen solid so that the coach pitched and tossed and the passengers were bruised from head to foot. "I was sea-sick," Horace said, "and when I got into Hartford I confess I was fairly Connecticut-sick."

There was little love lost between Massachusetts and Connecticut, and Horace was ready to find Hartford not to his liking. It was "an uncompact town of about 7 or 800," he said. The Hartford Convention, which had met in 1814 to protest against "Mr. Madison's war" with England, was high treason in Mann's eyes because secession had been discussed. Somehow Mann seemed to hold the city itself responsible, although plenty of Massachusetts men had taken part. "I saw the edifice where in 1814 were met together from the N. England States, the conclave of the Hartford Convention! Yes, I looked upon it and lived! I passed up and down the streets which at the same period of time were prohibited to the soldiers of the United States, who by a statute of this far-famed city were legally shoved off the sidewalks and cast into the middle of their streets to walk with horses and cattle!"

Having dealt with Hartford, Horace, for the first time on an overnight journey from home, proceeded to deal with this alien state. "Oh Connecticut! Connecticut! Land of Bigotry! Land of superstition! Land of Intolerance! May the increasing light and intelligence of the world liberalize thy character, and may a whole posterity attone for the crimes and follies of their ancestry."

Poor old Connecticut eventually rose high in Mann's esteem — but not next morning. He found that the stage for Litchfield ran but once a week and he congratulated himself on his good luck because he had arrived on the right day. Then he discovered that the stage-line proprietor, "consulting his own sordid views of interest, had sent down an open wagon." Snow and sleet were beginning to fall. There were two other passengers and they and their baggage could not all be crammed into the wagon. Fortunately the other two, "a gentleman and a lady," could afford to hire a sleigh, and they invited Horace to come with them.

And now Mann's opinion of Connecticut improved slightly. "The country is very picturesque, there are sudden elevations covered with woods, which are regularly cut through by deep vallies forming a precipitous descent on either [side]. The ground was covered with snow, no marks of cultivation appeared and at times I could almost see an old Indian, a native of these woods, darting through their gloom with his bow and arrow."

As soon as he arrived, Mann was greeted by the jocular Burgess and by "Rogers" — probably Henry Augustus Rogers, a Brown classmate of Burgess. Mann took lodgings with the two, at Mrs. Mary Lord's house. This was on North Street about opposite to Judge Gould's fine mansion with its little law school building in the garden. Mrs. Lord charged two-fifty a week for board and seventy-five cents a week for the room which Mann occupied. Laundry went on her bill at twenty-five cents a week. Even Welcome Burgess could not have claimed that Mrs. Lord was cheating and yet, when she presented the bill on May 30, 1822, the total of $55.75 looked large in Horace Mann's eyes.

During his last winter in Providence, Mann had been ill. The papers reported an "epidemick" — apparently of an influenza-like cold — and his had hung on, leaving him with a cough that caused him and his family a good deal of anxiety. Tuberculosis was believed hereditary and that cough was so like his father's! But the clear, cold air of Litchfield was just the thing. "You may banish all extra anxiety about my health," Mann wrote Lydia in April 1822, "it is much improved and improving." Fully as important as the invigorating climate of the Berkshires was the fact that Horace Mann was intensely happy in the knowledge that the work he was doing was right. He was finding what he had come to seek. He was on his way at last.

Judge Gould was a demanding master, arrogant at times, with a touch of the ruthless. Mann's own fighting spirit rose to the challenge and, if there were no particular affection between teacher and pupil, there was mutual respect.

The Law School itself consisted of two little wooden buildings each about the size of a crossroads schoolhouse. One, in the garden of Judge Tapping Reeve's colonial mansion, was the old one that had been, literally, his office, and then was the first school building still called "the Office." When Mann came to Litchfield, he found this building used as the library, and for "Moot Court." Judge Gould had built a similar building in the side yard of his big house with its Palladian doorway, and here the regular morning sessions of the Law School were held from nine till noon. Judge Gould lectured here at eleven.

Gould's lectures were particularly pertinent on "the Law of Contracts," on "Fraudulent Conveyances" and "Action on Debt" — all subjects his students would need constantly in everyday practice. Old Judge Reeve had lectured extemporaneously — talking at length when a point seemed interesting, breaking off to answer questions. Judge Gould spoke from a written manuscript; there would be no interruptions, and he expected his students to take down every word he said.

Gould sat himself down in his big chair before the fireplace, and his students, at rough wooden desks, scribbled away for dear life. They were writing what was to become their own law library — and for many of them, this would be all the library they would ever own. The Judge's dark eyes, under their black brows, watched and seemed to probe the mind of the lazy student or the dull one, discovering the slightest gap in this knowledge of the law that he was giving them so rapidly and so well. The lazy student came under the fire of his sarcasm but the young man honestly attempting to understand the intricacies of the law received patient help and brilliant exposition of every obscure point.

Judge Gould "studies, thinks and talks law," one of his students said. He also made his scholars live the law — by means of his "honor system." The rules were many but first and of paramount importance was this: "It shall be the duty of the members of the Office to inform the Chairman of all breaches of these articles, within two days after their knowledge of the same."

"The Conscience of Gentlemen may be appealed to, in all cases, to discover testimony, when sufficient testimony to convict one cannot be produced from any other quarter." There was a fine for "disorder," not exceeding twenty-five cents. But a student "directly or indirectly offering insult or disrespect to Judge Reeve, Judge Gould Esq." would be fined up to a dollar for his misdeed. The "chairman" to whom misdemeanors must be reported was a student, each student taking a turn at the chairmanship, in alphabetical order.

If all the "Gentlemen" had been saints, the chairman would have been gravely disappointed at missing a chance to call witnesses, to hear evidence, and to pronounce judgment. There seems to have been little or no difficulty about discipline, however. For one thing, almost all the students were over twenty and some considerably older. A good deal of leeway was allowed, especially in the matter of drinking, but all the students were intensely interested in their courses — most were earning their way with a goal in sight.

"Moot Court," which was held one evening a week, was the place where student reputations were made and lost. By April 9, 1822, Horace Mann had argued a case. "I made my first appearance evening before last & as I came off about half-middling, I know not as I have reason for complaint," he wrote. Judge Gould had been on the bench, ex officio, and a student elected by his classmates was attorney general. In the summer of 1822, Horace Mann was attorney general. However modestly he wrote about it to his sister, Moot Court was his joy from the very beginning.

Years later J. W. Scott, a Litchfield classmate, wrote, "The arguments of Mr. Mann were distinguished for clearness. . . . On one occasion when the side he sustained was opposed to the decision of the judge, previously written out, it was the general opinion that Mr. Mann made the better case." Judge Gould made a great effort to refute Mann's arguments and for once he was not reading from manuscript. The students thought old Gould took the whole thing badly — or, to put it in Scott's words, "showed . . . some improper feeling or wounded self-esteem."

On April 11, 1822, Horace wrote to Lydia that he had been to two parties and had made some calls. He had picked up a bit of gossip about the minister's daughter. "You may have heard that Professor Fisher of N. Haven has been *making love* to Miss Catherine Beecher." Professor Fisher was none other than Alexander Metcalf Fisher, the pride of Franklin. Despite Fisher's nervous breakdown, which Horace's brother Stanley had held up as a grave warning against overwork, here was the town boy (two years older than Horace) now much farther up that ladder of eduucation and of life. Mann would not have been human had he not envied Fisher a little. He did not envy Fisher his fiancée, however. "Miss Beecher is reputed a lady of superior intellect," Horace told his sister. "She writes very good poetry and will probably make the professor a very good help-mate." Personally, Horace found her dull. "We exchanged truisms on Scott's novels, but it was nothing tremendous on either side."

When this letter was written, Alexander Fisher was on his way to Europe to make that tour considered so essential to the scholar and the gentleman. But if envy ever entered Horace Mann's heart, he was quickly taught never to desire another man's fate. On April 22, the *Albion* was wrecked in a gale "on the coast of Ireland." Professor Fisher and all others save one were drowned. Franklin forgot her young genius but Miss Catherine Beecher never married.

Great was the fame of Dr. Lyman Beecher's preaching, and Horace Mann lost no time in going to hear him. "Dr. Beecher," Mann said, "published . . . a dolorous tale about the heathenish condition of the people of the U. States, six-sevenths of whom were, according to him, sitting in the . . . shadow of death because . . . they had not *hopkinsian* . . . ministers to dispense the light of the Calvinist creed, a light very much like the 'lurid light' of Milton's 'which far round illumined hell.' "

Emmons was a leader in the Hopkins school of theology, and Horace Mann, brought up on Emmons's sermons, was a connoisseur of hell-fire preaching. He wanted to see how Beecher rated by comparison — and Beecher did well, for in the first sermon Horace heard, he "divided sinners into several distinct classes . . . carried one by one through the dark valley of the shadow of death to the throne of God and then, personating the Almighty, he pronounced their terrible doom."

"I never heard such a sermon in my life," Horace told his sister. "It produced as great an effect upon my feelings as it would have to have heard a great tragedy well performed at a theatre! *No more upon my belief;* for belief belongs to the understanding and should not be biased by hopes and fears." Horace Mann was twenty-six years old. This was the point to which his earnest, careful thinking had brought him.

In spite of all the work and churchgoing as reported to sister Lydia, Litchfield law students knew how to have a rousing good time and Horace Mann joined in, as friends later testified. Litchfield had been given a special dispensation from providence in the form of Miss Sally Pierce's Female Academy, and Miss Pierce, little and bright-eyed, had amazingly modern ideas when it came to allowing young gentlemen of the law to entertain her young ladies.

Horace Mann, studying in his room across the way from Miss

Pierce's school, would be roused by music in the late afternoon of a summer's day. Down North Street would come a long procession of young girls, and he was young and human — he went to the window. The girls walked two and two, wearing floating muslins in flower colors, with soft heelless shoes on their little feet. Walking at their head was their music master — and in order that they should learn grace and rhythm, Miss Sally's girls walked to the music of a flute and a flageolet. The music taught many a young man that there was more to life than the study of law, as the girls came stepping sweetly, under the young elms.

Miss Sally was a maiden lady of fifty-five at this time and her school was at the height of its popularity. She came from a Litchfield family so numerous that apparently no one knew how many more than eleven children there were! When Sally was sixteen her father died, and her oldest brother, since he wished to be free to marry, set about with remarkable efficiency to establish his brothers and sisters in life. He decided that Sarah should teach. Accordingly, he sent her to New York where she was "not to miss a single dancing school" and where she was to overcome any awkward "country girl" ways and learn "a natural careless, genteel air." She was to "study the fashions, the art of pleasing to advantage."

A portrait of Miss Sally in later years shows her to be a very pleasing little lady indeed, with an exceedingly fashionable high muslin cap. It would be unfair to her not to add that her brother also bought her books. She was not to study them in New York but at home where her time was not so valuable.

Miss Pierce's girls worked hard under strict rules. They must "rise early, be dressed neatly and exercise before breakfast." They must be in church every Sunday unless they had so good an excuse for staying away that they would "dare present it at the Day of Judgment." School session was long and "two hours must be faithfully devoted to close study, while out of school." But Miss Pierce's girls also had more fun than most girls in Female Academies. To be sure, "no young lady is allowed to attend any public ball or sleigh party till they are more than 16 years old," the rules said — but what parties there were for the young ladies of the advanced age of seventeen! There was no vacation given at Christmas or New Year's, but a half-day was granted and off went the girls in sleighs, with bearskin rugs around them and floor stoves at their feet. They drove to nearby towns for a supper with fiddle music afterwards and a fast square dance to warm them for the return journey. They must be home by nine or woe betide them, so they played hard. On holidays such as the Fourth of July the law students gave a "Students' Ball in the Assembly room on the third floor of Phillips Tavern." In return, Miss Pierce's girls gave several less formal dancing parties at the school. Theatricals were the rage — the girls acting in excessively moralizing plays written for them by Miss Pierce.

Miss Sally's girls boarded in private homes just as the Litchfield law students did. Horace Mann mentioned one party "out of the house" where he lived, and "one party in it," for Litchfield people treated these young students like sons and daughters and entertained for them with elegance — a servant "handing around the wine." There was music and there were tables of whist, with Horace Mann "the best whist player . . . in the school," according to the testimony of his friend Scott.

"Two of my college acquaintances are here, with whom I spend many pleasant hours," Horace wrote. He probably referred to Burgess and Rogers but he made many more new friendships, some of which were to last for many years to come. There was James Sullivan of Boston, his father a prominent and wealthy lawyer. James had trouble with his eyes and Horace Mann read the lessons in law to him — thereby acquiring for himself a more perfect knowledge. Of importance to Mann in later years was Edward Greely Loring. Edward was a Harvard graduate, son of Edward and Frances Loring of Boston. He was five years younger than Mann and had already studied law with his distinguished cousin, Charles Greely Loring. Ten years earlier, Edward's cousin had also studied at Litchfield, had married Ann Brace, a niece of Miss Pierce. Edward had a ready-made introduction to Litchfield society, he had a talent for social life and money to support his taste. "Glorious Neddy," Horace Mann called him, with just a touch of mockery. But Neddy was good for Horace, loved and understood him about as well as any friend he would ever have.

Mary L. Wilbor, sixteen years old, must have been one of the most attractive girls at the Female Academy. On August 21, 1822, she wrote in her diary that she and her roommate "were awoke by music." They ran to the window "and found it to be Messrs. Loring, Burgess and Sullivan with flutes which were played with much skill and sweetness." It is a pity that Horace Mann's Litchfield bills carry no item for a flute and flute lessons. They do, however, prove that he was by no means a hopeless grind.

In June, Mann bought a leghorn hat which must have had a cockade or how else could the milliner have used two and a half yards of ribbon to trim it! He had a waistcoat of imported silk and a pair of white "imperial cord pantaloons." Charles L. Webb of Litchfield supplied these materials, $2.07 for the waistcoat and findings, $2.31 for the material for the pantaloons; and Ellis Hull of Litchfield made up the pantaloons for a dollar and a half — the waistcoat for a dollar. Here was gala clothing for an "elegant" young man.

It is true that in January 1823 Horace Mann burned four quarts of oil in his lamp, and it was doubtless the "midnight" variety that his later-life admirers liked to talk about. But what is more to the point in showing that Litchfield's special advantages were not lost upon him is the bill for three quarts of Madeira wine and "2 doz. Best Segars" — these last costing a total of sixty-four cents!

Horace Mann's account was probably one of the lowest carried with Charles L. Webb, for Horace was always careful of his expenses. He had no reason to suppose he would run short of money, having earned at least three hundred and seventy-five dollars a year for two years as Tutor at Brown. It seems possible that he sent his money home to his brother Stanley to take care of — perhaps to invest in Stanley's various activities. Certainly Horace wrote home for money without apology and without a doubt that he would get it. "If Stanley can remit to me a little of the 'root of all evil' without embarrassing himself, I wish he would do it. My full quarter's board will come due the last of the month & I should like to meet the demand with punctuality. Forty dollars will be sufficient."

"Make Stanley write me respecting his concerns," Horace went on, "I may be able to give him some hints, inasmuch as the circumstances of growing up into a lawyer & living in Connecticut are calculated to make a man wondrous keen for here the most common thing imaginable is to rise from your knees at prayer to cheat a man out of two pence."

But Stanley did not write of his affairs. He was no letter writer and his affairs were so complicated that it is doubtful if he understood them himself. In fact no one wrote from home very often, not even Lydia. "For the past several weeks I have been in a half delirious state, on account of receiving no intelligence from home," Horace said, heading his letter LITCHFIELD, *Sept. 17, 1822.* "It is now three months since I have heard a single lisp from home! & for a good part of that time I have been trying the experiment with respect to money, which ended so tragically in the case of the old man's horse! If the children of Israel were pressed half so hard for 'gear' as I have been, I do not wonder they were willing to worship the golden calf."

Little if anything was forthcoming and finally, in desperation, Mann was obliged to accept fifty dollars from Welcome Burgess. It was an anonymous gift, Welcome insisted. It was not, it was a loan, said Mann, and he repaid it the following November with interest. "I immediately paid over the money to the person of whom I borrowed it," Welcome wrote, "it was only a friendly act & what (had circumstances been changed) I should have expected from you."

By June 1823 Horace Mann was writing to graduate friends about prospects for a young lawyer. He asked about going South and a former classmate replied, "I may emigrate there myself . . . I believe it holds out tenfold encouragement to what the North does. To be sure, they have an idle habit of dying early from epidemics & also of making small holes thro' a man at the distance of ten paces. . . ."

Horace Mann decided to brave the lesser hazards of a town which "had a strong dislike to newcomers." But after all — he only returned to the home of his ancestors when he chose Dedham, Massachusetts, as his future home.

CHAPTER SIX
Turbulent Dedham

"RECENT events in this town have had a tendency to create an opinion abroad that here was a litigious and turbulent community," wrote Erastus Worthington, Dedham historian of 1827. Mr. Worthington described the lawsuit by which Dedham Parish retained the property of the First Church and upheld their right to choose a Unitarian minister. The Episcopal Church had been involved in lawsuits too, while "irregular practices" by the Dedham Bank had resulted in "public prosecution." This was a record which Mr. Worthington deplored but to Horace Mann — about to become a lawyer — what town could be more to his advantage than "litigious and turbulent" Dedham! [1] Mann made no mistake when, in the spring of 1823, he entered the law office of the Honorable James Richardson, President of the Norfolk Bar Association.

"The present village contains nearly one hundred houses," wrote Mr. Worthington in his Dedham history. "Nearly all of them are two stories high. . . . More than four fifths of the houses are elegant, so far as that term can be applied to a wooden house." Only partly elegant, therefore, was Alden's hotel [2] on Court Street, since it was built of both wood and brick. It was handsome — by anybody's standards. Here the coaches stopped to change horses and take on passengers for Providence or Boston. Distinguished visitors stayed here, President Monroe for example — and here came ordinary citizens, some of them in search of a lawyer. Again, Horace Mann made no mistake when he took a room at Alden's.

Captain Alden would supply horse and chaise when Mann's law cases took him out along the country roads. Alden would supply the occasional bottle of port with which Mann might entertain a guest. But the noise and bustle of an inn had its drawbacks too, and Horace, writing to Lydia from Dedham on May 3, 1823, said "I am as well as usual & only about half-pleasantly situated." He would be twenty-seven years old the following day but of that he made no mention. He sent his sister eleven dollars to pay a debt.

Beside the inn was a small green common shaded by carefully planted young trees. "The Square" they called it, and it marked the center of town. At the northern end stood a church, painted white with high columns and a graceful, unusually high spire. Built in 1763, this house of God was "elegant," although of wood. It was the "Lamson church," so-called after the present liberal pastor whose installation had brought both turbulence and plenty of litigation to Dedham. To this church Mr. Mann paid tax and pew rent and thereby (in the eyes of Dr. Emmons and his followers) declared himself a heathen.

Across the northeast corner, across the street but still facing the green, stood a new church, built in 1819. Sturdy and square, its spire less aspiring, the church was handsome nevertheless. Here the orthodox former members of Mr. Lamson's "First Church" were free to be as Congregationalist as they pleased. However, Dr. Lamson's flock were so incensed against their seceding friends that they opened a door at the back of their own building so that they could come and go of a Sunday without so much as a glimpse of their fellow Christians. Although commemorating Protestant dis-unity, the two churches created architectural harmony in spite of themselves, at the heart of this singularly beautiful New England town.

Around the green stood square white-painted houses with wide chimneys and small-paned windows. Judge Haven's mansion dominated them all — or tried to. Built in 1795, the original façade had a quiet dignity, but an additional story flanked by heavy Greek scrolls gave the house the look of a haughty dowager who had just raised her lorgnette. Beautiful twin elms guarded the front walk and masked, somewhat, this look of disdain.

It was very soon after his arrival in Dedham that Horace Mann made his way up the terraced front walk to the Haven mansion. He was accompanied by Dr. Fisher, who introduced him, as Catherine Haven afterwards remembered. Catherine was just twenty-one and she remembered forever the tall, rather thin young man with the deep-set eyes, the generous smile. But it was Catherine's sister Elizabeth who seemed to interest Mr. Mann.

The Haven girls had a younger brother, Sam, now at Amherst. He would later become a lawyer and he looked upon Horace Mann with a suspicion which might have been caused by jealousy.

There were already at least five lawyers in Dedham and it would not have been surprising if all of them treated Horace Mann, the newcomer, a trifle coldly. The rest of the citizens, on the other hand, hastened to pay him a high honor before he had lived in Dedham more than a few months. They asked him to be the orator at the Fourth of July celebration.

The Fourth was a holiday far more generally and joyously celebrated than Christmas. In Puritan New England, Christmas festivities were still too reminiscent of Old England and the established church, but to commemorate the nation's liberation from England was a patriot's duty. In Dedham there would be a big public banquet at Alden's hotel. There would be a procession with as loud a brass band as the town could provide and then the oration would be heard — not on the village green but with much greater pomp and solemnity within the Lamson church. It was understood that political leaders would listen carefully to the Fourth of July orator. And it was expected that the orator would paint a clear picture of his own political views — and place a flowery frame of patriotic sentiments around it.

Horace Mann knew all this, having been brought up on this sort of Fourth of July tradition. He had been invited well in advance of the date, so he knew that he was no second or third choice and that this event was of importance to his future career.[3] But on June 14, 1823, he wrote his sister Lydia. "That long Quixotic visage of mine" — was the way he described his face. It was now swollen strangely. He had the mumps!

How long would the mumps last? Dr. Fisher had been encouraging. And Horace told Lydia why the matter was of such importance. "I am expected to put a black gown on, the 4th of next month, and shall have a right to make a noise for half an hour for my own amusement, other folks in the meantime being bound to hold their tongues."

Mr. Mann labored hard on his oration. He began by blasting the monarchies of Europe and extolling the virtues of a representative government. This was a theme close to his heart and one in which his hearers agreed completely. But Mann did not miss this opportunity to sound an equally heartfelt warning. These blessings of freedom, which had been so hard-won, could be lost easily and imperceptibly. They could slip away, one after one, he said. How then could American freedom be guarded and preserved? "*Intelligence*, like the blood sprinkled upon the doorposts of the Hebrew houses, will prevent the destroying angel of despotism from entering," and Horace Mann's words, spoken in a little town in another century, would always ring true.

Oratory was still Mann's first love and the law, it must be admitted, was unexciting that first summer. Until December 1823 when he took the "oaths required by law to practice in the Court of Common Pleas," he was no more than a clerk in Richardson's office without the right — still less the opportunity — to address a jury. New friends made the first summer endurable. There were "boating and walking excursions" for Dedham young people, with the Haven girls[4] eager to include Horace Mann in their circle. Elizabeth Haven was all too often ill at home but her sister Catherine proved a lively companion. What a way she had of making a man talk — of laughing at his sallies and making him feel the very soul of wit!

Catherine, telling it later, described Horace Mann as she first knew him. "How brilliant he was in general conversation, with such sparkling repartee, such gushing wit, and such a merry laugh! . . . His droll sayings could never be recalled without exciting a hearty laugh at their originality."

When winter came, Elizabeth and Catherine Haven had no intention of losing Horace Mann's society even though the meandering Charles was frozen over and there could be no more boating parties. There was parlor entertainment, fully as satisfactory. It must have been the winter of 1824–1825 of which Catherine wrote when she said, "The beginning of a still more intimate acquaintance was during the second winter of his [Mann's] residence in Dedham. My sister and I and an older friend formed ourselves into a cozy little coterie for reading together and invited Mr. Mann to join us. One evening in each week we came together." It was the girls' idea that they should read novels and poetry aloud, and Horace Mann said not a word about the "permanent injury" the novel might do to their minds! He found the Haven course of literature much more persuasive than the one at Brown, and Catherine said she "learned to know the finer traits of his nature as well as the strong and brilliant ones."

Horace Mann was not again a Dedham public orator until 1826. In 1826 there were three men who had signed the Declaration of Independence still alive and active for the welfare of the nation. These were Adams, Jefferson and Carroll. On the Fourth of July of that year, Thomas Jefferson died "at ten minutes before one P.M." at Monticello, and John Adams died a little before six in the evening at his home in Quincy, Massachusetts. The whole nation was shocked and saddened. In New England, it was the loss of Mr. Adams that seemed the greater, because the more personal. Dedham people mourned a friend and neighbor.

Memorial services were held in every city and town in the vicinity with John Quincy Adams and his sons attending so many of them it is hard to see how they could have stood the strain. But if Mr. Adams would not refuse to go to Boston to hear Mr. Webster's "eulogy," — neither would he fail to appear in Dedham where a young lawyer by the name of Horace Mann was the orator!

"Cold and unfriendly," John Quincy Adams was sometimes said to be. His neighbors did not find him so. When a committee from Dedham asked him to check a list of people who wanted to meet him and indicate those he considered sufficiently important for him to see at Alden's hotel, Adams would not bother with the paper. "I want to meet everyone who is interested in meeting me," he said.

Dating his entry *July 31st, 1826,* John Quincy Adams told of the memorial service. "After dining at noon, I went with my brother, his son T.B. and my sons G.W. and John to Dedham. We stopped at Alden's Tavern where about two hundred persons, inhabitants of that place and of other towns in the County were introduced to me. Between three and four, we went in procession to the meeting-house where the funeral solemnities were performed. Two anthems, a dirge, and an occasional hymn, written by Horace Mann were performed by a choir of singers accompanied by the organ . . . and a eulogy upon John Adams and Thomas Jefferson was pronounced by Horace Mann, of splendid composition and lofty eloquence. . . .

After returning in procession to the tavern, I thanked the several performers of the day and we came back to Quincy."

Mr. Adams had already attended five such ceremonies "in the past week" but he did not praise any other orator as highly as he praised Horace Mann. Although he had now met two hundred of his Norfolk County neighbors, he would not forget Horace Mann, and there were those who said that this was the point in Mann's career at which he turned in the direction of politics and public life.

Dedham was a town with a mind of its own — not easy to please. For example, in 1784, Dedham townspeople directed their representative in Boston in no uncertain terms: "You are desired to attempt the reduction of taxes in the following manner. First by reducing wages and salaries of public officers. Secondly, by lopping off some unnecessary branches in some department." Lawyers came under this heading! "If they cannot be effectually regulated, we then desire that the order of lawyers be totally abolished." By 1827, Dedham had economy still in mind and felt that little had ever been done about it. But they could tolerate lawyers and the "republican farmers" were looking for a leader. Dedham had been Federalist, but now the town as well as the farmers wanted a young "National Republican" who could "beat our opponents at their chosen game of hard words and satire." Horace Mann showed promise. Hitherto his words had rarely been hard or satirical, but those who knew him felt he had it in him — if the occasion would warrant.

Representatives to the legislature, or "General Court" as they called it, were chosen by vote or by acclamation in the various towns on varying dates, in May. On the last Wednesday in May they all gathered in Boston — 313 of them in 1827. From Dedham came Richard Ellis, who had been chosen the previous year as well. A newcomer to Boston, his name for the first time in Boston papers, was "Horace Mann Esq.," of Dedham.[5]

Overnight, booths and tents had sprung up on Boston Common. Oysters, "egg-pop," gingerbread and rum were sold and a joyful crowd gathered round the booths — country people for the most part, come to Boston to see the parade, the governor, the mayor, the cadets and the lawmakers — as though the whole thing were a country fair. As the day wore on the booths where rum was for sale were more and more liberally patronized. The cows, still pastured on Boston Common, had to give up their grazing rights temporarily — or else develop a taste for rum and gingerbread!

It was all new and exciting to Horace Mann, and that warm smile which so transformed his face broke out often as he caught sight of constituents outside on the Common and met old acquaintances within the State House. At ten Governor Levi Lincoln and his council appeared and "the usual oaths of allegiance and fidelity were administered" to new members. To Horace Mann, there was nothing "usual" about the ceremony. He brought high ideals and a determination to work for the public good to this, his first legislative experience, and he took the oaths, not with his tongue in his cheek as so many did, but in all sincerity. He felt an intense pride in his country — where the son of a farmer could become a lawyer and then in four short years a maker of laws.

As soon as the formalities within the State House were over, the procession formed and members of both houses marched down the hill to the Old South Meetinghouse to hear the election sermon. The Reverend Moses Stuart preached from the text, "Where the Spirit of the Law is, there is thy liberty," and his sermon was long and by some unheeded. Horace Mann, who perhaps needed it least, listened closely. The church service over, the procession returned to the State House and "the rest of the day" was "devoted to festivity."

The exact nature of the festivity was best described in a letter to the *Boston Patriot and Mercantile Advertiser*. "The gentlemen will repair to . . . Faneuil Hall . . . and there eat and DRINK and fiddle and beat drum and roar and sing and clap hands, and some of them will tumble down, or keep it up till candlelight and then reel home."

Most certainly Horace Mann never reeled home from Faneuil Hall or anywhere else. But these were days when he enjoyed life to the full, entertained friends and took all proper steps in the direction of success. The Exchange Coffee House billed him for five bottles of port the day after New Year's, 1828, for example. There were tickets to the theater and dinners for a group of friends he called "the club." Edward Loring, the "Glorious Neddy" of Litchfield days, was a prominent member of the club. He was delighted

to take Horace around and introduce him to his Boston friends —
the Quincy family in particular.

These were days when Horace Mann had good reason to believe
that he was making not only a political name for himself but a
private fortune. The most important factor, both for and against
his chances of wealth, was his brother, Thomas Stanley. The first
indication of the direction in which Stanley's interests were taking
him (and his brother Horace along with him) comes from a receipted bill headed DEDHAM, *May 20, 1825.* Seventeen dollars had
been received from Horace Mann for "a lot of shuttles made . . .
for Thomas S. Mann and delivered the 16h of May Inst." Stanley
wanted the shuttles for cotton textile mills and Horace would see
to the financing when Stanley decided to buy two factories!

One of the first mills for the manufacture of cotton cloth was
located in Wrentham, where — before 1790 — a horse patiently
turned a sort of capstan to supply power for a loom. A year later an
Arkwright mill in nearby Pawtucket, Rhode Island (the one President Monroe visited) was operating with water power. The little
lakes and brooks of Wrentham and Franklin were ideal for providing just enough water power to turn a few spindles. In 1809 the
Eagle Manufacturing Company was incorporated for the purpose of
"producing cotton yarn and cloth," and in 1822 the City Manufacturing Company incorporated to produce "cotton and woolen
goods." The City Company had taken over the site of the old grist
mill, where Eagle Brook ran out of Pearl Lake, and the two mills
were not far apart. They used the same source of water power but
the Wrentham–Franklin town line ran between them. These were
the mills, one old, one new, that Stanley proposed to buy.

Stanley had a magnetic personality, he was exceedingly handsome
— and he could sell anything. Unfortunately, he detested pen and
paper, expressed himself with difficulty on paper and left only
enough letters behind to show that he was at one time a commission merchant, traveling in the vicinity of Franklin with a load of
goods on a cart. He seems to have done well. But if letters were
hard to write, he found accounts still more troublesome to keep —
and he had faith in the word of his fellow man that was all too often
misplaced.

Naturally optimistic, Horace admired and believed in Stanley and accepted Stanley's own estimate of his assets, of the value of the two mills and their alleged fredom from debt. Horace Mann proceeded to finance the buying of the mills with next to no capital of his own! In February 1826 he bought of his brother Stanley nine shares of capital stock in the Eagle Company, for which he promised to pay two thousand dollars. That same month, he bought seventy-five shares of City Company stock of John French and Otis Everett of Boston, the two original incorporators.[6] Mann paid French and Everett thirty-five thousand dollars, of which twenty-seven thousand was in ten notes, two maturing during each of the next five years.

A group of men were willing to go on Horace Mann's notes to French and Everett. He promised to indemnify them in case of loss and he transferred to them all his stock. He also promised that a committee of three should have "free access to the books while the loan stands." He agreed to keep thirty thousand dollars' worth of insurance in force on the mills and to offer all shares at public auction should the notes not be met on time. But Mann felt so certain of the value of the property that he added a clause whereby anything left after such an auction would be his, "for his exertions."

The men who were "co-sureties" on Horace's notes were from Franklin, most of them. They were of the generation of his father and several were related by marriage to his father's family. Horace Mann had confidence in his own legal ability and great confidence in Stanley's ability to run textile mills at a profit. Great family fortunes were being established — why should not Horace and Stanley establish the Mann family fortune?

Foremost in Mann's mind were his law practice and his political career, just launched. A fortune would come in handy, since the clients who interested him most were those most in need of him and least able to pay. And although a political office could be profitable, the devious means thereto were not for Horace Mann.

CHAPTER SEVEN

Dearest Miss Charlotte

A NEWCOMER to the House of Representatives could not expect to choose the committees on which he would like to serve — he was lucky if he were appointed to any committees at all. Horace Mann found himself "ordered to enquire if any and what alterations are necessary to be made in the laws respecting Hawkers, Pedlars and Petty Chapmen." Doubtless he did so, with all the zeal of the novice.

Like the good child among his elders, the newcomer to the legislature was expected to be seen but not heard. But the Dedham *Village Register*, in its support of Horace Mann, had made it clear what was expected of him. Richard Ellis, though his "services were useful and valuable" was "not excelling in debate." What the town needed was someone "qualified by talents and requirements to enter into the *discussion* of important subjects. . . ." And almost immediately the *Register's* support of Horace Mann was justified.

As far as the House was concerned, Mann's first entry into "discussion" was a bolt from the blue. A bill to incorporate the Trustees of the Ministerial Fund of the First Church of Blandford [1] came up. Similar bills had been passed without question. But this time, although no word appeared in the papers, friends of Horace Mann remembered that he sprang to his feet in that impetuous way so characteristic of him. The bill was against religious freedom, he said. No money should be set aside forever for the benefit of any given creed! There was surprise and consternation, especially among the orthodox ministers among representatives. Hastily, the bill was put over till next session.

The winter session of the legislature began on January 2 and although the year was now 1828, this was still considered the session

of 1827. The matter of incorporating the Blandford fund came up
again and now Mr. Boies, Blandford representative, proposed a clause
that really provoked debate. The money must be "forever applied to
the support of a learned, pious, *Trinitarian* Minister"! Plenty of
representatives favored this, including Speaker Calhoun, of Springfield. But now Mr. Mann was not alone against it. Those opponents
who dared stand up and be counted were "Messrs Saltonstall, Savage,
Mann, Appleton, Phillips etc." said the *Christian Register*, a Unitarian
publication. The fund, if incorporated, would establish an estate in
a kind of mortmain — or, translating literally, *dead hands* would have
a stranglehold on the money throughout coming generations. Mr.
Mann was heard often during the debate, which "occupied the
greater part of two days." Mann spoke of leaving "posterity as free
and unshackled as ourselves" and gradually the tide began to shift
in favor of freedom. But the subject was so touchy that the daily
press kept quiet about it and only the *Christian Register* told the
story. Finally, the House decided to defer the bill indefinitely rather
than to vote on it, one way or the other. They killed it this way
without going on record as orthodox or liberal; but it was noted that
the newcomer, Mr. Mann of Dedham, cared more for his convictions
than for political caution.

At this stage in Horace Mann's career, religious freedom was by
no means his only cause, however. What also kindled his imagination
and aroused his enthusiasm was the subject of railroads. How joyfully he welcomed the coming of the machine age! "Machinery is
the enlargement of human power," he cried. "Here strength of mind
makes up for the weakness of the body." With these words, he began
his first long, carefully prepared speech in the House of Representatives.

On June 9, 1827, Josiah Quincy, then Mayor of Boston, "and
2683 others, citizens of Boston," presented a petition, "praying for
the survey of a railroad route to the Hudson." The papers were
full of this fascinating contraption, the "steam cars." Letters warning
the public that the iron horse was a dangerous monster were followed
by articles on the "steam-pressure engine" telling how, in England,
passengers could "whirl at the rate of eighteen or twenty miles an
hour!"

In the legislature, a large group attempted to protect the interests

of canals and stagecoach lines. "The Commonwealth shall not subscribe to any railroad in any direction," they thundered. But Josiah
Quincy was a master strategist. He presented his petition on a
Saturday and at half-past eleven that morning the House adjourned
to inspect the railway at Quincy. Off they all trooped like a bunch
of schoolboys given an unexpected holiday, their transportation to
the neighboring town and their tour of inspection all carefully stage-
managed by the astute Mr. Quincy.

The Quincy Railway,[2] "the first constructed in this country,"
had been built in 1826. Stone cross-ties, eight feet apart, carried
wooden rails, and the line — three miles long — had cost over 33,000
dollars. It ran from the Quincy granite quarries to "the navigable
waters of the Neponset river," and it carried great blocks of granite
to be loaded on lighters for the second leg of their journey to
Bunker Hill — and the monument project. Before long, Bostonians
would point with pride to many new buildings of Quincy granite —
white and sparkling when it was first quarried, growing grim and
gray only with time and coal smoke.

"Cars of great weight, the wheels alone of a single car weighing
a ton," were hauled up and down an "elevation about 80 feet" but
so far the Quincy railroad was not fooling around with the Demon
Steam. The motive power was "a horse traveling about a shaft"! As
one car went up the grade, "suspended by a strong chain," another
went down and the chains passed around a drum "regulated by the
horse." On level ground the motive power was still horses — two
of them driven tandem.

Mann kept the manuscript of his speech in favor of railroads, dated
1827, among his papers. He began by pointing out that Massachusetts was dependent upon her sister states for almost every necessity
of life. The soil of Massachusetts "scarcely produces anything spontaneously, and scantily requites the most devoted labors of the
husbandman," he said, speaking from the bitter experience of early
years on his father's farm. "We do not even grow the grain for our
horses!" Transportation lagged far behind the factory and "the labor
of production can hardly be compared to the labor of transportation," Mann said — canal boats with slow-moving horses upon the
towpaths, and stagecoaches snow-bound in winter, being laborious
methods he would discard. On June 16, the House authorized a railroad survey to cost not more than $10,000. The resolution passed

166 to 47. But the battle was by no means won. It was not until 1829 that the "Worcester Railroad Company" was chartered to run "from the coal mines in Worcester to Quinsigamond Pond and the Blackstone Canal."

Absorbed in his new duties, charmed by the city of Boston, Horace Mann drifted away from the social life of Dedham. On February 16, 1826, the lovely Elizabeth Haven had died of tuberculosis, aged twenty-six. The Haven family withdrew from all social activities, including, of course, the little reading group which had given Elizabeth so much pleasure. Horace Mann no longer sprang eagerly up the terrace steps to the Haven mansion. When a reasonable period of mourning was over, Catherine Haven began to hope to see him again — but he came not. He had been deeply attached to Elizabeth, Catherine thought — drawn to her, it seemed, by her frail health and her need of strength and protection. But Catherine was a person of courage and resourcefulness.

When Horace Mann appeared on the streets of Dedham again, between legislative sessions, he was a more interesting figure than ever. Catherine Haven made it clear that she wanted to hear all about his experiences in Boston, and he began calling regularly at the Haven house. Catherine had a way of making Horace put his dreams and ambitions into words and sometimes he went home feeling that he had talked too much. But, as he said years later, "she was a most enrapturing person!"

It seems probable that Catherine would have been willing to share with Horace Mann the brilliant future that she foresaw for him. Mann never had any idea how attractive he was to women — now, nor at any time. But Judge Haven put an end to Catherine's dreams, in any case. According to Catherine's brother Sam, their father asked Horace Mann what his intentions were toward Catherine. Mann had none — beyond friendship.

Catherine held her head high in spite of her father's anger and the village gossip, of which she must have been well aware. She did not lack for suitors. She accepted her status as Horace Mann's friend and so she steadfastly remained. She said, however (understandably on the defensive), that she was the first to know when Horace asked Charlotte Messer to marry him.

Horace Mann had been a friend of the Messer family for thirteen years and had always been a welcome and a frequent caller. Natu-

Charlotte Messer

This silhouette of Charlotte Messer is the property of
Mrs. Manning A. Williams, descendant of Caroline Messer.

Brown University in Mann's Day

No other building was added until 1822. The well house
at the far right must be the one the students delighted to
burn when a sufficiently joyful occasion arose.

rally, Asa Messer would never have dreamed of asking Mann's intentions toward any one of his three daughters but Mann's experience with Judge Haven may have been somewhat on his mind when he wrote his formal proposal to Charlotte on June 9, 1829. Let there be no misunderstanding this time! When she did not reply to his first letter [3] he was bitterly disappointed, but there was no "wreck of hope" such as he had mentioned to her.

Mann proceeded with his journey to Hartford — conscientiously determined to study the Hartford hospital for the insane and build a better one for Massachusetts if he could. The governor awaited his report. But his evenings were his own. Placing HARTFORD at the top, he wrote Charlotte a second letter. It was still "Miss Charlotte" — although he had known her since she was a child! But it was "My dearest Miss Charlotte" and he let his heart speak rather than his legal mind.

"Hitherto my emotions, excited by your image in my mind . . . have been too sacred and tender to be breathed aloud, even in my solitary walks, or at the sleepless hour of midnight. I have bourne them about as a devotee bears his faith in a strange land, where others know not the object of his worship. . . . My heart has been torn by the conflict of desire and fear. . . . But if the path to your happiness can be the same with that to mine; what celestial light will burst upon my future being! . . .

"Write to me, my love — Do write!"

And still no letter came! But ten days later Horace was back in Dedham, having seen his beloved and learned the cause of her silence. It was not cruelty nor coquetry. Her parents, while they had no objection to Horace Mann, had misgivings, as all loving parents must. Charlotte was twenty — she was old enough to marry, they agreed. But they wanted her to take her time about making up her mind, and until she was engaged it would not be proper for her to write.

So it was still "Miss Charlotte" with "Dearest" underlined. Horace prepared his case for Charlotte's consideration with all the care and logic he had learned when preparing to address a supreme court judge. In all probability, Charlotte would be required to show his letters to her mother —which was enough to bring a touch of self-consciousness into any lover's efforts. So Mann wrote down the arguments he had thought out during his sleepless nights. They were lawyer's love-letters with classic sentences and similes. His very perfection might have lost him his Charlotte except that his ardor and sincerity showed through even the most measured phrase. Often his passion for her burst through his legal habit of mind — banished the picture of Mrs. Messer and even older sister Mary Messer reading over Charlotte's shoulder!

"Do not, I entreat you, believe that the fullness of my love can be compressed within the limits of these inexpressive sentences. . . . The words with which I fill these sheets are but as a short and narrow line, traced upon a map, which, though a thread can cover it, stands as the representations of a copious stream. . . . Such, my dearest girl, is the current of affection, such the tide of passion within me. . . .

"When I was with you, I thought I could more adequately delineate my feelings if I were absent, & now I am absent, my only desire is to be with you again. But when that time shall come, what am I to read in your looks, what to hear from your lips? I cannot view my fortunes as undecided. My mind escapes from the pain of suspense & takes refuge in the bright or dark alternative. When hope predominates, my feelings are sublimed into ecstasy, when fear reigns, they are aggravated into torture. This conflict of emotions is too painful to be endured. I break from its absorbing vortex & seek relief & solace in the prayer that your attachments may never be placed upon an unworthy object, nor even a worthy one, where they cannot be requited by an ardor worthy of you."

The next time Horace Mann called on Charlotte, she promised to marry him. Surely she could never have found an ardor more worthy of her than his. But Horace's first letter to her was full of self-reproach. When at last his "dearest, loveliest Charlotte" as he now addressed her, gave "encouragements & hopes," he feared he had seemed cold. He wrote to tell her all the things he had not been able to say. "It was not until after I left you that there came thronging round me the bright and beautiful forms of happiness, that your voice had spoken into existence; that the heart spontaneously sent forth its thousand revelations of bliss, before unknown & inconceived, & the earth & the heavens were filled with iris-colored visions of love & blessedness. . . . Would that it were in my power to create feelings in your breast, that should be kindred to these, that hold their jubilee in mine. Would that I were a magician, at whose touch new fountains of joy could be unsealed within you, which would flow out until the heart run o'er with the waters of gladness.

"Had another destiny placed you beyond the reach of hope, had the burning ardors of my love been constrained & pent up within me, I feel & know that the flame would soon have consumed the center at which it was kindled. Imagine then, if possible, the bliss that now pervades all my being. I feel its warmth and vigor circling round the sources of life. . . . May your heart ever dilate with emotions, that shall bring the smile and song unbidden to your lips. May not only the light & music & gladness of the external world pour their enchantments into your breast, but may a feeling go out from your heart, with power to emparadise all the realms of nature."

It was now September 1829. In spite of the "encouragements & hopes" Charlotte had given Horace, she still wrote not a word in reply to his letters. By the end of September, he was writing with resignation to say that whether she replied or not, he still must write of his love for her. "I know not indeed, how I could endure the privation of that relief, which is afforded by these endeavors to radiate some of that light of love, with which my soul is filled," he told her. "There are no recurring hours or seasons, with which habit or custom associates recollections of you; but when mingling with the busy tide of being, there is a voice, nearer to my ear than the din of business; or frequenting the circles of pleasure, there is a hope & a joy closer to my heart than the world, with all its promises & blandishments can bind about it. My mind goes forth on a strong pinion to meet you."

While writing this letter, Horace Mann had for once forgotten to watch for the arrival of the mail. And then it was that Charlotte's first letter was brought to him! "I will pass over that minute, nor tell how near I came to betraying both myself and you to strange ears. I could regret that you have overcome your repugnance to write, but that your letter gave me so much pleasure; I could most heartily rejoice at receiving it, but that it seems to have been extorted from you unwillingly."

It was true that Charlotte did not like to write. She was fond of people and her father's house was always full of friends. She was "particularly fond of dancing" she said, and her lively wit was the kind that sparkled best in conversation but refused to be captured

by a pen and put on paper. Horace Mann's large impetuous handwriting raced and tumbled over page after page while Charlotte's
neatly written words slanted strongly to the right as if eager to
reach the end of a sentence. Her first letter seems to have disappeared
— perhaps read into tatters by her lover who had awaited it so long.
The first to be preserved in the same small box with those of Horace
Mann is dated October 17, 1829. It was stilted — it was shy — yet
it had the delicate touch of humor which was Charlotte. "My
Friend," she began — and so she would always begin her letters until
begged and implored to be a little less impersonal — "I suppose you
will expect an *occasional* answer to your letters." Charlotte underlined "occasional" in the spirit of mischief. Mann, it seems, had "not
complied with the conditions upon which" Charlotte had "agreed
to write." She had made him promise to see her in a more realistic
light and not to extol at such length so many virtues which she felt
she did not possess. "You persist in saying that you have not exaggerated but as I am fully convinced that you will in time discover
your error, I am willing to let that discovery be your punishment.
Your letters, notwithstanding, give me much pleasure. . . ." But
Charlotte hoped that her fiancé would be "willing to overlook"
her "faults and to love" her as she was.

Horace set to work, affectionately and humorously, to correct
certain faults. "It cannot but occur to you that a just notion of economy forbids leaving any part of a sheet unoccupied." Charlotte was
to write at much greater length next time. Then she had referred
to the "interest" he had in her. This was not interest, it was love.
"Let that feeling awaken your *love*, for that is the wealth my avarice
thirsts for, the honor my ambition aims at."

Letter writing became easier for Charlotte but she loved to tease.
Sometimes she wrote in legal terms, mockingly. Sometimes she
wrote short letters and told Horace the blank page would rest his
eyes. Never would she take orders, whether in fun or in earnest.
Her blithe, independent spirit was her greatest charm.

Horace could not longer doubt that he was loved. He was su-
premely happy and his letters grew lighter and gayer in response
to Charlotte's light touch. In November he pretended to give her a
severe lecture. "I beseech you, my most dear Charlotte, not to be
alarmed when I tell you, that I have sat down to hold a serious expostulation with you . . . the thought of uttering a single chiding

word fills me with unspeakable emotions. I feel as though I could not send a harsh syllable to you without accompanying it with two loving ones to interpret its meaning. But there are truths that must not be concealed. Kindness sometimes dictates language apparently unkind. . . .

"My dearest girl, (for even in rebuking you, I cannot but remind you how dear you are to me) — why is it that, day after day, the moment I put myself in the posture of study . . . why is it that your form invariably whisks itself in, like a spirit, & stands fixed and immovable between my eye and the page I am reading? Why is it that when I am intent on the solution of some difficult question, or am framing arguments . . . why is it that you should whisper some witchery in my ear & send argument & analogy . . . back again into chaos? Were this done a hundred times a day, you should have no complaint from me. Or were it only when I am engaged in dry & unpalatable speculations that you should be so importunate, I should consider it of less moment. But even when Eloquence utters his burning periods — when Poetry kindles with her ravishing senti-ments . . . — it is still the same."

It was a very long letter full of delightful nonsense which Char-lotte was almost ready to believe — had she not known that Horace was getting a great deal of work done in spite of his thoughts of her. He had returned to the legislature as usual and his project for the Massachusetts hospital for the insane was receiving a great deal of comment. Then there was his law practice, growing rapidly now. One case had attracted a little more attention than Mann bargained for — it was a breach of promise case, with Mr. Mann representing the faithless lover! Charlotte, the minx, dared to twit him about it!

"Perhaps, however, I should not let you know with how much interest I think of you," Charlotte wrote. "It is *reported* I had better be careful how I rely upon your promises of constancy, fidelity etc., if you will undertake to defend a gentleman who has left a lady, to whom he was engaged, and sought and obtained another fair one! [4] You see we are not so far apart, but I *can* hear what is going on in your region, but although I may not wish you success in your pleas [here Charlotte relented and could tease no more] I believe I will wait until I have a better reason, before I doubt your sincerity."

Her sister Mary was hanging over Charlotte's shoulder reading her letter as she wrote it — a habit Horace must have hated! Charlotte was being silly, Mary said — she'd better say she had a headache as an excuse for writing that way. Laughingly, Charlotte refused and suggested instead that she might be "a candidate for your insane hospital" — but she would let Horace be the judge.

This breach of promise case had been going on since 1828. Horace Mann was defending one Hiram Spear in a suit brought by the father of a former sweetheart, Hannah Jones. It was Hannah's father's contention that Hiram had wounded Hannah's heart to the extent of two thousand dollars!

Mann had little trouble in finding witnesses for Hiram. One of them testified that Hannah had refused Hiram's company "going from the Baptist Meeting House" — had sent him packing and had told her friends that if Hiram courted other girls, "it was nothing to her." On the other side, Charity, Hannah's sister, testified that Hiram had come courting Hannah "as often as four times a week" and often stayed to breakfast! Hannah had gone to Boston to buy bedquilts. But under Horace Mann's close questioning it was agreed that Hiram "did not shirt her" — he bought Hannah no clothes. The case was decided in favor of Mr. Mann's client.

Hannah's father appealed and, at long last, a grand jury decided that Hiram Spear "did promise in manner and form as alleged" to marry Hannah — but they found the extent of the damage to Hannah's heart to be only a hundred dollars instead of two thousand!

Here was a fine case indeed for a young lawyer about to be married. Mann was by no means "humorless," as has been sometimes contended — but it took a superlative sense of humor to enjoy being laughed at by his beloved. He did not quite meet the test — but he was the better for trying.

CHAPTER EIGHT

A Fine Gold Ring

O F John B. Jones, Boston jeweler, Horace Mann bought "one
real stone and fine gold ring." He began the year 1830 with
a visit to his mother in Franklin to tell her the news of his engagement, and he wrote Charlotte that he had "a hundred questions to
answer" and that "since strong affection is proverbially contagious,"
his mother loved Charlotte "by anticipation."

Mann realized that he was on the threshold of a new life as he
walked out alone across the old acres cleared by his great-grand-
father. "What an Eden-like day it was, such a day as we imagine to
have shone upon earth ere the name of Sin was known or the first
page of the vast history of Sorrow was written." He climbed a hill
and "paused beside the tree, where, when a boy," he had "reclined
& held speculation upon . . . time and eternity." How intensely,
then, did his thoughts turn to "Charlotte, the embodiment of all
youthful visions, the exciter and sustainer of more mature hopes."

Edward Loring must next be told the news and no one could have
reacted more satisfactorily. "Hallelujah, Cherubim & Seraphim &
all glad things & gladdest of them all is no gladder than I — my dear
friend," wrote Loring in his almost indecipherable scrawl. "My first
emotions came out with a strong interjectional burst & ever since
a tranquil joy has pervaded my whole sentient man. It is glorious
news to me and totally unexpected." Ned spoke of Mann as having
been ill and said, "Never an angel of them all had half the healing
in his wings than the little profane Dan has flattered your soul with.
You've taken a 'bond of faith' (sealed no doubt). . . . Give my love
to Charlotte, thank her, for the happiness she has given you."

A few more days and Mann was back in Boston. He abandoned

the old Exchange Coffee House and stayed at the new Tremont House.[1] It was "a palace," he wrote Charlotte, "containing more than one hundred and fifty sleeping rooms." Four granite pillars at the main entrance were "fluted from top to bottom" — a departure in Quincy granite.

And speaking of granite, "the post-master must be a granite-hearted wretch," Horace said. "When I asked him for a letter, he looked them over with as much sang-froid as I would have looked over a young author's first novel. I saw no touch of humanity in him — even the last day I was there. There was no quivering of the lip, no suppressed breath, no anxious expression of his eye — in short there was no sympathy in him. But today, today it came, & solicitude and doubt were expelled to give place to a crowd of delightful emotions."

Mann's letters to Charlotte were always amusing these days, but after telling her about the granite-hearted postmaster he spoke for the first time of a dread that was before long to invade his heart and go hand in hand with his love and happiness. "But Charlotte, your health, why is it that I am doomed to suffer this misfortune? I entreat you, be well. These repeated colds may lead to — may lead to — but I cannot write it nor think of it. The value of my existence rises and falls with your welfare and happiness."

"I think it advisable for you to petition the President immediately to remove your Post Master," Charlotte replied. But no one had been able to take her letter to the Providence post office in such terrible weather so perhaps not all the fault lay in the Boston mail service. Her health was better of course. She always believed herself better and told Horace her cough was nearly gone — until he came to Providence to see for himself.

After he had been to Providence, "I cannot bear to have you look so interestingly pale," Horace wrote. "I am no amateur of delightful languors. Sentimentalists may dote on the half-closed eye of 'beauty soft reclining,' but if half of it be beautiful . . . the whole would be doubly so. The White Lady of Avenal never pleased me much, even in Scott, nor would a saint look to me any less saintly, though she had a countenance radiant with health. This last I set down for your especial consideration."

And now, to amuse Charlotte, Mann describe the "new woman" just coming upon the scene: "*Her* spirits were too extravagantly buoy (boy?)-ant [*sic*]. She should have been kept laying stone wall till she was forty at least. What museum of monsters, in this or any country, can exhibit such a horrid monstrosity as that 'two-fisted chap' Miss Royall, or Fanny Wright, Esquire." Anne Royall was a woman who earned her living traveling over the United States and writing about her adventures. She was a reformer — better known for her attacks upon existing institutions than for any improvements she ever advocated. The previous year she had been sued by the Presbyterians under the charge that she was "a common scold." As for Fanny Wright, she found no favor with Horace Mann because of her astounding contention that women should be allowed to vote!

Mann hastened to tell Charlotte that she was like neither of these dreadful women. But he came perilously close to criticism when he said that Charlotte had "a salient vivacity that seems springing beyond the bounds of propriety, when prudence suddenly arrests its course." Did he think that prudence could have stepped in a little sooner when Charlotte teased him about his breach-of-promise case? Proceeding with his description of Charlotte, "presiding over all," he said, "was a womanly dignity and grace that poet never transferred to page nor artist to marble." Charlotte's next letter contained a mischievous suggestion that "laying stone wall" might be what her future husband had in mind for her. And Mann discovered that he could as easily do without the sunlight as without Charlotte's "salient vivacity."

Charlotte's trousseau was now being made in an upstairs room in the great white house in Providence. Her mother, her sisters and the village dressmaker were all absorbed in silks, satins, muslins and lace. Horace brought Charlotte some beautiful straw for a bonnet — a gift from his sister, Lydia. But he felt sure that Charlotte herself was being neglected. Her cough hung on. Her parents never had a doctor for her. Horace could only console himself with thoughts of how well he would take care of her, once she was his. He could write her and tell her what to do — but she would do as she pleased at least until her wedding day when she promised to obey him!

Writing from Dedham on the 25th of May, 1830, "When I received your letter yesterday, pleasure took entire possession of me, & we had a fine holiday," Horace said. "The assurance of your affection animated me with a new life; & the account of your improved health relieved me from a grievous burden of anxiety. I had just been engaged in a melancholy affair — preparing a 'will' for a clergyman in a neighboring town. . . . He is a young man, has been settled but a short time, now rapidly wasting away with that most terrible of disorders — a consumption . . .

"I have a new notion in my cranium. . . . My project is to sink the law, turn physician and out of the deepest depths . . . of art and science to obtain some 'grand specific' for your case. . . . But as something ought to be done immediately, allow me . . . to call in the aid of others & to prescribe the following. . . ." Horace had been reading a book by a doctor who had studied in Germany and had concluded "that singing is to young girls who by the customs of society are debarred from any other kinds of exercise . . . a means of preserving health." German girls "exercised the organs of breathing by singing" and this contributed "to defend them from those diseases to which the climate and other causes expose them. 'The Germans are seldom afflicted with consumption,'" said this doctor, and Horace went right around to the music master of the nearest academy! The music master (at the local academy) "furnished me with an observation still more in favor of this opinion," Mann told his Charlotte. "He informed me that he had known several instances of persons who were strongly disposed to consumption, who were restored to health by the exercise of their lungs in singing. . . .

"What a charming elixir!" Mann said. "Take seven pills, fa sol la, mi, fa, sol, la! Swallow this gamut at one draught. Extract strength from a song, & from a chorus length of days."

But Charlotte laughed at being made the subject of a survey as though she were a problem such as the number of insane in Massachusetts. She replied, "Had you sent me the voice of a nightingale, I would have made use of it with much pleasure and it might have had the effect desired." But Charlotte claimed to have the voice of a raven. "It strikes me if ravens have any nerves, their own voices would send them into a nervous fever, if not a consumption."

Charlotte could use the dread word lightly! Mann allowed his fears to subside, and when he returned to Boston for the brief May session of the legislature the city seemed more beautiful than ever before. Allowing generously for the fact that he was in love — he was still right. Summer Street, arched over with trees, was a street of famous gardens. Marshland along the foot of Beacon Hill had recently been filled in to make a new street — Charles Street. Beyond it, the blue waters of the Charles River basin stretched away to wooded hills, with a white church steeple marking the center of a little town. On Beacon Hill the gardens were giving way to handsome city houses, for in 1830 fortunes were being made and there was a scramble to buy lots. Mann loved the activity, the ring of hammers, the rumbling drays full of Quincy granite and red brick. He liked to watch the crowds and speculate about the lives of strangers he saw passing in the streets. The thing to do was to try to describe all this to his "dearest, loveliest Charlotte" in the hope that she too would love Boston and would like to live there some day.

"My attachment to a city-life, like a certain other attachment I wot of, grows with indulgence," Mann began. "From every point of view, a city displays innumerable objects of interest and pleasure." There was "the mass of human, sentient, intelligent beings gathered together within a city" and Mann marveled at the way in which "the common passions of our nature" affect the mass mind of the city until it is "agitated & swayed to & fro, like the heavings of the ocean beneath the influence of the moon." There was the "wealth, the intelligence, the power concentrated within [the city's] borders; the strength of its physical, its commercial & its intellectual actions" as the city absorbed "within itself the productions of every soil, the labors of all the arts . . . the wisdom of all past ages; and then, by its powerful pulsations," sent "them abroad again through a thousand channels to the extremities of the realm of civilized man. . . .

"I love to break down the mass into the individual atoms that compose it," Mann went on, "to make conjecture busy with the motives that activate the individual parts of this stupendous whole." Mann's thoughts turned particularly to "the most obscure & wretched, the outcasts from fortune . . . swept away by adverse circumstances. . . . After such reflections, I feel my desire for humane and benevolent effort invigorated. If I have been blessed with the possession of any good, or the exemption from any evil, an obligation has accompanied the blessing, to use the immunity for the benefit of my kind."

Never before had Horace Mann written so intimately to anyone of what went on within his most secret soul. He had just put down the philosophy of his entire life, and here was a letter which would give Charlotte complete understanding of the man she had promised to marry. It is to be hoped that she read it not once but many times. But Charlotte was so young, and she had led such a sheltered life, that she had not thought much about human misery or anyone's obligation to society. She replied that she preferred the country. She was not unfeeling or selfish about it. She was "a simple country damsel," she said, and she spoke of rising early to listen to the song of birds, of walking out in the fresh morning air. Horace would be asleep, she felt sure. He was to dream of her.

The wedding had been set for early September. It was "a certain September I wish would change places with July," Horace said. "Before the time of Augustus Caesar, the month of August was unknown in the Roman calendar. He interpolated it & it received his name. I always hated him — a feeling which for some reason or other I have lately perceived was growing more intense."

But Horace would have to hate most of September as well as August, for Charlotte postponed the wedding. As was to be expected, Horace took it hard. He demanded to know if Charlotte really loved him. And Charlotte replied, "I have acknowledged to you that I loved you, I have given you what I consider *very* strong proof of love in consenting to leave family and friends so dear to me as mine are, to share with you the happiness, or misery of life." It seemed as though for once her sister Mary was not looking over her shoulder and as though Charlotte had decided to grow up. "Could I do this without such love for you as would insure my own happiness, and above all to enable me to ensure yours? If, in an unguarded moment, I have said or done anything which has given you pain, believe me, it was the *frailty of human nature* and do not pain me by attributing it to a diminution of my affection for you. I never doubted the sincerity of your love, — do me the justice, I beg you, to place equal confidence in my sincerity. Without *mutual* confidence we can never be happy, we should be without an anchor. If, as I sincerely hope, you have banished and forgotten all the sad thoughts which dictated your letter, do not allow this to bring back even the remembrance that they have been, but *bury* them altogether." This was not Charlotte's customary light vein but it was the real Charlotte — as Mann must have known.

Charlotte's home was already waiting for her in Dedham.[2] Mann had found a house for rent which was certain to please her. Square and substantial, it was built before the Revolution with broad beams, fine paneling within and having a graceful balustrade at the roof's edge without. One door opened on Church Street and the other on Church Square. Small and unadorned Trinity Church occupied the square while just a few steps up Church Street was Horace Mann's law office. All around the square were other old houses full of quiet dignity and unpretentious charm. Church Street and the square was not a neighborhood of mansions but of homes where a bride would be sure to find a friendly welcome. The owner of their house was doing some painting and repairing, Horace said. Did Charlotte care? he asked — still grieving that he must live without her one more month. Of course she cared! What were the colors? How large were the rooms? Horace was to measure and let her know.

There was shopping to do. Carpeting was a substantial item with fifty-six and three quarters yards of one pattern costing seventy-five dollars; and sixty yards of another, forty-eight. Horace had been selecting furniture with loving care, buying in Boston from John Dogget and Company. There was a "mahogany French Bedstead" and a "Grecian worktable," a square looking glass and two bureaus. Most of the furniture was listed as "Grecian" — meaning French Empire pieces made popular in America by Duncan Phyfe. There were ten "Grecian Fancy Chairs" and chairs listed simply as "Fancy" — perhaps painted in gold. The rocking chair for Charlotte's own particular pleasure was to be kept in the bedroom. Everything had been set in place, down to the last "tea kettle, bake pan, kitchen shovel and tongs."

Horace visited Providence to make the final arrangements for the wedding. He planned to take Charlotte to New York by way of Hartford, coming back through Worcester. It was a honeymoon he found means to pay for by postponing the purchase of books for his law library. Charlotte was delighted with the plans and agreed to everything.

As soon as Horace left, however, Charlotte's family took over and Charlotte was obliged to write — doubtless with sister Mary looking on again as usual. "I found after you left here the other day that I had entirely mistaken my sisters' plans. They said they had no idea of giving up the *party*, and Ma says she cannot consent to my leaving Providence without it. You know, such little things are sometimes of great importance. You see, therefore, it is necessary to contrive some new plan, and our wise heads, always fertile with expedients, have invented the following. It is that we should go to Newport on *the* Wednesday and stay there a day or two, return to P. and have the party Friday and take the boat Saturday for N. York. Pa and Ma think they will feel easier to have us take the boat here, than at Hartford, as they would be more sure of a good boat and good weather."

It must have been hard for Horace to understand just why Providence weather was sure to be better than the Hartford variety. But Charlotte said meekly that she would give up the plan if Horace objected, so he said nothing. "I thought it would be more convenient for us . . . and much better to have the party in a moonlight evening," Charlotte went on. "We might go in the boat to Newport, or take a chaise and explore the country, just as would be most agreeable to you. If you approve the plan and we go by water, why will you not ask your sister to accompany us?"

In a postscript, Charlotte added, "Pa thinks after *mature consideration* that it would be better for him not to perform the ceremony as he has been so long out of the clerical line. Next to him, I should prefer *your friend* Mr. Pattison."

With wonderful patience, Horace replied, finding "all our arrangements are again disarranged." The "party" seems to have been a wedding reception and he should think they'd have the wedding "towards evening and the party on the same day and then the journey" — a sensible idea, surely. But "as the plan you propose is 'agreeable to yourself,' I have no personal objection to it." Charlotte could almost hear the resignation in his voice by way of the words on the paper. He enclosed a letter to the Reverend Mr. Pattison with the hour of the wedding left blank for Charlotte to fill in. The date was "Wednesday, the 29th inst." About one matter, however, Horace Mann was firm. His sister was not going on his honeymoon!

The Messer family seemed to think that they were lending their youngest daughter to Horace Mann, not giving her to him; but Wednesday the 29th was agreed upon at last. Charlotte, twenty-one years old, was lovingly arrayed in her merino wedding gown.

The day dawned clear and mild — Providence weather of course! The steam packet *President* left Providence for Newport that day at twelve noon. But now that Horace and Charlotte were no longer writing letters to each other there is no telling whether Mr. and Mrs. Horace Mann were on board the packet — or whether a private chaise set out, "exploring."

Firmly corded chests, trunks and flowered bandboxes arrived in Dedham by cart via the Providence Road. Charlotte put away her wedding china, the teapot, the wineglasses, and spread her best bedspread on the French mahogany bed. She hung her pretty dresses in the closet and she was as happy as a child playing house.

The days grew short and as Horace Mann left his law office he could see the lamps being lighted in homes along the street. Now there need be no lonely walk such as Mann used to take into the country, and no return to town in the early darkness to see lights in all the houses but never a home that was his own — no lamp lighted for him. "When the work of the day was done, how cheerful and glad was the light that shone from the window, as I returned," Mann said. "How tender and affectionate was her greeting, what hallowed light she shed around my home!" Charlotte! It still seemed unbelievable that she was at last his own, his "ever dearest wife."

The neighbors called, and Charlotte had calling cards engraved with her new name, MRS. HORACE MANN. She looked at the name for a long time, trying to make it seem really her own. Would the time come when she would take her new name for granted? Perhaps — but she would never cease to be proud of it. Proudly, Charlotte slipped the new cards into her case and set out along Dedham's lovely tree-lined streets. Maples were turning scarlet and gold, there was a smell of ripening leaves in the air, of drifting smoke from bonfires. Charlotte returned the call of a neighbor, Mrs. Swett, who had two little girls, Fanny and Esther.

There was another caller at Mrs. Swett's that afternoon — a Miss Sophia Peabody of Salem.[3] She was an artist, visiting the Havens, yet living by herself in a room she rented — so as to be free to paint. This, Miss Peabody explained to young Mrs. Mann. But the little girls absorbed most of Charlotte's attention. When she asked their mother to let them come to see her anytime, they flung their arms around her neck in delight. Charlotte raised her dark eyes to find Miss Sophia smiling at her — enjoying the charming picture she made with the children.

When Horace Mann came home at night, Charlotte laughingly threatened to "jog his elbow" if he turned to his books and his briefs before she had time to tell him all her day's adventures. But, over their glass of Madeira, it was apt to be Horace who did the talking after all. "I loved success but it was because it increased my means of adding to her enjoyment," he said. As he told of his victories in court or the speech he was preparing for the House, he watched "the light of pleasure — half expressed, half concealed, as it gleamed through every feature of her face."

Mann had every reason to consider himself successful. His law practice, he said, brought him between twenty-five hundred and three thousand dollars a year and in terms of the dollar's purchasing power, this was a good income. This is not to say that Mann's income was exactly easy to calculate. For example, in 1831, neighbor Fales delivered a load of wood — in return for legal advice! And George Brown upholstered an armchair, made an eight-foot pew cushion for Mr. Mann's pew in the Unitarian Church. Mr. Brown also carpeted the pew and made "one pr. crickets with trimming" so that Horace and Charlotte could get their feet up off the cold church floor in winter. Brown's bill came to $11.79 or just ten cents more than he owed Mr. Mann in legal fees! It took talented bookkeeping for Mann to figure out just where he stood, but fortunately enough clients paid in cash so that he could buy Charlotte lengths of gleaming silk for a dress, and, for himself, forty dollars' worth of much-needed lawbooks.

There was one factor in his marriage which Mann had overlooked. He was away from home a great deal in the course of his legal practice; he was often in Worcester serving as Commissioner for the hospital for the mentally ill, and he was in Boston while attending Legislature. He had supposed that Charlotte would soon be well and strong under his loving care — able to go with him on all his journeys. But Charlotte was unable to stand the jolting of even a private chaise over the rough road to Worcester. She was lonesome and afraid if left alone at Dedham, for she had always lived in a large family with friends constantly about and servants to wait on her. In December, Charlotte was ill and Dr. Jeremy Stimson called — gentle, kindly and reassuring in his black frock coat, carrying his gold-headed cane. He prescribed "powders" and came on the eleventh, twelfth and sixteenth, but his powders did

ttle good for on the twentieth he was summoned in all haste in
he night.

It was agreed now that Charlotte was never to be left alone. But as
lways, she struggled hard to be well and in January she was able
o go to Boston with her husband when the legislature convened.
he winter of 1831 was severe to a degree. Snowdrifts were "up-
vards of eight feet" deep so that some of the streets "were abso-
itely impassable." The driver of the Providence stage got lost in
he storm. But Charlotte and Horace were happy, snug in their
omfortable room at the Tremont House. It was no problem of
heirs to keep the snow from the door and if fires were extra there
vas no chilly journey to the cellar or the woodshed for another
hunk of neighbor Fales's firewood. Charlotte discovered that there
vas a great deal to be said for city life.

On January 17, Edward Loring was married to Harriet Boott, a
;irl extremely wealthy in her own right. Mrs. Curtis, Ned's mother,
iad promised to be "a friend to Charlotte," and she kept her word,
eeing that Charlotte was invited to all the festivities before the
vedding and afterward. Charlotte had Boston friends of her own as
vell — among them the Marshall girls, one married and a frequent
isitor in Providence, one the beautiful Marion, to whom half the
oung men in Boston were writing verses. Charlotte was well — so
ntirely well that she walked out upon the Common every day un-
ess the snow were too deep, so she said in a letter to her sister-in-
aw, Lydia.

But Charlotte followed her stay in Boston with a visit to her
arents in Providence, where she caught cold and became ill again.
A new series of letters began between husband and wife — more
ender, more deeply affectionate than any Charlotte and Horace
iad written before their marriage. Charlotte had learned what love
:ould mean. Horace wrote of all his daily doings and her replies
howed that there was nothing else she cared to hear.

CHAPTER NINE
Major Mann

IN 1832, the Massachusetts legislature convened on January 4, for the first time, under a new ruling which abolished the short spring session. But January is no month to set up booths on Boston Common and hold a country fair in honor of legislators. The parade would take place as usual, and with the usual military escort; but few would gather to see it march down the hill to the Old South Meetinghouse, and few would wait around for the return of the dignitaries when the church service was over. The papers deplored the passing of a colorful day and temperance workers rejoiced in the disappearance of the rum-selling booths, forgetting that the taverns might be able to pick up a bit of trade.

No one expected that the day would be particularly notable — but in this all were mistaken. Horace Mann wrote Charlotte about it, for she was visiting her parents as usual.

The streets were snow-covered as the First Division of the Independent Cadets under Lieutenant Colonel Grenville-Temple Winthrop drew up in front of the State House to escort the "Executive and Legislative branches of Government" to the Old South. Down the steep slopes of Beacon Hill they went, all of them trying hard not to lose their dignity by falling on the ice. The "Government" filed inside the church, grateful to feel the pleasant warmth. The cadets, too proud even to shiver in their handsome uniforms, felt relieved none the less because their short march was over. And then the church doors were shut in their faces! No seats had been provided for them, inside the church!

The cadets knew their duty — it was to remain on guard outside, then, in accordance with ancient custom. But the Indians had long since ceased to threaten Boston town. Even the Redcoats were gone for good, while that old demon east wind — oldest of all their enemies — remained. After some deliberation Lieutenant Colonel Grenville-Temple Winthrop dismissed the cadets, telling them to come back in half an hour. Where they went was up to them and they showed good sense when they made straight for the Exchange Coffee House. They ordered the most immediately warming beverage — which was not necessarily coffee!

The half-hour went by and the militia dutifully turned out and marched back to the Old South Meetinghouse. The doors were still inexorably closed. It was the custom for the legislature to vote for chaplain, and as each senator and each representative loyally voted for his own minister, 29 names had been put up this year, RALPH W. EMERSON coming out ahead with 63 votes. But as HOWARD MALCOM had 62 votes, both were chosen and both were entitled to admonish the "Government" this bitter January morning. When one of the militiamen managed to tiptoe inside the church and return, the word was that the service could go on indefinitely. There was no end in sight.

Back to the Coffee House went the cadets, leaving someone at the church whose duty it was to run to tell them when the sermon came to an end. Naturally enough, the cadets were now chilled all over again and they required another dram all around. After that, time seemed to go very fast — at least for the militia. They became increasingly optimistic about everything, and when their messenger arrived to say that the discourse had finally ended, they turned out, confident that they had plenty of time to draw up their lines outside the church while the last hymn was sung and the benediction pronounced.

At that very moment, however, fateful words were being spoken at the Old South: "Owing to the lateness of the hour, we will omit the final hymn." When the cadets arrived, the Governor and his staff were already part way up the street — all unescorted!

But the cadets were still full of optimism. The thing to do was to get in front of the Governor somehow, form and march, and when the Governor arrived at the State House he would not notice that anything had been amiss. Accordingly, the cadets ran madly through the side streets, they cut across gardens and vaulted fences, shouting encouragement to each other as they ran. Governor Levi Lincoln walked fast — feeling the cold, august personage though he was. The cadets "intercepted him at the new Park Street Meeting-house."

With the State House just a steep, icy block away, Lieutenant Colonel Grenville-Temple Winthrop "did order his company in front of the Commander in Chief and his party." The Independent Cadets, far too independent for their own good, "thereby impeded . . . his Excellency and the Legislators . . . and obliged them to change their course from one part of the street to the other in order to return to the State House." It was a pity the usual crowd was not out on the Common to watch the Governor dodging up Park Street. As it was, the windows of the elegant houses lining one side of that comparatively new street were surely full of fashionable spectators who would enjoy the laugh and spread the story. Out in the snow on the Common there must have been at least a few hardy citizens who got a good money's worth.

Gathering the remnants of his dignity about him, Governor Levi Lincoln ordered the militia to disperse. But Lieutenant Colonel Winthrop flung discretion to the east wind and chose valor! He formed his company, and marched up Park Street in the rear — since he could not quite manage to get in front. And on arrival, before the Governor's temper had a chance to cool, an adjutant appeared in the Council Chamber for further orders — just as if all had gone according to custom. The adjutant was sent away. Just where he was told to go is not a matter of record.

The previous July, Mr. Horace Mann had received an official communication from the Governor. It was his appointment as Judge Advocate of the Militia of the Commonwealth of Massachusetts.[1] So now, in 1832, it was Major Mann who received official notice to appear at the court-martial of Lieutenant Colonel Grenville-Temple Winthrop, accused of "unmilitary and unofficer-like conduct."

Young Winthrop defended his honor with more ardor than wisdom. He retained Dexter and Gardiner as his lawyers and they were the ones who had defended the Knapps in the famous Judge White murder case in Salem the previous year. The Cadets were all socially correct young men and they had gotten themselves thoroughly laughed at. The public would have gone to the trial anyway — but this pair of famous lawyers assured "a full house, day after day."

Major Mann described his own dramatic appearance at this affair. "Tomorrow comes the 'pomp & circumstance' of the Court Martial. I have got to appear in uniform, cap-a-pie, a glorious transformation! Imagine me, surmounted by such a *chapeau bias* as once crowned the head of Napoleon himself — lofty and wide-spread as a banyan-tree, — a coat, the breast of which swells with emotion and padding, — and a sword, hungering & thirsting because it never has tasted blood or flesh, — & rattling along enough to scare away the millenium."

Charlotte replied that Sydney Williams (recently married to her sister Caroline) had attended the trial one day and reported that Major Mann looked very handsome in his uniform.

Long before the trial was over, Mann was heartily sick of it. "I would that there had been no 'Winthrop,' or if that must be, no 'Grenville-Temple Winthrop,' or if that must be, that there had been no 'Company of Cadets,' nor any 'Lieutenant Colonel' of same, nor any militia to be ordered out, nor any escort service ever invented, nor *anything* nor that either, to keep me away from you for another week. But so it must be, & I could eat my own sword for dinner, through vexation and impatience."

Life in Boston was not entirely without its distractions, however. "I dine with Loring about half the time," Major Mann told Charlotte. "Ned gave a dinner to club last Friday evening. The entertainment was not profuse merely, but profusion itself. We had a capital time, not less on account of what *appeared*, than of what *disappeared*." The following week, "club" met with a friend by the name of Baker. And on March 23 it was Mann's turn to entertain, at the Tremont House. He paid for "9 suppers at $1.50, Moselle, $1.50; 3 bots Hock, $6.00; Madeira $2.00; cigars, .75" and again "Madeira $3.00." Surely "club" had a "capital" time again!

The court-martial dragged on until the end of March. "Messrs Dexter and Gardiner read an argument of an hour and a half in length," and then Horace Mann "replied to both sides in one which took . . . an hour to read." Mann told Charlotte how he felt about being a judge. "I stand between the parties and take a pride in the consciousness that it is my duty to see justice done." In the end, Winthrop was found guilty of all charges except that of sending the adjutant to the Council Chamber. The adjutant seemed to have acted upon his own inspiration there. The unfortunate Winthrop had given Boston a good laugh and his sentence was light. He was "reprimanded in orders." Governor Lincoln wrote the reprimand and it required 6000 words to say all he had on his mind. But Winthrop published a book at his own expense — stating his side of the story in 565 pages!

Major Mann laid aside his sword and Napoleonic hat with relief. It was already too late for Charlotte to join him in Dedham before circuit court began, but he hoped she would go to their home with her sister Mary and wait for him.

Mann's practice was still very much that of the country lawyer. He drew up an agreement between neighbors concerning the sale of a "yearling heifer," and he adjusted difficulties when one man's cow wandered into another man's "grounds." The turnpike was not without its hazards and its attendant lawsuits. Horace Mann questioned Miss Priscilla Lewis, who testified that she had seen a chaise pass her house "at a moderate jog." Then the stagecoach rumbled by at such a pace that Miss Priscilla ran to the window again and saw the chaise "overset." A lady, thrown out of the chaise, was given "camphor and hot drops" but when she seemed "inwardly hurt" a doctor was summoned who prescribed a "mustard-seed poultice." Mr. Mann had no trouble showing that the stagecoach had been speeding!

It was all very similar to that "satirical play" "The Country Justice," which Mann had written as a schoolboy. Now he had become his hero, "Lawyer Ellery." But he was also a member of the legislature and a judge, like "Judge Meanwell"! One court session "continued fourteen days, during which I tried thirteen cases, most all of them of considerable importance," Mann wrote Charlotte. Bringing intelligence, integrity and education to the role, Mann was the opposite of that mythical judge — butt of his schoolboy satire. The law from the lawyer's point of view was what he still loved best, however.

The case which brought Mann attention from the world outside his own community was that of the "Inhabitants of the First Parish in the town of Milton against the Rev. Mr. Gile." Mr. Gile was excessively orthodox. He believed in protecting his flock against heresy by seeing to it that they heard no other preacher but himself. The parishioners, on the other hand, said that Mr. Gile had promised "occasionally and from time to time to make exchanges." They also felt that "a just and fair proportion" of the ministers invited into Mr. Gile's pulpit should be "liberal or those now denominated Unitarian."

Discontent had been simmering for ten years and it must be admitted that what brought it to a boiling point was Mammon and not pure theology! The Reverend Mr. Gile had "acquired an apparent title to certain real estate belonging to said Parish." Mr. Mann's first moves were the conciliatory ones of the good lawyer. In behalf of the Milton Parish, he offered Mr. Gile five hundred dollars for the real estate and his resignation. Mr. Gile refused.

A mediating council was finally chosen, consisting of a majority of Unitarian ministers, each with a deacon from his own church. They met at "Mrs. Atherton's tavern" in Milton, where the warmth of great hearth fires dispelled the January cold and the pleasant aroma of ale from the taproom was a reminder that, if any of the clergy needed a medicinal draught, no one would think the worse of him. The Reverend Mr. Lamson was there, pastor of Horace Mann's own church. The Supreme Court ruling which secured to Mr. Lamson his pulpit and to Dedham Parish the First Church property was the precedent upon which Mr. Mann based his argument and won his ultimate victory.

Mann's argument, however, was more than an exercise in debate — it expressed his personal point of view. "When a minister comes before his people, his face should radiate with moral light as did the face of Moses before the Children of Israel when he first came down from Sinai. A light from heaven should fall upon his countenance and be reflected from that to his people, warming through pity and love. . . . But if clouds of jealousy and suspicion and distrust intervene . . . no light from his face can ever reach their eyes to be a guide and blessing to them as they pursue their pilgrimage through the shadowy paths of earth."

The council, after listening to Mr. Mann, voted unanimously that Mr. Gile "had lived in habitual violation of the understanding between himself and his parish." The case was celebrated, and great was the rejoicing over Mr. Mann among the Unitarians. It is to be feared that the Reverend Dr. Emmons, who was still living, had a few difficult moments explaining how a boy who grew up in his parish could persecute the faithful!

"How I would like to *assist* you in your preperations [Charlotte's spelling was never as reliable as her husband's but he never complained] for the Supreme Court. I should think you would *miss* me so much in that respect as to feel yourself unqualified to appear. . . . I fear that you have not appeared in the House as you did formerly, that your reports have not been properly *drawn*, since you have had no one to criticize your style."

Heading his letter COMMONWEALTH OF MASSACHUSETTS, Mann told Charlotte how things were going in the House while she was no longer his critic (surely the kindest he ever had). "I must commence, my ever dearest, dearest Charlotte, in the language of a Report, because I am writing to you from a snug corner of a gallery in the Representatives Hall. Below me are three or four hundred men, who make as much clamor as so many bees, as the bodies of one are larger than those of the other. Calhoun is putting motions. Messrs. Every Body [2] are debating the questions pro & con, hands fly up in the affirmative or the negative & the current of business sweeps along below me without drawing my attention from you. All, all put together, what are they, compared with you alone. 'I hope that air motion won't not prevail.' Oh, I beg pardon, I began to turn reporter for a moment. . . . Suppose my sheet should slip off the desk, over the edge of which it hangs, what would the ignoramus say to it, think you?"

For Charlotte's sake, to cheer her in her frequent illnesses, Mann wrote mostly of the lighter side of his work in the legislature. This would have surprised his colleagues because the bills he sponsored were always serious in the extreme. As a member of the Committee on the Judiciary, Mann worked to abolish capital punishment "of persons convicted of stealing, in certain cases." It is a shock to discover that there was opposition to such a measure on the grounds that it was too lenient. Mann also moved that his committee be empowered to "look into the possibility of passing a law to have capital punishment inflicted in as private a manner as the faithful execution of the law will permit." There would be no more public hangings in Massachusetts if Horace Mann had his way.

In 1831, Mann was at work upon changes in the law "allowing imprisonment for debt." Long and bitter were the battles as Mann tried to get the law to differentiate between fraudulent debtors and those who through misfortune could not pay. He attempted to liberalize the laws concerning the attachment of property. A man's family must eat, a man must retain the tools of his trade if he were to pay off indebtedness.

Horace Mann was the most prominent member on the committee to change the license law so that county commissioners could "grant licenses to public houses without the right of selling ardent spirits." His first move was to send out a questionnaire and his speech made news for the press. He had found that "one preacher, or physician or lawyer, was considered sufficient to take charge of the morals or maladies or legal business of at least a thousand people [but that] there was one person in every fifty male adults now set apart by licenses under the law of the Commonwealth, to distribute distilled liquors to a community. . . . Grog shops spring up by the road-sides. Property values go down, life itself is rendered less valuable."

Mr. Mann's speech was "a shower of eloquence," an opponent sarcastically remarked, but the bill for regulating licensed houses passed, 155 to 69. A provision passed, requiring "a special license 'costing $4.00' for the sale of beer and ale." "Many poor persons gain support in summer" selling "ale, a healthful beverage," cried the opposition — in vain.

"Mann's license bill" they called it, and there was far more popular opposition to it than the vote in the House would indicate. Jackson clubs, which had started up among the laboring people of Boston, met in "reading rooms" where very little reading was done and plenty of drinking. The Irish immigrants arrived starving, with the habit of drinking heavy upon them. Conditions of overcrowding and starvation wages or unemployment soon drove them to further depths of desperation, and the "grog shop" with its cheap drink was their consolation. Mr. Mann felt a particular sympathy for these people and their families; but since most of them could not read, his speeches printed in the papers never reached them. It was not hard for Jackson men to organize this mass of people with their honest grievances and make them believe that anyone who wanted to take away their grog shops was their enemy.

"You'll have a stormy time," Ned Loring wrote to Mann when the 1831 legislative session was over. "Much is expected of you . . . against a ferocious and reckless opposition."

But with Charlotte by his side, Horace Mann had the strength of ten. If much were expected — much would he accomplish.

CHAPTER TEN

A Light upon Earth

WHEN the date of their first wedding anniversary came around, Horace Mann was in Dedham, Charlotte with her parents in Providence. Her visit, planned to last a fortnight, had been continuing now for six weeks. Dinner at the Lorings the night before in Boston, pledges to Charlotte in a glass of wine, had failed to raise Mann's spirits. He had returned to his empty home and, writing late in the night of September thirtieth, he wondered if Charlotte really wanted to return to him.

"Of the year that is past, I hardly know how I ought to speak, & still less how I ought to feel. To rejoice in that which has given me the means of the highest happiness . . . to dote upon having the object I most love present with me, only while she is absent from others, with whose claims to her affection, I hardly dare compare my own, might seem too selfish a point of view of our relation to each other. But if it be any sacrifice on your part now, let me hope, that at some time it will be amply requited. . . ." It was the sort of letter Mann had written when their wedding was postponed. Charlotte understood the love and longing which prompted it. Her own letter, written that same night, was all that Mann's heart could ask.

"I thought Oh! how much I thought of that dear absent 'friend who is more than a brother,' to whose care, one year since, I committed all my happiness, and who has so amply redeemed his promise to 'love and cherish.' I say 'Love' and I believe it, for I rest so *secure* in your affection that I cannot dream of change. As those thoughts rested on my mind I could not but acknowledge to myself that I was most happy, that every wish of my heart was gratified and I could not stop thinking how little I had done to deserve so much happiness."

Charlotte still did not tell her husband how ill she was — perhaps from some of the cures her friends recommended. Mann continued to expect her daily. "Time wears clogs," he said. "I have no one to comb my head and sing to me & coax & pother me & *sich like*. What shall I do? If you stay away much longer I shall have to marry you over again."

Unable to sustain the light vein, however, "sometimes, my love, I can hardly help repining at your protracted illness, at the privations of enjoyment to which it subjects us . . . the suffering which it inflicts upon you. That, I *hope*, is the only cause which shuts you from what is attainable of human happiness. Why should we be brought so near to the bounds of felicity & then find an impassable barrier? Why should pleasure, the highest of pleasure, suffer itself to be pursued so closely & then elude our grasp?"

Another lonely month went by. "I had half promised my arms you would be here tonight," Mann wrote, "but when that sovereign trio — 'Father & Mother & Mary' decree the contrary, I know I must submit, though men & angels were on my side. I approve sincerely of your purpose to 'err on the side of caution, if at all,' — you ought surely to lean toward caution, but *I* am caution, ergo, you ought to lean toward me. If you can ride six miles a day, it would take you but five days to come here, & yet I wait, week after week, & very soon it will be month after month."

When Charlotte had left her home for Providence, promising to be back in a fortnight, she had been suffering from what she called "my ailment," but to which her husband referred more frankly as "continual loss of blood." He had called Dr. Stimson, who prescribed a mustard-seed poultice! After Charlotte reached Providence the resulting "blister" gave her great pain and her ailment was no better. As a result of her husband's entreaties, she finally called a Providence doctor but soon gave up his nauseous medicines. Charlotte grew better, took short rides in her father's carriage in preparation for those rough thirty miles from Providence to Dedham. But just as her hopes rose, she would be taken ill again. Someone suggested that port wine would give her strength and Charlotte drank it dutifully till she could stand no more of it. She tried a diet exclusively of oysters, recommended by a friend. Too weak to leave her room, she sat by the fire and wrote to her beloved husband. She had come across a copy of "don Quixote" which struck her as silly at first but the more she read the better she liked it — she found herself laughing out loud over it. Horace must read it. Charlotte's delicate handwriting grew weaker but her spirit was strong.

At last, in the spring of 1832, it seemed that Charlotte was well in every way. The old house on Church Street was now a smiling place because of her happy presence. Once more her light step was on the stair and she sang softly to herself as she went from room to room, dusting, arranging her dear possessions — making her house a home again. The "square looking glass," blank and empty for so long, came alive with her dark eyes as she passed by. The "Grecian worktable" was in use, the "fancy chairs" were polished. No need now to write to Horace and beg him to fold away the best bedspread. Charlotte would fold it away herself and get it out if company were coming. She would worry no longer about the damper in the parlor fireplace, but see to it herself and never let a drop of rain leak in to spoil the carpet.

Belowstairs, a "Mrs. Goody" had wrestled none too successfully with iron pots and pans. She had been succeeded by others and Horace had even talked with the great Daniel Webster on the subject of a cook! Mr. Webster had been kind, condescending, but of little help. Charlotte was so well now that she was sure she could learn to cook — but whether she could have lifted the kitchen shovel and tongs was another matter! A neighbor woman had been found, strong of arm, to come in by the day.

It seemed strange to Charlotte to write from her own home in Dedham to Horace in Boston. And he would return so soon. "Dearest, you see I obey and write," she began — her letter to go to Boston by messenger on April 3. "I am very well and have been out gadding all afternoon. . . . Caroline Stimson came in to see me immediately after dinner and accompanied me to Mrs. Lamson's and from there to Mrs. Fairbanks's which astonished all the good people here who say I am *going* on *too* fast, but *I* say I feel all the better for the walk." Charlotte was not afraid of being alone — a friend was coming to spend the night. It was a gay and confident letter. Surely "human happiness" was "attained."

"There was a light upon earth brighter than any light of the sun and a voice sweeter than any of Nature's harmonies," Horace

Mann wrote. He felt that "the happiness which was boundless in present enjoyment would be perpetual in duration."

Dr. Stimson approved of Charlotte's being out of doors and May and June were ever the loveliest of months in Dedham. Horace left his law office early to stroll with Charlotte along the streets flecked with the shade of tiny leaves. They paused to admire the gardens, heavy with the perfume of lilacs. Almost before they knew it there were roses in the gardens, shade was dense along the tree-lined streets, and this, the second summer of their married life, was passing all too soon.

On the second of July, 1832, Mann wrote his sister Lydia. "Charlotte was taken very unwell,[1] & it will be a fortnight tomorrow since she has been out of her chamber or scarcely off her bed. She is much more comfortable today than she has been during her illness but we cannot anticipate at best a very speedy recovery. But she bears her illness with the stoicism of a philosopher and the resignation of a saint. Mary is with us and makes Charlotte's illness as little painful as possible."

Two weeks later, in reply to letters urging him to come to Worcester on state business, Mann refused, saying he could not leave his wife. When she was able, he lifted Charlotte gently and carried her to her rocking chair by the window where she could see the summer sunshine and look into the trees on Church Square.

How light Charlotte was to lift! How lovingly her arms clung to him, enjoying his strength and silently thanking him for his tender care! Each day, Charlotte assured her husband that she was better, or if not much better today, that she would surely improve to-morrow.

Edward Loring wrote, dating his letter July 25, and it would seem that Horace had told him something not put down on paper. Loring wrote,[2] "I have been before you in this path, and tho' I have seen my wife suffering as yours suffers — I have seen from similar suffering, improved health and renovated system and exquisite joy — all arise and grow strong together. So be it with you in God's good time. Hope, my dear friend — there is comfort in it and ground for it." The Lorings had a little daughter and it would seem possible from Loring's letter that Horace and Charlotte hoped for a child.

Dr. Stimson began his calls on the twenty-third of June and came daily through July fourth — bringing "powders." But then his visits

ceased; Mary Messer went back to Providence. Hope did indeed
shine like a light in Horace Mann's heart — it was as he had always
said — if he had Charlotte in his keeping he could make her well.

Then "suddenly, in hour of fullest fruition & certainty," hope
vanished. The doctor's daily calls were resumed — his last visit was
on the thirty-first of July, a Wednesday. Horace Mann relived that
Wednesday night on each recurring anniversary for many years.
"The clock strikes eleven. It was about this hour, as I watched over
her and sought to relieve her distress, that signs of mental alienation
became visible and sunk as dismaying omens on my heart." Charlotte's delirium increased. Two hours passed. It was "a scene of
anxiety, of dismay, of struggling, — of death!" Unable, in the end,
to recognize her dearest husband, Charlotte died in his arms.

"Oh my love . . . should you speak to me, how would you say
the word 'farewell'?"

CHAPTER ELEVEN

Somerset Court

THEY said that Horace Mann's hair turned white during the night, while he watched alone beside the dead Charlotte. But the neighbors who saw and talked about him soon saw him no more. It is ever the impulse, in the midst of grief, to attempt to escape by closing all doors upon the past and turning away from scenes once happy.[1] So Horace Mann left Dedham — that town which he had supposed would always be his home.

Dutifully, Mann carried Charlotte back to Providence and laid her in her father's family plot in North Burying Ground. Charlotte visited her old home forever now — no return.

Her lovely clothes, her almost bridal wardrobe, her china, the furniture, Mann offered to Charlotte's family. Asa Messer's reply was full of kindness. His "dear son" should keep everything of Charlotte's "for his own comfort." Although Messer was not reputed a generous man, "I wish nothing to be done that will make me the richer or you the poorer," he said.

Again with that impulse to destroy everything that brought painful remembrance, Mann sold his household goods with the exception of a few pieces that went to the Messer family; the "best bedstead," a "looking glass," the "dressing table" and the "entry lanthorn." The proceeds of the sale Mann put into lawbooks. "We are much pleased with your determination to devote the proceeds of your furniture to the fulfillment of the wishes of our dear daughter," wrote Asa Messer — for he knew that Charlotte had always wanted that law library for her beloved husband.

Mary Messer came to Dedham to dismantle the house on Church Street.[2] She packed Charlotte's prettiest bonnets and dresses for

Mann's widowed sister Rebecca Pennell and her three little girls. But Mann wanted his sister Lydia to have "the light silk," the first dress he ever bought Charlotte — and "the merino in which she was married."

Charlotte's brother-in-law, Sydney Williams, urged Mann to come to Taunton and become his law partner. Sydney and Caroline welcomed him into their home, but Mann realized how painful it would be to come within the circle of their happiness with the loss of Charlotte all the more poignant by contrast. Moreover, he would hate to bring the shadow of his grief into their happy world, to darken it. Sydney wrote often for advice in matters of law and they collaborated on many cases.

Edward Loring, the "glorious Neddy" of Litchfield days, was also urging a partnership. Ned had been in the office of his cousin, Charles Greely Loring, and now he wanted to hang out a new shingle — LORING AND MANN. They would do wonders together, Ned said, and Horace Mann agreed to the plan. The Lorings were a wealthy clan — almost every one of them said to be worth over a hundred thousand dollars. Wealthy people would be their clients, for Ned specialized in the handling of estates.

Ned and his wife loved lavish entertainment, and they expected, as a matter of course, that Mann would be at their home often. In due course, Harriet Loring would introduce a proper young lady. But the Lorings' affectionate hopes waned as Mann tried in vain to recapture his old enthusiasm for the career of a successful lawyer. Without Charlotte, the game was simply not worth the candle!

The journey from Dedham to Boston, once so stimulating, was now completely dreary — but for one interesting sight. As Mann's stagecoach rumbled into Needham, he saw the "excavation" for the Boston and Worcester Railroad, a project he had always ardently championed. But upon giving up his residence in Dedham, Mann relinquished his seat in the House of Representatives. It no longer mattered whether he supported railroads or not, and it was just one more melancholy thought to realize how well the legislature got along without him. It was "Metcalf of Dedham" now and "John W. Ames," in all the papers. Measures which Mann had sponsored fared well at their hands. But there were times when Mann would have liked to stand again upon the floor of the House and speak out. There was the day when the papers quoted a former colleague as saying that "It is perfectly right and proper that the offices of government should be distributed as spoils of victory." Mann would have liked to register a loud "nay" to that remark!

There was one public service which Mann had not relinquished with his change of residence. When the appropriation for building the "State Lunatic Hospital" finally went through, Horace Mann headed the committee of three appointed to oversee the work. "You got us into this," Governor Levi Lincoln told him; "you'll have to see us through." Mann was appointed Commissioner and then, from 1833 until 1838, he served as Trustee — writing the annual reports for the hospital.

As the building progressed, Mann was delighted with the new inventions which he and his fellow Commissioners were able to install. There were "water cisterns in the garret" which made "the apparatus of water closets seem to operate perfectly." There was a ventilation system, something almost unheard of — with air ducts opening into that same garret. A "windlass" carried food from the basement kitchen to the dining room on the first floor. The pauper insane of Massachusetts would have everything essential to their health and comfort — while Horace Mann was on hand to direct the project.

But Mann was shocked by the efforts of laborers and suppliers alike to cheat the state. Somehow, public money seemed to them to belong to no one. It was to be had for the taking — like blackberries in a pasture! Mann angrily demanded that defective lumber be replaced. Laborers were not to get drunk on the job. And bedsteads "a meaner width than you ever saw from any shop" and "only 5½ feet long" were not acceptable.

There was a demand brought forward in the legislature for a gilded dome on the "State Lunatic Hospital" on the grounds that it would be good advertising. It would be "incongruous," said Mr. Mann. There would be no waste of public funds for mere display — and no cutting-down on essentials.

By the middle of January, 1833, Governor Lincoln issued a proclamation. The hospital at Worcester would soon begin to receive patients and methods for liberating the insane in jails and work-houses and transferring them to Worcester were outlined. Each county could send six patients and each community must supply "a new suit of strong woolen or satinet cloth . . . stockings, new shoes." This directive was in itself a step forward since most of the insane prisoners had been in rags for years.

Mann had obtained the services of Dr. Samuel B. Woodward, whose pioneer work at the Hartford Retreat made him one of the two best-qualified physicians in the country. By spring, 1833, Dr. Woodward was accomplishing miracles — as Mann wrote to his sister Lydia. "Individuals who for years, while subjected to the severe rigors of confinement in jails & Houses of Correction, have been so frantic & ferocious that their keepers had not dared to go into their cells, had not been at Worcester a week, before the powerful & reviving influence of good air & suitable diet & cleanliness & warmth, with expressions of kindness on the part of their attendants, had so far transformed them into men, that they became quiet & manageable & declared themselves happy under their new conditions."

So optimistic were both Mann and Dr. Woodward that no cells for the restraint of the violent had been built. And then a patient named Trask declared that "he had been deceived and that medicine had been administered in his food for the purpose of destroying his health." He began to talk of revenge against his imagined enemies and it was decided to keep him from free access to the galleries — broad hallways on each floor where patients exercised. Trask's persecution complex is perfectly familiar today. In 1833, doctors had everything to learn. Reluctantly, Mr. Mann proposed the building of a few barred and "solid cells of stone," but what proportion of patients received would need close confinement, no one knew.

While the problem was being considered, Trask escaped. Now there was alarm among Worcester residents and the whole project, which depended upon public support, was suddenly unpopular. A reward was offered for the capture of Trask and Mann saw the Governor and had the reward doubled. Trask took refuge among the New Hampshire hills in what was at that time almost a wilderness around Keene. He was finally returned to custody without having harmed anyone, but it would take time and patience to restore public confidence in the new hospital.

The sorrowful discovery that illness of the mind could not be cured as easily and as quickly as he had hoped added to Mann's depression and loneliness. Ned Loring watched his friend with affectionate concern. Horace went no longer to "club" and entertained no group of friends over a cheerful bottle of port at the Tremont House. This was understandable. But he also refused Harriet Loring's invitations to dinner — he was seeing no one except clients, and going nowhere except to the Worcester Hospital! Ned appealed to his mother, Mrs. Curtis, who was fond of Horace Mann and to whom he would surely listen.

Just before Charlotte's death, Mrs. Curtis had proposed Mrs. Clarke's boardinghouse in Boston as the place where the Manns should live during the coming winter. Charlotte would be "cossetted and cared for," Mrs. Curtis had said. She now proposed Mrs. Clarke's as "a cheerful home" where Horace Mann would find "pleasant companions."

Mann admitted that the advice was sound and went accordingly to Number 3, Somerset Court — now Ashburton Place. He found a quiet street of modest city homes behind the State House and almost within the shadow of its dome. Snow lay along the slopes of Beacon Hill except where excavators still worked at leveling the summit. Mount Vernon had already been decapitated, to provide fill for Charles Street; Pemberton Hill was soon to go, and already most of the second peak of Boston's distinctive "tri-mountain" was filling the old Mill Pond to the north. In a little park opposite Ashburton Place a monument would eventually appear — a replica of the demolished Bulfinch shaft on Beacon Hill and arising to about the height of the old summit. There were those who deplored the disappearance of Boston landmarks, but Mann was not one of them. A filled-in Mill Pond would provide a site for a new North Station, and Mann felt that Beacon Hill summit could not be better employed! He knocked at Mrs. Clarke's door, found he was expected, and took the room Mrs. Clarke had hopefully set aside for him.

Once installed, Mann looked about him with interest. He had promised to try the efficacy of pleasant companionship and he would give himself a fair chance to recover from excessive grief. All Mrs. Clarke's boarders ate together at a long table.[3] Mann assessed them, one by one. There was Jared Sparks and his bride, the former Frances Allen. But Mrs. Sparks was nowhere to be seen and Mann was told that, after her first dinner at the long table, she chose to take all the rest of her meals in her room. Poor girl — the table-talk had overwhelmed her. Her husband soon took her to be mistress of beautiful Craigie House in Cambridge, but her illness had been no pretense and she had but two more years to live.

Jared Sparks became a valuable friend to Horace Mann during the years just ahead. There were many similarities between the two men — Sparks had struggled hard for his education, as had Mann, for example. After graduating from Harvard, Sparks had studied for the ministry and it was Dr. William Ellery Channing who preached the ordination sermon — a sermon so full of a new doctrine that the ordination of Jared Sparks was called "the Pentecost of Unitarianism." In 1833, when Horace Mann and Jared Sparks met at Mrs. Clarke's boardinghouse, Sparks was forty-four and Mann thirty-seven years old. Sparks had completed two careers and begun a third — resigning from the ministry to become owner-editor of the *North American Review;* then beginning his work as a historian with his *Life of Gouveneur Morris,* praised in all the papers. At this present moment, Sparks had in his room at Mrs. Clarke's "20,000 letters of Washington's, only 5,000 of which" had ever been published. One more career lay head of him. He would become President of Harvard, a position most of his Boston contemporaries regarded as more desirable than that of President of the United States!

Horace Mann already knew Jared Sparks by reputation, for he could hardly open a newspaper without coming across his name. It was interesting to discover that Sparks was handsome — the delight of such painters as Stuart, Sully and Peale. He was still called "Reverend" — for who could address otherwise a man responsible for a Pentecost? Sparks was charming when he chose; he could be impatient and brusque in an argument, having come to consider himself an authority — as indeed he was.

In marked contrast to Jared Sparks was Samuel Downer and, as Mann looked at his fellow boarders, he was immediately attracted to Downer — a young fellow just starting out on a business career. It was plain from Downer's speech that he had little or no formal education. But he spoke very little, being given to listening instead; he had intelligence and he was remarkably free from egotism. He had an insight into politics which was uncanny — a sort of intuition born of a knowledge of human nature and worth any amount of book learning. In 1833, Downer had just gotten a toe hold in what he called his "oil business." He sold high-quality whale-oil for spindles, and a rapidly growing textile business supplied him with plenty of customers. He soon hired two salesmen, paying them a 50 per cent commission and founding both their fortunes as well as his own. In 1852, when kerosene was discovered, Sam Downer was one of the first in the field, selling "kerosene spindle oil . . . superior to sperm." He made more than $20,000 a year, he told Horace Mann — still his close friend ever since their friendship began at Mrs. Clarke's.

The other men at Mrs. Clarke's were a Mr. Nisson, a foreigner and probably a student, a Mr. Rand, described as "horrid stupid," and George Hillard — "sick and melancholy." Twelve years younger than Mann, Hillard had just graduated from Harvard Law School and this was the year he was admitted to the bar. But the law never enchanted him as it charmed Mann. Young Hillard was blessed with too many gifts and at the moment he thought that a writing career was what he wanted. He was at work upon a *Life of Captain John Smith* for Jared Sparks's "Library of American Biography." He also contributed more than twenty articles for the *North American Review*, but one of several causes for present melancholy was lack of money. Jared Sparks could buy the *North American Review* on speculation and double his investment. George Hillard had not this Midas touch.

Since Mrs. Sparks no longer graced Mrs. Clarke's dining room, there were only four women at table, and most of the conversation was carried on by two of these. Mrs. Clarke herself led the field in "clamorousness." She talked about her late husband and his unfortunate ventures with merino sheep — and about his factory which burned down, uninsured. She talked about her son, James Freeman Clarke, soon to graduate from Harvard Theological Seminary and to follow in the footsteps of his famous step-grandfather for whom he was named. She told of her daughter Sarah's prowess as an artist and there at the table sat Sarah — blushing often and painfully at her mother's flow of words.

Mrs. Clarke talked about Horace Mann — behind his back. "How delightful it is," said she, "to see anyone really polite — and who you are sure will never say anything unkind."

"Mrs. Clarke far out-talks all of us, even Elizabeth!" So said Mary Peabody of Salem, herself the quietest among all the boarders.

"Elizabeth" was her sister. And Miss Elizabeth Peabody was un-like anyone who had ever crossed Horace Mann's path before.

In the first place, Elizabeth was indeed the talker that everybody said she was, but she was brilliant and full of originality. At the moment she was entirely absorbed in the Greeks because she was writing a book about them. Her interest centered around their social customs and their home life rather than their military defeats and victories. To Lizzie, the Greeks were real people who had once led private lives — an approach to history almost unheard of! Horace Mann was astonished to find that Miss Peabody rekindled his own boyish enthusiasm for the Greeks. Somehow, she made him feel again the thrill of his first discovery of the classic world in those books in the Franklin library!

Miss Peabody could read Greek — and she a woman! She could also read French, German and Latin, but all that seemed less re-markable to Horace Mann. She could outquote him in the classics, and it had been years since Mann had met anyone who could do that.

Being perfectly normal and human, Mr. Mann preferred that the women he had to look at often should be beautiful. Miss Peabody was not. Perhaps her only beauty was her abundant, naturally curly brown hair; but at the moment, being so intensely interested in the Greeks, she was attempting a Psyche knot, held (partially) by ribbon bands. By the end of the first argument at table, Elizabeth would have shaken her head once too often and her curls would begin to escape like revolutionists from their foreign fillets. Her face was anything but Greek since it was inclined to roundness with a nose not Greek nor even Roman but short and shapeless.

These would be but first impressions of Elizabeth Peabody in repose, however. Since she was almost never in repose but always alight with some new enthusiasm, her friends could never attempt to describe her — save to say that she was fascinating. Her blue eyes flashed "bright as a diamond," friends said. Color would come into her cheeks as she talked of some plan — usually for helping someone else — someone not yet aware that he needed help. How old was Elizabeth? People never thought about it. She had been "Miss Pea-body" since she began a teaching career at eighteen, and she was now twenty-nine; but probably Horace Mann thought of her as his own age or older.

There was one guest at Mrs. Clarke's to whom Mann found himself drawn more than to any other. This was Mary Peabody — Miss Lizzie's younger sister. Mann had buried his heart in the grave with Charlotte, but he had not lost his eyesight by any means. And Mary was beautiful. It was Mary's poise, the natural grace with which she moved, the sweet turn of her head, which first attracted attention. "The association of beauty" could "never be separated from" her. She had lovely color in her cheeks — a "rich damask bloom" in no way dependent upon artificial aid, which was at that time denied a gentlewoman. And when the lovely color faded with the years, there would always be Mary's fine features, the deep-set eyes, the handsome Roman nose inherited from aristocratic ancestors.

This is not to say that Horace Mann saw all this at first. He was at first pleasantly aware of her good looks yet far from acquainted with her, she was so quiet. But one day at dinner Mary Peabody chanced to say something in favor of the abolition of slavery in the South. The Reverend Jared Sparks spoke sharply, pointing out her ignorance of the subject and her faulty argument. Mary's color rose and her gray-green eyes blazed for a second. But when she spoke it was with good humor and she took her scolding "meekly." Horace Mann took up the argument in her behalf and did not forget the lady he had championed against "the Right Reverend Rude Rough" — as he afterwards jokingly called Sparks. It is probable that Mann thought Mary was younger than she was. Mary's twenty-seventh birthday was November 16 of that year, for she was born in 1806.

Horace Mann found himself enjoying the "pleasant companions" at Mrs. Clarke's just as the Lorings had hoped he would. He was carried out of himself and he was able to thrust sad thoughts aside as he sharpened his wit for those long table-talks. Sometimes Elizabeth, carried away by her own enthusiasms, would make too sweeping a statement. Mary would ask Mr. Mann for an opinion and Mann, in the most courteous yet faintly courtroom manner, would shorten Lizzie's flights of fancy. More often than not, this only served to set Elizabeth off again on another tangent and at a still more reckless pace, and Mann would be led into such a brilliant argument that it seemed a shame no judge and jury could hear him!

But in the midst of it all, Mann would glance at Mary Peabody and catch a gleam of mischief in her eye! Had Mary led them both on for her private diversion? Mann more than suspected that she had. Before long, Mann began to look for the gleam of approval with which Mary Peabody rewarded his best efforts. But he was both pleased and amused to notice that Mary was contrite if she goaded Elizabeth too far and made her look ridiculous. Mary was "like the 'Boy apprenticed to an Enchanter'," Mann said — sorry and a bit frightened at the mischief she had done.

It did not take Mann long to learn that Mary and Elizabeth Peabody were teachers. They had a little private school at Mrs. Clarke's with scholars coming to them from homes nearby — from the new Mt. Vernon Street, from Beacon Street, and from Louisburg Square. It was a fashionable school for girls — except that mere fashion was disregarded and lessons taught in new and original ways. It was an exclusive school — to the extent that snobbery and vulgarity were rigorously excluded. Elizabeth was headmistress and pioneer. Mary was her reliable assistant, patient and tactful but with ideas of her own, none the less.

There was a great deal about the Peabody sisters that Horace Mann could not know, of course. The girls made very little money with their school and most of what they earned must be sent home to help their father, who found dentistry in Salem far from lucrative. There were younger brothers with an aptitude for getting into debt. Then there was the third sister, the invalid Sophia, who in spite of a formidable and overprotective mother, struggled hard to earn her own living by painting.

"I hope you will find the Naples Yellow good, — I happened to have the money," Mary would write Sophia, whom she dearly loved. This extra money came from a project which would now be called "adult education." It was new and original when Elizabeth and Mary Peabody promoted "the idea of our historical school" — a series of lectures. "I think it will succeed nicely," Mary told Sophia, "and then we shan't be such poor rats any longer."

Mary had just cut over and fitted for herself a lovely foulard dress given her by a close friend, an elderly spinster of Salem, Miss Rawlins Pickman. Horace Mann, meticulous in his dress himself, could not but notice how pretty Mary looked in the green silk — how careful she was of every detail of her appearance from smoothly brushed hair to polished shoes. By contrast, Elizabeth was hopelessly untidy even with Mary at hand to sew on missing buttons and baste straight the little white collar which Lizzie always pinned askew.

Watching the two sisters together, Mann could not but observe the contrasts, guess at occasional conflict between them — but for some time to come he would know nothing of their private lives and their home in Salem.

Least of all would Horace Mann have suspected that, from early February 1833, letters written by Mary and Elizabeth Peabody to Sophia in Salem carried more about the new boarder at Mrs. Clarke's than anything else! "And then Mr. Mann is so intolerably witty, and has an anecdote, a story or a saying for every emergency and tells them with such full effect that he well nigh destroys me," wrote Mary. And when Mr. Mann was away attending court, Mary found that "people's ideas get into a strange jumble without him. Everything is referred to him when he is here — it is inexplicable, but he seems to be a point of union to all the heterogeneous mass — all defer to his opinions which he gives with great lucidness and doing ample justice to the rights and brains of all. It is astonishing to see the power of a fine mind especially when united with fine manners."

It was Elizabeth who set to work to find out all about Horace Mann. Who was he — where had he come from, and above all why was he so witty at one moment and then at intervals so suddenly grave and sad? Elizabeth had all the instincts of a novelist and she sensed a story. One evening, she and Mary sat talking with Mr. Mann in Mrs. Clarke's parlor long after the other boarders had gone to bed. Elizabeth, ever direct in her methods, asked Mr. Mann the nature of the grief from which she could see he suffered. Horace Mann told of the death of Charlotte.

"I listened speechless — I wept — then every power of my soul was taxed to console and finally to cheer," said Mary Peabody in a diary written long later.

Elizabeth took it otherwise. She discovered that Horace Mann, in his bitter grief, had cast aside Christian hopes. "He does not believe in revelation at all. He does not believe that Jesus Christ rose from the dead or any of those things," Elizabeth discovered, and she was profoundly shocked, for she herself never suffered from doubts. She was no child and heaven no longer lay all about her — but it was still only a step away, over a threshold that held no fear. She had yet to lose anyone extremely dear to her but she was certain that the spirits of the dead in Christ looked lovingly upon the living. Mann told Elizabeth of his Calvinist upbringing and "his horrible associations of the deity" and Elizabeth then and there set her generous and loving heart upon making Mann see God as a loving father.

Now here was drama which Elizabeth Peabody enjoyed to the full. And Horace Mann would not have been the fine lawyer that he was, the impassioned antagonist in debate, had he not been endowed with a dramatic sense to equal or even to surpass Miss Peabody's. Ever the teacher, Miss Lizzie decided that the thing to do was to educate Mr. Mann in the newest theology as a means to restoring his Christian faith. Mary was not so sure it was a good idea. To Sophia, Mary wrote: "I am going to read Benjamin Constant's 'Religion of the Greeks' and Cousin's 'Analysis of Locke' to Mr. Mann. Don't you think I shall be a candidate for *his* Insane Hospital?" Elizabeth and Mary took turns, reading aloud, but before long Horace Mann discovered that Mary had a lovely voice and that, during a brief period of family prosperity, she had taken singing lessons from a famous Italian teacher, living in Boston. Cutting the theology lessons short, Mann urged Mary to sing to him.

Mary agreed readily and sang all the songs she knew for she felt sure that this was better for Mr. Mann than "metaphysical arguments long enough to exhaust all common minds." But alas for Mary's hope to "console and finally to cheer." One night, unknowingly she chose a song that Charlotte used to sing. She later received and kept all her life long the letter Horace Mann wrote her.

My dear Mary,

I regret exceedingly that I had so little command over my feelings last evening as to suffer them to betray me. But I was taken unawares; and the song itself was one, which that departed spirit, angel as she is, could not now sing more spiritually than she used to.

I do not regret the occurrence myself, for I know I must pass through such scenes till feelings are cauterized, if indeed that can ever be, and it is less painful to pass through them with friends than with strangers.

H.M.

In spite of this single failure in her efforts to cheer, Mary was happy and hopeful. Spring came with peepers in the Frog Pond and mud on all the paths across Boston Common — then sudden flowering of all the famous gardens on Summer Street. Bostonians went to walk or ride in Mt. Auburn Cemetery — a suitable Sunday outing. Mr. Mann went with the sisters, to Newton and to Mt. Auburn. He looked "radiant," Marry told Sophia. He climbed a cherry tree to pick a blossom for her and she dared to laugh.

All this, Mary wrote to Sophia. But Elizabeth wrote of activities along metaphysical lines — or so she imagined. She wrote of Mr. Mann being "plunged into the profoundness of remembrance" — of other boarders leaving Mrs. Clarke's parlor, of Mary leaving last, and of scenes alone with "dear Mr. Mann." Elizabeth, with her storytelling gift, set down the drama as Mr. Mann "still held my hand till Mary had gone out of the room — and then drew me nearer and throwing his arm around me — let the tears flow, which seem ever to wait this touch of sympathy."

It seemed strange to Elizabeth that her sister Mary should be angry with her for invoking emotional scenes. And it was still more strange when sister Sophia wrote a letter full of anxious warnings. Sam Haven of Dedham had married a close friend of Sophia's, they were visiting in Salem and, under vow of secrecy, they had told Sophia tales which she eventually passed on. According to Sam, Mr. Mann was a philanderer who had trifled with the affections of both Elizabeth and Catherine Haven! Mann was "Irresistible to women," Sam said.

Elizabeth overwhelmed Sophia with page after page in proof of Mr. Mann's innocence. "I know Sam Haven is very much prejudiced against him," Sophia replied. Hastily she added, before Lizzie should write her another ten-page argument, "At any rate, I shall think as you do now. . . ." It was no fault of Horace Mann's that women fell in love with him — particularly sisters!

But early in the summer of 1833 a blow fell that neither Mary nor Elizabeth Peabody expected. Mr. Mann left Mrs. Clarke's boarding-house! Mary took it meekly without asking questions. To Sophia she wrote of "Mr. Mann's sudden and unexpected departure."[4] Mann had been in Taunton all week "attending the court, and returned today and concluded to go from here immediately, took away all his things and has actually commenced his solitary life at the French lady's rooms where he is to take his breakfast and his tea alone, and dine at the Tremont."

"I think it is best for him to go since he has taken up with the

idea so decidedly," Mary went on. She would always think that Mr.
Mann knew best. "But it is dreadful to think that he feels just such
a change necessary." Mary searched her heart to discover how her
effort to "console and finally to cheer" had failed. "I cannot help
thinking of him there all alone, feeding upon those overwhelming
thoughts, contemplating that one theme." Not for the world would
Mary have said any of these things to Mr. Mann, however.

Elizabeth, as usual, shared most of Mary's thoughts but took an
opposite course of action. She wrote to Mr. Mann to ask what she
had done or said to force him to leave! It seemed more than probable to her that Mary had been to blame. What had Mary done?

Mann replied at great length to "My dear Miss Peabody . . . I
cannot pardon myself, were I to allow an impression so strong as
your letter indicates, & at the same time so erroneous, to remain
on your mind *one moment* without an effort to remove it. . . .
Allow me to say that the generous sympathy you have evinced in
my sorrows has not been thrown away, that it has done much toward
relieving the burden of *life* at seasons, when it would otherwise
have seemed intolerable. . . .

"When I first went to the house . . . I had hoped that the intellectual and refined society of its inmates would do something toward
filling up the void in my life. I found every female member of the
family more agreeable than I had anticipated, I only found so much
of that which I mourned as to be a perpetual remembrance of it.
Often, I have retired from the gratification of their society to weep
over the blessedness of that I had lost. But soon the form of my grief
was changed. Physical nature was overwhelmed by the moral stimu-
lus that pain had given it. One image became more & more fixed
before my eyes & I had less & less power to remove it. My faculties
became congealed. I was transfixed to stone. I occupied the most
frightful situation of grief, *powerless* but *conscious*. I know upon the
confines of *what it is that that condition of mind lies*. I found myself more and more incapacitated for business daily."

If Elizabeth shared this letter with Mary, it must have been at
this point that Mary was torn between pity for Mr. Mann and anger
at her sister. Had she not warned that those long religious discussions
were bad for him! And — in spite of Mann's polite assertions — the
proof that he was escaping from too much sympathy lay further on.

"I saw the necessity of effort," Mann said, "and in the hope of

eing able to break the spell that bound me, I resolved upon the
proposed change. I need to reverse this fatal current of tho't. The
ies of association must be broken. If it is possible, I must re-edify the
uins of my mind. . . ."

The letter went on and Elizabeth, at least, drew complete reas-
urance from it. "Let me then, my dear friend, beseech you not to
disquiet yourself on my account & do not ever again indulge in any
uch injurious imputations against yourself, as you seem to have
done."

There was a special message for Mary Peabody and the generous-
earted Elizabeth must surely have let her read the sentence. "Above
ll, do not blame your sister, who is incapable of doing anything
deserving it."

CHAPTER TWELVE

The Honorable Horace Mann

THE most cogent reason for leaving Mrs. Clarke's boardinghouse was one which Mann did not mention in his letter to Miss Peabody. He was suddenly faced with financial disaster [1] and he could not afford Mrs. Clarke's genteel accommodations. But this was a matter Mann did not care to discuss any more than necessary and he must have discovered that Miss Peabody's gift of "communication," as she called it, extended to the affairs of all her friends, whom she endeavored to help by advertising their troubles.

On April 3, 1833, Mann's brother, Thomas Stanley, had left Franklin for Louisville, Kentucky. He went to make a new start in life but he left chaos and ruin behind him. On June 18 four men, "in behalf of themselves and of the other mortgagees . . . made open and peacable entry upon all lands, mills and buildings . . . except the Thomas Mann farm." The Eagle Manufacturing Company and the City Manufacturing Company had failed. Horace Mann had barely managed to save his mother's dower rights, his sisters' and his own claim to Mann's Plain.

When the two cotton mills were seized "for breach of conditions of said mortgage" Mann discovered what a terrible instrument of self-destruction he had created when he drew up the contracts for himself and his brother and the men who lent them money. Horace Mann was personally liable for thousands of dollars. The last drop of bitterness in his cup was the knowledge that he had himself to blame. He had once written his family that he had "grown up to be a lawyer" but where his own interests were concerned he was not a good one! The City Manufacturing Company was ost but Mann's efforts to salvage something from the wreck of the Eagle Company continued for the next twenty-five years — providing little except liabilities and litigation.

Thomas Stanley persisted in assuming that his affairs were not desperate. He wrote home for money, certain that goods from the mills had after all been sold and that friends and customers to whom he had made loans or advanced goods on credit had now paid up and that he must have money in the bank. But his accounts were in a hopeless tangle, and goods supposed to have been delivered were reported gone astray while money owing the mills proved impossible of collection through careless handling of bills. It was not surprising that Stanley Mann had begun to seek the taverns a little too often before he left home. In Louisville, he was once more overwhelmed by debt and disaster and he drank to excess.

Horace Mann had become increasingly prominent in the temperance movement. After Charlotte's death, his very temperate enjoyment of a glass of wine had ceased and "total abstinence" — an expression just coming into use — was now his watchword. It hurt his personal pride that his brother should have a "weakness." It was bitter, indeed, that a perfect stranger from Louisville should write and tell of it!

In December 1833 Horace Mann sued his brother Thomas Stanley for $794.35 in the Court of Common Pleas in Boston. The purpose was to recover a few acres of land in Franklin but in the cruel wording of the law, the sheriff was "to take the body of the said Thomas and him commit unto our Gaol in Boston or Dedham." The body of Thomas was well out of reach in Kentucky; but there must have been twenty men in and around Franklin who could have had the body of Horace Mann seized for debt under the contract he himself had drawn. It was ironic — since Mann had been for years at work in the Legislature to abolish imprisonment for debt! There is no pride like the subtle one which a man feels when he endeavors to raise the fallen — all the time feeling sure that he himself could never fall so low!

It became a point of honor with Mann not only to pay back every cent of indebtedness but to do it as rapidly as possible and in as painful as possible a manner. He soon left "the French lady's" and moved a cot into his law office, where he lived, day and night.

Dinner at the Tremont House was out of the question and Mann recorded in his diary that he followed a plan of dining only every other day! His clothes grew frayed and rusty but he bought nothing new. Inevitably, he became ill, but the deathbed he believed he sought eluded him.

One luxury Mann allowed himself. So strong was Elizabeth Peabody's magnetic personality, so tenderhearted and persistently friendly was she, that he could not give her up. Mary's sweet low voice,[2] her charming glances — shy at first, then becoming more confident — drew Mann to Mrs. Clarke's and before long he was calling on the Peabody sisters regularly every Sunday evening when he was in Boston.

Horace Mann could not know when it happened, but a day came when a simple gesture of courtesy changed the current of Mary Peabody's life.[3] "I had not been able to look him fairly in the face and could not have told the color of his eyes," Mary wrote long later. "One day he opened the door for me to pass out before him. I meant to give him only a courteous look of thanks . . . but the smile with which he accompanied the gentlemanly attention . . . was an earnest to me that the capacity for happiness was not exhausted, even though he thought it was. I know I returned [the smile] for I felt the glow permeate every fibre and vein. I knew nothing more till I was seated by the window in my own apartment." There was a glimpse of the State House from Mary's window. How beautiful it looked — how beautiful everything seemed and yet how sad as she tried to face the fact that she had fallen in love with a man who had, so far, shown nothing more than friendship for her!

"It was not long before my life passed out of myself into him," Mary confessed years later. "The idea of human love is so associated with marriage . . . that altho' I did not suppose *he* would ever marry again, from that hour, my mental ejaculation to him was invariably, 'my husband.' My interest in life was now more intense than I ever imagined it could be. My own ideal of human perfection had been brooded over till I had substantially given up the expectation of seeing it realized but I found myself overpowered by the conviction that not only its main features were before me but with something else added."

In the autumn of 1833, Sophia Peabody's ever precarious health took a turn for the worse. Elizabeth, the family manager, decreed journey for health and arranged everything so that the family resources, which were slender, would not be strained to breaking. She found a wealthy family in Cuba willing to take a Miss Peabody as governess for their children, pay her next to nothing, but allow Miss Sophia to live at their haçienda as a guest. It was understood that Sophia might die very soon or she might have to live in Cuba always for the sake of her health. One of her sisters must accept exile and a life of self-sacrifice to take care of her. Years later, Mary Peabody gave her reasons for offering to be the one to go.

"My state of feelings became at last so impossible to be borne that I hailed [the opportunity] which offered to accompany my younger sister to the tropics. . . . I loved her most dearly and perhaps I could have had the courage to go with her at all events, but it was no question of courage now. My only thought was to take myself away from his sight who was daily becoming so indispensable to my happiness that I feared he would discover my feelings. . ."

Perhaps, as Mary firmly believed, Horace Mann "had no conception of the estimation" with which she "regarded him." But it seems hardly possible that he could have missed entirely the admiration in her eyes. He wrote her a letter of farewell but in this, his second letter to her, he addressed her as "My dear Miss Peabody" instead of the "Dear Mary" of that treasured first epistle. Here was a new note of caution in a letter which contained little to comfort one who had lost her heart. Mann mentioned "that delicious climate" of Cuba and spoke cheerfully of Mary's return home. She was to "enjoy all the happiness" she deserved.

This letter was written in October when it was supposed that Mary and Sophia would sail on a ship called the *Red Rover*. That plan fell through and they did not leave till December, on the brig *Newcastle*. Mann did not write Mary another farewell letter but wrote to Elizabeth instead with "tell her" this and "tell her" that. Hidden deep in Mary's heart and confessed only in later years was the conviction that Horace Mann already loved her sister Elizabeth and that letters from home would soon bring the news of their marriage.

In her "Journal of Remembrance" Mary recalled her voyage "Nothing less than the Ocean could hold my soul. . . . In its waters I sowed my heart. . . . I longed for storms but we had none to meet my cravings. I was insensible to danger; my timid nature slept & I do not believe any contest of the elements would have caused an emotion of fear."

With her assistant gone, Elizabeth could no longer handle a school large enough to pay for the rooms at Mrs. Clarke's. Beset by financial difficulties, she moved from pillar to post, always hopeful that the latest move would solve her problems. She made certain that Mr. Mann always knew where to find her and he continued his Sunday-night calls. Of much greater interest to Elizabeth than her own troubles were those of Mr. Mann and she continued her efforts to restore his faith. After each call, so many things occurred to Elizabeth she had not thought of saying that she wrote Mann long letters, turning over all her unturned stones!

"Can love spring from the bosom of suffering?" she wrote on December 21, 1833, just after Mary left. She answered her own question. "Yes, and you have experienced it — *For me*, my dear friend, — you have expressed a very affectionate friendship. Before you did it in words, you did it by the most confidential manner. And yet — if I do not mistake, the very words of mine which attracted you . . . touched chords whose slightest vibration was pain — not one word that I said of comfort did you believe . . . you laid your poor suffering head upon my bosom — and pressed *the inflicter of pain* to your breaking heart — *and why was this?* It was because you believed that sympathy and tenderness dictated the painful words. . . . And so, if you believed in God, you could take pain and love him better."

It was an excessively long letter, extremely hard to read, and it must have been fairly alarming to a lawyer who wrote circumspectly! But Horace Mann understood Elizabeth better than anyone ever had before or ever would again. He replied to her long letters, in charming, informal notes undated but addressed to her various abodes. He told her of a speech he made. "I went to Lowell, & in the evening of Sunday, who do you think *expounded* & *explained* on the subject of Temperance . . . ? I smote the cushion with no inconsiderable vehemence, nor can I tell how many hearers I may have had . . . outside of the house."

Mann hated cold weather and told Elizabeth, "I have felt lighter and freer during the hot days and my *mortal coil* sits more easily upon me. But in such a day as this, I feel tightly swathed in cold bands & my nerves are all at so great a tension as to endanger their cohesion. All easy and flexible motion is screwed out of me.

"My spirit has suffered like my body. *Once* it was warm, elastic, expansive — now it is unimpressible and torpid."

But when it came to answering Elizabeth's long theological arguments — Mann sometimes ignored them; sometimes refuted them too well. Lizzie decided that she needed help. Dr. William Ellery Channing, with his famous voice, his personal charm, had long since opened the gates of heaven for Elizabeth. She prevailed upon Horace Mann to go with her to call on Dr. Channing.

Channing and Mann liked each other at sight. But to Elizabeth's disappointment, they talked "colonization" instead of religion. There had been articles in the papers about "a large and very respectable company of agriculturalists of color" who had sailed for Liberia "aboard the splendid ship *Lafayette* — a name auspicious to freemen." The emigrants were "under the auspices of Maryland" and both Mann and Channing saw hope in this that the South would in time settle for herself the question of slavery. It made spirited conversation for two optimists!

Mann began to go to Dr. Channing's church fairly regularly and at last, in 1834, Elizabeth's hopes were realized. Mann heard Channing's Easter sermon and a new, mature faith came to him. He spent Sunday evening with Miss Peabody and told her that Channing's Easter sermon "gave laws to the imagination and landmarks to the affections — what [he] had never before known." Joyfully, Elizabeth related the whole story in her next letter to Mary in Cuba. "Dear Mr. Mann" had "said a good deal about himself and his destitution of right views and habits of thought in regard to the other world — and did not suggest a doubt of Dr. Channing's views nor call them visionary. He said many times that he was never so overcome by a sermon — that he felt himself borne on the wings of an angel."

Elizabeth would not have been Elizabeth had she not rushed to tell her wonderful Dr. Channing all about it. "I never saw him so much gratified," she said. She copied the sermon (aided by her phenomenal memory in translating Channing's hieroglyphic handwriting) "to give to Mr. M. for his friends in Providence."

Mann's business often carried him to Providence and to Dedham. But in Dedham he went only to the courthouse, avoiding Church Street, because he was not yet able to look calmly upon the once loved corner house. The railroad, which he had so enthusiastically championed, was advertised alongside of the stagecoach companies, in the daily papers during August 1834. "From and after Monday the 28th inst. the Passenger Cars, with Locomotive Engine *Whistler* will, until further notice, be dispatched daily (Sundays excepted) from the depot at the foot of the Common to the Sprague House, Dedham Low Plain." Tickets cost a quarter and a stage would carry passengers from Dedham Low Plain to Dedham Village. There was only one train a day, however, and sometimes that one was "delayed by a strong head wind in her passage up." Mann rejoiced in the railroad, none the less. It brightened a dark mood, brought on by a return to Dedham, to stop and admire the *Whistler* or the *Meteor* or the *Yankee* and have a word or two with the engineer. Mr. Mann always knew the trainmen by name.

Occasionally, "on the cars" and elsewhere, Mann met former political associates. The talk was all to the effect that "the wheels of our factories move languidly or are still." There was a serious depression and it was a comfort, although a cold one, for Mann to realize that his cotton mills were not the only ones to fail. For the most part, however, Mann saw little of his former friends and took little part in the world beyond his law practice.

On July 4, 1834, Horace Mann sat alone in his room writing a letter which began, "My very dear & Sisterly Friend . . ." Mary Peabody, in faraway Cuba, was this "Sisterly Friend," and since she was now "almost on another planet," Mann set himself to tell her of "the great jubilee day of America" which was ending. "There is what is called a 'Whig' celebration," Mann said — "a revival & application of an old name to all who are opposed to Gen. Jackson's administration. They have a beautiful pavilion on the East side of the Common, just without the Mall. It is a large semicircle & will accommodate, or rather I should say, is accommodating two thousand at this present." Although invited to join "the throng," Mann told Mary, "I preferred to avail myself of the opportunity . . . to do what I am now doing, so that you may hereafter be very certain that on this day, while you was [*sic*] thinking of your home and country . . . there was one at least here, to whom the recollection of you & his desire for your welfare was so strong, that in the hour of festivity, he was thinking only of you. Would that his *thoughts* were *powers*, & happiness would fill the circle of which you should be forever the center."

Mann knew that Mary was homesick, and he wrote on, to amuse and please her. There had been a "procession" — he would tell her of that. It was part of "an unwonted celebration by a new party, with a new name, which has sprung into sudden existence here & attained maturity at once. It is the party of 'Trades Union!' "

In the middle of the "Trades Union" parade was a float, evidently the first Mann had ever seen. "The shipwrights" had "provided themselves with a splendid ship built for the occasion. . . . It was no child's toy either, being nearly as large as one of those in which Columbus crossed the Atlantic." Mann was boyishly delighted with the full-rigged ship, "drawn by twenty-four (I write out the words" — he said — "lest you should think I have made a mistake) white horses." But Mann's approval of their float did not extend to the party which had sponsored it. "The bond of association among these men is mutual support and defence against what they denominate aristocratic institutions & manners. This principle is rapidly extending itself in this country & if something be not done to check it, the advantages of possessing wealth will find what to me would be more than a counterpoise in the envy & dis-social feelings which it will occasion."

Mann said nothing of any personal leanings toward politics. The Lorings and the Curtis family were urging him to proclaim himself a loyal member of the newly formed Whig party and run for office. If all who opposed Jackson's administration were Whigs, then Mann was certainly a Whig, but he found honors so empty now that he could not bring himself to make much of a political effort. It was as well that he could not read Elizabeth Peabody's letters to Cuba, written daily and dispatched in batches whenever a boat sailed. Immediately after Mary and Sophia sailed away on the brig *Newcastle*, "I went down to Mr. Henry Lee's to tea and spent the evening," Elizabeth wrote. "He said a great deal about

Mr. Mann and says he wants him to go into the senate and that he certainly would be chosen if set up — and would be set up if he would let his friends know he was willing."

Mr. Henry Lee was a Boston banker, prominent in politics. His wife's father was Jonathan Jackson, first president of the Boston Bank; the two men were associated and the whole family connection was, as a matter of course, Federalist. The Lees knew that Mr. Mann had been a National Republican. Could they all become Whigs together? Miss Peabody felt able to cope with political difference. "We talked of the old Federalist party and he [Mr. Lee] admitted that all that Mr. Mann blames about them to have been true."

On went Lizzie — campaigning for Horace Mann, though, fortunately for her, without his knowledge. Most useful to Miss Peabody were balloon ascensions during August! The balloons were inflated and rose from Boston Common with crowds gathering to watch them. Among the crowd on the Common was Horace Mann, his heart rising within him in a sudden surge of joy at this one more sign of great things to come. Elizabeth was invited to the housetops of various Beacon Street families, there to watch the scene — and from the housetops she proclaimed Horace Mann, her senatorial candidate! . . . A sudden hush fell upon the people out on the Common, Mann told Elizabeth. She had not noticed it, Elizabeth said — and in all probability there was no hush on Elizabeth's rooftop.

Lizzie talked to Mr. James K. Mills for two hours "about Mr. Mann," and defensively Elizabeth added, "Mr. Mills introducing the subject." Mr. Mills, a banker, said that if Horace Mann "would be nominated for any public duty, it would be *carried* without a doubt" — so Elizabeth reported.

The Dwights, where Elizabeth was always welcome, listened to praise of Horace Mann. They were a Springfield, Massachusetts, family, their fortune having been founded in trade along the Connecticut River. Edmund Dwight had married the daughter of the great merchant, Samuel Eliot, and their children were pupils of Miss Peabody. The Dwights had not only a large fortune but large hearts, and Elizabeth had no difficulty in interesting them in Mann, the crusader — who had built the hospital at Worcester. Elizabeth's faculty for bringing the right people together bore fruit when a devoted friendship developed between the Dwights and Horace Mann.

On went Miss Lizzie, to the Tuckermans, to Henry Rice, to the Forbeses, to the "F. Cabots" — all old friends through scholars, past and present. That most of them were "State Street," or the moneyed group, did not matter to Miss Peabody, who never set a cash value on her friends, one way or the other. What mattered right now was that Federalist State Street was ready to support a former National Republican. Mann would have found it an unwelcome task to explain himself to State Street — but Miss Peabody was only too glad to do it for him. There may have been a little laughter behind her back but people listened to her just the same.

Horace Mann was comparatively unknown in Boston but just at this time a terrible occurrence humbled Boston's pride — and for a short time brought Horace Mann in personal contact with city leaders. *RIOTS IN CHARLESTOWN* was the headline in the *Boston Advertiser* on August 12. "The alarm of fire last night about 11 o'clock was from the burning of tar barrels in Charlestown," the account began. "It was doubtless with a view of attracting persons from this city and vicinity to join in an attack on the Ursuline Convent. The attack was commenced with disgraceful shouts and by breaking of windows but up to 12 o'clock the work did not appear to proceed with much vigor and it is probable the rioters desisted, although there did not seem to be any peace officers present." So the account went, as though the shouting mob, the flying stones and the crash of broken glass were all in the day's work. But before the complacent *Advertiser* went to press an item headed "Postscript" had to be added. "Our anticipations were incorrect. The convent is completely wrapped in flames." Parents whose children were in the convent school lashed their horses in a frantic attempt to reach Charlestown faster than horse and chaise had ever made the trip before.

Next day, Mayor Theodore Lyman issued a call for a mass meeting at Faneuil Hall. Boston citizens, deeply sensible of the disgrace of mob violence, voted an inquiry and the death penalty was promised the instigators of the riot — if they could be found. The mayor appointed Boston's most prominent citizens to a committee of investigation.

On the nineteenth of August, Elizabeth Peabody wrote to Mary in Cuba. "Mr. M. is solicitor to the Committee of Investigation which is seeing about the convent affair. This is an office bringing his law knowledge, and equity of mind into high play and it was a great compliment to be chosen and Mr. Lee speaks of him as displaying the highest principles. . . . The committee consists of fifty of the first gentlemen in town [According to the list in the paper, there were thirty-eight, but Lizzie liked higher numbers]. Mr. Lee says nothing can be better for Mr. Mann than to be thus displayed."

A member of the committee had questioned whether Mann might be "too orthodox" and therefore unfair toward the Catholics, Elizabeth said. This, she quite rightly considered "a comical idea."

Mann was happier while at work for the Convent Committee than he had been for over a year. He had little time to dwell on private sorrows, for the investigations began at once. A great wrong had been done and Mann felt a return of his former crusading spirit as he sifted evidence and tried to allocate the blame. An ill-tempered convent gardener with a ferocious dog had stirred neighborhood enmity. A young woman, suffering from "brain fever" and probably of unsound mind, had wandered away from the convent, had returned, but was reported a prisoner. Wild rumors of her torture and death spread among the neighbors until the Charlestown selectmen had visited the convent, seen the young woman, and convinced themselves that nothing evil went on there. Six or seven nuns were teaching about twenty little girls in school and that was all.

The words of the report Horace Mann signed sound very much like him. The Ursuline Order was "extensively beneficial" in their "services in the cause of Christian charity." Fear, born of ignorance, had caused the outrage. Jealousy between immigrant Irish laborers and native laborers fanned the flames. It was only by the grace of God that the Mother Superior had been able to lead her charges to safety in the garden while the vandals ransacked the convent, smashing musical instruments, throwing books and church ornaments out of the windows — and finally burning the building. As Mann signed the report, he wondered how many would ever read it and how many readers would be educated thereby.

The investigations continued, but in September Mann was taken ill.[4] It was necessary for him to give up his work for the Convent Committee and Elizabeth said that "Mr. Lee was lamenting that Mr. Mann was taken off the solicitorship, it being very important."

Mann had a "slow fever" and Elizabeth thought "the disease was probably choleratic." Whatever it was, Mann had finally succeeded in breaking his health through overwork and alternate days of starvation.

Elizabeth sent grapes and flowers and finally announced that she was coming to see "Dear Mr. Mann" — ill upon his cot in his law office. Mann replied firmly but with a light touch. He was not on his deathbed, and till that time, "Miss P." must be discreet and stay away. But the boy, Willy, who carried messages back and forth, could give no assurance that Miss Peabody might not be behind him on the stairs almost any day! Mann went away — leaving no address. It was the first time such a thing had happened since their friendship began, Elizabeth told Mary. She was greatly distressed and at a loss for the reason!

Early in November the Whig caucus took place and Horace Mann's name was put in nomination. How unfair it seemed to Elizabeth that women were not allowed to go to a caucus! She had to depend on her friend William Rice for the news and then send it all to Mary secondhand. Mr. Charles Curtis had made a speech, "defending Mr. Mann" who, he said, "was charged with two crimes — having projected a lunatic asylum was one of them." Mann "acknowledged it — he had projected and erected it" and then Curtis "gave the whole history of the hospital" and Mann's "action" and "was applauded with uproar." The other of Mann's two crimes was "his being a friend of Temperance."

All very well — Dr. Channing, to whom Elizabeth went at once expecting him to help her gloat over Mann's nomination for senator from Boston, was "pleased," but was also "grieved that the grocers, distillers &c had congregated to split the ticket — which would probably defeat" Mr. Mann "entirely." Elizabeth was disappointed — why was it that her beloved Dr. Channing was forever acting like a kite string and bringing her down to earth?

What Channing had not counted upon was the ingenuity of the Whigs. So new was their scheme for getting out the vote that Horace Mann himself wrote all about it in one of his not too frequent letters to Mary in Cuba. "Young men of Boston took it into their own hands," Mann told Mary. "A civilian committee of 100" were appointed and "each ward of the city" covered. "Every house (was) entered and the name of every Whig voter marked down and on election day carriages were ready to bring every man, who had not voted, to the polls. . . . Every department of the State government is Whig! Whig! Whig!"

Mann left it to Elizabeth to tell of his own night of victory and she did so on November 8. "All evening the people in large crowds were thronging the streets and calling out the elected gentlemen to make speeches. There is no doubt that Mr. Mann is elected notwithstanding the distillers' ticket against him."

Returns came in slowly but before Elizabeth sealed her letter she added, "I see by tonight's paper that Mr. Mann's majority is nearly three thousand and he is now the Honourable Horace Mann."

CHAPTER THIRTEEN

To Present to the People

IT was "Mann of Suffolk" now, instead of "Mann of Dedham," as the year 1835 began. The new senator was "in good spirits," Elizabeth Peabody reported. "He seemed much gratified with his triumph and encouraged to pursue his objects."

Few members of the legislature would now need to ask the name of the new senator in the black, rather clerical-looking coat, but many might turn to look again at Horace Mann — white-haired now, and with the radiant smile so many remembered now but rarely on his lips. Mann was placed upon a committee at once — it was Probate and Chancery. The matter of guardianships came up, and Mann strengthened the law, for he felt that it was not enough for a guardian to take care of a minor's inherited funds. The guardian should also see his ward at least once a year and try to determine whether or not the child was happily situated and in healthful surroundings.

"Mann of Suffolk" put forward "a resolve for enlarging the Lunatic Hospital" [1] and no one now was surprised to hear him speak eloquently upon the subject. The hospital at Worcester had been inadequate almost before it was completed, the reluctant towns having first failed to report their "pauper insane" and then, when the hospital fulfilled its promises to take over the liability, having inundated Worcester Asylum with applicants for admission. The new appropriation would have a hard struggle in the House, Mann told Elizabeth Peabody during his rather more infrequent Sunday-evening calls. If the appropriation failed, then only such cases as might be curable were to be taken at Worcester and if, after a certain period, the patient were not cured, back he must go to the terrible conditions of almshouse or jail again.

Miss Peabody determined to go to the Senate to hear Mr. Mann speak. Then how eloquently she in turn would speak to all her influential friends about the wonderful work of the Honorable Horace Mann! To be sure, no woman ever entered the sacred halls of the legislature, but there was no law against it — not that Miss Peabody knew of. She made the mistake of writing dear Mr. Mann that she was coming.

Mann was horrified. He must head Miss Peabody off before she got both of them thoroughly laughed at — and yet she was truly his "very dear Friend" and he would deal gently. "I have so much regard for my colleagues and for myself too," he wrote, "that I should be sorry to have you present at our meetings. The gallery is not open, so all spectators are obliged to come upon the floor of the Senate Chamber." (*That* should keep Miss Peabody away. Imagine a woman on the *floor* of the Senate! But Mann knew he must think of still better reasons.) "Then there is not one chance in a thousand that you would hear anything by which you would be in the least gratified. Our debates are very irregular and desultory and nobody thinks of making the sort of speech, which has a beginning, a middle, and an end. So, I guess you will give up that notion. . . ."

Mann signed himself "Yours affectionately" and hoped fervently that Miss Peabody would take his strong hints. When he signed himself "Yours *very* affectionately," Elizabeth "kissed these sweet words." This time she could only put the note away with a sigh. "I have forty letters from Mr. M." she told Mary — "counting each note for one." She waited dutifully at home till Mr. Mann came to tell her that the Worcester Hospital appropriation had gone through.

"The stern decree of human suffering, which had gone forth, was recalled," he told her. "The tears of sorrow which would have been shed shall be tears of joy. For me, it has lifted the burden of life."

A task now came to Mann's hand for which he was particularly fitted and which again lifted the burden of life. Four years previously, he "and a colleague got up the project of having all the state laws revised and a commission of three very able lawyers" had been appointed to look into the matter. Their report now came before the Senate and, as a member of the committee on Probate and Chancery, it fell to Horace Mann to complete, in the Senate, work he had begun in the House. Statute Law was one of the subjects best taught at Litchfield and Mann had studied it with youthful enthusiasm.

In the beginning, Mann visualized the project as one to make the work of lawyers easier. He now saw it in a larger light. The law ought to be understood by the client as well as by his attorney. The object of the revision ought to be "to present to the people, in methodical and luminous order, in clear and precise language . . . the Statute Laws of the Commonwealth which had been enacted in all the years of its history."

To present to the people . . .[2] There was Mann's personal feeling about the law. He had set himself a stupendous, probably an impossible task, but to give the people their law shone in Horace Mann's mind like a holy vision. The daily newspapers now rarely carried his name. He was heard from only once, when, with George Bliss of Springfield, he moved that the Committee on the Revised Statutes be permitted to "sit during recess." All through the summer months, as chairman of the committee, Mann labored to make "luminous" the law. Writing to his sister Lydia in June, he described his work.

"I know not when I shall see you. The Committee on the Revised Statutes is now in session and the labor is almost beyond description. You know that, ever since the adoption of the State Constitution in 1780, the Legislature has been enacting law after law, to enlarge, abridge, or amend the existing code. When any inconvenience was experienced from an old enactment . . . then some provision of the former law has been repealed, or some addition has been made to it. Hence, to ascertain what the law is upon a single subject, it has been necessary to look thro' half a dozen volumes, and to see how far one provision had cut in upon a former — where new provisions began & where they ended." Mann's task, he explained, was to take up each revision of a law and to "compare it with existing provisions, as they are scattered over the books for the last half century, & see that we allow nothing to be left out & nothing to be put in, unless in cases where the old law was defective or its provisions otherwise objectionable."

When the revision was finally completed, Theron Metcalf — also a native of Franklin — was credited with editing and indexing the statutes. It was Horace Mann who wrote the marginal notes and the references to judicial cases. The hours of labor, the difficulties ironed out in committee, and most of all the "clear and precise language" of those marginal notes, raised Horace Mann high in the estimation of his profession.

But alas for the aim that lay closest to Mann's heart — that of giving the law to the people! Few if any outside the legal profession ever read the revised statutes and few indeed ever knew who had labored to prepare them. In later years, when asked for autobiographical material, Horace Mann always mentioned his work upon the Massachusetts laws. The information was usually received with blank incomprehension and left out of the projected sketch of his life.

Sometimes, long after midnight when his day's work upon the law was done, Mann would rob himself of one more hour of rest to write to Mary Peabody in Cuba. And along with Elizabeth's impetuously scrawled pages, he kept Mary's letters written in her delicate slanting hand.

"Once in a while, dear Mr. Mann, I take out all your letters and read them," Mary wrote, "and with that renewed impression of you and certain little items I get from Elizabeth, I take my pen to write you. I must confess I often put it down again. . . . When I write home, I have no ideas, only a *feeling*. . .

"I want to write you very much today but I have nothing to say. I am tired of telling you how beautiful the avenues are — I am even guilty of thinking them very monotonous. Orange time has come again, too, golden orange time — but I told you about that last winter." Mary had been ill and someone had given her a book to read, Silvio Pellico's description of his imprisonment by the Austrians. She was a good student of Italian and Pellico was a good poet. "If I did not think you would in your secret mind call me a little fool, I would tell you — shall I tell you? — that when I read Sylvio Pellico's lament over his lost happiness, I did not weep for him alone but for myself too, as if I were in a desert island just as he was in that Castle of Spielberg, with Sophia as my Maroncelli — did you ever know anything so ridiculous? — but I did really feel so, knowing all the time I was too absurd."

Mary's term of exile was nearly over, however, for her sister Sophia's health was better. Mary allowed herself to imagine how it would be to come home. She realized that she must have a clear understanding with her sister Elizabeth concerning Horace Mann. Elizabeth had been living temporarily with her friends the Rices, who had fitted up a little private parlor for her where she could receive Mr. Mann. It was a hard letter for Mary to write but she put the question — What must anyone think of those long and intimate Sunday calls? Was there a secret romance?

By sailing ship at long last came Lizzie's answer. MONDAY MORNING, Lizzie headed her letter. "I left off last night, being called down to see dear Mr. Mann who spent a most beautiful evening. He was not well and he was full of feeling and affection and we talked very delightfully about a great many things — and the difference between love and friendship. And delicate as the subject was, the conversation was perfectly unembarrassed and pleasant, and I feel a great deal more certain than ever I have done that no misunderstanding can come between us, however affectionate we may be. It is a brother's and a sister's love on both sides — and now I *know* he will never think otherwise. It would be impossible to write the conversation but if you were here I could tell it you. My friendship is a great comfort to him and he needs its constant ministrations. I only wanted to be sure that he would never feel that I felt *more* than friendship for him. . . . Not that it would not be possible for Mr. M. to make me love him exclusively. But I could not do that unless he had or did try for it. And his situation, his grey hairs and his sorrow has ever precluded from my imagination that possibility. I know what the feeling of love is for I have been sought and all but won — and this knowledge has always given me assurance that, strong as my friendship is, — deep as my interest is in Mr. M. it is a totally different feeling."

What a load of sorrow lifted from Mary's heart as she read this letter! She smiled at the assertion that a woman could not love Horace Mann unless he should "try for it." He might try to win Elizabeth's heart after all, but this was a chance she must take. She sat down to write of coming home. "Sometimes I sit lost in a dream of happiness," she confided to Horace Mann, "at the anticipation of meeting with those I have learned to prize so dearly, only I am sure that they will not, cannot be one thousandth part as glad to welcome me back again as I shall be for one look at them."

It was in May, 1835, that Mary later said she returned "home after all my wanderings." In her still later diary, she told of seeing Horace Mann. "When I saw him again, he destroyed nearly all the fabric of caution and reserve I had erected for my defense . . . by his deeply expressed joy at seeing me. . . . My prophetic hope returned." It was to be hope deferred.

"My old love of letter writing has returned upon me in all its original force, dear Mr. Mann, since I touched these charmed shores," Mary wrote from Salem, "and I cannot let Elizabeth return [to Boston] without a letter telling you how delightful it was to see you look so much better in health. I was so occupied in thinking of it, that I forgot to tell you of it. It is one of the happy changes that I remark since my return. . . .

"They tell me, especially the ministers, that society is very bad here, & that signs of the times are dark & evil, but I do not yet realize it & hope that the testimony of the lawyers will be a brighter one.

"In regard to philosophy, & all these great matters that interest the public mind here, I feel quite behind the age, dear Mr. Mann, so you must remember to use simple language to me as a novice. I am not quite clear about *Transcendentalism* & if you know, I wish you would give me some intimation of it. Elizabeth says that she is the only practical transcendentalist there is, but even that does not clear my vision entirely."

Mary's delicate hints that Mann continue his letters to her now that she was at home and could not, therefore, be homesick, went all unheeded. In the months immediately ahead, his work on Statute Law was increasingly heavy. Yet he could not find it in his heart to neglect her entirely — she wrote so faithfully, so pleadingly and with such charm! Mann answered at last:

My very dear Friend,

I have received your mournful letter of last Sunday, which described your perception of things on earth as they appear when seen in a light from Heaven. . . . Why should the thought ever come to you not to write to me, because I do not reply to your letters? Surely it is impossible you should ever suppose your letters not to be most welcome. I long for them. I read them again & again. They seem to me like messengers from a happy land.

Mann was re-elected to the Massachusetts Senate in 1836, a fact "not without gratification to me," he said. It was the Senate's first duty to elect a President and ten names were put in nomination. Second on the list was that of Horace Mann but on the first ballot he received only eight votes. No one got a majority, however, so the voting continued. On the fourth ballot, Mr. Mann had fifteen votes but he was not elected until the eighteenth ballot when he finally collected twenty votes. You could not call it a landslide but Mann had reason to be gratified again. One cause for gratification, although he did not say so, was the fact that he would now receive four dollars a day for every day of legislative session instead of the two dollars paid other senators!

In 1836, a new governor addressed his message to the Massachusetts legislature. This was Edward Everett. Son of a minister, himself Unitarian pastor of the Brattle Street Church before he was twenty, Edward Everett was now forty-two and an ex-clergyman, world traveler and former Greek Professor at Harvard — recently a member of Congress! He was Boston's most admired orator, with his "grace of language, the music of his voice, and the magnetism of his presence" charming his contemporaries. Everett was married to the "socially elite" Charlotte Brooks, daughter of wealth.

Boston's high opinion of Everett was not entirely understood by Thomas C. Gratton, British Consul in Boston, who drove to Watertown to the governor's house, expecting to find "dignity and classical polish." He found a wooden "box" of a house "close by the roadside" — a "rough-clad stable boy" to take his horse and only a "woman servant" incapable of "announcing" his name properly. There was no drawing-room — just a parlor, into which walked Governor Everett, wearing a "black coat and green slippers." The British Consul said he could "not imagine" such a man "being fitted for public office." He had, of course, stated some of the reasons why Governor Everett was exactly what Massachusetts wanted for public office.

Edward Everett was one of those New Englanders "born to be educated." He believed all things of education as a regenerating force and it was of great importance that the orbit of his varied career should swing, at this particular time, into that of Horace Mann. In Everett's first message to the legislature, he praised Mann's work on the revision and re-enactment of Statute Law and proposed that "it would be expedient to incorporate into a uniform code . . . those numerous principles of Common Law, which are definitely settled and well-known." The Governor appointed Mann, with others, to see to this. Horace Mann now supposed that he might be remembered as a codifier of Common Law.

Miss Elizabeth Peabody found it increasingly difficult to engage the time of a cheerful and busy Mr. Mann. Miss Peabody was herself occupied, though by no means gainfully. She was teaching in Temple School, most of the children for which she had "gathered" for herself and then turned over to Bronson Alcott with characteristic generosity. Temple School opened September 22, 1834, with 30 pupils. By March 1835 Alcott set down in his journal that "Miss Peabody is now occupied during the mornings of each day in preparing the *Record* for the press." Mr. Alcott said nothing of the fact that he had somehow never managed to pay Miss Peabody her promised salary but added, "I anticipate an interesting and useful volume from these *Conversations* and exercises."

It was on an afternoon in early October that a note from Elizabeth Peabody was handed to Mr. Mann as he set out for the State House. "I put your note into my hat," he wrote her, "and as I had three or four bills to report during the afternoon, I had not time until this present, even to break the seal of your letter, & could only steal a look towards it once in a while as a hungry schoolboy does to his cake, before the hour comes when he is allowed to eat it."

But the news in Elizabeth's letter was of a personal disaster. A warehouse in Boston had burned and she had lost *Record of a School*. The burning of the books had "swallowed up not only the profits of the whole edition but left her in debt."

"It seems as if she were fated to make no money by books," her sister Mary said; but Elizabeth, in her letter to Mann, somehow managed an optimistic view.

"I most sincerely regret your loss & shall find some difficulty in making myself believe 'it is all for the best,'" Mann said in reply to Lizzie's letter. ". . . You will smile when I remind you that you are a common sufferer with Newton; whose little pet, Diamond, burnt all his manuscripts."

In April 1836 the Alcotts moved to Front Street, where they

"took a family of boys to board" — and also Miss Elizabeth Peabody, who was to consider her tiny parlor and a rather eccentric bill of fare as part of her still unpaid salary. Elizabeth was miserably unhappy, not the least of her griefs being that her parlor was too small to accommodate Mr. Mann and the guests she liked to invite to meet him from time to time. Such meetings must take place at the home of friends, now.

Most congenial of these were the Dwights, who shared Elizabeth's passion for the writings of the French educator, Victor Cousin. Edmund Dwight (with his brother Jonathan) owned most of the land occupied by the village of Chicopee Falls, Massachusetts, and he had dammed the Chicopee River and built four cotton mills. Dwight had capital, both his own and that from his wife, which had enabled him to weather the storms that wrecked Horace and Thomas Mann in their textile-mill venture. He built still more mills, controlled the Holyoke water rights, and was interested in the Worcester Railroad. He must already have known Horace Mann as an advocate of railroads, so their talk could have been about business. But at the Dwights' the subject of conversation was education, and what education could do for a nation already suffering from growing pains.

Edmund Dwight had worked on the farm and in his father's store — had sent himself to Yale. Young people worked in his mills and this did not trouble him, since he himself had worked hard as far back as he could remember. But the fact that mill hands and the children of mill hands were illiterate worried him greatly. There should be good schools and laws about school attendance. Sometimes his brother reproached him for being more interested in education than in making money.

Horace Mann and Edmund Dwight were friends made to order. Their experiences had been similar, their tastes were alike and their ideals were high so that Mann was always at his ease. One evening Horace Mann talked so brilliantly on education that Miss Lizzie rushed home and jotted down everything he said. Then she urged him to let her publish this conversation.

Mann remonstrated. "And now I entreat you to save me from being shown up — like the wrong side of a tapestry . . ." Conversation being about the most fleeting of all the arts . . . "to print it & send it out to the whole world is about as wise as for a man to

tell sober people the joke which made a tipsy company laugh!"
Elizabeth swallowed her disappointment and took comfort from
the affectionate tone of Mann's note.

But soon these intimate little notes ceased through no fault of
Elizabeth's.[3] She told her sister Mary what happened. "Would you
think that Mrs. Alcott came in to my room and looked over all
my letters from you and found your last to me and the one to
Sophia and carried it to Mr. Alcott and *they* have *read* them!
. . . Mr. Alcott attacked me without telling me he had read the
letters." Alcott accused Miss Lizzie of gossiping about him but
gave himself away by quoting a phrase in Mary's latest letter —
about his "never paying poor mens' bills." So Elizabeth knew
what had happened and the story came out but instead of being
covered with confusion, the Alcotts continued to upbraid Miss
Peabody!

Mary urged Elizabeth to tell Mr. Mann all about it. And now
Mr. Mann's letters, once so frank and affectionate, became mere
cryptograms — lest prying eyes should read them. He wrote freely
to Elizabeth only when she was at home with her parents in Salem
— where Mary also lived and taught a little school. At such times,
Mann's letters were always to both sisters.

On February 7, 1837, Horace Mann wrote to his "very dear
Friends," underlining the *s*. "In a day or two, a debate will come
on in the Senate with reference to the Surplus Revenue from the
state, & a few of us have set our hearts upon its being redistributed
to the purposes of education. We mean if possible to turn it into
ideas."

Fantastic as it sounds, Massachusetts actually had a surplus
revenue from several sources. When the Province of Maine became
a state, lands belonging to Massachusetts were purchased and in
1834 a law provided that all money which should be in the Massachusetts treasury on January 1, 1835, received from sale of lands
to Maine, would go into a School Fund — together with half of
all funds from future sales. Then there was the "Massachusetts
Claim." During the War of 1812, President Madison had ordered
the Massachusetts Militia to Washington. But Massachusetts had no
use for "Mr. Madison's War." They ordered out their militia to
be sure — but citizens were in daily fear of attack upon their coast-
line by the British Fleet, so the Massachusetts Militia stayed at

home! Afterwards, the National Government, with reason on their side it must be admitted, refused to pay the Massachusetts Militia. Pressure was brought to bear, however; the claim was paid, and "money not otherwise appropriated" went into the School Fund. Here then was the cash that Mann and his friends had their eye on. Why not spend some of the School Fund which was accumulating and why not turn the Massachusetts claim into ideas?

Edmund Dwight, Josiah Quincy, Jr., and Governor Everett were among those Horace Mann referred to as his friends who favored new ideas in public education. This is not to say that they were the first in the field. There was Thomas H. Gallaudet of Connecticut, Walter R. Johnson of Pennsylvania and James G. Carter of Massachusetts, to name a few of the pioneers. By 1827, James G. Carter was teaching the art of teaching in an academy provided for him by the town of Lancaster, but his project could not be made to pay its way even with the town's assistance. In desperation, he petitioned the Legislature "for aid in establishing a seminary . . . for teachers." The motion lost by one vote in the Senate. Although this was the year when Horace Mann was first elected to the House, the proposal came up during the session before he took his seat.

In March 1837 it was ordered in the Senate that the "Committee on Education enquire into . . . appropriating $2500.00 for a seminary for the education of the Teachers of the Common Schools. . . ." A month went by; and then, on April 20, 1837, the State Board of Education was created by an act of legislature. It was as though the wood were arranged upon the altar of Elijah — waiting only the divine spark.

CHAPTER FOURTEEN

Let the Next Generation
Be My Client

BEFORE Charlotte's death, Mann had written to her telling of his love for a city and its people — especially the less fortunate. "If I have been blessed with the possession of any good, or the exemption from any evil, an obligation has accompanied the blessing, to use the immunity for the benefit of my kind." With the loss of his beloved wife, Charlotte, Mann's "good" had been changed to misfortune and his "immunity" lost. During the first months of frantic grief, all the old impotent anger against the avenging Jehovah of Nathanael Emmons's preaching must have invaded his mind — magnified a thousandfold. If God had taken Charlotte, then there was no justice — anywhere.

It was at this period, just after Charlotte's death, that some of Mann's friends spoke of him as an atheist. He was not. It made him angry in later years to be told of this. That he came close to it, he did not deny, but he found great comfort in his friend, Josiah Holbrook — who found God in the study of the world around him, in geology particularly, with its amazing story of past ages.

Persuaded by his "sisterly friend," Mary Peabody, Mann had attended Emerson's lectures. "I heard his lecture last evening," he wrote. "It was to human life what Newton's 'Principia' was to mathematics. . . . [He] discovers harmony and order when others can discern only confusion and irregularity." Mann gradually began to see his own grief in less overwhelming proportions — though no less bitter.

With the help of his friends, Mann tried to take up his old

life. And now, five years had passed since Charlotte's death — he had accomplished much. Mann had been born with a "desire for humane and benevolent effort," he felt, and now a new idea came to him. If "blessings" received made his obligation toward others greater, then blessings taken away made a life devoted to others the only solution. Most people make new resolutions on New Year's Day but Horace Mann always chose a day particularly his own upon which to survey his past life and evaluate his future.

Selecting an ordinary cardboard-bound notebook[1] and dating the first page *May 4th, 1837*, Mann wrote that he was resolved to keep a diary. The date was his birthday and the new year it ushered in for him was the forty-second year of his life. He was embarking upon his true career — the work which was to make him nationally and internationally known as Horace Mann, the Educator — founder of the American public school system! But this was outside the range of his prophetic vision. "My future days are like the succeeding pages of this book, untouched, alike receptive of good and evil," he wrote.

On May fifteenth, Mann recorded an evening call upon Dr. William Ellery Channing. "Suppose what is sometimes said, to be true — that he is a man of one idea. Yet is not one life well spent, developing one idea . . . if it be a good one?"

Another evening call, or rather a series of them, brought Mann to the point where he was ready to write in his diary that he had found the one idea by which he himself was ready to live. "Mr. Dwight again urged upon me a consideration of my being Secretary of the Board (of Education). Ought I to think of filling this high and responsible office? Can I adequately perform its duties? Will my greater zeal in the cause than the others supply the deficiency in point of talent and information? Whoever shall take that task must encounter privation, labor and infinite annoyance from an infinite number of schemers. He must condense the steam of enthusiasts and soften the rock of the incredulous. What toil in arriving at the true system himself; what toil in infusing that system into the minds of others! How many dead minds to resuscitate!"

Mann's remarkable power of prophecy was serving him well as he foresaw the difficulties of the road ahead. The path would be still more steep. But in this new year of 1837 and during this month of May, which was the time of Mann's personal Pentecost, he also saw the glory. "But should he succeed . . . should he be able to teach even a few generations how mind is God over matter, how in arranging the objects of desire, the subordination of the less valuable to the more is the secret of happiness . . . what intensity, what perpetuity of blessings he would confer. How would his beneficial influence upon mankind widen and deepen as it descended forever!"

With the glorious vision still upon him, Horace Mann wrote to Edmund Dwight on the twenty-eighth of June accepting the Secretaryship of the Board of Education. When the names of the first State Board of Education were announced, Mann copied them in his diary. They were "James G. Carter, Emerson Davis, Edmond [sic] Dwight, Horace Mann, Edward A. Newton, Robert Rantoul Jr., Thomas Robbins and Jared Sparks," in that order. There were future enemies among them — and future friends. But Mann's prophetic gift did not serve him here, and only time would tell.

"Faith is the only sustainer I have," he wrote, "faith in the improvability of the race." Here was a touch of Miss Peabody's transcendentalism perhaps, but after all "improvability" is a human quality. Belief in the improvability of the race gives man the right to look upward and not down — forward and not back.

Collecting everything that he could lay his hands on that had been written on the subject of education, Mann went back to his old home in Franklin to study for the new life that was opening before him. He was like one taking holy orders — he renounced the world. Other great causes had kindled his enthusiasm before, but never like this. Once he had loved the law but now the law had become dust and ashes. "The interests of a client are small compared to the interests of the next generation," Horace Mann wrote. "Let the next generation be my client."

It must be admitted, however, that Mann's conception of what he meant to do for his new client, the next generation, was legal first of all. A lifelong habit of mind may not be discarded overnight, but it may be of use in the service of a new idea. "The laws which sustain our system of Common School instruction are scarcely better than they have been for a century and a half," Mann said, resolving to remedy this situation at once.

Hidden away in Franklin with his books and pamphlets, he was happier than he had been since the loss of Charlotte. "Could I be assured that my efforts in this new field of labor would be crowned with success, I know of no occupation that would be more agreeable to me. Nay, could I accomplish in this cause all I desire, I may say that if I had the power to make a world and to prepare a station of duty for myself in it, I could not devise one more desirable than this!"

By the end of summer, Mann's self-education was complete as far as theory was concerned. He felt, he said, "like a sailor approaching a new land." At first he saw only "lofty summits," then "hills, cities, towns and plains" began to appear. He laid out a campaign for himself — to visit key towns and cities in the state and deliver an address on education which he had written with heart and soul. He sent out a circular to all communities asking for information about public schools. "I can only hope that all communities are on a poise, and ready to be swayed one way or the other, according to the manner of putting on the weight," he said.

But Mann had already suffered one disappointment. His friends were inclined to blame him for throwing away a promising legal and political career. He had expected praise, not blame! "All men but one, so far as I know, thought me a fool and most of them said so," he complained. Dr. William Ellery Channing was the one exceptional man and his letter had an apostolic ring, like the charge given by an older clergyman to a young missionary.

"I understand you have given yourself to the cause of education in our Commonwealth," wrote Dr. Channing. "I rejoice in it . . . You could not find a nobler sphere. Government has no higher one to give. . . . If we can but turn the wonderful energy of this people into right channels, what a new heaven and earth might be realized among us! And I do not despair. Your willingness to consecrate yourself to this work is a happy omen."

Mann cherished this letter. But when he looked for a similar one from Elizabeth Peabody, he did not get it. It must be admitted that Miss Peabody loved to solve another's problems; and here was Horace Mann abandoning politics, which was the career she had chosen for him! He had taken up public education without so much as a word to her beforehand.

"It appears to me," Horace Mann wrote half-playfully, half-reproachfully to Elizabeth, "that you don't seem to be very much sky-lifted about my new appointment. I expected you to emulate an anthem at least. You surely know that education is the lever — nay it is the fulcrum, lever and all. But perhaps you think my mechanics will not operate; — well, I fear very much so too, but I will try nevertheless; and if I can get things well adjusted and then let some heavier man jump on, I am content therewith."

The news of the new direction which Horace Mann's life had taken seems to have reached Mary Peabody in Salem by round-about means. Mann wrote to Mary just three days before accepting the secretaryship of the State Board of Education, but not one word did he say to her of future plans. He did make it clear that he had decided to be a person of "one idea" — like Channing. Referring to slavery — "On this subject," he told Mary, "I am ready to hear a great deal but I do not believe it is the *only* evil now extant, nor that the abolitionists are about to eclipse all other apostles of humanity."

Mann ended his letter with affectionate solicitude: "And now, my dear friend, I am sorry to have you answer so faintly when I ask if you are happy."

But there would be no real happiness for Mary Peabody as long as her secret hopes concerning Horace Mann continued to be deferred. When she finally learned of Mann's new crusade her hopes grew still more dim, but he could have had no complaint at the praise she gave him. It was some time, she said, before she knew "what a change had come o'er the spirit of your dream," and before she realized that Mann was "actually to be the High Priest of Education in our land. . . . I had thought of it with so much pleasure for your sake that I had not begun to take the other view of the subject. I am so thankful that you no longer count yourself an attorney, that you are not bound to that wearisome routine, that no client is drawing upon your head or your heart, and no sentence pending upon your judgment — that I have had comparatively no thought of the public good. . . . Your occupation is with beautiful theories of good, and how to prevent rather than remedy evil. You cannot but enjoy the change."

Mann set out on his first tour of the state and by the sixth of September he was with "E. Dwight, Esq. in Chicopee Village" — having arrived there the day before on horseback — a fifty-mile ride! This was indeed a change from the sedentary life he had been leading but Mann did not say how stiff and lame he must have been when he spoke in Springfield next evening. He did mention that very little work had been done by Edward A. Newton to secure him an audience. Newton was a member of the State Board of Education and head of the newly formed Education Association of Berkshire. With grim humor, Mann wrote in his diary, "If there is not more life in the body than in the head, it will soon decompose."

Early in October, Mann found himself in Taunton and remarked, "Today is Militia muster-day — an *animal* day!" He wondered if such holidays would ever be "superseded by intellectual & moral days" and felt that it was his mission to set such a trend. But how to make the subject of education draw a crowd without a brass band and a barrel of rum! "Dr. Channing came over from Newport to give me a lift," Mann said — "otherwise I must have come away without much to modify unpleasant impressions."

Skies were brilliant blue and maples were turning red and gold as Mann left Taunton and turned his face toward Cape Cod. Whether he traveled on horseback or by public conveyance he did not say, but beside the road the cranberry bogs spread a deep scarlet carpet. The planted elms and maples of the village streets gave way to native pine for mile after sandy mile of country road and soon the pines were a low, sturdy variety with all their limbs reaching in one direction — away from the wind. The wind was a living thing, a force to be reckoned with as Mann climbed aboard a little sailing vessel bound for Edgartown. He was never a good sailor and Martha's Vineyard seemed as far away as France before he landed. But once arrived, Martha's Vineyard and Nantucket became beloved islands.

"Delegates even from the Orkney Islands of Chilmark" had gathered in Edgartown to hear Horace Mann. Here was none of the coldness and indifference with which Mann had been received in Taunton. The Islanders made a "most attentive and goodly audience." Mann said he had been "most marvellously disappointed one way in Taunton and about as much the other way here."

There were three churches in Edgartown: orthodox Congregationalist, Baptist and Methodist. Since he could not go to one without offending the members of the other two, Mann decided to spend Sunday to suit himself. "I thought I would go over to Chapoquiddie and see the Indians," he said. He called on several families "with their guardian, Mr. Thaxter" and learned that there were about fifty children in the village with "next to no schooling among them, except a Sunday School."

Mann returned to Edgartown revolving plans in his mind for helping these Indian children. But "one Ebenezer Chase, reverend by courtesy and Christian by assumption" was not interested in the plight of the children but only in the shocking discovery that Horace Mann was a Sabbath-breaker! Mann should have gone to church morning, afternoon and evening — attending each denomination in turn. He had the "alternative to hear three orthodox sermons in one day or be burned," Mann gathered. "I confess I had rather be burned — at least a little," he said.

Again taking ship like Saint Paul, Mann sailed to Nantucket to preach the gospel of education, and here his reception was all he could have desired. "Every part of the meetinghouse was rammed, crammed, jammed." Even so, not everyone who wanted to hear Horace Mann had been able to squeeze into the building and he was asked to repeat his talk. Mann consented reluctantly. "It will be 'cabbage twice boiled,' I fear, to all: — certainly to myself & I am doubtful where I can get enough of the actor to cover my own apathy. But I'll try." Mann need not have worried. The second audience was even more enthusiastic than the first and their approval awoke the natural actor within him so that he did not have to strive for effects but reached their minds and hearts without effort. The magnetic current between him and his audience never once broke and when he finished they crowded the platform to shake his hand.

The little town of Nantucket, climbing its hill and looking ever seaward, roof over gray roof, became dear to Horace Mann. It was here that he met Cyrus Peirce. Indeed Peirce was largely responsible for Mann's enthusiastic reception — having prepared the ground. And Peirce was responsible to an important degree for Mann's ultimate success in the great crusade for education. Peirce was six years older than Mann — tall, ugly, with a great beak of a nose and a mouth too large even for his large head! His was an endearing sort of ugliness which made strangers smile and decide to trust him. Children were always drawn to him and his pupils called him "Father Peirce."

On graduating from Harvard with honors, Cyrus Peirce took

charge of an academy in Nantucket. He remained only two years, having set his heart on Harvard Divinity school and the ministry. But after an interval in the ministry he realized that his calling was to teach and not to preach, so he returned to his Nantucket academy. But now a new revelation in regard to education came to him, and with leading citizens of his town he outlined a system of public education for Nantucket, from primary school through high school, and saw it put into effect. In 1837, when he and Horace Mann met, Cyrus Peirce had given up his private school and was Principal of the Nantucket High School.

It was a peculiarity of Mann's genius that he could select the best among the ideas of others, use them and fuse them with his own. He talked long and late with Cyrus Peirce about such strange ideas as special methods of teaching for very little children, of graded classes and of girls — allowed to study high school subjects! Mann accepted or rejected ideas gleaned from Cyrus Peirce's experience. He added them to his own during the coming years so that eventually there would be created, not a Cyrus Peirce school system for Nantucket but a Horace Mann system for Massachusetts, which would serve as a model for the nation — for Europe — and for South America.

But at the present moment another of Mann's gifts asserted itself. He was able to inspire utter devotion on the part of a few kindred spirits. Cyrus Peirce was his first disciple. This was not the gift of conciliation, which makes well-wishers of many, close friends of few. It would be Peirce who would conciliate and soothe the injured pride of many men whom Mann accidentally antagonized in the course of his headlong drive toward his objective.

Nantucket shone like a light in the gloom as Mann made his first circuit of Massachusetts, holding a convention in each county. Salem came close to the end of his year's journey. Here Mary Peabody was living and feeding her starving heart upon the hope of seeing him. She wrote of the good talks they would have in the schoolroom she had fitted up in her father's house and where she taught a handful of neighbors' little girls.

But "dear Mr. Mann" could hardly have been cheerful company for Mary when he discovered that Salem had nothing but the coldest indifference toward the cause of public education. Mann described his Salem reception: "November 10. Went to Salem as proposed.

Met the convention; though that is almost too great a word to apply to so small a number of men." It always seemed to Mann a personal insult when members of the State Board of Education failed to show up at his meetings when he reached their home towns. "Mr. Rantoul did not come at all, Mr. Saltonstall but little. Things had not been arranged beforehand & everything dragged & stuck — one of the poorest."

"A friend who was there" (this was the way Mary Peabody always referred to herself) told more of what happened. "One gentleman, who made one of the first speeches, questioned the expediency of endeavoring to get the educated classes to patronize the public schools. He spoke, he said, in the interests of mothers who preferred . . . to have their children grow up with those of their own class. No one spoke on the *American* side of the question."

Someone proposed that Mr. Mann ought to spend a day visiting each public school in the state. This sounded well coming from Salem — where only a handful of citizens were willing to spend so much as one evening in behalf of their public schools! But Mr. Mann replied good-humoredly — "that it would take him sixteen years to do that." And "a general stir in the assembly indicated that suddenly the immensity of the work to be done had struck their minds for the first time."

Horace Mann had long been a close personal friend of Josiah Holbrook and in 1837 Holbrook's Lyceum lecture system was sweeping the country. Mann, with his colorful turn of expression and his dramatic delivery, was a popular Lyceum lecturer right from the start. He had been asked to open the Lyceum series in Salem, which he realized was an honor. Thriftily he arranged to have the Salem school convention come at the same time so that he could attend to both assignments for the same amount of traveling expenses. And now that the convention was over it was time for the lecture. Mann had a special lecture prepared — but such a small handful had heard his convention speech, why not repeat it? This time, Mann had no misgivings about "twice-boiled cabbage." The Lyceum Hall was crowded and the audience, who came with their tickets in their hands, had very few of them appeared when Mann served his cabbage the first time — free of charge! The ticket-holding audience had come for two purposes — entertainment and instruction. They got both.

"If the system of national instruction devised and commenced by Charlemagne had been continued, it would have changed the history of the French people," Mr. Mann began. "Such an event as the French Revolution could never have happened with free schools; any more than the American Revolution could have happened *without* them!" The Salem audience looked gratified. This was educational — all about history.

But Mr. Mann brought them right back to their own day and age with sobering effect. "The mobs, the riots, the burnings, the lynchings, perpetrated by the men of the present day, are perpetrated because of their vicious and defective education. We see and feel the ravages of their tiger passions now, when they are full grown; but it was years ago when they were whelped and suckled. And so too, if we are derelict in our duty in this matter, our children in their turn will suffer. If we permit the vulture's eggs to be hatched, it will then be too late to take care of the lambs."

Mann brought the animal kingdom heavily to bear in support of his argument but his hearers were highly entertained. Tigers and vultures kept them right on the edge of their chairs. They wanted him to go on.

Some people found the present state of public education good enough, Mann said. Others wanted improvements. "Let us waste no time in compromising this strife!" And if there had been pulpit cushions Mann would have pounded them now, for in this sentence he revealed the whole attitude of his mind. "Let us waste no time!

"Nothing is so good it cannot be made better — nothing so bad it might not become worse. . . . No community should rest content with being superior to other communities, while it is inferior to its own capabilities! . . . The very thought of improving is the germination of improvement."

Mr. Emerson would soon appear on Salem's Lyceum platform. He would not be able to offer a more practical working plan for his "perfectability" than this. The Salem audience understood these things, for was it not a search for perfectability that led the ship designers to build the fastest clipper ships afloat?

It was a very long address but Mann's audience would have felt cheated if it had been any shorter. And now was defeat turned into victory, for the Lyceum subscribers were profoundly impressed by Mann's ideas on education. The time was not far off when Horace

Mann would be invited to Salem to attend the celebrations planned for the opening of a new high school. Mann would soon speak with pride of Salem as having some of the finest public schools in Massachusetts.

The first circuit of the state was over now, and Mann returned to his rooms in Boston. "I confess life begins to assume a value which I have not felt for five years before," he wrote in his diary — referring to the fact that five years had gone by since his wife's death.

On November 16, however, he faced a new but yearly recurring task which would always seem to him like the stone of Sisyphus. "Today have examined the returns in the Secretary's office, of which an Abstract is to be made & find they look very formidable. What an ocean of work lies spread out before me! Well, I am ready to plunge in."

Thanksgiving found Mann still at work upon the resumé of all those figures sent in by the various towns in Massachusetts — the number of children in school, number of teachers employed, amounts spent by the towns — the facts were as endless as they were dull, and Mann's fiery spirit always chafed under a routine task. He must spend Thanksgiving alone and he forgot for the moment all the friendly homes that would have been open to him. His friends could only have intensified his mood, because Thanksgiving to the New Englander is the one festival dedicated exclusively to home and family. "I have no domestic hearth," Mann wrote. "I have no friends before whom to take away the entire veil that now lies like a pall over my heart. One such friend was mine. We passed two Thanksgivings together & then the day of darkness & of mourning came & that cloud still envelops the whole sky."

On the first of January, 1838, Mann appeared before the State Board of Education to read his first report. He then withdrew so the Board could discuss him — their employee. This was a new experience, and not an entirely pleasant one. He was "not in the shallows but the deep waters of the fidgets," he said. He could not tell how his report "squared with their notions, for that is their test of right & wrong." He had withdrawn at his own suggestion. "Whether I should have been run down or crushed, rail-road fashion, had I been there, I know not." The following day, as the

Board continued to discuss his report behind closed doors, Mann was "extinguished by a headache."

In spite of nervous headaches, in spite of occasional fits of depression, Mann wrote in his diary the story of a greatly improved state of mind. "Tomorrow, the legislature convenes. Till today, the last General Court was prorogued. Till today, my senatorial life lasts; today it ends. With good sleep, I shall wake up unsenatorial. So be it. I would not exchange this life, toilsome, anxious, doubtful as it is, and may be, to be at the head of the 'grave and reverend senators' tomorrow."

Mann's state of suspense over the reception of his report was not entirely laid at rest until the middle of the month. On January 18 he "received an invitation to preach a preachment, in the Hall of Representatives." He had "a pretty full house, though the weather was unpleasant" and he "held them one hour and a half, stiller than still." Here was compensation for whatever coldness and indifference Mann had encountered on his statewide tour. If he was pleased with his success, he was always equally severe in self-criticism, recording in his diary when he "was too much disconcerted" by a small audience, or when there were "some evident hitchings on the seats now and then."

It was good to be back in Boston once more and to spend congenial evenings at the Edmund Dwights' again. In January a conference took place there, among the "friends of education" — the subject, "whether or not to petition the legislature for aid in establishing teachers' seminaries." The majority felt that here was a lost cause. If James G. Carter had failed, who could succeed? And it would never do to try again — at least not right now.

Mann remained behind with his host after the others had left. And now Edmund Dwight made an offer that lifted Mann once more to the heights of exaltation. Dwight would give ten thousand dollars for a normal school, if the state would match the sum. Mann was to make the offer and Dwight insisted upon remaining anonymous. "It is now my intention to make a descent upon the two Honorable Bodies & see if they cannot be so rubbed as to emit the requisite spark," Mann said.

On April 18, Mann got his twenty thousand dollars for his "seminary." "I think I feel pretty sublime!" he exclaimed. "Let the stars look out for my head!"

CHAPTER FIFTEEN

Lost ... Two Golden Hours[1]

MANN had every reason to walk with his head among the stars after his first year's achievement as Secretary of the Massachusetts Board of Education. But people who walk among the stars are apt to stumble over lowly obstacles, and so it was with Mann. His "Common School Library," a star of an idea in itself, caused trouble because of human greed and jealousy.

The campaign for the school libraries began with a survey of library facilities in the state. In all the cities and towns, Mann found only about ten or fifteen public libraries. There were 299 libraries belonging to societies where people owned shares and made contributions — with the noncontributing public excluded. Then there were the college libraries, Harvard leading the list with 50,000 volumes by no means at the disposal of the public. "For the poor man and the laboring man, the art of printing seems hardly to have been discovered," Mann remarked. He conceived of school libraries as having two sections: books for adults which the children could bring home to their parents, and books for the children themselves. The legislature authorized the towns to raise money for libraries by direct taxation.

Mann suggested to the State Board that a commission should be appointed; and Jared Sparks, one of the Board members, promised to inquire among booksellers "respecting terms on which they would make and supply sets" of books. Sparks, in a verbal report, recommended that the Secretary come to terms with a publisher and, when the Board agreed, Mann approached Marsh, Capen and Lyon, who thought they could publish fifty titles to be sold to the schools for $57.50.

In the spring of 1838, authors and publishers began to send in manuscripts and books. Mann, preoccupied with thoughts of the pleasure that good books would bring to a community, forgot that he was also promoting a business deal in which many people would like to profit. Almost the first book Mann was requested to read was submitted by Frederick A. Packard; "Editorial Secretary of the Sunday School Union" was his title but he was actually one of the most persistent, unscrupulous and sharp-dealing book agents that ever lived! The book Mr. Packard offered was *The Child at Home* by the Reverend John Stevens Cabot Abbott. But Horace Mann had to acquire a copy from his own bookseller.

Mann sat down to read the book with a pleasant smile of anticipation. This very shortly turned to a scowl! In the text, a little boy of six or so who had gotten into childish mischief was told: "But we must not forget that there is a day of most solemn judgment near at hand. When you die, your body will be wrapped in a shroud, placed in the coffin and buried in the grave. . . . How awful must be the scene when you enter the eternal world! . . . You will see God seated upon that majestic throne. . . . Oh what must be the confusion and shame of the deceitful child. . . . The angels will see your sin and disgrace . . . the Savior will look upon you in his displeasure. . . . You must hear the awful sentence, 'Depart from me into everlasting fire!' " Mann must have been sorely tempted to throw the book into the nearest fire as he recalled his own childish terrors under the preaching of Nathanael Emmons and imagined a child taking such a book home from school. He wrote to Mr. Packard in haste and with more heat than was politic.[2]

"I cannot hesitate a moment in saying that it would not be tolerated in this state as a District School library book. . . . There is scarcely anything in the book which presents the character of God in an admirable or loving aspect." Mann pointed out that the author denounced "eternal perdition for the most trivial neglects or acts of disobedience, committed in the thoughtlessness of childhood." Mann also said in his letter that he did not know who Mr. Packard was — and Frederick Adolphus Packard thought he was a pretty important person!

Packard was furious but concealed his anger for the time being and sent a primer and a spelling book. The spelling book seemed old-fashioned, Mr. Mann thought; and as for the primer — the pictures in it were hideous. They would "inspire fear instead of admiration." The primer was full of stories of the dreadful fate of wicked little boys and girls! "How can a child who has adopted such a view account for disastrous terminations which happen to the enterprises of good boys, or for the fortunate ones which crown the exploits of the wicked?" Mr. Mann wanted to know. "The falling of a brick depends in no degree upon a boy's moral character, but wholly upon the laws of gravitation!"

Mr. Mann wrote Packard a long and patient letter, explaining in particular the "law of 1827" which guaranteed religious freedom to the public schools. In this law, the use of sectarian schoolbooks was forbidden and Mr. Mann felt that sectarian library books were therefore also barred. Although the law was passed the year Mann entered the House, he had not helped to write it, because it was passed on March 10 and Mann did not begin his duties until May 30. But religious freedom was something Fred Packard was incapable of understanding — especially when it interfered with the selling of his books.

Packard called on Mr. Mann, at Mann's invitation, and they had a long talk. Mann gave him the letter he had written but had not had time to send. Next day, Packard went to New Bedford to the meeting of the Massachusetts General Association, where were gathered about a hundred orthodox ministers and as many laymen. Packard asked permission to speak and proceeded to do so after first arranging his display of books for sale — on the steps of the pulpit in the church where the meeting took place. Then he went to work to sell books by attacking Horace Mann. He told the clergy that their influence was on the wane because of the "so-called improvements in education." It was all a plot "to delude them." He had sent Mann *The Child at Home* to prove that he was "prejudiced in his views" — a test case and a trap into which Mann had fallen. Getting excited, Packard pulled Mann's letter out of his pocket and said he was going to read some shocking sentiments. But at this point there were objections from the floor. Wasn't it a private letter? Did Packard have permission to read it and did it express Mann's views as Secretary of Education or as an individual? These acute questions came mostly from the Reverend Thomas Robbins, orthodox minister to be sure but a good friend to Horace Mann and a member of the State Board of Education. Packard was astounded. He had not supposed Mann had an orthodox friend in the world! But the moderator ruled that the letter was not to be read. Packard was worried and now begged everyone to forget about the letter. He proceeded to extol the virtues of his "library for Common Schools" with its wooden case and key — all for thirty-three dollars.

The scene which Packard played with Mann's letter, flavoring so strongly of Shakespeare's Mark Antony and the will of Caesar, was by no means kept secret! It was too good a story. There were those who really believed that Horace Mann's unread letter contained a vengeful attack upon the Congregational Church! Clergymen still remembered that Mann had won the well-known Gile case for the Unitarians against the Congregationalists and that, in the legislature, he had been in favor of religious freedom. In 1833, the Congregational Church was disestablished as the Massachusetts state church and this was still a sensitive point with some. Perhaps Packard should have been allowed to read the letter. But he would certainly have lifted sentences from context and Mann's meaning — that children should be spared the knowledge of "the creeds which divide one Christian from another" — would have been lost.

The story of the unread letter reached Mann promptly and he wrote Packard, this time like a lawyer. Mann sprang to the defense not of himself but of the Board, which Packard also attacked. " 'Improvements if they may be called so,' is the Language you use in reference to measures they have adopted," Mann said, "and what Cause of denunciation have you against the Board, except that they may not aid, as you suppose, in the propagation of your dogmas, & the sale of your Library?" But if Packard was condemned, Mann thought that "before passing sentence," a "tribunal" should "enquire into" Packard's "*sanity*."

This parting shot of Mann's was all too close to the mark. Packard dropped active promotion of the books, super-salesman though he was, and devoted himself to attacking Horace Mann personally with all the virulence of a madman. He prepared letters, two of which were published in the *New York Observer*. They were addressed to the Reverend Dr. Humphrey, President of Amherst, and were signed with a pseudonym. Dr. Humphrey knew nothing whatever about the letters, but readers of the *Observer* would suppose that he received them from a friend and approved their contents so highly that he sent them to the paper! Horace Mann was referred to as an "incendiary" and the Board of Education was made to appear malign and secret — an "invisible all-controlling influence."

Mann had not one but many friends among the orthodox. This time, Emerson Davis of Westfield wrote to Dr. Humphrey, found that the President of Amherst not only knew nothing about the letters but was sympathetic to Mann's work in the cause of education. Dr. Davis then wrote the *Observer* and no further letters were published. Mann received a letter from Dr. Davis which was heart-warming. "It is said that you may know a good apple-tree by the number of clubs and stones that lay [*sic*] about it. I think our tree will have this sort of evidence to prove that it is good. Be not discouraged."

It seemed as though the affair had terminated and meanwhile books continued to pour in. Miss Catherine Beecher recalled that she once knew a young law student in Litchfield by the name of Horace Mann and she sent him a volume. Miss Elizabeth Peabody wrote: "I have a manuscript, 'The Story of the Pilgrims,' written by my mother, which I have used a great deal with many children and it has proved extremely interesting and instructive." Elizabeth had another book to offer. It was " 'Twice-Told Tales,' by N. Hawthorne."

Mann felt doubtful about Hawthorne. "I have read several of the 'Twice-Told Tales,' " he said. "They are written beautifully — 'fine' is the true word. But we want something nearer to duty & Business." Mann thought there were better authors for his purposes — for example, "Miss Sedgwick has her eye on the true point."

When the school library was finally advertised for sale Miss Beecher was not listed but Miss Sedgwick was. Under "Works Proposed for Consideration" was *History of the Pilgrims* by a Lady." At first, it was only under "individuals engaged as writers" that the name of "N. Hawthorne" appeared. In this same category was "Miss E. P. Peabody" herself.

After his first too hasty appraisal of *The Child at Home* and his overvehement first letter, Mann proposed that the entire Board of Education approve all other books for the school library. Edward A. Newton, Board member, now angrily resigned. He was orthodox Episcopalian, had attended the General Association meeting which Packard made famous but was absent while Packard was holding forth. Newton was not only opposed to Mann on religious grounds

but on political grounds as well. His father had been a Tory refugee
from Boston at the time of the American Revolution and when
Newton returned as a young man, he was employed by Stephen
Higginson and Company to be their representative in India. He
lived in India for nine years and then retired with a fortune to live
in Pittsfield. He was opposed to everything Mann stood for in the
way of public education. His resignation was "glorious," Mann's
friends said. But Newton retired from the State Board to fight
Horace Mann with personal animosity almost equaled by that of
Fred Packard.

With the resignation of Newton and the suppression of further
Packard letters, Mann hoped that the school library project would
proceed in peace. But the first "controversy" had begun and Mann
could not have stopped it with the winning of one argument any
more than he could have stopped the first hot flash of a forest fire
with one bucket of water.

The establishment of the normal schools [3] was of immensely more
importance than the school libraries, and was now uppermost in
Mann's mind. The history of the libraries was repeated to a certain
extent, for as soon as it became known that the state had a little
money to spend, all sorts of offers came to Horace Mann through
the mails. It seemed as if every town had some moribund academy
which had long ceased to pay its way but which was suddenly po-
tentially successful — and just the thing for the state to acquire for
at least twice the value of its abandoned buildings.

Mr. Mann made himself clear — and to Miss Peabody, who,
naturally enough, had a friend with a school for sale. "The Board of
Education have not given, nor is it their intention to give, the
slightest encouragement to the establishment of a Normal School,
except some strong inducements are offered by those who may desire its location in their vicinity. Did they not adopt that course,
their whole means would be exhausted at once, and they might well
be compared to the boy who gave away his all to buy a purse. In
those cases where the Board has encouraged the applications made,
it has been upon the basis of their being gratuitously furnished with
Academy buildings, and a Mansion house or houses sufficient for the
lodging of a hundred pupils."

The resolution appropriating the money for the normal schools was signed by Governor Edward Everett on the nineteenth of April, the anniversary of the Battle of Lexington. Mann noted the coincidence with amusement when the village of Lexington was chosen as the site of the first normal school. Citizens had promised to raise a thousand dollars for the school, and a vacant academy building standing at the corner of Lexington Common was rented for a nominal sum. The building was "fifty feet long and forty feet wide," two stories with "suitable outbuildings." A cupola with columns and a weathervane gave it an air of dignity — but within, the building left much to be desired. "Carpentering, painting and whitewashing" proved to be the first Principal's first duties.

When it came to the choosing of a principal, the effect of Packard's attacks and Newton's barrage of criticism of the Board was immediately visible. The position was first offered to Gallaudet in recognition of his work and writings on education, to be sure — but also because he was orthodox, a graduate of Andover Seminary. Gallaudet had a successful school for the deaf and felt he could not leave. And now the next choice was the Reverend Jacob Abbott — unanimously appointed by the Board. He was orthodox to the core and none other than the brother of the Reverend John who wrote *The Child at Home!* Here was the way to draw the teeth of the opposition! The Reverend Jacob Abbott had been principal of the Mt. Vernon School for Girls, and he was the author of the "Rollo Books." But there was no sufficiently orthodox church in Lexington — and the Reverend Jacob Abbott thought he would not be happy in such a town. He was later offered the principalship of the normal school at Barre, where there was a church to suit him, and again he said no — this time giving the reason that the whole normal school project was too risky.

Three more orthodox gentlemen were approached in behalf of Lexington, and all refused. Now, at last, Mr. Mann was free to make his own choice regardless of religious bias. He took ship for Nantucket Island to see Cyrus Peirce. Peirce thought nothing of the risk and the personal sacrifice but came with his wife and worldly goods to start life anew where difficulties would spring up in his path at every step. For his services as principal, sole lecturer, director of the model school and janitor, Mr. Peirce was to receive fifteen hundred dollars. Governor Everett said that he personally would be "willing to vote an additional gratuity of three hundred dollars for the expenses of moving," and the Board was being princely — since their Secretary of Education was now getting fifteen hundred and no "gratuity" for anything.

With his fine sense of the dramatic, Mann chose April 19 for the opening of the Lexington Normal School. Appropriate allusions to the Battle of Lexington and the new battle against ignorance must have occurred to him as he thought of the speech he would make, of the people gathered on Lexington Common — the music, the flags. But globes, maps and books did not arrive. A new innovation, the blackboard, was easier to plan for than to acquire, and delay followed delay.

It was July 2, 1839, when Mann wrote in his diary: "Tomorrow we go to Lexington to launch the first Normal School on this side of the Atlantic."

After all — it was close to Independence Day and Mann could make a Fourth of July speech of far more importance than his maiden effort in Dedham so long ago. "Much must come of it, either of good or of evil," he wrote. "I am sanguine in my faith that it will be the former. . . . But the good will not come alone. That is the reward of effort, of toil, of wisdom. These, as far as possible, let me furnish. Neither time, nor care . . . shall be wanting to make this an era in the welfare . . . of our schools . . . then it will be an era in the welfare of mankind."

The next day came. Rain fell in torrents. There was no festive air, no gathering of townspeople. Worst of all — there were only three students who "presented themselves for examination." With the courage supposed to belong only to youth, Mann wrote: "What remains but more exertion! More and more! Until it *must* succeed."

Students began to appear by twos and threes, and on July 10 Mary Swift of Nantucket arrived; she was accepted as the seventh pupil — and dutifully began a journal of her school life in accordance with her teacher's request. Cyrus Peirce was himself setting down his steps in creating the first normal school, and, read together, the two journals make a charming counterpoint.[4]

Peirce longed to teach the theory of teaching. For this, he had given up his successful work in Nantucket — and if he could but kindle that pure flame of service, that sense of teaching as a high calling, his sacrifice would have been well made. It caused him understandable impatience when he found himself forced to teach spelling and simple arithmetic to young ladies who, he had supposed, would be well grounded in all fundamentals. He must begin with girls who were themselves the product of poor teaching and bad schools and turn them into fine teachers capable of reforming bad schools and preparing excellent students! Peirce's task was painfully like trying to find the beginning or the end of a circle and grievously did he suffer in spirit! September 9 is the date of entry in Peirce's diary which reads as follows:

"The school now consists of twelve scholars. They seem industrious and interested; and nearly every one of *fair* capacity. But many of them are yet backward . . . they want language — they want the power of generalization and communication." Then a few days later Peirce bemoaned "a great deficiency in reading and spelling." By December, "There are two or three scholars who do little or nothing in Arithmetic and Grammar."

Beginning on the same day — Monday, September 9 — Mary Swift of Nantucket, aged nineteen, contributed her melody to this counterpoint in education. Her spelling was excellent and she "communicated" freely and easily. Was she not brought up in Cyrus Peirce's own Nantucket schools? But she admitted shortcomings. "The problem in the globe was rather too deep for me to fathom but I succeeded in 'making land' as Mr. P. said. The lesson in Moral Philosophy was badly recited. The subject as yet seems to excite but little interest."

Cyrus Peirce had no children and at times a daughter or two of his own would have helped him. He was very desirous that his students should have good health, insisting that they read "Bakewell's Philosophy" and lecturing them on the health rules laid down therein. "Held much conversation with my pupils," he said. "I gave them to understand that I thought there were but few of them who did not violate the Laws of Physiology in the matter of tight-lacing. I hope it may do some good."

To which Mary Swift replied in her journal: "The lesson in Physiology was very practical and our teacher made some remarks in connection with it, upon tightness of dress, apparently thinking that it was the fashion at present to dress tightly. He has not probably heard that the wisdom or some other good quality of the age has substituted the reverse fashion for the time present."

Cyrus Peirce issued many warnings, taken from his text, concerning the dangers of an innovation called "ice-cream." But his girls were educating him just as surely as he was educating them. In August, he allowed them to go to a nearby county fair, joining them there later himself. Mary Swift said that "when we had become wearied with standing we descended to the refreshment room where Mr. P. treated us to ice-cream and cake. Contrary to the principles of 'Bakewell's Philosophy,' we felt much cooler after eating the cream."

The pupils of Cyrus Peirce kept their journals with the understanding that their teacher would read them at intervals. What, then, became of the girl who gently admonished her teacher in the matter of feminine fashion and gave her own ideas on the effect of eating ice cream? Upon graduation, Mary Swift received one of Father Peirce's highest recommendations and went to teach at Perkins Institute for the Blind under Dr. Samuel Gridley Howe. She continued her habit of keeping a journal, which this time became "an important book," called *The Life and Education of Laura D. Bridgman.* Mary Swift was a famous teacher of the blind and deaf, and many years later she "inspired Helen Keller to learn to talk." And this was not all — Mary was married to Edwin G. Lamson of Boston, had four children and lived to be ninety!

Not all the pupils were the equal of Mary Swift, of course. There were days when Father Peirce would write in his journal, "some failures and not a few tears." But all his "Normalites" would spread the gospel of fine teaching and an important feature in the success of Lexington Normal was the "model school." It was begun October 21, 1839, and Father Peirce described it as having "about 30 scholars: ⅓ girls. — All sorts of odds and ends."

Peirce had yet to appreciate one factor in his size-up of the children who were to serve as guinea pigs for his would-be teachers. They were drawn from families who were personally interested in the Normal School experiment. Little Charles Follen was a typical example. His father, Professor Charles Follen, was first professor of German literature at Harvard and now lived in Lexington because Harvard had dispensed with his services as a result of his antislavery activities. Charles's mother was Eliza Lee Cabot, herself a teacher and a devoted friend of Elizabeth Peabody's. Here were highly intelligent and very vocal parents ready to spread the news if Charles was doing well in school. Here were parents ready to bring a long string of distinguished visitors to the model school as soon as they saw how fine Peirce's teaching of teachers really was.

Peirce's daily schedule now went as follows: classes at the normal school, 8 to 9; teaching in the model school with normal student assistants and observers, 9 to 11. At eleven the model school was dismissed to return from 1 to 3. Normal school recessed from 11 to 12, "came to order at 2 and continued Session until 5." As for Cyrus Peirce, he recessed never. He rose before dawn to set the fires going in the cast-iron stoves in his little school building, and in winter he arose at intervals all night to keep the stoves going. He sat late over his desk, writing down the events of the day and the progress of the great experiment. "I am glad . . . to learn that the Parents of the pupils are beginning to be interested in the school," he wrote. He could have added that the whole state was interested, and that word of Lexington was spreading far beyond the boundaries of Massachusetts.

Edmund Dwight arrived to see the first tangible results of his ten-thousand-dollar gift. Governor Edward Everett came, senators and representatives followed, and educators arrived — new friends of Horace Mann. A shy, very respectful man appeared, who said his name was Henry Barnard. He had been in correspondence with Horace Mann. He had been a lawyer, then in the Connecticut legislature, and his career was so similar to that of Mann's as to seem almost an echo. Now he found himself newly appointed Secretary of Education in Connecticut. Barnard, on Mann's invitation, had come to see how a normal school was run.

Of course Bronson Alcott came over from nearby Concord. All the other visitors had come to learn something — from the gifted young Barnard on down. But Alcott came to instruct, though uninvited to do so. It was one of those off days for the little Normalites when they did badly at the blackboard and burst into tears upon being reproached by Father Peirce. Peirce told of the scene. He felt he had "much reason to fear that" he had not "manifested the proper temper under my trials. . . . Mr. Alcott gently rebuked the Principal for his impatience. This may not have been very agreeable; nevertheless it may have been strictly Just. It is not often, I suppose, that a teacher receives a rebuke from a visitor in the presence of his own school."

One visitor came oftener than any other — and never offered a rebuke. "Mr. Mann spent the day with us," Cyrus Peirce wrote not once but many times. "The School did well — Mr. M. was pleased to express much gratification in his visit — the state and prospect of the school; and we all felt benefited and cheered by his presence."

At the beginning of the second term, Mr. Mann appeared with two nieces to enroll. They were the Misses Rebecca and Eliza Pennell, aged eighteen and seventeen respectively. They were earnest, hardworking, grateful to their uncle for giving them an education — and they were both unusually pretty. Rebecca outshone Eliza. She was as frail and slender as the fashionable romancers could wish but she was also as brilliant mentally as the new woman that her era was attempting to produce. Cyrus Peirce made little mention of her in his journal, but in his letters to her he called her "my Jewell" and covered her with glory. "Your industry, your attention to order, your success in lessons and general improvement, your constant cheerful regard to all my wishes, the salutary influence which your exemplary conduct shed upon others and the deep concern you felt and manifested for the character and prosperity of the Institution . . ." how could a man say more and yet this and more Cyrus Peirce said in praise of Rebecca. It was hardly surprising that Rebecca was well aware of her own worth!

Rebecca was "feeble and sickly" when she "came to Lexington." Both she and Eliza developed feverish colds immediately and Eliza wrote home, desperately homesick yet pathetically afraid she might seem ungrateful to a generous uncle. In response to her letter, her Uncle Horace, her mother and her Aunt Lydia all came hurrying over from Wrentham! It was Miss Lydia, the faithful maiden aunt, who stayed to nurse the sick and sorrowful. She found four girls ill and cared for them all for two weeks. Her departure, Cyrus Peirce noted, "caused much sadness of heart."

Horace Mann, once he was sure his nieces were in no danger, lingered to enjoy the school an hour or two and then hurried about his business. The major projects which he started at this time and carried on simultaneously would have furnished full-time occupation for several men. When he found himself a trifle weary, Mann reproached himself and never stopped to rest unless forced to it by occasional attacks of nervous indigestion.

In 1838 Mann made his second tour of the state, holding school conferences. He campaigned successfully for the state grant for normal schools, decided to start three of them, selected their sites, planned their courses and found leaders for these all-important outposts of his educational campaign. He made Lyceum appearances, accepting every possible chance to hold forth on his great theme, education for the people. And on October 20 he prepared the first number of the *Common School Journal*.

The *Common School Journal* was an innovation in publications, designed expressly for the school system which Mann was creating with the speed and mental excitement of an artist at work upon an enormous frescoe. The artist must get his great conception painted all complete in line and color before the plaster dries. And Mann must present to his state and eventually to his nation an entire public school system before the recently awakened public interest flickered out and died.

Marsh, Capen and Lyon, publishers of the school library, undertook to publish the *Common School Journal* and foresaw much profit to be derived therefrom. They promised to find an editor and a staff and pay them well. It was Mann's understanding that he would contribute only occasionally. But as it turned out, he was for ten years the sole editor, paid only in promises. Mann was often the major contributor — and he was final victim of the firm's remarkable financial ineptitude.

There were advantages on Mann's side. He could print what he pleased and did so — giving more thought to what his readers ought to know than to what they might like to read. Sometimes he printed nothing but his own school report, running it in several numbers. He replied to the various enemies that rose up against him with such vigor that the *Common School Journal* was often the most talked-of publication in Boston. Unfortunately, few people paid "1 dollar per annum or 6 copies for 5 dollars" — they just borrowed a *Journal* when a controversy flared up. Teachers were the *Journal's* best customers, of course, for Mann published lessons in geography, drawing or spelling, signed A TEACHER — and written more often than not by Miss Mary Peabody. Miss Mary received for her efforts the priceless reward of being able to serve Horace Mann.

In the first number, November 1838, Mann addressed the "Citizens of Massachusetts" at greater length than he might have been per-

mitted to do had someone else been his editor. Yet he had something
to say and he said it well. "None of you is so high as not to need
the education of the people as a safeguard; none of you is so low as
to be beneath its lifting power." In a Republic like ours, "children
must be educated," Mann urged, so as to be "above pride as well as
above abasement, to be master instead of slave of accident. . . ."

Mann told in the *Common School Journal* of the progress of his
work. For example, he had been struck by the plight of the children
of Irish railroad hands. "On the line of the Western Railroad, at no
great distance from its summit, skirting the town of Middlefield, are
temporarily located, within a distance of three or four miles, about
one hundred families, mostly immigrants from Ireland . . .

"Here was an extent of road, stretching from the Connecticutt
river to the western boundary of the state, passing most of the way
through a mountainous country, alive with laborers from one end
to the other and, except here and there and for short distances, out
of reach of churches and schools. Did wealth consist in children,
it is well known that the Irish would be a rich people. . . . Hence
it was that along this extensive line of road, the children of this
people might be seen, peeping from behind every bush and playing
beside every stream. They were too young to be employed; they
were not recognized by local authorities as having any right to the
privileges of the public school . . . and there, in the midst of a
Christian people, no more public care was taken of their instruction,
than for that of young foxes in the neighboring mountains."

Our country owes "a vast economical debt to that class of people,
whose labor has been mainly instrumental in rearing the great material structures of which we so often boast. They have materially
changed the surface of the earth for our profit and delight, building
piers and wharves for our commerce, turning the bed of ocean
into dry land for the enlargement of our cities, cutting down the
mountains and upheaving the valleys, to smooth the pathway by
which distant and alien people might hold communion with one
another. Were all considerations of social and Christian duty out
of the question, an equitable and fair-minded man ought to blush
to receive such benefits without any other requital than just enough
food and clothing for the laborers. . . . It is impossible for us to
pay them in kind; but there is a compensation . . . which we have
the ability to bestow. We can confer the blessing of education upon

their children. And the impulse of duty to do so may lawfully derive additional energy from the reflection that every wise, humane measure adopted for their welfare, directly promotes our own security. For it must be manifest to every forecasting mind, that the children of this people will soon possess the rights of men, whether they possess the characters of men or not. There is a certainty about their future political and social powers — while there is a contingency depending upon the education they receive — whether these powers will be exercised for weal or woe."

One fact Mr. Mann left out of his article. He did not tell his readers that he had personally contributed a hundred dollars out of his meager salary for the education of these immigrant workers' children. He praised instead the town of Middlefield which had built the children a school from private funds. Mann suggested that hereafter the state should grant railroad charters only if there were a proviso for the education of the laborers' children.

The *Journal* was not always deadly serious. Almost every article sparkled with humorous touches. "It was lately remarked by a gentleman not over-sensitive in his sympathies for the mass of mankind . . . that on the subject of education there seemed to him to be a good deal of 'cant.' We replied that there seemed to us to be much more of 'won't.' " And Mann congratulated New York State upon its school system "of recent origin [1839]. . . . Unlike Massachusetts," he said, "they have been exempted from the immense labor of boasting about their ancestors, and have more time to devote to posterity."

Famous for its vein of satire was Mann's report and article on schoolhouses as he found them. "We can now call to mind several cases which we have witnessed in travelling over the state, where barns, piggeries and other outbuildings have been erected according to the most approved style of Gothic Architecture, and the abode of brute animals decorated with the profusion of ornament that belongs to that finical order. But models of the old schoolhouses did not come from the classic land of the East; their origin was aboriginal, — not copied from Greece or Rome, but rather from the Pequots and the Narragansets. Not only, as we have before said, would many of our schoolhouses furnish us an illustration in geography, because four steps would carry a pupil through the five zones;

but astronomy could also be studied in them to advantage, for through the rents in the roof the stars may be seen. . . ."

The need for filling up a line or two at the end of a page taught Mann to shorten and sharpen his wit. He began to experiment with the aphorism and so, after various trials, in the *Common School Journal* of November 1844, appeared the lines learned by many a schoolboy — lines now to be found in Bartlett's *Quotations:*

"Lost, yesterday, somewhere between sunrise and sunset, *two golden hours*, each set with *sixty diamond minutes*. No reward is offered for they are gone forever."

CHAPTER SIXTEEN
Political Madmen

ALTHOUGH no longer in politics, Mann was still alert to every-thing that went on under the dome of the State House, because of possible profit or loss to his education crusade. The political weather forecast for 1839 seemed calm and pleasant. To be sure the "license law" was causing a few clouds to gather — nothing more. This was a law limiting the sale of liquor to quantities not less than fifteen gallons, and it was rather a backhanded scheme for reducing the sale of hard liquor by the dram to people of low income — hard-pressed, some of them, to provide food for their families. "The antis are straining for a repeal of the late law and for that reason they wish to change the character of the Legislature in the ensuing year," Horace Mann observed. "Hence their agitation — their clamor about 'inalienable, home-bred, fire-side rights' of getting drunk. But if our friends do half their duty we are safe."

It would seem that Mann's friends did just a trifle less than half their duty at the polls in November! Marcus Morton, Jacksonian democrat candidate — unsuccessful for the past sixteen years — de-feated Governor Edward Everett by a majority of just one vote!

Marcus Morton addressed the legislature, his curiously high and narrow forehead contrasting with his fat chin that looked for all the world like a picture of Humpty Dumpty. He started in by at-tacking the Western Railroad — which was now completed as far as Worcester, Massachusetts. The farmers would get nothing out of it, he said, while Western produce would soon roll in by rail in ruin-ous competition. Morton was for economy. He cried fraud and cor-ruption against the previous state government for lending money to the railroad when private funds failed as a result of Jackson's bank-ing policy.

Mann read the new Governor's address from beginning to end with careful attention. Previously, Governor Everett had devoted a good deal of space to the State Board of Education, to which he had given well-deserved praise. Mann was not looking for praise from Governor Morton, but he was unprepared to find that Morton had "cut the Board of Education entirely." Mann was "full of gloom and apprehension," he said — yet willing to give Morton the benefit of the doubt. "Probably he did not know of its existence. He has got to know it. He has made a mistake on his own personal account as I believe. But time will make further developments."

Horace Mann and Marcus Morton had curiously similar educations, from which they emerged with ideas diametrically opposite. Like Mann, Morton entered Brown as a sophomore by reason of brilliance and was class orator at graduation. Morton also studied at Litchfield Law School and, although never in the Massachusetts legislature, he went twice to Congress. Morton said that his sympathies were with the farmer, the laborer and the immigrant. So were Mann's. Morton went even further than Mann in his enthusiasm for temperance, becoming the first President of the American Temperance Society. But in 1839, Marcus Morton rather suddenly discovered that the license law "discriminated against the common people."

Irish immigration would not reach its peak until after 1845 when the "potato rot" brought starvation to all Ireland. But already Irish absentee landlords had so exploited their tenant farmers that the slightest crop failure caused famine and the more enterprising Irish spalpeens managed to reach Boston, a Promised Land. Here they gutted the labor market in spite of expanding textile mills and new railroad construction so that they found life in America hardly less miserable than in the old country. In Ireland, whisky was at times cheaper than bread! The Irish had come to rely on it and opportunist Irishmen set up "grog shops" in Boston — "grog," a word of interesting origin, having come to mean any kind of cheap liquor. Now came the "license law."

Of course there were ways of getting around the law — of buying a drink without paying for fifteen gallons of whisky! In Dedham, an enterprising vendor put up a tent, printed a sign and invited all who would pay a small fee to come in and see the "blind pig." It was no violation of the law when "free" drinks were served inside the tent. "Blind pigs" became popular. And it all proved, Marcus Morton argued, that the "fifteen-gallon law" was not the will of the people. He went into office on his promise to fight the liquor law — but even if Morton's majority of one must rule, Horace Mann did not like it.

Morton's first appearance as ex officio chairman of the State Board of Education was anything but a happy occasion. He attempted to put a stop to the school library project, once and for all, by refusing to endorse any book. The Board made new rules to circumvent this move, but this did not improve the atmosphere.

Morton now attacked Mann's public school system still more directly. Economy was his watchword and the thing to do, he said, was to put public education back into "the hands of town and district meetings." The schools would then relapse into the state of neglect where Mann found them and a young person wanting to prepare for college would find it extremely difficult unless his parents could send him to a private academy. But Morton was on solid ground with his constituents. For generations, the Irish peasantry had been forbidden to attend school. Many immigrants could neither read nor write and there was trouble in the home as their children aired book knowledge and tried to outsmart the older generation.

Mann wanted to make school attendance compulsory, and he was proud of the marked increase in numbers of children attending school regularly. He called attention to this in his reports. But again Morton was sensitive to the will of his party. The immigrants were bitterly opposed to compulsory education and called truant officers "kidnapers." The Irish were so miserably ill-paid and so poverty-stricken that they depended upon the few pennies their children could earn for them. It was useless to tell them about the great gift of free public education. These parents were too hungry to listen. Marcus Morton, with his majority of one, had a pressure group behind him when he moved to cut off the funds for the education program.

"Political madmen are raising voice and arm against the Board," Horace Mann wrote in his diary on the fifth of January, 1840. Mann referred to something more than Morton's suggestion that a State Secretary of Education was a reckless extravagance at a salary of fifteen hundred dollars a year! The move Mann referred to was a plan to close the normal schools, refund to Edmund Dwight his gift toward their support — and hand the duties of the Secretary of Education over to the Secretary of State, abolishing the State Board of Education.

It was some time before Mann was able to trace the whole plot; but his old enemy, Fred A. Packard, was at the bottom of it. Packard had written four letters supposed to be to Dr. Humphrey of Amherst but he got only two into the *Observer* before his fraud was discovered and the *Observer* refused him further space. He now put his four letters into pamphlet form and sent them, anonymously, to "all orthodox clergymen in Massachusetts." In other words, a pamphlet went to all but Unitarian ministers, and Packard's missionary effort must have cost him money. In an unsigned review for the *Princeton Review,* Packard praised his own anonymous pamphlet!

The pamphlets "caused great excitement," Mann said. They "sowed seeds of jealousy against the Board" although "the letters of Mr. Packard were as wicked a libel as ever were published." The general idea of Packard's pamphlet was that the State Board of Education, and Horace Mann in particular, plotted to teach the children of Massachusetts to become Unitarians. All other denominations must band together to save the children's souls from Satan's power!

The whole idea seems ridiculous, but to Edward A. Newton the Packard pamphlet was gospel truth. Newton had resigned from the State Board in angry protest over the school library, but he was now a member of the legislature where he could proceed directly against Horace Mann. Packard was Mann's first enemy and Newton was the second, with little to choose between the two.

Newton had no books to sell but he had a doctrine to uphold, and this raised him in his own estimation to the status of Christian warrior. Mann had always been proud to remember that his maiden speech in the legislature had been in favor of "religious liberty." Because of Mann's efforts, the little church in Blandford, that Berkshire hill town, could choose either a trinitarian or a "liberal" minister and still enjoy the use of their endowment fund. Word of this triumph of heresy could not have failed to reach Newton in nearby Pittsfield, where he was establishing an extremely orthodox Episcopal church. And now here came Horace Mann invading Berkshire County with still more wicked ideas — namely that the common people should have free schools! In Mr. Newton's opinion, the common people should be educated in church schools, where they would learn to accept the estate to which God had called them — no matter how far down the ladder they might find themselves. It must have been a trifle shocking to the wealthy Edward A. Newton to find himself in accord with Irish immigrants, but politics make strange bedfellows, and he saw his duty — to defeat Horace Mann.

Allied with Newton was the Reverend Allen W. Dodge, representative from Hamilton on the opposite side of the state from Newton's Pittsfield. Also believing every word of the Packard pamphlet, Dodge had the advantage of being on the House Committee on Education. Moving fast, he wrote a report for his Committee asking the legislature to abolish the Board of Education, close the normal schools, get rid of Mann. A majority of the Committee signed the report.

Everything so far had happened with the speed of a military *coup d'état*. But now the news was out. Horace Mann gathered his forces, and they were formidable. Ex-Governor Everett entered the fray in behalf of public education and in spite of his minus-one showing in the election he surprised Governor Morton's cohorts by his extensive influence in the House. Dr. Samuel Gridley Howe wrote letters to the press and Dr. William Ellery Channing spoke out from the pulpit. Henry Barnard, now Secretary of Education in Connecticut under a law of his own proposing, came to Boston to help Horace Mann, who had been his inspiration. Theodore Lyman was particularly effective in Mann's behalf, being an ex-mayor of Boston and until recently a Jacksonian democrat.

Now everything had been done that could be done. When the debate on the Committee's report to abolish the Board came before the House, Mann was in the visitors' gallery — like a general watching to see if his strategy would prevail as his forces were joined with the enemy. A minority on the Education Committee had presented a report favorable to Mann. It was having its effect.

But just as the debate began, Horace Mann was obliged to hurry away to fulfill a lecture engagement in New York! He was "most anxious," he said — and he put it mildly.

* * *

Cyrus Peirce

This portrait hangs in the assembly room, Framingham Normal School. In a letter to Horace Mann, Peirce objected to having his "ugly" face immortalized, but Mann had no sympathy with the complaint.

Rebecca Stanley Mann

Horace Mann's mother looks out upon a world which fills
her with misgiving.

On March 21, 1840, Mann wrote in his diary: "Yesterday heard news from Boston that the bigots and vandals had been signally defeated — 182 in favor and 245 against" destroying the work for education which Mann held so dear. Letters began to reach him in New York, "all filled with shouts and exclamation points!" Perhaps the best was from Dr. Samuel Gridley Howe, beloved fellow warrior, but "they all come like a feu de joie and are sincere and hearty."

As so often happened men of ill will, instead of injuring Mann, succeeded only in bringing new friends to his side. Packard's pamphlet, so unwarrantably using the name of Dr. Heman Humphrey, President of Amherst, brought Dr. Humphrey into the ranks of the education crusade — sincerely orthodox though he was in his religious views. Dr. Humphrey became Mann's personal friend and admirer, accepting a place on the State Board of Education in 1841, where he soon saw for himself that the Board was and always had been nonsectarian.

No less gratifying was the change of heart on the part of the Reverend Mr. Allen W. Dodge, the man who had framed the report to abolish the Board. Dodge had been called "stubborn," with "prejudices which were inexpugnable" — but he was nothing of the sort. Discovering how false was Packard's "wicked libel," Dodge now became the friend of public education and of Horace Mann. Here was as happy an ending to the plot against the common schools as even Mann himself could have wished.

So completely immersed in the cause of education was Mann that he must have seemed to have no private life at all, these days. Yet he had griefs of a personal nature and there were family claims upon his time, his purse, and most of all upon his heart. On March 20, 1837 — three months before he was made Massachusetts Secretary of Education — Horace Mann's mother died in Franklin. Knowing that he must soon lose her, Mann had visited his mother as often as he could. In the hope of brightening her melancholy moments, he tried to rally her about her grim Calvinistic faith. If there were one person certain of fore-ordination to Heaven, it was his mother, Horace Mann told her — but Mrs. Mann could never permit this with a smile. No longer able to lead an active life, she spent many hours reading her Bible and brooding, not so much over her own eternal future as over the probable fate of her sons, Steven and Thomas Stanley. Her son Horace, for all his good works, could as easily be foreordained to outer darkness — as his persistent preference for the Unitarian doctrine seemed to prove. Lydia,[1] Mrs. Mann's faithful nurse during her last illness, tried to reassure her mother. Horace was "not *really* Unitarian," she said.

At some time during Mrs. Mann's married life, a local or a journeyman artist had made an attempt to paint her portrait. She had worn her best lace cap and the matching collar, to which the artist did justice with meticulous care. But through iron-rimmed glasses, Rebecca Stanley Mann peered at the artist with an expression sad and somewhat severe — her lips shut tight in an uncompromising line. Perhaps she suspected that the artist might be a heretic! The artist rendered the spectacles all too faithfully yet somehow he managed to paint the eyes behind them with sympathy and understanding. There was a spiritual quality and a mysticism which lived again on canvas so that all who loved this simple, devout woman would remember how she looked. People must have said that Horace had his mother's eyes.

After her death, there was nothing to hold Horace Mann in Franklin.[2] The farm now belonged to him and to his sister Lydia and in 1838 they sold Mann's Plain — the acres which had been in the family for a hundred and eighteen years. It was not without regret that they left the old homestead and closed a chapter in family history; but on July 29, 1839, Mann recorded an event in his diary which gave him great satisfaction. "I have this day caused a deed to be put on record, conveying a small house & plot of ground situated in Wrentham, to my sister Rebecca, having advanced and become liable for the sum of eight hundred dollars. If by this I can furnish a home for the remnant of our once united family where quiet & harmony may be enjoyed, no money ever spent by me will have yielded a sweeter reward."

The little house which Mann had bought stood close to the road from Wrentham to Foxborough, not far from the center of Wrentham village.[3] It was indeed a small house, having one story and surely no more than loft space above the first floor. But there was a wide, welcoming front door with charming side lights and flat, engaged pilasters in perfect scale and perfect simplicity. The roof line came close above small-paned windows, two to the side with the front door in the middle. A chimney at each gable end proclaimed the comfort of fireplaces within and at the corners of the house lilacs grew tall enough to set their purple blossoms in handsome contrast against the dark shingle roof when springtime came.

Mann kept a furnished room in Boston — now here, now there. In 1838 he was living at Mrs. Bean's, Number 47 Mt. Vernon Street — in spite of Elizabeth's and Mary Peabody's affectionate urgings that he go to the George Hillards' and let Susan look after him. He had no home, he often said — but Wrentham was the place to which he turned in search of rest. There were reasons which made rest in Wrentham impossible. Packed into the tiny house with their mother were Calvin, Rebecca, Eliza and Marcia — for whose support their uncle had been at least partially responsible since their father's death in 1824. The children were painfully grateful and anxious to please — but it was a large family.

Rebecca remembered what a gay young Uncle Horace she had once had — a laughing young man who would swing her off the ground into his arms. She was twelve when her Aunt Charlotte died and the tragic change in her Uncle Horace, who no longer laughed, made a deep impression on her. In imitation of the lovely lost Charlotte, Mann's niece Rebecca would comb his hair and sing to him to relax his taut nerves as he sat in the corner of the family sofa of an evening. Mann's sister Rebecca and all her children, young Rebecca particularly, were fiercely jealous of their place in his affections.

The Pennell family kept alive the memory of the lost Charlotte — doubtless without the conscious thought that Horace Mann might someday love another and remarry. Their pitiful insecurity and dependence upon him would be enough to foster such ideas. In any case, the atmosphere was bad for Mann as is amply shown by an entry in his journal dated Dec. 29, 1839. "Went to Wrentham on Thursday & have not done a particle of work. . . . Thoughts of homelessness, uselessness, friendlessness — the very elements out of which suicide is born, press on me with almost overwhelming intensity."

This mood was of course partly the result of anxiety and would be replaced by one of exaltation as soon as there were some fortunate turn in favor of the cause of education — for of such mercurial stuff was Mann's spirit made. Fortunately a foreign visitor arrived in Boston whose influence may very well have prolonged Mann's life. This was George Combe [4] of Edinburgh, Scotland, a "phrenologist" whose book, *The Constitution of Man*, was popular on both sides of the Atlantic. Combe's theories were a sensation because he advocated such new ideas as the value of fresh air, daily baths — and even outdoor exercise for women! He was a heretic because he did not believe that illness was a punishment meted out by an angry Jehovah but was instead the punishment for ignorance of God's laws of right and healthful living. This was enough to cause him to be looked at askance by some and looked upon as a prophet by others.

Unfortunately, Combe also proposed the theory that if the human mind were capable of development in a given direction a raised area, or bump, would appear upon the skull at a given point. He and his fellow-phrenologists drew pictures of human heads, making them look like maps of a crowded subdivision with tiny house lots set aside for every possible characteristic and trait. They went about blithely measuring heads and coming to conclusions about the criminal type, the intellectual and plenty of other types in between. This would have been bad enough, but they developed a lingo of their own — just as the modern psychologists (whose forerunner they were) now speak a neo-Greek jargon of their own concocting.

Combe had heard in Scotland of Horace Mann as the founder of the first American state-supported asylum for the penniless insane. As soon as he reached Boston, Combe sought out Horace Mann and one look delighted him — phrenologically! Mann's high forehead indicated intellect, but above the forehead Mann's skull continued to arch handsomely and this indicated "spirituality," which was better still. Mann's face was narrow with no noticeable extra width in front of the ears, which indicated that he lacked "alimentiveness" or "love of eating"! Combe's quick and practised eye noted no bulge at the back of Mann's head just above the collar — so Mann was not over "amative," while a small "philogenitive" bump just above indicated little or no desire for children! Bursting with enthusiasm, Combe told Mann of all the splendid intellectual traits his rather bumpy forehead proclaimed. Mann had "causality" — or reasoning power — "very large." If this were true, then it was remarkable that Mann could be led to suppose that two bulges over his eyes had anything to do with it! But so he believed.

The effect on Mann's vocabulary was deplorable. But the effect of George Combe on Mann's health and mental outlook was everything that could be desired. In early August 1839 — that time of year when Mann usually gave himself up to morbid thoughts of Charlotte — he visited Mr. and Mrs. George Combe at Cape Cottage, a summer resort three miles south of Portland, Maine. It was the first vacation of Mann's life, and lasted seven days. Mann arrived with "health . . . very unsound," troubled by sleeplessness. He enjoyed nights of deep sleep and he spent his days in "the society of Mr. Combe who is on the whole the completest philosopher I have ever known." Mann learned that Mr. Combe obeyed "the laws of his nature" and "by submitting to the limitations which the Deity has imposed on his nature, he is enabled to perform the duties which the Deity requires of it."

This rule Mann would now try to make his own. In proof of his having turned over a new leaf, he promised to go west with Mr. and Mrs. Combe for a much longer vacation the following spring. He could not have realized how desperately he would need this rest after his battle to save the Board of Education, but it came so providentially that he knew Combe must be right. Hitherto, Mann had deliberately overworked, feeling satisfaction in being a martyr to the cause. He now saw that this was a puritanical idea he should discard along with other Calvinistic severities. On March 25, 1840, he set out from Philadelphia. Behind him lay victory to raise his spirits to the soaring point. Letters of congratulation — "Huzzahs" he called them — followed him as he discovered his own glorious country, all the way to the Middle West!

Mann had never before been much farther from home than New York City. He was forty-four but a farm boy at heart, and his delight at every new sight increased the pleasure of the much-traveled Mr. Combe. "The great National Road" was an engineering miracle that filled Mann's heart with pride. The Cumberland Mountains were the first high mountain range he had ever seen and they left him "lost in amazement." Once over the Divide, it was "as though a great curtain had been withdrawn" and "the great valley of the West burst upon us. Away in the horizon, far as the eye could reach & as far to the South & to the North . . . we saw all that the convexity of the earth's surface would allow."

In North Bend, Ohio, Horace Mann and Combe went to call on General Harrison, first "log cabin" candidate for the presidency — whose campaign Mann was watching with a certain amount of skepticism. Did Harrison merely affect the homespun?

Harrison's health had been broken by his long campaigns in the West against the Indians and by his more recent assignment in Bogotá as United States Minister to Colombia. He had now but one year to live. Mann found his "appearance feeble, thin, his skin shrivelled & his motions weak. He entered into conversation, however, & seemed to gain strength & vivacity, as he proceeded. . . . His conversation was sensible without being profound . . . his manners had the utmost simplicity . . . he spoke of events in which he had borne a conspicuous part without the slightest elation & referred to his own frugal & homely life without a hint that his poverty was a thing either to be proud of or to be ashamed of. His dwelling is humble . . . I should think that half the farmers in Norfolk County had a room quite as well set off as the best room of Gen. Wm. H. Harrison, the leading Whig candidate for the Presidency of the United States. The billiard room of a certain gentleman in Boston would have bo't the General out of house & home."

General Harrison told his guests that Webster and others had been to see him lately. He had no wine to offer them, "had none in his cellar for twenty years — if he had got it, probably should not have been able to pay for it. After Mr. Webster went away he had enquired of some of his fellow guests if it were really true that the General did not keep wine." And Webster "then remarked that he tho't he should have it, whether he could pay for it or not." This anecdote alone would have made a Harrison supporter out of Horace Mann.

The Ohio River aroused Mann's admiration. He wrote gloatingly of "2200 miles of steamboat navigation on the Ohio and the Mississippi." Mann had never before visualized the actual size of the United States. "What will this country be!" he exclaimed. "It has been created on a splendid scale of physical magnificence. Are its intellectual & moral proportions to be of corresponding greatness? We trust in God they are."

CHAPTER SEVENTEEN

The Auspicious Years

MANN returned to Boston early in May 1840, much refreshed by his three-thousand-mile Western trip. "I now resolve never to undertake to do so much work in so short a time again," he wrote in his diary. This was an annual resolution, broken annually. Such good resolutions are better made and broken than never made at all, however, and Mann was reaching out toward a more normal, happy existence.

The year 1840 was a presidential election year and Mann, in his circuit of the state, had competition he resented. "Politics [1] are the idol which people have gone after and the true gods go without worship," he said. "There is a roar of politics in the land above whose din my own voice cannot be heard." Nevertheless, on November 9, Mann set out to do his own political duty — particularly in the Massachusetts election. "BOSTON; after a most tedious drive in a severe northeast storm, I have landed in this city. Nothing but the desire to give one vote against Governor Morton could have induced me to run such a risk. . . . He came in by just one vote, by just force enough to bring him within the official circle: he will be sent out by a force sufficient to propel him across the earth's orbit."

The vote against Morton was not as overwhelming as Mann wished but John Davis, former National Republican and now a Whig, was elected. Politically, Davis should have suited Mann better; but after Mann had seen and talked with him "on the great subject," education, Davis did not "burn with zeal." Mann thought that "when other things are off his mind this may come in, but probably many others are hosts while this is but a guest." A sponsor such as Edward Everett had been too much to hope for, but Mann went to work on Governor Davis.

Three normal schools had been established on a purely experimental basis and in 1842 their probation period would end. Forewarned by the close call his whole education program had just experienced, Mann set about grooming the normal schools to pass the most rigid test. Sometimes it seemed to him as if he were the only one who really understood how critical the situation was. After the Lexington school was opened, July 3, 1839, a normal school at Bridgewater was started September 9, 1840, with Colonel Nicholas Tillinghast as principal. The Board had been successful in getting an orthodox principal at last and fortunately Colonel Tillinghast had other qualifications. He was a graduate of West Point, a veteran of five years' active service in the West and South, professor of natural science and ethics at West Point. But Colonel Tillinghast was forever demanding an assistant — and he was right, he needed one. He would not take a woman, however, and much correspondence passed between him and Horace Mann while Mann pointed out to him that this was not the time for extravagance. A woman's services were easily acquired for half the price of a man's, so Tillinghast must put up with a woman or no one! Tillinghast won the argument, acquiring a male assistant for about twelve dollars a week.

A normal school at Barre had opened September 5, 1839, with twelve boys and eight girls as students and the Reverend Mr. Samuel P. Newman as head. He was an orthodox minister who had been teaching at Bowdoin and was Bowdoin's acting president when he accepted the position in the Barre school. Unfortunately the school at Barre continued to attract only a few students while calling forth violent criticism from the townspeople. The young gentlemen did not behave themselves properly, was the complaint, although they seem to have been only a little too noisy and cheerful. Mann wrote sharp letters, for he was aware of the danger of criticism — and Professor Newman soon felt that all he wanted was to get out of the whole business. The school must leave Barre, Mann thought, and he looked about, considering Springfield as a good location because the Dwight family had done so much to make friends for education in that city. A truly brilliant principal must be found and Mann believed that Henry Barnard would be the perfect choice.

Mann approached Barnard in 1842 because the fate which Mann escaped in Massachusetts in 1840 had overtaken Barnard in Con-

ecticut. The Connecticut legislature had voted an end to Barnard's
ntire education project. It was a terrible blow to a man of thirty-
ne, embarking on what he had hoped was a career of public service.
Mann's sympathy was the more deeply felt because of his own
xperiences — yet he could almost rejoice if it meant that Massa-
husetts would acquire Barnard's services. The plan seemed to suc-
eed, for on July 30, 1842, Barnard wrote to Horace Mann from
Westfield. "I am now here to confer with Mr. Bates and have told
im that I was prepared to go to Springfield and organize a Normal
chool, and remain at the head of it for one year, provided we
ould agree on the preliminaries. He thinks there will be no diffi-
ulty on that score and proposes to have a meeting in Springfield of
ourself, and Humphrey, himself and myself on Thursday or Friday
f this week."

A final paragraph contained the seeds of ultimate disappointment.
I almost desire that you will not agree to my terms, for I assure
ou, I never took, or decided to take a step in my life, with so much
istrust in myself. You must be responsible for my failure, for were
: not so that I am to be a fellow-laborer with you, I should not
hink of leaving Hartford at this time and for this object."

Terms could not be agreed upon and Barnard did not come. It
as as well. Horace Mann was not an easy person to work for and
Barnard was too much the leader himself to work under him. Mann
llowed the Barre school to lapse, so that, in the spring of 1842 when
he final testing time drew near, three normal schools was the official
umber but only two existed.

Lexington under Cyrus Peirce was still Exhibit A. This does not
ean that all went smoothly at Lexington. The house where the
irls boarded was poorly run, there were complaints about the food.
Mann had recently become acquainted with Dorothea Dix, who was
king up the work for the insane where he had left it. Miss Dix
ound conditions as bad or worse than when Mann built the Worces-
er asylum; she seemed unaware of Mann's work, but he did not
ind — he admired her greatly. The thing to do was to get such a
onderful woman to help with the Lexington normal school. Miss
Dix proposed to "take a house, hire a steward, and pay him a salary;
lso put in a young lady of 24 as a sort of supervisor of the estab-
ent and counsellor to the young ladies, — Miss D. proposing to
ome up 2 or 3 times per week to Lexington to give directions and

see how matters go." Miss Dix had been to see Cyrus Peirce and told him all this, which he in turn related to Horace Mann.

But Peirce had misgivings. He thought the plan was too expensive and complicated — "rather too much wheel within a wheel" was how he put it. And Miss Dix's idea of how young ladies should behave struck Cyrus Peirce (who was himself considered strict) as rather "too strait." Miss Dix "thinks, for instance, that young ladies while connected with the school," should be forbidden "to ride or walk with young gentlemen visitors," and should "not even receive a call from them unless they are relatives. . . . Miss Dix objected to the girls going to the Post Office for letters. I mention this just to give you an idea of her views or notions. But the good lady must not expect to make these Normal young ladies, ladies in the sense in which her own scholars were. They are designed for a somewhat different sphere, and must so encounter more of the roughness of life." Regardless of how rough it may have been down at the Lexington post office, it was a blessing that Miss Dix decided not to run the Lexington boardinghouse after all.

Cyrus Peirce was seriously ill and asked to retire. But he was prevailed upon to stay one more year — until the danger point was passed and the legislature had decided whether to continue the normal schools or to snuff them out of existence with a vote.

On March 3, 1842, Mann recorded in his diary the outcome of all his planning and hard work. "The brightest days which ever shone on our cause were yesterday & today. Yesterday resolves were passed in the House for granting $6,000 a year for three years to the Normal Schools. . . . Language cannot express the joy that pervades my soul at this vast accession of power to that machinery which is to carry the cause of education forward."

On March 8, Mann was still exulting. "The joy I feel on account of the recent event . . . has not begun to be exhausted. It keeps welling up in my mind, fresh & exhilarating as at the first hour of its omniscience. I have no doubt it will have an effect on my health as well as on my spirits. The wearisome, depressing labor of watchfulness I have undergone for years has been a vampire to suck the blood out of my heart & the marrow out of my bones. I should, however, have held on until death for I felt my grasp all the time tightening, not loosening. I hope I may now have the power of performing more & more labor."

On April 24 Mann wrote: "I understand that eighteen thousand copies of my last Report to the Board have been printed in Albany for distribution. This will carry it to many minds & may be the means of doing some good. If so, I shall be paid for all my labor. It is also translated into German."

Honors were now heaped upon Mann, the culminating one being an invitation to give the Fourth of July oration in Boston. It was an invitation sometimes given to Webster, Edward Everett or Josiah Quincy — all Boston's favorite orators. Mann would have been justified if he had paused to consider what a point he had reached since his first oration in Dedham at the start of his career. But his uppermost emotion was anxiety. "I find that expectations in some quarters are raised high & it will be difficult for me to satisfy them."

Mann looked into his heart and wrote. When the address was finished he said, "All that strength & time can do, I have done & all that remains is to submit it to the terrible ordeal of public opinion. Before twenty-four hours have passed" Mann thought he would know whether he had achieved "the great object" he had in view — that of "favorably influencing the public mind on the question of education."

When the time came to stand before his fellow citizens, Mann spoke with fervor and conviction. The audience warmed to him and he responded with that electric quality which brings the fine speaker close to each listener. At intervals, he found words better than those appearing on his prepared pages, as that mysterious thing called inspiration came to him.

Horace Mann spoke for his own time but also for all time when he said:

"The great experiment of the capacity of man for self-government, — is to be tried anew, which, wherever it *has* been tried, — in Greece, in Rome, in Italy, — has failed through an incapacity in the people to enjoy liberty without abusing it. If in all governments, wisdom and goodness in a ruler are indispensable to the dignity and happiness of the subjects; then in a government like our own, — where all are rulers, — *all* must be wise and good or we must suffer the alternative of debasement and misery.

"It is not enough that a bare majority should be intelligent and upright. We need general intelligence and integrity as we need our daily bread. By the vote of a few wicked men, or even of one wicked man, honorable men may be hurled from office and miscreants elevated to their places; useful offices abolished, and sinecures created; the public wealth which has supported industry, — squandered upon mercenaries. . . . If votes come from ignorance and crime, the fire and brimstone that were rained on Sodom and Gomorrah would be more tolerable.

"Select schools for select children should be discarded. Instead of the old order of nobility, a new order should be created — an order of Teachers, wise, benevolent, filled with Christian enthusiasm and rewarded and honored by all."

It was, of course, a very long oration. The applause was tumultuous — but Mann had no idea whether his words had really reached the minds and hearts of his listeners and, as always when suffering from this sort of anxiety, he was stricken with nervous headaches and dyspepsia. He was asked to visit his good friends the Josiah Quincys at their summer home in Quincy and, while there, he "rec'd an invitation from the city authorities to give them a copy of my 4th of July oration for the press." This was gratifying but the real verdict came later, in August. "About seventeen thousand copies of my oration have been published & another edition of ten thousand is to be published this week."

"Auspicious," Mann termed the year 1840, and he was right — for everything was going his way. Most people might have rested on their laurels a little at this point, but Mann found success an incentive to harder work. On the first day of June, 1840, he wrote to Mary Peabody, whom he still saw more often, perhaps, than any other woman friend of his.

"I meant to have treated my eyes to a sight of you last evening," Horace Mann told Mary, who was visiting in Boston. "Yet old time was too fast for me & I had to send my heart supperless to bed. . . . If you have aught to say to me, you know you have not only my permission but my request to say it as freely as tho' I were a part of your consciousness. I feel as tho' I might take the liberty of thinking aloud to you on any subject that concerns your welfare, or of thinking on paper, for your perusal; cannot you do the same to me?

"I have a summer of solid work before me, which will allow my imagination but little playtime; which, being interpreted, is only saying I shall think of you less than I would. But I go to work with a heart full of alacrity & zeal, for I know that whatever befalls me, the effects of the work shall spread wider & deeper, until they are felt thro' every nerve of the body politic. This is the solace & the impulse of which none of the opposers that obstruct my path or the maligners that pursue me in it, can deprive me.

"But I must bid you goodbye. When you have leisure, transcribe your heart & send it to me & I will do the same to you."

This was a letter of farewell and Mary Peabody had received so many from Horace Mann! But it was signed, "Yours very affectionately" and most certainly Mary transcribed her heart and sent it to him who had possessed it so long.

In 1843, Marcus Morton again became Governor of Massachusetts and Mann again faced the possibility of defeat in his crusade for high standards in free public education. This time, Morton did not win a majority in the election and the choice of governor went to the legislature. He was elected by one vote in the senate — "a certain B. H. A. Collins" having abandoned his Whig party to cast the fateful democratic ballot. Collins received, as his reward, the appointment by Morton to be keeper of the Eastham Lighthouse. It was probably the only place where he could escape from the wrathful Whigs!

Morton came out for education this time. He was for it, he said — only the State Board had been increasing inequalities instead of decreasing them. With the aid of such wealthy citizens as the Dwights, cities, such as Springfield and Salem, were building fine schools while the country schools remained inadequate. Morton's solution was to lower standards to meet the meanest level, while Horace Mann looked for the day when every American boy or girl would be able to attend a school that was the equal of the finest "academy." This time the Board of Education was well defended and Mann was upheld in his desire to give his "clients, the next generation" that academy-quality schooling which he himself had been denied.

But Morton was out for economy again and Mann went around to the State House to see how he stood. "The Retrenchment Committee passed all offices & all salaries in review," Mann said. "Nobody they doomed escaped. I went to a surgeon to see if my own head was on . . ." but Mann had not been fired. In spite of the success of his work, no one had ever proposed increasing Mann's fifteen-hundred-dollar salary and a few days after Morton was elected, Mann wrote, "Old mouser introduced an order . . . to consider the expediency of applying the shears to one side of my salary." But "old mouser" Morton got nowhere for, as Mann put it, "All the committees of both houses are friendly to the cause, my two best friends, Mr. Quincy & Mr. Kinnecut of Worcester, being respectively President of the Senate & Speaker of the House. If they do not give me a good committee, of what use would it be to have friends in office!"

It was Josiah Quincy who was first mentioned among Mann's particular friends in this case. He was at this time Speaker of the House and would soon become the second Mayor of Boston to bear the name. And he was fourth in a line of Josiahs so distinguished that their admiring friends and relatives (who spoke of them constantly) needed special titles to tell them apart.

First came "Colonel Josiah," born in 1709. He engaged in ship-building in Boston with his brother Edmund and his brother-in-law, Edward Jackson. The Partners owned a trading-ship, the *Bethel*, which they sent into the Mediterranean. But the year was 1748 and Great Britain was at war with France and Spain so the British Colonial partners in Boston prudently took out a letter of marque for the *Bethel* and armed her. There was no use squandering money on over-armament, however. They gave her "14 guns besides 6 wooden ones," guaranteed to fool an enemy who kept his distance. Isaac Freeman was Captain, a man who knew how to make the most of his defenses both real and otherwise. He had a crew of 37 men.

The *Bethel* had a lucky voyage until she emerged from the Straits of Gibraltar and entered the Atlantic, just at nightfall. There the Spaniards were waiting for her. But Captain Freeman ordered lanterns aloft, sailors' coats and hats stuck up scarecrow-fashion on his decks, and then he "bore down upon the Spaniard."

The "*Jesus Maria and Joseph*, register ship" of 26 guns and 110 men, "surrendered without firing a shot. At Daylight we had the last of the prisoners secured, who were ready to hang themselves when they saw our strength," wrote Captain Freeman to his owners. "You may easily imagine we had Care and Trouble enough with them till they were landed at Fyal."

There were "161 chests of silver and 2 of gold, registered, besides cochineal and other valuable commodities" in the Spanish cargo, and descendants of the Quincys long remembered how "chests of doubloons and dollars" were escorted by sailors "armed with pistols and cutlasses" to the home of Colonel Josiah, where the treasure was lodged in the wine cellar.

Colonel Josiah had established the family fortune at the age of 40, and he soon retired to Braintree to live the life of a country gentleman. His son, Josiah, Jr., was a brilliant young lawyer who was associated with John Adams in the defense of Captain Preston, British officer, at the time of the Boston Massacre. But while his father lived on, this Josiah died at the age of thirty-one, forever known as "Josiah, Jr.," though he left an infant son of the name.

The third Josiah Quincy became Mayor of Boston and afterwards President of Harvard. "The President," the family always called him — as did Horace Mann, who knew him well. But it was "Young Josiah," born in 1802, who was Mann's particular friend. This Josiah was married to Mary Jane, the daughter of Samuel R. Miller, a girl wealthy in her own right. They had, of course, a son Josiah — one of the most remarkable of the children in the school which Elizabeth Peabody had gathered for Alcott.

In Mann's friendship with the Quincy family, Miss Elizabeth was as usual the benevolent promoter. She dearly loved to bring together the right people. But of late, Miss Lizzie had been "discovering" a wonderful young genius from Salem named Nathaniel Hawthorne. It proved difficult indeed to get him to meet the people Lizzie thought he should. And at the young Josiah Quincys' house it was another friend Mann saw more frequently. Miss Mary Peabody had become the close friend of Mary Jane Quincy — and this time it was Horace Mann who brought two friends together!

CHAPTER EIGHTEEN
On Earth No Other Treasure

HORACE MANN was well aware that Mary Peabody wanted nothing so much as to come to Boston to live. As far back as 1838 he had tried to help her start a school in Boston, writing to tell her what he had accomplished. "I have seen the Lady, who is desirous of making your acquaintance in reference to her own three very beautiful children, & of course of some others to make up a company. It is Mrs. Josiah Quincy Jr.[1] I believe you do not know her though the Lady we call Elizabeth Peabody does. But whether you know her or not, she is an *excellent*. She loves her husband, she loves her children. She is kind & sympathizing &, as I believe, has a heart that flows far beyond the circle of her visiting cards . . .

"What other children, besides her own, she expects to find & put to nestling under your wing, I do not know, but I think she has this further right notion — that it is best for children to be considerably in the society of children of their own age, & that it is only under such circumstances that the social nature will pop its head out from under its covert or hiding-place of fear. . . .

"She wishes to have an interview with you, which is all right, & may be to talk this very matter of young plants & sunshine & shade all over; & she will welcome you to her house at any time, but will expect you in particular next Wednesday, as I told her you would probably come up that day.

"The Board of Education meets on Wednesday . . . & I fear I shall be cheated out of Mr. Emerson's lecture on that account. If I am at the lecture, I will arrogate to myself the honor of escorting you . . . if not, you may feel perfectly at liberty to call at Number 4 Park Street. . . . Thus I do not see but I have arranged the whole affair." In a postscript, Mr. Mann added, "Mrs. Quincy asked me what compensation I tho't you would expect, but not recollecting the sum in your note, I did not mention it. I think they care infinitely more about having the thing well done than about the cost."

Mary Jane Quincy and Mary Peabody liked each other at sight, just as Mr. Mann had known they would. Although Mary Jane had five sisters-in-law — or perhaps because of this — she was rather a lonesome young woman in need of Mary's friendship. Many were the affectionate letters, signed M. J. Quincy or just "M. J.," which would reach Mary Peabody in the course of a long friendship; but for the time being plans for a school came to naught. Parents Mrs. Quincy approached had made other plans — it was a little too late in the season.

It took Elizabeth Peabody's powerful talent for managing the affairs of others to uproot the entire Peabody family from Salem — and transplant them in Boston at Number 13 West Street — before Mary could have her Boston school. Elizabeth opened her magical bookshop in West Street on the last day of July, 1840. With Mother Peabody in her chair by the window, studying German at the age of seventy-two and watching for customers; with Dr. Peabody more or less reluctantly dispensing homeopathic drugs in the corner of the Book Room — Elizabeth held sway and bought all the books she had always wanted. Surely customers would share her tastes, or if they did not she could convert them. The practical Mary got her school under way as quickly as she could; for while Lizzie lived on golden dreams, someone would have to bring in a little silver to pay the bills.

Elizabeth, having "discovered" Hawthorne in spite of him — having tried to sell his books to Horace Mann for the Common School Library — now became Hawthorne's publisher. In 1842, Sophia, that youngest Peabody sister, was married to Nathaniel Hawthorne in the parlor on West Street. Now Elizabeth and Mary were left to create a booklovers' paradise and hope that enough people would patronize their shop to give them a living. Proceeds from Mary's flourishing little school were gratefully received.

Every morning early, Mary dusted and tidied the West Street house while her mother went to "keep store." Then Mary met her little scholars till one in the afternoon, "relieved by half an hour's racing or sliding on the Common with the children." School was over for the children at one, but teaching was not over for Mary. "Three days a week Mrs. Greeley comes at one to take a French lesson — two afternoons at three, I have a drawing class of twelve pupils," she said. And she was both amused and pleased when Father Taylor, the famous spellbinding preacher at the Seamen's Bethel, came to her for drawing lessons. His friends were sending him on a voyage for his health and he wanted "to take sketches in Asia." Mary Peabody taught him her "new plan of perspective."

The *Common School Journal* would soon blossom forth with drawing lessons illustrated by plates, the text (though unsigned) by Mary Peabody. Assorted cubes and cones were arranged in progressively difficult groups and drawn with delicate ink lines. Many boys and girls grew up with the idea that they "couldn't draw a straight line" — since success in art now seemed to depend upon that and nothing more. But on the other hand, here were children being allowed to draw in school without being rapped over the knuckles for it! Horace Mann often recalled how he had longed to draw, and again he was giving his clients of the next generation an opportunity which had been denied him. Schoolteachers could buy a set of cubes and cones for their pupils to draw "at 13 West Street" — so said the *Common School Journal*.

Of course Mary took her turn tending shop, and she had a book of her own for sale in the Book Room. It was *Flower People*, a book for children based on some Sunday School lessons which her sister Elizabeth had prepared, brought down to earth and made practical with botanical information — retold by Mary. She was now at work upon a geography, which would come out in installments in the *Common School Journal*. Long titles were the rage and Mary was right in style, calling her articles for the *Journal* "Letters from a Teacher to Her Young Female Friend Just about commencing to keep school." (This curious use of capital letters was probably the printer's idea, not Mary's!) Of course Mary received no pay beyond the priceless boon of being able to do something for Mr. Mann. She pinned her financial hopes upon sales in book form of the geography, to the common schools — that pot of gold so many were seeking.

Mary's daily work seemed light, her lot a happy one, because she was at last in Boston where she might chance to meet Horace Mann upon the street almost any time — or at the house of a friend.

She almost persuaded herself that she had all she could ask of earthly happiness when Mann began to come often to West Street, his hands full of letters, memoranda covered with figures — all sorts of papers to be worked into his school reports.

First, Horace Mann would stop in the Book Room (which was the family parlor after hours) for a word with Mother Peabody, with whom he was a favorite. It was not everyone who was well received by that formidable lady — for her own son, Nathaniel, who admired her greatly, said that she had "a tinge of aristocratic demeanor," which appeared in marked contrast to the genial democratic character of her husband." Mrs. Peabody took a great interest in politics, was an ardent Whig, and invariably regarded the opposition as "unprincipled." She considered Horace Mann a prophet in Israel and read all his speeches, cutting them out of the newspapers and sending them on to her daughter Sophia Hawthorne after Sophia was married. Mr. Mann always had a bit of news for Mother Peabody, or an anecdote to make her laugh.

But Mary was always prompt to remind her mother that Mr. Mann had come for help with his work. They would soon retire to her schoolroom and Mary would reduce to order all that welter of papers Mr. Mann had brought. Horace Mann was full of ideas for sending out questionnaires to every city and hamlet. How long should children under eight be "confined" in school without a recess — did factory workers who had been to school do better work than illiterates? Only Mary Peabody could have had the patience to sort out the answers Mann received, tabulate the results and put the material into shape. Mary's eyes must have smarted with fatigue many a night. It was hard work, and few people besides Mary would have found it romantic!

Now in 1843, with the school system again under fire because of the election of Marcus Morton, Mann worked with increasing tension. He was forever falling ill; and on March 20, 1843, he spoke of a visit to the Quincys' where he had been cared for and nursed back to health after "a severe cold." Mann was now living at the Hotel Albion,[2] just across Tremont Street from the Tremont House, that hotel he had so greatly admired when it was new. It was the Albion that was new now. It was built of red brick with bastion-like bay windows referred to in newspaper advertisements as "swell-front." Wrought iron ornamented the Albion; it was an apartment hotel for men, and a spot much favored for men's literary gatherings. Doubtless Horace Mann's room was among the less expensive, but he realized that he was fortunately situated. In spite of this, the friendly but paid-for greeting of hotel employees, the room with its comfortable yet impersonal furnishings — all intensified his feeling of homelessness and loneliness. Sundays, alone at the Albion, were Mann's most difficult days.

It was Sunday evening, March 26, 1843, when Horace Mann pulled toward him the now well-filled notebook with its marbleized board covers — the diary which he had begun when he entered upon his crusade for education. The self-conscious tone with which he had begun his diary had long since yielded to a natural style with characteristic touches of humor. But now Mann wrote solemnly again:

"This day of my life, I trust is worthy of the Cretan mark. I have engaged myself to be married to Miss Mary T. Peabody, a lady whose noble & elevated character, whose just & pure sentiments, whose capacities & attainments, & whose unfathomed depth of affection have long since won my admiration & my love."

It is to be hoped that Mann paused and looked over what he had written. Was it really that remarkable collection of virtues that made him love Mary at last — or was it that one thing, her "unfathomed depth of affection" for him? If she had "long since" won his "admiration and love" why had he kept waiting? Mann felt he should explain.

"Circumstances have hitherto rendered it improper that I should avow my secret affection for her, but certain affairs of my life are approaching such a crisis that it could not well be delayed longer without being smothered forever. I have projected a voyage to Europe in company with Dr. Howe & we propose to sail next month. I have felt as tho' it would be too painful to go & leave so lovely a being & one in whom I had such an interest, behind me. The voyage will be of tenfold pleasure & service to us in company; & it will promote my ulterior views which are concentrated upon advancing the great work of education. In this cause, I know the object of my affection will be the greatest help I could possibly have. The range of my acquaintance does not afford such another. In this relation & in my future purposes, I now have high & holy objects in view. God grant that I may wisely pursue & successfully win them all."

Did Mann's proposal to Mary run on exactly those lines? It is to be feared that it did! Mary loved him so dearly that she would have taken him on any terms however and the warmth of her love, now at last avowed, began to work its magic at once. A week later, Mann wrote, "I feel even more secure in the justness of my choice than when it was made. I could view it then prospectively only, — from one side. I now have seen it from both sides and hope is passing into reality."

Mann had not forgotten and never would forget his beloved Charlotte, but for several years his grief for her had been growing less bitter. In 1840, after his trip West, he went to Providence on business and recorded in his diary a visit to North Burying-ground. "Tonight I visited the sacred spot — the grave of my beloved wife. No tears would flow as I called to mind the bereavement which all the world has not charms to solace. Her spirit — where is it? Shall I see & know it again? It was starlight, when I leaned over her grave. Her spirit must be like that starlight peace. Was it like that, shining on me from such a distance — that its power over my feelings was lost?"

Charlotte's starlight spirit still shone upon Horace Mann now, two years later, and he felt a sense of guilt in the midst of his dawning happiness. "My feelings, of course, are not what they once were, indeed it is impossible that the ardor of a first love should ever be rekindled within me."

It was clear that for Mary Peabody this was first love with all its ardor. She went to Salem to see her old friends and tell them of her happiness. This was Sophia's first year of marriage and in Concord with Hawthorne she lived in such a rose-colored atmosphere of happiness that Mary could not help envying her. But now Mary wrote to Sophia more freely than she had done for years. Mary told first of her Salem visit and of Miss Rawlins Pickman, her old friend. "Sister Rawlins rejoiced over me with smiles & tears & blessings — glad that I was happy & sure that I had reason to think myself so. She told me she had often thought of it & hoped that it would be so for she knew my friendship for him and his worth." Mary felt a little guilty because she had never confided her secret love for Horace Mann to this intimate friend. "I told her I had felt as if she thought me wanting in love & gratitude but she said *never* & that if I had had anything of this sort in my mind & kept it to myself & behaved so well, I was a wonder — & so the darling praised me. . . . She gave me the little bank book worth $500.00 and wished it was more." All of Mary's friends seemed not too surprised at the news — though delighted.

"I believe no one is quite astonished but you, lovey, no one that knew Mr. Mann's intimacy with us I mean," Mary told Sophia. "How nicely I dusted the little eyes, Sophy! I would not have had you know that the large joy of knowing and loving him stood so near the large sorrow of apprehension that I should never dwell wholly by his side. . . . I could only bear it because it was *my* sorrow & had never infected anyone else. I do not think I shall ever realize how happy I *know* I am."

Mary was hard at work, during the few weeks at her disposal, to make herself more than ever the ideal wife for Horace Mann. "I have found an intelligent German lady who is to come every day & talk with me all the time." Mr. Mann was also coming for German lessons — since he planned to study schools in Germany — but he must soon have seen that he could safely leave the language to Mary who had studied it for years.

On the day before her wedding, Mary wrote once more to her sister Sophia. "I wonder I have nothing to say to you, but I have held my pen a long time & nothing flows into it or through it out of my full heart. I remember you did not feel the hour of *ratification* to be anything added to your true marriage in Heaven, & I thought I should not, but as it approaches I am overwhelmed with the thought that when that hour is passed there is no escape for *him!* I have been so long presumptuous in thinking I could make him happy. . . ."

Once Horace Mann had known the mingled pain and joy of giving more love than he received. The tables were turned now. He saw it with sorrow and anxiety. "The ardor of love that once filled my youthful mind is indeed no more," he wrote in his diary when his wedding day was set. It would be May Day. On Sunday, April 30, he made his final entry in this, his first diary:

"I have a true & generous heart, to sympathize with, to rest upon; & surely on earth there is no other treasure to be compared to this. Oh Mary, I think you will bless me, I trust I shall bless you."

CHAPTER NINETEEN

Accompanied by His Lady[1]

MAY DAY, 1843, in Boston was the opposite of everything that such a day is supposed to be. It rained heavily during the morning. Seeing the violence of the storm, Sophia Hawthorne gave up her hope of journeying from Concord to the shop in West Street where, in the parlor up one flight, a wedding would take place. Miss Rawlins Pickman, an elderly lady long the affectionate friend of Mary Peabody, gave up her projected trip from Salem to Boston. Miss Lydia Mann decided that Providence was too far from Boston to travel in the rain, and Mrs. Rebecca Mann Pennell felt the same way in regard to Wrentham. The Misses Rebecca and Eliza Pennell, who had promised to come from New Bedford, came not nor sent word. "The pouring rain prevented all guests."

But Elizabeth Peabody was at her sister Mary's wedding, her generous heart full to overflowing because her "dear and brotherly friend" Horace Mann was to be her brother-in-law. Elizabeth wrote descriptions of the wedding for Sophia, for Mrs. Pennell — for almost all the expected guests who failed to appear.

"My sister, Mrs. Mann . . ." Elizabeth wrote, using Mary's new name for the first time on May 1. "This morning at half-past eleven, all things being completed and without hurry, too, the minister said the sacred words. . . . No one was present but my father and mother, myself, my brother and his wife and two children. My sister Mary was dressed in a plain white grassecloth gown without any ornament, and a little piece of embroidery with lace around her neck, the wedding gift of one of her scholars. Round her head was a gold chain band, the gift of Mr. Mann.

"Mr. Mann looked delightfully during the ceremony — so sweet and bright and happy. It was to me the greatest adornment of the wedding to see his face. I am rejoiced for him that the daily, hourly comforts of such a home as I know my Mary can make, is again his; and so rejoiced for her who loves him so dearly and deeply and did for so long love him so disinterestedly, that now it is her duty to make him as happy as she can forever. . . ."

Elizabeth went down to the Cunard dock with the bride and groom and there was time for her to go aboard their ship, the *Britannia*. "Their stateroom is one of the best," she reported, "but it seemed very small. . . . At the foot of each berth was a little cupboard and Mary, being rather short, — put a large satchel containing all her clothes for the voyage at her feet. Under the lower berth, which was Mr. Mann's — were two drawers which she filled with the things most necessary for him." Of course the lower berth was Mr. Mann's and of course all the storage space was his! This was the supreme happiness Mary had longed for, and if her satchel rolled over on her feet in the night she would be glad to lie awake and think about being married at last to the man she had so long loved. Mary finished arranging the cabin "in reference to Mr. Mann's comfort" and came on deck just before the ship sailed.

Mann had been on deck all this time with Dr. Howe and Dr. Howe's beautiful young bride Julia Ward — tiny, red-golden-haired, exquisitely dressed. Julia's sister Annie had come along on the wedding trip, being delicate in health! Dark-haired and pale, Annie was as lovely to look at in her own contrasting way as her sister Julia. Mary would not have been human had she not felt a faint twinge of envy because of the beautiful and wealthy Ward girls of New York.

Horace Mann told the story of the ship's departure. "At 7 minutes past 2 the cable was loosed & we started from the shores of America. The crowd of spectators & friends upon the shore gave us three cheers, which the company of passengers returned. I joined in the first two, but the third stuck in my throat."

Miraculously, the sun had come out after the storm and now happy was the bride the sun shone on. Mary looked at her sister Elizabeth and love for her welled up in her heart. Once she had thought that Elizabeth would be Mrs. Mann and she Mary Peabody forever. "You looked perfectly satisfied," Mary wrote her sister. "I shall think of you with that look very often."

* * *

"As soon as we got below the islands in Boston harbor, we encountered a pretty rough sea," Mann said. The sea "made fun of us all that day & the next. We had dinner at four P.M., Mary being the only live lady in the ship at that time. But she succummed very soon & we retired to our room where we remained until this morning. We are now all out on deck & enjoying ourselves." This was a letter written by Mann to his sister Rebecca and as he dated it May 2, both Mary and her husband had proved themselves good sailors. They gave the credit to Dr. Howe and his special prescription for seasickness. "You must not tell the Tee-to-tallers that we have all drunk brandy all around this morning but we considered ourselves out of the jurisdiction of the American Temperance Society & under the law of Neptune & Nations. So much of my crooked hand as you cannot attribute to my writing in my lap, in a rolling & pitching ship, you may attribute to what you please."

On shipboard, Mann began a new diary [2] — not a notebook this time, but a series of sheets of letter paper which, at intervals, Mary neatly sewed together. This second diary would contain his impressions of all the schools, orphanges, prisons and asylums he was on his way to visit. The new journal would provide the basis for Mann's famous "Seventh Annual Report" but between paragraphs about social conditions were personal observations in a humorous vein. He said no more of his doubts concerning a second marriage but his cheerful rejuvenated spirit spoke for him.

All of Mann's friends urged him to make his European trip a real vacation and a true honeymoon [3] — but he had been given leave of absence from his post to study educational systems abroad and he hung grimly to his purpose. He hoped to bring back a great store of valuable ideas and put them to work in his own country. And everything of which he disapproved would be useful as a warning.

The first schools Mann visited were those of Halifax, and he had little good to report. The new fort at Halifax was costing a great deal too much money, he thought — far too little was being spent on schools.

When the *Britannia* docked in Liverpool most of the passengers made for Chester to see the fine old town with its walls and cathedral — or they hurried to London. Not so the Manns. They visited a Blue Coat School in Liverpool, where they saw "a church service conducted by the boys & girls" in which, Mr. Mann said, "Kneeling seemed to be the *standing order*." They watched the children march to the dining room to receive "a big piece of bread & very little cheese." Next day, at the Blue Coat School, they found the boys "copying down the liturgy by heart." This was Mann's first experience of the functioning of church and state with church-supported schools, and he was by no means pleased.

When the Manns finally set out for London, even the railroad — which Mann admired as being in advance of those in his own country — shocked him from a democratic point of view. "Some part of the passage was very rapid — say 40 miles an hour." And there was "an admirable device by means of longitudinal springs" which prevented "shocks when the cars stop." So much for the credit side. But there were, also, "three classes, the lowest or third class being entirely open — indeed nothing but lumber wagons, & therefore, in the opinion of the community here, good enough for the human lumber which they convey."

After a long search, the Manns and the Howes found lodgings in London at "Number 31 Upper Baker Street." Mary would have been just as well pleased if "Dr. Howe, Lady & her sister" had not been with them — and so doubtless would Dr. Howe's "Lady" — but their husbands made the plans. But Mary "enjoyed highly, pulling everything out of trunks and carpet bags and arranging them in closets and drawers." It was "quite like housekeeping." On May 21, she wrote her sister Elizabeth to tell her of married life, so far. "Today Mr. M & I shut the door of our little dining room & sat down together alone for the first time & it seemed a little bit of a home feeling. The only evil in my lot, thus far, has been this living in public. When I am married to Mr. Mann the next time I will not go on board a steamer immediately but retire into the country for a time where I can cosset him to my heart's content without being looked at. I did cosset him somewhat in spite of the multitude for he needed it and I was so glad to have a legal right to comb his hair and hold his head but I shall not expatiate any more upon this theme. I will only add *when* we are at house-keeping what a pleasant season that will be!

"Do not suppose that I fail to appreciate London town. On Friday afternoon we walked through Regents Park to the Zoological Gardens and there Mrs. Howe and I rode on an elephant! We afterwards saw a caged elephant twice as large as our dobbin."

"The differences of condition here strike me constantly and most painfully," Mary told her sister Elizabeth. They lived "close by Regents Park" and they saw "such splendid mansions and equipages and such squalid misery side by side." Parts of the park were barred to all but "glass coaches" and Mary said that "Mr. Mann boils with indignation and rejoices that he is not an Englishman." Mary did not see all the poverty and misery her husband saw — it would not have been safe for her to go into some of the sections he visited.

Horace Mann and Dr. Howe took "a police officer" with them when they visited the rag market where "sacks & bundles of old clothes were displayed" and "a more deplorable sight than the fetid, squalid wretches" who bought and sold "can hardly be exhibited." They visited the "Jews' quarter . . . what a place to lie in immediate proximity with so much luxury," Mr. Mann exclaimed. And to Billingsgate they went, where Mann saw the "genius of the place" in evil faces around him.

What really touched Mann's heart most deeply was the plight of London's children of the poor. He "saw great numbers of children . . . committed to Bridewell prison . . . children of twelve years of age who had been imprisoned there repeatedly before, & make the heart bleed. There are certain quarters in London, where children are born, educated, trained to go to Bridewell . . . or to be hanged . . . as certainly as poultry are raised to be eaten."

It was at Mary's insistence that she and Horace did a little sightseeing. Mr. Mann, she had discovered, had an "anti-love of the past" which was difficult to overcome, but he permitted himself to admire St. Paul's. They climbed high into the dome, stepped out upon one of the highest outside galleries and saw the vast city of London stretched at their feet. Mann was astonished. "Five New Yorks would not make it!" he exclaimed.

A concert was given at St. Paul's by children from all the Sunday Schools in London, and this, for Mann, was the happiest of his London experiences. Again the Manns climbed into the dome but this time they stayed within it and went no higher than the "Whispering Gallery," where they could look down on row upon row of children seated in stands built for them on the floor of the basilica. There were "said to be 10 or 12 thousand children collected together." As Mann listened to their pure young voices, rising high and clear, amplified by the great dome above them, he found himself thinking of the future — as always. "Had there been a sudden revelation of all future history of that company, who could have borne it? But these musings are useless only as they stimulate one to great exertions for the welfare of the young."

There were social events in which Mrs. Howe with her beautiful New York trousseau very naturally took more interest than did Mary Mann. But Mary went along fairly often. "I wore my velvet Spencer and my white muslin and looked 'very nice,' my beloved said. He even said 'pretty'!" Mary confessed in a letter home. The other women at the "Fancy Ball" for the benefit of the Poles did not fare as well at Mann's hands. He would let the ladies describe the costumes, he wrote, but only "about 20 ladies were beautifully & decently dressed. The money of the others apparently did not hold out, for their dresses arose but just above the waist — all the rest was *common*, — that is as open as the Boston Common." Mann saw even the bosoms of great ladies through Boston eyes.

The Manns left London with little regret and headed north; and now the picture changed and they liked almost everything Scottish — the schools especially. To be sure, Mary had a severe disappointment. She longed to visit Abbotsford, being an ardent admirer of Sir Walter Scott. There was not time, even on a wedding trip! "I would gladly have made the pilgrimage," Mann wrote — "but we are looking to the future rather than the past. . . . I confess it was a sacrifice for which it is not probable that posterity will ever repay me."

But those Scottish schools soon erased all disappointment from Mann's mind — and Mary's too, since she wanted nothing so much as to see her husband happy. Mann described many classroom procedures in detail but it was the spirit of the teachers he most admired — it was "the activity of mind with which the exercises were conducted," on the part of teacher and pupil. "The most active & lively schools in my own country might be regarded as dormitories in comparison with them & both teacher & scholars as hibernating animals just emerging from their torpid state. . . ." In the Scottish schools, the teacher did "not stand immovably fixed to one spot, nor are the bodies of the pupils mere blocks of wood, resting immovably in their seats, but . . . the custom is for each pupil to rise when giving an answer." The children jumped up so quickly and joyfully — the first to rise being given the honor of answering the question — that Mann said there were "exciting scenes." Only one thing troubled him. Prizes were given to the best scholars and Mann felt that this put the children under too great a strain. That each pupil should be ambitious to outdo himself, not his classmates, became one of Mann's firm beliefs.

From Hull across the Channel went the Manns, miserably seasick for forty-eight hours. But Horace Mann admired German school-masters right from the beginning. His mood was happy since he felt sure he was gathering the inspiration he had come to seek, and he allowed himself the relaxation of going outside the city gates one Sunday to see a fair. The crowd reminded him, "in their dress & boisterousness . . . of one of our old muster days. . . . There were persons standing at stalls with all kinds of small wares exposed for sale which they were crying at the top of their voices, — others walking along with such commodities as could be carried in the hand & thrusting them before the eyes of the passers-by. There appeared a little sentry-box by the side of the road for the exhibition of puppets . . . there was a caffe [*sic*] with seats enough within & before the house, to accommodate 500 people. . . . Groups of men & women sipped coffee or some stronger beverage. Hard by was a monkey theatre, a place where the part of Fanny Elsler [4] was performed not only a la monkey but by veritable monkeys themselves. . . . The next group marked the place of a circus go-ing by machinery, that is a circular platform, on the outer edge of which were four *artificial* horses, made to revolve rapidly. . . ." There were shooting contests which Mann watched for a while, but he had seen better at home. The whole thing, "with the excep-tion of the theatres," looked to Mann "more like a militia muster day, before the Temperance movement, than anything else I ever saw." But "these scenes of festivity or carousal were not allowed till after the close of the afternoon churches."

Mary was not at the fair, and how she would have loved to go! She had caught a severe cold in London but she had insisted upon visiting schools with her husband — in sickness and in health. Now she was no longer allowed to tire herself. Mary said nothing of the reason but wrote of her happiness because her husband took such loving care of her.[5] "Instead of being the nurse as I expected, I am the nursee & no old woman who has practiced the art for half a century is equal to my beloved one in this department. I know not whether he is better practically or theoretically, he is so perfect in both. I am learning not to wink a een without his advice." It was sweet to have her husband so tender to her but he was anxious also and Mary assured him that there was nothing to fear — no cause for anything but joy, because they were going to have a child.

One of the pleasures that Mann had looked forward to on this European trip was the meeting once more with Mr. and Mrs. George Combe. He had expected to find them in Scotland but they had gone to the Continent leaving a sheaf of letters of introduction to their friends and many affectionate personal messages. The Manns were to come to Germany and meet them at Baden if not before. "Thrice welcome my very dear and much esteemed friend," Mr. Combe had written. "And thrice again to your wife. Our inmost souls rejoice that you have done this wise thing. . . . But, my dear friend, you have forgotten to tell us who she is; what feminine name she bore before she became a *Mann*." At last in Leipsig, "the happy consummation has taken place," Mary said, "and good, ugly Mr. Combe arrived this morning."

Mr. Combe took one look at the Manns and told them they were not obeying the rules of health laid down in his books. They were working too hard and not resting and enjoying life half enough. If Mr. Mann had "dyspepsia" it was his own fault — and off to Baden went the two families "to take the waters." So famous was the cure that practically every resort called itself a "watering place," but Mr. Mann had little use for the whole idea. It was "trying to drown disease . . . as people drown a woodchuck," he said. A walking trip among the mountains of Saxony, which Mr. Combe next proposed, was much more successful. One could visit schools in every tiny hamlet.

Mann was valiantly trying to learn German these days — so that Mary need not go with him to every school session his enthusiasm led him to attend. Mary had begun the study of German when she was twenty and had published a German translation. She wrote home of Horace Mann's prowess. "You don't know how I talk about my husband right before his face, he not knowing the whole by reason of his ignorance of foreign tongues, & when he talks, I listen & put in a word or a termination when he places it out. He asked for stewed churches at dinner today, instead of stewed cherries. If the inquisition were in existence, who knows what would be his fate, for he once asked for the Lord's Supper, instead of his own, & now proposes to eat churches & all!"

German schools met with Mann's approval everywhere he went and, as in Scotland, he particularly admired the teachers for the enthusiasm they showed in their work — for the lively, cheerful classrooms they maintained. "The teacher does not sit, neither does he stand aloof from his pupils in sullen dignity, but he mingles with them, passing rapidly from one side of the class to another, breathing life into the less active, assuring the timid & distributing encouragement & endearments to all. This mode, of course, prevails where the children are younger but I have seen a teacher clap his hands for joy when a boy of twelve has made a bright answer."

Mann tried to put down, for his own satisfaction, exactly what it was that pleased him so in Scottish and German schools and what was lacking in much of the teaching he had seen in his own country. Naturally, he turned to his law experience for a simile. "Suppose a lawyer in one of our courts were to plead a cause of the most interesting nature, before a jury, but instead of standing & extemporizing, & showing by the energy & ardor of his whole manner that he felt an interest in the theme, instead of rising with the subject & radiating flashes of genius & wit, he should sit himself down in a chair, read from a book which scarcely a member of the panel could understand, & after droning away for an hour, should leave them without coming to any logical conclusion, — would it be any wonder if he left them half asleep, — & would it be any wonder . . . if he lost not only the cause of his client but his own reputation as well!"

By the time the Manns reached Holland they were completing the circle of their intended journey and were turning toward home. They made an afternoon excursion to Leyden, the town where the Pilgrims took refuge before setting sail for America. "I have often been at Plymouth in my native state," Mann wrote in his diary, "& looked out from shore eastward, as it were to see them coming, for freedom's sake, to a strange & inhospitable shore. Here, I looked westward to see them departing & it seemed as though my spirit could follow them on their desolate course. . . . I found in this town no memorial of their residence, no monument marked the spot where they departed, no antiquarian knew the place where they resided." But in fairness, Mann added that the landing-place of the Pilgrims in Plymouth was no better marked. "The spot where they first trod is now ten feet below the surface of the wharf where Commerce plies its occupation." It made no difference whether there were monuments or not, Mann thought, because "the capacity of human improvement, opened throughout this boundless Western world, are monuments & testimonials of their worth."

Horace Mann's spirit was begging to turn westward with the Pilgrims and so was Mary's. Homesickness had dulled even Mann's appetite for visiting schools and he would have liked to sail directly home from Holland. But France was the country where normal schools originated and whence came their name. It would not do to leave for home without going to France, and Mann visited several schools in and around Paris. He was disappointed because the schools seemed stereotyped and the young men students trained in memory alone, with little opportunity for original thinking. Mann spoke only one good word for the school at Versailles — "The buildings . . . were the dog-kennels of Louis 14th & 15th & a Revolution which can turn a dog-kennel into a Normal School has at least one argument in its favor."

It was October now, not a good time to cross the ocean. Mann described his voyages. "We suffered from Dieppe to Brighton, from Milford Haven to Waterford, from Dublin to Liverpool & from Liverpool to Boston . . . the worst passages that have been experienced since St. Paul's shipwreck." And Mary, telling her side of it — "Mr. M. has suffered much & I more than usual & how we long for Boston Harbour no words can by any magic express, magical as words constantly are. Right glad are we that America, with all its youthful faults, is our native land."

Horace Mann found lodgings on Bowdoin Square in Boston and went to work at once on his Seventh Annual Report. Mary worked by his side, translating the many German books and pamphlets they had brought home. The Seventh Annual Report must be ready on time, and Mary seemed to think that the child she was expecting would await this more inportant event. She made a few plans, however, as her sister Sophia found out.

Dating her letter February 11, 1844, Sophia Hawthorne said:

"Mary Mann wrote me the other day that she was all ready for her confinement. Her loving friends in Boston have done all her baby's sewing. One took the little robes, another all the flannels, and another . . ." Here Sophia subsequently blacked out some indelicate words! Sophia said she was worried about Mary, "for she is so busy with the Report."

The Seventh Annual Report was presented to the legislature on January 17, 1844. At the end of February, Horace Mann started a new and special diary. This time he chose no simple schoolboy's copybook nor loose sheets of paper, but a handsome leather-bound volume.[6] He headed the first page "BOSTON, BOWDOIN SQ. (the old Coolidge House, so-called) *February 28, 1844.*

"Yesterday at ½ past 10 o'clock P.M. a male child was born to me. Another Spirit was ushered into being; another unit added to the countless host of existences. As yet, not a day has passed, & yet his journey is for eternity. So helpless now, but with an undeveloped wing that will soar thro' immensity . . . whether it shall soar or sink, whether it shall rejoice or mourn, — oh how much of this depends upon the guidance which he will receive, before his own will takes any part in directing his conduct! What a responsibility!

"His mother's sufferings were fearful. Does any child ever think of this as one of the bonds of filial attachment, some of the motives of filial duty? I fear not, at least until it is too late.

"Let God be thanked that the child is perfect, in its physical conformation. . . . The child is of good size & seems very healthy & well. . . . As yet, in anticipating the future, I feel nothing but a trembling joy. Hope and Fear are competitors in weaving bright & dark threads into the web."

A few days passed and Mann wrote, "Almost every person whom I meet, congratulates me on the event of his birth. It is with very melancholy feelings that I rejoin. I cannot but think a thousand times more of the responsibilities of training than of the pleasures of having a child. So deeply am I impressed with this sense of responsibility, that I can hardly dare to be glad."

The child's name was Horace but his father had yet to call him by it. The baby was nevertheless making his way straight into his father's heart. "Tonight it is just a fortnight, since my boy was born. I find myself more & more interested in him, my feelings more & more alive to his welfare, to his fortune — his future unknown fortune. Considering my own age and his [Mann was almost forty-eight, Mary thirty-eight] it is hardly probable that I shall see him through his period of minority. He may be left fatherless, as I was, at the age of thirteen or younger. . . . Still more necessary is it, then, that . . . he be conducted into the right path."

In spite of himself, Mann began to enjoy his child and to realize what a family can mean in terms of human happiness. "Henceforth our happiness & his, while we all live, must be to a great extent bound up together. There is no such thing as earthly happiness for one that is not for all." And at last, in July, Mann wrote lightly and humorously. "Today, the little boy found his feet & was in raptures at the discovery. The only trouble was, they were a little too far off. By much twisting & turning, he succeeded, in the common phrase, in making *the two ends meet*." During that same month, Mann added to the story of his son. "His most prominent trait is an ecstasy of laughter into which he is sent by a kind of loving look or smile. I cannot look in his face but . . . he bursts into what is commonly called a horse-laugh; — his however, can be nothing more than a colt laugh."

The pressure of work continued as heavy as ever upon Horace Mann and he could not spare the time to continue long entries in the diary of his first-born. His "interest" increased, however — which was his way of saying that he loved the child! In January 1845 it was "my dear boy" — now almost a year old, who had been "ill of a sudden & severe cold" which was followed by "a violent humor" — apparently an allergy. "There is something dreadful in the sufferings of an infant, their innocence, & their incapacity to describe . . . their wants, excites a tenderness for them, which makes our pain as great, if not greater than their own."

The diary was intended as a record of young Horace, but Mann paused to comment on Mary, the mother of his son. Truly she "lived to bless" him beyond all his hopes. "I am sorry to say that the temper of the boy is sometimes irritable or fractious; but his mother's gentleness & patience are inexhaustible. She bears whatever comes & uses the softest words to smooth down his excitement. Such a store-house of love as is laid up in her heart is to me a daily marvel."

In January 1846 Horace Mann made a new and important entry in his journal. "On December 27, 1846 [so he wrote but should have said 1845], at about ½ past one o'clock in the morning, my dear wife produced another son. It was a fearful scene, tho' far less severe than at the birth of the first. The pain was mitigated by joy at the birth of a child & by affection for it. My sympathy for the mother, after the hour of peril was over, passed into anxiety for the offspring. Another son! It is wholly impossible for me to express the emotions which fill my mind in contemplating this fact. I have not philogenitiveness very large, & therefore my mind turns to duties and responsibilities, far more than to pleasure. . . . What may he be! . . . There is not one chance in a hundred that I shall live till he arrives at years of discretion. . . . God grant that his mother may live to guide his footsteps along the paths of early life."

Mann decided not to attempt a journal of the new little son — who was named George Combe Mann in honor of Mann's dear friend Mr. Combe of Scotland. Mann "obtained a book for his mother" to "record his development from time to time." Said Horace Mann, "we shall preserve an enduring record" in this way — but if Mary ever found time while taking care of two babies to keep a journal the book has since disappeared!

Meanwhile Mann viewed little Horace (aged two) with alarm. "Generally speaking, he has been willing to obey . . . but with this obedience, there has arisen in his mind, the idea of doing prohibited things. For instance, if he wants to open a box & scatter around the contents, he will carry it round behind our chairs. . . . This is a very serious matter. Here is the game of deception & the laying of a plan to make the deception successful. How should this be overcome? . . . Such a habit would lead onward to dishonesty, from which may heaven save him."

Could Nathanael Emmons have been right about children being born with the seeds of evil — ever since the fall of Adam? Horace Mann had spent a lifetime refuting such a theory and here was little Horace originally sinful! Fortunately Horace found more favor in his father's eyes as he grew older. "This is my little boy's birthday. He is three years old," Horace Mann wrote. "He has given me much more satisfaction this year than he did last. He behaves better. His paroxysms of passion are far less violent. . . . I believe he had originally a temperament & a disposition which might easily have become hostile to his own happiness. . . . But great care has given him fine health & with it has come cheerfulness & joy & kind, steady

& firm treatment has softened his passions & developed his affections. He is full of affection & social feeling. He loves approval. . . . His great sensibility runs into irritability, but seems to be an affection of the nerves, in part at least."

It seems not to have occurred to Horace Mann that his little son was the image of himself!

CHAPTER TWENTY

Owls in the Sun

MANN was proud of his Seventh Annual Report, and it turned out to be famous — but not for the reasons he would have chosen. In April 1844, "My report, generally speaking, has met with unusual favor," he wrote George Combe, "but there are owls who, to adapt the world to their own eyesight, would keep the sun from shining. . . .

"Most teachers have been activated to greater exertions by the account of the best schools abroad," Mann continued. "Others are offended at being driven out of the Paradise which their own self-esteem erected for them."

Thirty-one exiles from Paradise were even then preparing a most vicious attack upon Horace Mann. These were "the Boston School Masters," determined to discredit Mann and throw him out of office before he exposed their methods. "The flogging in the Boston schools, as everybody now knows and as few will deny, had been atrocious," Mann charged. The Masters would never be able to deny it.

The "Principals' Association" sponsored the attack and published a pamphlet. In a private letter to Theodore Parker, Mann called the group "this association — alias *Club* for eating & drinking & telling bawdy stories." He fought the School Masters as he would have fought criminals brought into court against his client, and there were those who claimed that his words were too hard, his wit too caustic. But now Mann's client was the next generation, and how could any weapons be too keen for its defense?

Mann's "Reply" was neither unfair nor vindictive. "Last month a pamphlet appeared, entitled 'Remarks on the Seventh Annual

Report of the Hon. Horace Mann, Secretary of the Massachusetts Board of Education.' I have read the production with astonishment and grief. It introduces my name more times than there are pages, in connection with sentiments that I never felt, and expressions I never uttered." Mann had been accused of "disparaging" the Massachusetts schools and of being hostile to teachers. These foolish generalizations he immediately disposed of. "On schools and teachers I rely, more than on any other instrumentality, for the prosperity and honor of the State, and for the reformation and advancement of the race," Mann said. He defined his attitude toward teachers. "I have sought to elevate their standing and rank in the community, to cluster noble associations around their sacred calling."

Mann's "Reply" was published in a pamphlet of 176 pages which make good reading today. He took up many of the technical problems of teaching. The School Masters attacked a certain primer! It was obvious that they objected because the author was Mrs. Mann. She had been Miss Mary Peabody at the time the book was written, a point the Masters did not bring out — but Mann defended his theories on the teaching of reading without rancor.

The writing of the "Reply" cost Mann much nervous energy, however. No sooner did his head touch the pillow at night than new and better arguments flashed through his mind and he rose to jot them down. Old letters, bits of scrap paper, were covered with scribbled notes. Writing to his friend Dr. Jarvis, Mann said, "Can you do anything for a brain that has not slept for three weeks? I can feel the flame in the center of my cranium, blazing & flaring round, just as you see that of a pile of brush burning on a distant heath in the wind. What can be done to extinguish it?"

It did not quiet Mann's nerves to have his old enemy, Edward A. Newton, again in the field against him. Mann had been severe with the British because he had seen the children of the poor in common schools, "filthy in the extreme," while the sons of nobility enjoyed fine buildings. And Mann objected to the requirement that the Church of England catechism be taught to all British school children. Newton wrote an anonymous article for the *Christian Witness and Church Advocate*, denouncing Mann.

Girard College had recently been established as a school for orphan boys with the proviso in the will of Stephen Girard that no religion be taught and no clergyman be allowed within its gates!

Relatives who had hoped to inherit Mr. Girard's large fortune hired Daniel Webster to try to break the will — and the whole country was talking about the case. Mr. Newton, borrowing some of Daniel Webster's eloquence, wanted to know "how our Board of Education, or rather its Secretary, differs from . . . Mr. Girard" who "laid the axe at the root of Christianity itself while pretending to lop off the branches of sectarianism."

"The 'Christian,' commonly called 'False Witness' is out upon me again," said Horace Mann when a second article appeared. "Newton, knowing that he is known, has signed his initials this time." Mann asked his friends Howe and Dwight whether or not to answer these attacks and "what is best to do with these men who . . . serve God as tho' the devil were in them?"

Mann's friends thought he had better do nothing. But another article came out and Mann prepared a reply. "Being thrice called, I appear. . . . Though you deny me the character of a Christian, I shall endeavor to speak as one." He pointed out that while it was illegal for children to receive sectarian teaching in the Common Schools, it was required by law that they be taught "a sacred regard to truth, love to country . . . industry and frugality." About all Newton could think of to say in return was that Mann was "a political Jesuit"!

The School Masters' controversy raged all through 1844, with a "Rejoinder to the Reply" written by the Masters, followed by "Penitential Tears, a Cry from the Dust by the 'Thirty-one'" — a long, heavily sarcastic opus. But two of the original signers of the attack upon Mann repudiated their stand, and the remaining twenty-nine fought a losing battle.

The religious controversy died down, only to flare up again in 1847, when "a child of sin and Satan came out in a fierce . . . attack upon the Board . . . and myself," Mann said. This was the Reverend Matthew Hale Smith, preaching at the Church of the Pilgrims in Boston, from the text, "And they set the Ark of God upon a new cart." Smith attracted such a crowd that he repeated his sermon a second time to a full house and published the inevitable pamphlet. Starting with the premise that all men are sinners, Smith first went to work on Boston in general where "Sabbath desecration" was more and "more bold" with "newspapers now thrown with great impertinence into the doors of Christian people" on Sunday.

After warming up through "fourthly," Mr. Smith came to grips with the cause of Boston's sinfulness. "Modern reformers have taken the education of youth under their special care. . . . Throwing themselves across the word of God, they ridicule as well as forbid the use of the rod." The Reverend Mr. Smith made it clear that the Board of Education had put the Ark of God on its new cart, that Horace Mann had laid his hand upon it to steady it as Uzzah had done — and ought to be struck dead like Uzzah!

Matthew Hale Smith dealt with sectarianism in the schools of course, his idea being that his beliefs were the right ones and that all who held other views were "made liable to the pains of hell forever." There were replies in the press, some of them suggesting that it was Mr. Smith who should take the part of Uzzah.

Mann's answer was humorous! "Suppose they do have sectarian teaching in the schools," he proposed. Suppose the state should rescind the law "and local schoolboards . . . should decide from year to year, and depending on their personal preferences, what religion should be taught in the schools! One sect may have the ascendency today; another tomorrow. This year there will be three Persons in the Godhead; next year, but One. . . . This year the everlasting fires of hell will burn to terrify the impenitent; next year, and without any repentence, the eternal flames will be rekindled forever, or quenched forever — as it may be decided in town meeting! This year the ordinance of baptism will be inefficacious without immersion; next year one drop of water will be as good as forty fathoms. Children attending district school will be taught one way; going from district school to high school they will be taught another. . . . Will not fiery zealots move from place to place to turn the theological scale, as it is . . . sometimes done now to turn the political one?"

It was all in fun but Matthew Hale Smith did not think it was funny. This, however, was the last of the "Common School Controversies." As always, jealous, vindictive attacks brought friends to Mann's side, but he was injured none the less — by becoming oversensitive to criticism. Teachers who worked under him often found him hard to please, so anxious was he that every part of his school system should be above reproach. Every move he made was under scrutiny, and well he knew it.

When Cyrus Peirce was forced to resign from Lexington because of ill health, the choice of a successor was of great importance. The Reverend Samuel J. May, brother-in-law of Bronson Alcott, was decided upon; but Mann had grave misgivings. Mr. May was an ardent abolitionist and the cause of antislavery was by no means popular in Boston at this time. Bringing out the fact that the school system was continually under fire, Mann exacted a promise from Mr. May that, while May was Normal School Principal, he would suspend all antislavery activities. Everything went well, but in 1844 — while the School Masters were raising their furor against Mann — the Reverend Mr. May forgot his promise. An antislavery meeting was held near Lexington and he attended, taking with him several of his pupils!

An irate parent arrived from Boston to remove his daughter from a school where she was exposed to such wicked propaganda. Mr. Mann wrote the Reverend Mr. May a sharp letter to which May replied, mildly, defending himself. After all, he had not *spoken* at the meeting! But May resigned in September 1844. He did not like teaching very well and he could not, with a clear conscience, give up antislavery. Mann sincerely admired May, and they parted friends, although some fairly frank remarks had been exchanged.

The town of Lexington was now in arrears in its promised support of the normal school and Mann learned that the "Fuller Academy" in West Newton could be bought for fifteen hundred dollars although said to be worth "almost thirty thousand." Josiah Quincy, Jr., told how Mann rushed to his office in Boston and said, " 'Quincy, do you know of anyone who wants the highest seat in Heaven, — for it is to be bought for $1500.' " Instead of making a donation for the school, Quincy gave Horace Mann the money personally and told him to buy the West Newton academy in his own name if that was what he wanted. He refused to allow Mann to tell of the gift although Mann begged to publicize this generosity.

The town of Newton contributed six hundred dollars toward renovating the old academy, with its Greek revival columns, its high square-paned windows. Mann asked the Board of Education for an additional five hundred, which was reluctantly granted, and Cyrus Peirce, still far from well but able to teach again, took over the task of remodeling the school. Once or twice, Peirce wrote to Mann anxiously. The new ventilating system would prove expensive — was it all right to go ahead? And it seemed as if they would have to install two furnaces to take the place of the cast-iron stoves and heat the drafty old building properly. Mann came out to Newton and approved all Peirce's ideas. Then Peirce sent in the bills and the total was $2396.66. "This is more than twice what we expected it would cost," Peirce wrote. "Yet I know not where there has been any extravagance."

Mann knew that what Peirce said was true but he was nervously exhausted and he had no idea where to turn for money. He wrote hastily and angrily. "I confess I do not see what can be done. I have not examined the bills as to prices . . . but is not $2.00 a day for labor extravagant? I also saw a charge for trees. . . . The whole strikes me as a very serious matter, and I have not been so alarmed about anything this long time."

Cyrus Peirce was heartbroken. He had worked for nothing along-side his two-dollar-a-day workmen, as carpenter, painter and even tinsmith! In an excess of pride, he borrowed the money and de-clared he would pay the whole deficit himself. Mann also borrowed money and in the end each of them paid half the amount due.

When the Lexington normal school was fitted up, Mann had sold his law library in order to make the boardinghouse for the students more comfortable. These were the lawbooks which he had bought in Charlotte's memory from the proceeds of their furniture in his first home. Now that the Lexington school was being given up, Samuel May, who had stayed on to help in the work, wrote to Mann: "I apprehend all the clothespresses put up at your expense at the Normal House will be accounted fixtures and claimed by the owner. I have not yet made any attempt to sell the furniture be-cause, if sold apart from the building, it must be sold at great sacri-fice." Eventually, a small sum came back to Mann which he put into the West Newton school — but it was hard to see this particular fund diminishing.

Mann's moods of sadness were often replaced by moods of elation, however — and with good reason. In 1845, for example, and as a direct result of the School Masters' attacks upon him, a group of Horace Mann's friends banded together to honor him in the way that would please him best. The names of the thirty-one who at-tacked Mann were soon forgotten but the names of those who rallied to his side are still illustrious: Longfellow, Howe, Sumner — the list was long. It was Charles Sumner who wrote the "memorial o the legislature" asking for five thousand dollars for permanent normal school buildings at Bridgewater and Westfield. Sumner promised to match the amount with private subscriptions and the money was granted. The letter announcing the grant and the donation was written by Sumner and it expressed the gratitude of Massachusetts o Mann for his education crusade. Mary Mann, writing to her sister Sophia, said, "My husband did weep sweet tears and wished his mother were still alive to read the letter." Mann immediately ordered work to begin on the two schools, but mindful of the West Newton experience, he warned that strict economy must be the watchword.

With renewed faith, Horace Mann set about making 1845 even more "auspicious" for education. It was time to give up his annual missionary journeys from one end of the state to the other, he felt. He must find some new means of awakening the public, and he began to hold "Teachers' Institutes" — a sort of extension normal school. Mann's letters to a young Unitarian minister, the Reverend Mr. Edmund B. Willson of Grafton,[1] describe the system. Mann began the correspondence by asking if Mr. Willson could "give reasonable assurance" that "not less than seventy of Common School teachers" would be willing to "assemble" in Grafton and stay there "not less than ten working days." They would need "schoolroom accommodations & board for members."

The Reverend Mr. Willson was delighted with the idea but he was not certain that as many as seventy teachers would come. However, Mr. Mann felt that "the Southern half of Worcester County" must be reached because "the statistical returns . . . do not show a very satisfactory state of public schools." He explained that the "doors of the schoolroom will be open at all times to all people, — *who behave well*" and "the people in the neighborhood should attend that their interest in the schools may be increased." The end of September was selected as the time for the Institute, and the lecturers were chosen not only with reference to their teaching ability but also with reference to their church affiliation. Three out of four were to be orthodox and then there would be no "jealousy" if Mr. Willson (though Unitarian) addressed the group, not as a lecturer, but informally.

The young minister (still in his early twenties) put his heart into the project but response was meager. Mr. Mann's letter of encouragement shows not only his method but the reason why, if he had a few enemies, he also had many friends. "I have rec'd your *desponding* missive of yesterday. I see you are sensitive; you have not got case-hardened yet; you have not been rebuffed & neglected & seen any mountebank & hand-organist, & monkey-show & military company running away with your audiences. I have been accustomed for years to yield precedence to every puppet-exhibition or hurdy-gurdy mendicant. But I always transmute this discouragement into encouragement. . . . If you cannot get seventy teachers together at a Teachers' Institute in the great county of Worcester, I know you will work the harder for the cause of Common Schools as long as you live. . . . I have infinite faith. It is part of my religion to believe in the ultimate success & triumph of the cause."

It is not surprising that the Reverend Mr. Willson worked for the cause of education all his life, serving on school committees in Grafton and later in Salem. Mann's last letter to him in 1845 suggested that he visit the normal school at West Newton and perhaps he would feel moved to influence some "young ladies" of his parish to go there.

Horace Mann, taking his own advice and visiting the West Newton school often, was charmed by the pretty little country town where the school was located. He hated to see his boys cooped-up in the city all winter and obliged, during the summer, either to board in Concord or go to Wrentham where the house he had given his sister was by no means big enough to hold two families. In May 1846 Mann wrote to his faithful friend Cyrus Peirce: "What should you think of my coming out to W. Newton & trying to make a home there? I have so much a notion of it, that I wish you would see what the price of an acre of land would be, up on the hill. . . ."

To this, Peirce replied, "There is land enough on the hill for house sites, to be had for money enough, — from 400 to 1000.00 per acre. Mr. Mead has a beautiful grove of 2½ acres on the hill . . . which he offers for sale at 950.00 for the whole lot. It would make two fine building sites." Mann had no idea of paying such a price but he came to see the land and fell in love with it. The railroad had reached West Newton; prices were rising, and he could sell off the second house site and make a profit, Mann told himself. In any case, he must have it.

The house, when the plans were completed, was everything Mann wanted — with wide verandas from which to enjoy the view over the valley; with that wonderful new contrivance a furnace, and with — of all things most modern — a "bathing room," where water could be pumped into a tub instead of being carried there by the pitcherful! "I employed a trusty man to buy all my materials & build the house at days' work, paying him good wages," Mann said. "Not an unsound timber or bad brick went into it. During the time a great part of it was going up, I lived at Mrs. Lamb's on the hill, almost within a stone's-throw . . . & used to visit it twice every day. It was worth a third or a quarter more than a common-built house." [2]

But the garden was even more after Mann's heart than his house! Leaving a grove at the back, he cleared the land in front and at the side and had an orchard planted. There were "10 Roxbury Russet apple trees, 45 Baldwins, 4 Rhode Island Greenings, 2 Porter apple trees, one Gravenstein, one Benoni and one Red Astrakan." There were plum trees too, and a strawberry bed which it would be Mary's delight to cultivate, teaching her little boys to work by her side. Eventually there would be "2 horse posts" and stone posts for the two gates and the fence which surrounded the property to keep out the neighbors' cows. A summerhouse and trellis were built and painted — all with the loving care that people bestow upon a home of their own.

"We came into the house on Christmas eve, & who had a happier one?" Mary wrote to her sister Sophia. "We did not envy the shining halls of the city, for there was a feeling of permanence, of stability, in short of being settled that was inexpressibly satisfactory. Our life, hitherto, has been like that steamboat voyage — a toss here & a toss there, & my poor husband bearing the inconveniences like a saint, — never having a really comfortable moment to himself. . . .

"You must not think because we have built this beautiful house, dear, that we are rich or independent in it. A kind friend has lent Mr. Mann the money to build it, & although it has cost a great deal more than he expected, the place is so beautiful, & the locality now rising so much in value, that there is no doubt it will sell for more, should such an emergency come. It is not yet paid for & that must come out of the future. It has cost my husband some sleepless nights because it cost so much . . . & because he feels anxious that it should be *mine*, as he is pleased to say. But I had rather sell it now

& go back to lodgings than have him sleep the less . . . on my account."

The "kind friend" was James K. Mills and, judging by the receipted notes which Mann left among his papers, the loan was for four thousand dollars. John Meade, owner of the land, received five hundred and fifty dollars and a promise of four hundred dollars in one year. David B. Bartlett, builder, received $4,031.50 through January, 1847. These were all modest sums to pay for a home and land but Mann's salary had never been anything but nominal. He added to his income by lecturing, but many lectures were given free and his time in which to travel for the Lyceum was limited. Mary worked miracles of economy. Occasionally, it troubled her husband that she should give drawing lessons or organize a small class in French conversation. But Mary held that a woman of ability would be positively sinful if she did not put her brains to work for the benefit of her family. Bills for such items as "one pair of small shoes for your son" could be paid by a mother as well as by a father.

Besides her other projects, Mary was of course teaching little Horace because his father wanted to see certain theories put into practice. It was a disappointment to Mann when, at the age of three, Horace made slow progress in learning to write. "He prefers," said his father, "both on the blackboard & on the slate, to make random, unmeaning strokes or marks which we call 'nonsense marks.' " When remonstrated with, little Horace proved "very excitable." But he had "made some progress in reading which is taught by the phonetic method."

The new home in West Newton opened its hospitable door to visitors from other states and from other lands as Horace Mann's words and writings inspired others to enroll in the education crusade. One of the most brilliant and interesting of these visitors was Domingo Faustino Sarmiento,[3] afterwards known as the "Schoolmaster President of the Argentine Republic."

Mary Mann acted as interpreter for Mr. Sarmiento and her husband as they sat together in that study described by Sophia Hawthorne as "elegant." Mr. Sarmiento spoke English[4] quite well but was not until later that he admitted this, and only later did he discover that Mrs. Mann spoke Spanish. The two of them spoke French, which Mary translated into English, hour after hour during a visit lasting two days. Mr. Sarmiento was entranced when they all walked down to the Normal School together. Later, he wrote, "I saw, not without astonishment, women who had paid tuition fees to study mathematics, chemistry, botany and anatomy to round out their education. They were poor young women who had had to borrow money for their instruction, undertaking to repay it as soon as they were placed as teachers. . . ." Mr. Sarmiento was further astonished. On looking over figures he discovered that "the number of school-teachers in this state is greater than the entire standing army of Chile."

Domingo Sarmiento knew a thing or two about being poor. He was the son of impoverished Argentine landowners and his mother had set up a primitive loom under a spreading fig tree where she wove cloth which she sold to monasteries for monks' habits — till she had enough money to build a house. Sarmiento went to a village school — his uncle, a curate, taught him Latin. While clerking in a store, Sarmiento got hold of a life of Benjamin Franklin and, inspired by the story of the struggle for freedom in the United States, he joined the forces against Rosas, Dictator of the Argentine Federation. This landed him in jail, where he learned French! Later, as an exile in Chile, he worked in a mine and spent a few of his coppers for lessons in English. Chile became Sarmiento's adopted country, he became an editor, a teacher — and in 1842 he established the first normal school in South America. No wonder he was delighted to visit the first North American normal school!

The Chilean government sent Sarmiento to Europe to study education and in England an account of Horace Mann's journey "starting from the North of America precisely on the same errand" ultimately led this dynamic gentleman to the door of Mann's "humble residence."

Sarmiento arrived first in Boston, where "the public schools . . . are veritable temples in the magnificence of their architecture and every person pays $1.00 a year to educate his fellow-creatures' children. . . ." Even this was not enough to satisfy Mr. Sarmiento, however. "The chief object of my visit was to see Mr. Horace Mann . . . the great reformer of elementary education. . . . As he lived outside of Boston, I had to go by train to East Newton, the little village where his home is."

It made no difference if Mr. Sarmiento had his points of the compass a little mixed. He found what he came for. Horace Mann gave him copies of the *Common School Journal*, the school abstracts, as well as a collection of his speeches to public meetings and his valuable oral instructions.

And eighteen years later, Domingo Sarmiento would add, "I have done nothing but to follow his steps, taking as a model his great labors. . . . My safest guide, I found it, in the digest of laws and ordinances regulating that beautiful system of schools."

This foreign visitor and many other visitors left the Manns' "humble residence" full of gratitude and admiration for Horace Mann. These were happy years — even though Mann gave his enemies battle with more of his strength than they deserved.

One specter haunted Mann's pillow on sleepless nights — just as Mary knew it would. This was the problem of making money enough to support the home that was to him not humble but dearly loved. And there was the problem of educating the boys — when they finally learned to read and write!

Mann was still helping his nieces and nephews with their education, begrudging nothing so long as they were willing to become teachers. Young Thomas Mann alone proved a reluctant student.

In January 1846 Thomas was in Cabotsville in school, under the supervision of his cousin, Calvin Pennell. "I find Calvin the same person he used to be only much more," Thomas told his uncle frankly. "He does not think I had better take any recess . . . he does not think it best for me to form any acquaintances in this place."

By March, when the term ended, Thomas had made up his mind. He would leave school and learn to be a jeweler. His uncle wrote in dismay, even though young Thomas's decision lightened Horace Mann's load. And why *jeweler*, of all frivolous things? Why not machinist or carpenter, if trade it must be?

"In your letter, you asked me if this idea I had about being a jeweler was one of my own originating or had it been put into my head by some other person," Thomas replied. The idea was his own, he said, and he stuck to his guns although it was some time before he got a job.

Aunt Lydia voiced family sentiment when she wrote to Horace Mann. "I would inform you that Tho⁵ has at last got to work in jewelry, if trinkets made of copper deserve that appellation. He is at the Falls here, in A. [Attleboro, Massachusetts] & it is said with a very good man, but I cannot conceive of a man of sound moral principles . . . making articles of copper, with the supposition that they will eventually pass into poor, silly girls' hands, as gold."

In spite of family foreboding, young Thomas did very well. He eventually married the prettiest girl in town [5] — who happened to be the boss's daughter. The shop became a factory, and Thomas Mann succeeded where his father had failed. . . . All this was still far in the future, however. Horace Mann was anxious now, lest he had not done enough for his brother's child.

On February 25, 1848, the bells in Boston tolled from twelve noon till one o'clock. Flags of all shipping in the Harbor were at half mast. John Quincy Adams was dead. He had been a member of Congress at the end of his long career of public service, and he was in his seat in the House of Representatives on February twenty-first. He responded to roll call, but almost immediately afterwards suffered a stroke and died on the twenty-third without regaining consciousness. Horace Mann mourned the loss of a personal friend. He did not realize that the death of John Quincy Adams would affect his own career.

CHAPTER TWENTY-ONE

Mann of Massachusetts

THE Commonwealth of Massachusetts must now find a representative to fill the vacancy in Congress left by the death of John Quincy Adams. The *Boston Daily Advertiser* suggested Charles F. Adams, son of John Quincy Adams, or William Jackson, or Theodore Lyman. In all, eight names occurred to them but only in a sort of postscript at the bottom of the page did they add, "A correspondent suggests to us the name of Horace Mann." They seemed to think little of the idea.

By early March, however, Horace Mann had been hearing from friends, and in reply to one of them he wrote: "If you were not a sober man, I should in this case be a little waggish. . . . To ask anybody in this district to fill Mr. Adams's place is a good deal like asking a mouse to fill an elephant's skin. . . . To the question whether I would be a candidate for the vacancy, how can I with propriety say 'no' till some responsible body has made an offer, & how can I say 'yes' before I am asked? . . . I do not see that I can do more than say that, were such a proposition made to me . . . I should give the subject the consideration which its importance deserves."

The formal offer was made and there were two reasons why Mann found himself seriously considering it. First and foremost in his mind was his education crusade. He wanted to improve the common schools throughout the nation and where but in Washington could he put such a plan in motion? Already, countless letters had come to him from all over the country, asking for help in starting new state-wide school systems. If Mann could become national Secretary of Education, he could hope to do, for the country as a whole, as much or more than he had done for Massachusetts.

Mann's second reason for considering a place in Congress was financial. His personal finances were in a critical condition and he could not afford to continue to underwrite so many Massachusetts projects. The Bridgewater normal school building, for example, had cost seven hundred dollars more than the state provided. "An individual in the town of Bridgewater had paid a hundred dollars and Mr. Mann the residue." An old academy building had been found in Westfield, so Westfield had been chosen instead of Springfield as the site for the transplanted Barre school. But Westfield Normal School was completed with the same story of deficit. After canvassing "Dwight and each of the three Lawrences and one or two of the Appletons" Mann found that "not one of them would give a cent." He had asked such faithful contributors as Quincy and had received all they could spare him. "I had to become personally responsible for the whole," he said (or a total of about two thousand dollars). No wonder he told Cyrus Peirce, "I live by tapping my own veins and sucking my own blood."

If this had been all, Mann might have been able to go on. But there was another force almost as important to education as the normal schools, and that was the educational publications. Financial clouds [1] had been gathering for some time over the firm of Marsh, Capen, Lyon and Webb, who published the school library in 1840. The firm was dissolved and Mann lent money to Nahum Capen, taking a second mortgage on Capen's Dorchester estate. The firm became Capen and Fowle — but failed, and Fowle took over. To follow the Fowle correspondence with Horace Mann is heartbreaking. At first, William B. Fowle said he only needed Mann's name on a few notes — he was temporarily embarrassed but would have plenty of cash in a few days. Mann signed for five hundred dollars and then for another five hundred with Fowle full of promises but always short of cash. Fowle approached Dr. Howe, who refused to be "bondsman" and warned Horace Mann. "I cannot refrain from saying to you — what you will not relish — that neither you nor I should take any part in Fowle's publishing business."

"But I cannot let such a man as Fowle go down," was Mann's reply, and the date of this correspondence was 1846 — the year Horace Mann was building a home. By 1848, Mann was painfully aware that something must be done to ease the strain on his credit. There was one more urgent need for money in the near future. Mann tried to conceal his financial worries from Mary — for she was again expecting a child. This time, she said, she would surely have a little girl "to comb your hair and kiss you dearly."

Horace Mann accepted the invitation of the Whigs when it was formally made, and on March 16, 1848, Josiah Quincy wrote: "My dear friend, I cannot refrain from expressing the gratification I felt in seeing your name at the head of the list as the Whig candidate to fill the place of John Quincy Adams in the House of Representatives. I am gratified, not only on your account but on that of the public, on account of every child that now is, or that for centuries will be." Mann was elected by a majority of 904 votes.

But Mann himself was not sure he had made the right decision. He arrived in Washington the second week in April, "in a state of collapse," he said. He "felt miserably about this whole change." But of one thing he felt certain: "The Common School cause in Massachusetts" was " 'consolidated' " so that "nothing could overturn it."

As Mann walked toward the nation's capitol on April 13, 1848, to "take his oath of office and his seat," he must have remembered another day, twenty-one years earlier, when he had first presented himself at the State House in Boston. The building which he now approached was larger but it had an uncompleted dome. A partially finished colonnade rose above the middle portion like a broken crown, while the columns that were to grace a portico lay strewn in sections on the grass. The capitol looked more like an ancient ruin than like a classical rebirth, and Mann was to find the disunion within more appalling even than the chaos without.

But spring was in the air. "Peach trees are in full bloom," Mann said, "& the grounds around the capitol are as green as ever Boston Common was." As he took this new oath of office, his heart was stirred, almost as it had been twenty-one years ago in the springtime of his life.

Below the capitol, the city of Washington sprawled in half-reclaimed marshland knee-deep in mud all winter and in summer choking with yellow dust. Mann found lodgings "in very good quarters, — two rooms, a beautiful western aspect away from the dust & noise of Penn. Ave., & within three minutes' walk of the capitol."

Now he began a series of daily letters to Mary, his "Dearest" and "Ever Dearest." Often he would have time for only a line or two; the mails would be delayed and Mary might not hear for several days, but she could depend on it — the letters were on the way. And Mary, in return, would write of all that went on at home, what the children did and said — but most of all of how she missed her husband, whom she loved still more dearly with each passing year.

Mann had done everything he could think of for Mary's comfort and safety before leaving her. Her father — gentle, ineffectual Dr. Peabody — was summoned from the shop in West Street where his apothecary corner could be brightened rather better by that tower of strength, his wife. Characteristically, Dr. Peabody did not trust himself to deliver Mary's child when her time came. He would look after his two little grandsons, make toys for them and take them out into the garden to watch while he cut the hedge. Dr. Fisher was to come out from Boston to attend Mary. Also summoned were Mann's sisters, Rebecca Pennell and Lydia Mann. They disapproved of the way little Horace and Georgie were being brought up; they objected to Mary's faithful cook and refused to believe that she "never wasted bread." But Mary was the very essence of tact and only told her husband these details so that he could laugh with her a little. Lydia, in particular, was a great comfort to Mary.

Horace Mann had it carefully figured that his child — the promised girl — would be born May 4, but by April 18 his letters became increasingly anxious. "Send me word by telegraph, as soon as possible after the event, & also again the next day after." And the next day, "Remember that the least imprudence now may be productive of serious consequences. . . . Let the unborn child that cannot now speak, control you as with a sovereign command. And do not try to get well too fast." It did Mary's heart good to read these and other loving words and to know that her husband was "Ever & ever" hers.

All the excessively sad thoughts which Horace Mann had succeeded in banishing from his mind these recent years came flooding back. April 30 was a Sunday. "It being delightful weather, I took a solitary walk," he told Mary. But where must he go but "down to the Congressional burying ground"! He spent some time walking about and comparing it to Père-Lachaise, which he and Mary had visited in Paris. "As I was coming out of it, just about six o'clock," Mann said, "I met a funeral train just entering, having a coffin from which it was easy to infer that it bore a child to its last home. I followed it & heard the Episcopal burial service read. I could think of nothing but you & what might be passing in our home. I no longer saw nature; — I was absorbed in one thought & one notion. Oh what would I give for power, even for one moment to pierce the curtain of space that separates us from each other."

It was at six o'clock on the thirtieth of April that Mary Mann gave birth to a third son. It was not until May 1, the anniversary of their marriage, that Horace Mann received the good news that his third son was strong and healthy and his wife doing well. Even now, his fears would not cease. So many mothers died on the second or third day — he had asked for a second reassuring telegram but none came.

Mann waited in agony till a letter from his sister Lydia put an end to his fears. She had decided that another telegram would merely be a waste of money! Mary had only been in labor three hours; she had refused the chloroform at the last moment although her doctor had recommended it and friends had reported sleeping through all the pain. Suddenly, Mary had decided that the chloroform might hurt her child and she had pushed "the cylinder" aside. And on the very night of her child's birth she had insisted upon writing a few lines to her husband. Who could worry about a woman like that, Lydia thought!

On the fifth of May, Mary was able to write her husband a long letter. "I too, dearest, had more pain in the thought that I might never see you more, than in all beside . . . and all the pain is over now, so we will not think of that any more. Wings at my shoulders play when I realize that I am safely launched again with another little immortal of such noble proportions, daughter tho' it be not. But perhaps we now know how to invoke a daughter, one of these days, if we think best, and we will manage the chloroform better . . . This is the quietest, most comfortable baby we have ever had he only sleeps & eats . . . turning his large blue orbs to the light Father sees to his bathing every day at morning & night."

Knowing that her husband was away from her most unwillingly

and for her sake and the children's, Mary wrote next day, "I never realized how beautiful & convenient this house is. You must enjoy all you can the thought of the luxury you have left us in. It seems as if nothing were wanting to make it a bower of bliss. The birds bathe it in music. Soft showers are transmuting everything into emerald — the baby comes like a little angel upon the children's hearts. The memory of dear papa's love & kindness is a shrine upon which all good purposes and loving thoughts are laid every day — treasures laid up in heaven."

Miss Rawlins Pickman of Salem, for many years Mary's friend and fairy godmother, and her sister-in-law, Mrs. Benjamin T. Pickman, came out to see Mary and the new baby. They brought a handsome silver cup, the gift of Mrs. Pickman, whose husband had been Speaker of the House until his death — and whose place Mann had taken. Horace Mann's third son was named Benjamin Pickman Mann, and Mary said, "My baby's name melts her to tears as well as Sister Rawlins."

Mann made no record of the birth of his third son in the book which he had bought to fill with the story of his first-born. The leather-bound notebook was doubtless back home in West Newton and it was without doubt filled with more blank pages than written ones. From Mann's reactions to the advent of his first two boys it is safe to say that his feelings were mixed. Certainly he was relieved and happy that all had gone so well. Mary was, after all, forty-one. He had reason for anxiety. And once more he could rejoice that he had a physically perfect child. But he and Mary had such plans for their children's education — they wanted college for them of course, and European travel and studies in Germany. Where would the money come from?

For the present, Mann had eight dollars a day for his services in Congress for as long as the session should last. There was no telling how long that would be, but a most conservative estimate would give him around twelve hundred dollars' income in addition to the School Secretary's salary. Mann had been asked to remain Secretary for the rest of "the official year." He could not be called over-optimistic if he saw himself able to pay off some of his debts and the interest on the West Newton home.

And then, just as light seemed to break on the horizon, Mann's affairs took an unexpected turn. He was kept in Washington on business in which he never expected to see himself involved — and the Board of Education, growing impatient, replaced him with another Secretary before his year was up.

In all the years of close, confidential correspondence with Dr. Howe, Mann had never spoken bitterly about the state of his finances. He spoke not bitterly now, but frankly, and Howe lived up to the name of "Chevalier" by which his friends loved to call him. Rounding up Mann's friends, Howe put it to them that the State of Massachusetts should pay at least part of its debt to Horace Mann. The real debt of gratitude could never be repaid, but a few dollars should at least be forthcoming. It took time, of course, but the Honorable Charles Upham of Salem, chairman of the Joint Committee on Education, moved that his Committee find out how much money Mann had paid out of pocket for the normal schools, and other projects. Mann was loth to present an account.

"I cannot present myself in the form of a petitioner, asking for the return of what was voluntarily given," he said. "If the state chooses to consider any part of the sums I have paid on its account, — as paid for property of which it now . . . enjoys the use and possession, — it will be gratefully received. . . . But let what will come, no poverty, and no estimate of my services however low, can make me repine that I have sought with all the means and the talents at my command, to lay broader and deeper the foundations of the prosperity of our Commonwealth."

In the end, Mann was awarded from the state treasury "the sum of two thousand dollars." The "remuneration" came in May 1849 and Josiah Quincy, Jr., spoke for all Mann's friends when he said that it was "but partial payment."

Meanwhile, there was school business to finish. Mann wrote his final article for the *Common School Journal* and his last Annual Report. Of all Mann's twelve reports, the "supplement to the first" — on the "subject of schoolhouses" — was perhaps the most often quoted. The seventh was certainly the most violently contested. And the eighth was strangely prophetic. Looking at his own nation in the light of history, Mann foretold its fate — unless education became available to all.[2]

"Men wait until the tide of evil rises and desolates the land, again and again, before they will erect barriers against the deluge. Men will not hear the wind; they wait for the whirlwind. Men will not take warning from the cloud, they wait for the tempest. And the calamities which spring from ignorance, and a neglect of the social condition of the masses of the people, are no exception to this rule. Republics, one after another, — a splendid yet mournful train, — have emerged into being; they have risen to greatness, and surrounding nations have sought protection beneath the shelter of their power; but they have perished through a want of intelligence and virtue in the masses of the people. They have been delivered over to anarchy and thence to despotism; and because they would not obey their own laws, they have been held in bondage to the law of tyrants. One after another, they have been blotted from the page of existence, and the descendants of a renowned and noble ancestry have been made bond-men and bond-women; — they have been dishonored and trampled upon, on the very soil still choral with the brave deeds of their forefathers. Has a sufficient number of these victim-nations been sacrificed, or must ours be added to the tragic list?

"If men had been wise, these sacrifices might have been mitigated or brought to an end, centuries ago. If men are wise, they may be brought to an end now. But if men will not be wise, these mournful catastrophies must be repeated again and again for centuries to come. . . . The question for us is, has not the fulness of time NOW come? Are not the sufferings of past ages, are not the cries of expiring nations, whose echoes have not yet died away, a summons sufficiently loud to reach our ears, and rouse us to apply a remedy for the present, an antidote for the future? We shall answer these questions by the way in which we educate the rising generation. If we do not prepare children to become good citizens; — if we do not develop their capacities, if we do not enrich their minds with knowledge, imbue their hearts with love of truth and duty, and a reverence for all things sacred and holy, then our republic must go down to destruction, as others have gone before it; and mankind must sweep through another vast cycle of sin and suffering, before the dawn of a better era can arise upon the world. It is for our government, and for that public opinion, which, in a republic, governs the government, to choose between these alternatives of weal and woe."

Although it seems to have been written for today, this prophecy of Horace Mann's is dated December 10, 1844.

CHAPTER TWENTY-TWO

Turning Point

"I RISK my fortunes on an untried and hazardous voyage," said Horace Mann, as he began his duties in Washington. Yet, remarkable prophet though he was, he could not foretell how far he would be swept away from his endeavors of the past twelve years. He could not know that on the night of April 15, 1848, the winds of destiny were blowing and the course of his hazardous voyage was changing toward a port of no return.

Pennsylvania Avenue was illuminated that night. Candles burned inside many-colored paper lanterns which were hung from the trees. Drums beat and bands played. There was "a great torchlight procession" and "bonfires blazed in all the public squares." In front of the Union newspaper office "a great outdoor meeting was held" all "in honor of the French Revolution, the expulsion of Louis Philippe and the establishment of a republic in France." Mr. Foote, Senator from Mississippi, was the orator, and he "extolled the French Revolution as holding out to the whole family of man a bright promise of the universal establishment of civil and religious liberty."

Mr. Mann of Massachusetts went early to his rooms that Saturday night, for he cared little for such scenes. He could read all the speeches later in the papers. What had interested him, however, was the crowd. There were many Negroes, listening intently to the words of Mr. Foote. These Negroes were not all of them slaves by any means, although at this time Mr. Mann probably assumed they were. Many of them had earned and paid for their freedom and others had been manumitted by their owners. Such a Negro was Daniel Bell, for example, who had purchased his freedom while his wife and eight children had been given theirs according to the will of their late master. The heirs had contested the will but the judge had decided in favor of the Negroes and they had supposed themselves free for several years. The heirs were appealing the case, however, and Daniel Bell now listened to this talk of civil freedom with little hope, for he had recently been told that the higher court was sure to send his family back into slavery.

Also in the crowd was a young man about to be sold — and his sisters who worked for wages but were slaves. Their father was free but their mother was a slave who was allowed to live with her husband in a little house on the edge of town on condition that all their children should belong to her owner. Their name was Edmondson.

The oratory continued but, one by one, these Negroes and others dropped away from the crowd. Dark shadows joined them from darker doorways and soft, hurrying footsteps could have been heard — if the brass bands had not played so loud. A cab rattled over the cobblestoned street. At last the speakers took their final round of applause, the bonfires died down to embers and the band went home. No one had thought to follow the cab and the hurrying figures, which had all trended in the same direction — to "a lonely place called White-house wharf, from a whitish-colored building which stood upon it. The high bank of the river, under which the road passed" hid from view a small vessel. She was the *Pearl*, a sloop of the kind known in Chesapeake Bay as a "bay-craft." [1]

"Something past ten o'clock," Daniel Drayton,[2] the captain of the *Pearl*, went on board and told Chester English, a young man who was "cook and sailor," to cast off "and get ready to make sail." Sayres, the owner of the *Pearl*, also came on board. But there was a dead calm and they managed to drop down the river only a mile or so before they met the incoming tide. The *Pearl* anchored until "about daylight" when a north wind arose and at daybreak they passed Alexandria. Now Captain Drayton went below to have a look. He found he had seventy-four passengers and he gave them bread and tried to make them comfortable. Among them were Daniel Bell and his family. Richard and Samuel Edmondson were there and their sisters, Mary and Emily.

The wind was rising "and hauling to northward." At noon the

Washington-bound steamer from Baltimore passed the *Pearl* and
"for the idle passengers of a steamboat" the little bay-craft was "an
object of some curiosity." It was too early in the season for bay-
craft, which were by no means seaworthy. Captain Drayton had
been urged against his better judgment to attempt the voyage because Daniel Bell had approached him and urged him to hurry —
lest it be too late to save the Bell family. At sunset, the *Pearl* passed
a schooner loaded with plaster. And now the *Pearl* reached the
mouth of the Potomac but the "wind hauled to the north" and they
could neither go "up the bay" as they had planned, nor out to sea,
"the vessel being unfit to go outside." They came to anchor at
Cornfield Harbor, "A shelter usually sought by bay-craft en-
countering contrary winds."

"Soon after dropping anchor, we all turned in," said Captain
Drayton. "I knew nothing more, till, waking suddenly, I heard the
noise of a steamer blowing off steam alongside of us. I knew at once
we were taken."

The *Pearl* would have slipped away safely but for the Negro
driver of the cab that carried two fugitives to White-house Wharf.
Judson Driggs, the cabman, told his story, and "a Mr. Dodge of
Georgetown, a wealthy old gentleman originally from New England, missed three or four slaves from his family." Dodge quickly
gathered an armed posse and set out in his steam launch in pursuit
of the *Pearl*. The Baltimore steamer reported seeing her and so did
the plaster-laden schooner. But when Dodge reached the mouth of
the Potomac, he was sure the *Pearl* had slipped away. He could not
take his launch "outside" without forfeiting insurance, so he
turned to go back. "As a last chance, they looked in Cornfield
harbor."

When Dodge and his men opened the unlocked hatches of the
Pearl and saw the Negroes, Captain Drayton came very close to
being shot on the spot. He was constantly threatened but at last,
on Tuesday, April 18, the steam launch with the prisoners reached
Washington. Drayton and Sayres were "tied arm-and-arm, and the
black people also, two-and-two." They were marched to the jail
and "as we went along," Drayton said, "the mob began to increase;
as we passed Gannion's slave-pen that slave-trader, armed with a
knife, rushed out . . . and made a pass at me which was very near
finding its way through my body." They "met an immense mob"

near Pennsylvania Avenue, and "Lynch them! Lynch them!" was the cry.

Sitting peacefully in his room at Gordon's, Horace Mann wrote a letter to Mary. Dating it April 18, "Yesterday," he said, "there was a great commotion in the city. A ship in the river, from N. Jersey I believe, took a large number of slaves aboard . . . and attempted to escape with them. They were pursued by a steamboat, overtaken & brought back, & all parties this morning are committed to jail. So might prevails over right. It will not always be so."

Before the month was out, letters began to reach Horace Mann from Boston and gradually he discovered how closely the fate of the *Pearl* concerned him. Dr. Howe, Charles Sumner and Samuel E. Sewell, abolitionist lawyer, all wrote to Mann begging him "to undertake the defence of the Capt. and crew of the *Pearl*." "I hope you will consent to act as counsel for these men," Sewell wrote. "I have no doubt ample funds will be raised." And others hoped that Mann would receive "Webster compensation" which was synonymous with high fees.

But Mann's letter to Dr. Howe told of misgivings in which his fee played no part. "I had indeed proposed to myself to render . . . any . . . service in my power, before receiving your letter, but I have been so long a stranger to the courts . . . and should be so dull on points where sharpness is required, that I should probably be about the worst counsel the poor fellows could have."

In the end, Mann's friends prevailed; he took the case, and visited Drayton, Sayres and English in the Washington jail. He was particularly impressed with Captain Drayton's story and wrote to Howe, "What do you think of sending on a reporter? I am inclined to think that a book might be made that would sell." Drayton's life was indeed stranger than fiction but Mann's excellent suggestion was not followed. Six years later, Captain Drayton wrote out his own life history, much as he had told it to Mann in prison.

Daniel Drayton was born in New Jersey in 1802, not far from Delaware Bay. His father was a farmer and Daniel was "youngest but one" of nine children. When he was twelve, Daniel's mother died and his father married a widow with four children. Soon there was no room for Daniel and he began a vagabond life, apprenticed here and there — taught little and always overworked. He was drawn to the sea, and by the time he was nineteen he had become captain of a bay-craft. "My trading up and down the bay of course brought me a good deal in contact with the slave population," Drayton said. "No sooner, indeed, does a vessel known to be from the north appear . . . than she is boarded . . . by more or less of them, in hopes of obtaining passage . . . to a land of freedom. During my earlier voyages . . . I had turned a deaf ear to all these requests. At that time too, according to an idea still common enough, I had regarded all negroes as only fit to be slaves."

But Drayton went through many experiences — he rose to be captain of his own coastwise schooner, lost her in a gale — and finally found himself, at the age of forty-six, back where he had started at nineteen — captain of a humble bay-craft again. He had experienced a religious awakening and his "views had undergone a gradual change." Drayton had learned "that it was asserted in the Declaration of Independence, that all men are born free and equal" and he had "read in the Bible that God made of one flesh all nations of the earth."

"I had found out," Drayton said, "that negroes had the same desires, wishes and hopes as myself. I knew very well that I should not like to be a slave even to the very best of masters. It is not a great while since the Algerines used to make slaves of our sailors, white as well as black. I should think it right of anyone who would have ventured to assist me in escaping out of bondage."

"I know it is sometimes said . . . that the slaves at the south are very happy and contented if left to themselves and that this idea of running away is only put into their heads by mischievous white people from the north. This will do very well for those who know nothing about the matter personally. But there is not a waterman who ever sailed in Chesapeake Bay who will not tell you that, so far from the slaves needing any prompting to run away, the difficulty is . . . to make them take no for an answer. I have known of instances where men have lain in the woods for a year or two, waiting for an opportunity to escape on a vessel."

In the summer of 1847, Daniel Drayton had sailed to Washington with a cargo of oysters. While there, a Negro approached him in behalf of a woman and five children. The woman's husband was free, Drayton was told. And the woman, "under agreement with her master, had more than paid for her liberty; but when she asked him

for a settlement, he only answered by threatening to sell her."
Drayton listened to the tale with a sympathy that was new to him.
He saw the woman and agreed to take her, "the five children and
a niece. We were ten days in reaching Frenchtown." But the
woman's husband was waiting for them and long later Drayton
heard that they "were established in a free country and doing well."

Now Drayton was often contacted and told many stories of
families "expecting daily and hourly to be sold." But the risk was
great and he tried to harden his heart as he had done when he was
a much younger man and "fond of visiting, husking-frolics and
rabbiting" during the winter months when the canals and bays were
frozen and the bay-craft laid up. It was Daniel Bell who had finally
broken through Drayton's caution even concerning the early spring
weather. Drayton chartered Captain Sayres's boat, Sayres came
along to keep an eye on his property and they "proceeded down the
Delaware and by the canal into the Chesapeake, making for the
mouth of the Potomac."

When the slaves were caught and returned to Washington, the
excitement in the city was so great that it is surprising that Mann
wrote so little about it to Mary. Perhaps he was afraid of frighten-
ing her. A mob milled around the jail all day and at night left it
and gathered around the office of the *National Era*, an antislavery
newspaper, threatening to destroy the presses and burn the building.
The house of Dr. Bailey, the editor, was surrounded by a mob,
while a committee called on him and urged him to take his press
and leave town. "I am one man against many," said Dr. Bailey, "but
I cannot sacrifice any right I may possess." The police managed to
protect the press building.

Joshua Reed Giddings, member of Congress from Ohio, called
on the prisoners the night of their arrest although an attempt was
made not to admit him. In the House next morning he moved an
"inquiry . . . as to why seventy-six people are in jail in the District
for attempting to vindicate their inalienable rights."

Senator John Parker Hale of New Hampshire called for additional
laws against rioters. Formerly a democrat, Hale had broken with his
party over the slavery question and was in Congress through a
coalition of Whigs and antislavery Democrats. The law which Hale
proposed was already in effect in Maryland but the pro-slavery

paper, the *Washington Union,* said that Hale's was "a firebrand resolution" and that Hale and Giddings were "two abolition incendiaries." Senator Foote of Mississippi, who had been orating about "civil liberty" the night the slaves slipped away, invited Senator Hale of New Hampshire to come to Mississippi to visit him — and be lynched!

Into this whirlpool of attack and counterattack stepped Horace Mann of Massachusetts — new to Washington, well-known as an educator but unknown as a lawyer. Mann wisely asked for a Washington attorney to assist him, and J. M. Carlisle was retained because of his knowledge of Maryland law. This was the law in force under which Drayton and Sayres would be tried because although Maryland had ceded the territory now the District of Columbia no new code of law had been agreed upon because of dissension over slavery.

The District Attorney charged that Drayton had provisioned his ship for a month's voyage, that he planned to run the Negroes off to the West Indies and sell them there! The prosecution attempted to invoke a Maryland act of 1737 which carried the death penalty for stealing slaves. One hundred and fifteen indictments were brought against each prisoner.

When the trial began, "the men who cocked pistols and drew dirks upon Drayton" were as close to the "counsel for the defense" as they could get. These were details which Mann did not write to Mary but to Theodore Parker. "For the first days of the trial, the court room was packed like a slaveship," Mann said. "Within springing distance of me, on my left hand, [was] the man who drew his pistol on Drayton . . . ready to preserve order a la Warsaw." Some of the spectators amused themselves by snapping the hammers of their pistols and leaving it to the defense council to imagine which guns were loaded and which not.

The first trial began on July 27, and Drayton was tried first.[8] Mann jotted down notes as the witnesses for the District Attorney were called. "It was a starlight night," and there was a "hermaphrodite brig about three miles away." The steamer *Salem* reached the *Pearl* about two in the morning, and a witness testified to opening the hatches and letting down a lantern to see Negroes huddled together, cowering in fear.

It did not take Horace Mann long to show that the *Pearl* was not provisioned for a month but had only bread enough on board for the passengers during a short voyage — and that the little bay-craft could never have made it to the West Indies across the open sea in any case. So here was where the District Attorney's "hermaphrodite brig" came in: he now accused Drayton of enticing the slaves away with the intention of putting them aboard her. But — countered Mann — would Drayton have left the hatches unlocked and un-guarded if he had been about to deliver stolen slaves on board a slave ship? Under Mann's close questioning, confusion arose as to the starlight night, and before long both stars and brig had faded from the minds of the witnesses.

For the present, Mann could not even consider freedom for his clients. His present aim was to keep Drayton alive and to reduce the threatened jail sentences of Drayton, Sayres and English to reasonable proportions. As matters stood, Drayton was accused both of stealing slaves and of helping them to escape. He could not be guilty of both, so which had he done? As to that death penalty for slave-stealing, Mann pointed out that the law had been amended by act of Congress in 1831 to read "not less than twenty years in the penitentiary," rather than death.

In showing that neither Drayton nor Sayres had "enticed away" the slaves, but that the Negroes had attempted their own escape, Mann reminded the court of the celebration in honor of the French Revolution which took place in Washington the night the *Pearl* took on her passengers. Speeches had been made that night which had given the slaves ideas, Mann said, and he began to read aloud. "The age of tyrants and of slavery is rapidly drawing to a close . . . and the recognition in all countries of the great principles . . . of equality and brotherhood, was at this moment visibly commenc-ing . . ."

Judge Crawford banged angrily on his desk. He would not permit a harangue against slavery in his court, he shouted.

Mr. Mann said he was only showing the "exciting influences" the slaves were exposed to in the District.

"You'll have to prove that such a speech was ever delivered," thundered the judge, still very angry. Mr. Mann had the proof in his hand — a daily newspaper. "What newspaper is that from which the counsel reads?" demanded the District Attorney. Mann showed it to the court. It was the pro-slavery *Washington Union* of April 19.

And whose were the words Judge Crawford had just called "an antislavery harangue"? Why, that was the oration delivered by Senator Foote — the man who had so recently invited Hale of New Hampshire to come to Mississippi and be lynched! "Without further objection, Mann was allowed to read more extracts," and he must have enjoyed it thoroughly.

The first trial lasted a week and the jury was out all night, unable to agree. It was said that four favored acquittal but they came in with a verdict of "guilty." A second trial lasted four days and again the verdict was "guilty." Over Mann's protest, the Drayton case was now dropped and the Sayres case taken up. He was found first "not guilty." But the District Attorney, "surprised and vexed," tried Sayres on another indictment — and again the verdict was "not guilty." In the end, Sayres was fined on seventy-four indictments (one for each slave found on board his vessel) and the fine came to seventy-four hundred dollars. As he had no money, he remained in jail.

It was fortunate that Horace Mann could not see the long hard road ahead when he undertook the defense of Drayton and Sayres. His letters to Mary told of his alternate hopes and fears. On August 5 he wrote, "Dearest, we had a verdict of 'guilty' returned yesterday against Drayton. . . . We understand that those who stood out for the prisoner were at last induced to surrender by fear of losing all patronage & esteem in this city . . . but this is not the end . . . I stand the labor very well."

On August 9 Mann wrote, "Spoke yesterday two hours & a half & it was as good as horseback exercise. Don't feel anxiety for me. I am told public opinion in this district is undergoing a change." But the next day, . . . "It seems impossible at the present time, to have an impartial trial." Although Mann constantly held out hope that he would be home soon, the trial dragged on. His letters were full of longing for Mary, the children — and the little son he had never seen!

In the end, the young man "English"[4] was acquitted. Drayton was finally given fines and costs amounting to ten thousand and sixty dollars and sentenced "to remain in jail till the bill was paid." Drayton was penniless and not all the abolitionists in the north could raise the amount of his fine so there was nothing left but to try for a presidential pardon. It was necessary to wait for the right president however, and not until Fillmore became president was the pardon signed. The minute the papers were ready, Drayton and Sayres were smuggled hurriedly North lest the State of Virginia start new prosecutions. "Our imprisonment had lasted four years and four months, lacking seven days," Drayton said.

The case of the *Pearl* received widespread publicity among abolitionists, particularly after some of the slaves who had attempted to escape were sold into the Deep South. Great efforts were made to raise money and buy their freedom — which of course raised their market value. A grandson of John Jacob Astor gave nine hundred dollars to buy Richard Edmondson and free him, but Edmondson's sisters, Mary and Emily, aged sixteen and fourteen, were sold to Bruin and Hill, who refused a thousand dollars apiece for them, saying that the girls would fetch twice that in New Orleans. They were taken to New Orleans and exhibited for sale there, but the yellow fever broke out in the slave market and the girls were too valuable to risk. They were hastily shipped back to Washington and lodged in jail again, for safekeeping.

Paul Edmondson, the girls' father and a man now about seventy, journeyed to New York in the hope of raising money to buy his daughters' freedom. The price agreed upon was 1250 dollars for both girls, and the old man went to the Anti-Slavery Society, where his story was checked and found true. He was told to go to the Reverend Lyman Beecher and ask for help. But when Paul Edmondson reached the minister's house, his courage failed him and Dr. Beecher found the old colored man sitting weeping on the doorstep. Beecher persuaded the old man to go to the churches and tell his story. Meanwhile, Mary and Emily had been given calico and told to "make show dresses for themselves" in which to be again exhibited for sale. Their father arrived in Washington with the money just in time! Later, the girls' mother went to New York and raised the money to buy her two youngest children.

With slaves to be bought and set free, the resources of the Northern abolitionists were pretty well expended. The Washington lawyer who had assisted Horace Mann demanded and received a substantial fee. As for Mann — it was while he was in Washington for one of the many *Pearl* trials that his place as Secretary of Education in Massachusetts was filled and he lost a month's pay. He also lost his "per diem" pay in the House while attending court, and found that he was "out of pocket" about a hundred and fifty dollars "besides expenses," at a time when he could ill afford such extravagance.

Writing to his close friend Dr. Howe, Mann said, "This is rather a large fee, — not for the client to pay his lawyer but for the lawyer to pay his client. But it is my luck. I do not think it ever happened to me in my life . . . to have my dish right side up when it rained porridge. This I have got used to. But in the present case, a few spoonfuls that were in it, have got spilled out." It took all of Dr. Howe's best efforts to get Mann's bare expenses paid for by the committee which had urged the case upon him and who all agreed that he had done a brilliant job. As for "Webster compensation" — Mann received no fee at all.

But the *Pearl* case had cost Horace Mann something far more important to him than money. All through the years as Secretary of Education, he had never permitted himself to take sides publicly on the slavery question. The orthodox, who so bitterly opposed him, favored slavery, going back to their Bibles for proof that God had created certain races to be "hewers of wood and drawers of water." Had Mann made known his sympathies, the orthodox would have used antislavery as another count against him and his cause would have suffered. He was now almost as well known as an antislavery sympathizer as an educator, and in Washington he could never hope to unite North and South under his banner in the cause of education. The South would be forever against him, and Horace Mann would never be national Secretary of Education.

Mann made no complaint at this turn of fate. It was clearly something beyond his power to control and to his "dearest" Mary he wrote, "Do I think my fate hard? I feel in this case, as tho' I were not working for Drayton and Sayres only but for the whole colored race."

CHAPTER TWENTY-THREE

Free Soil—Question of the Age

A S SOON AS Mann arrived in Washington his mail began to be enlivened by frequent and urgent letters from Charles Sumner. Why had not Mann made his maiden speech, Sumner wanted to know. And Sumner had so many suggestions as to what Mann ought to say and how he ought to say it that Mann's replies were remarkable for their good-humored patience. "I would pay great deference to your judgment," Mann said, "but I hardly think that . . . any discreet man could expect that a private soldier, not yet two days in camp, could rush forward & assume a post among leaders. . . . Such a presumptuous act, as everybody here would have deemed it, would have neutralized the effect of the best speech any man could make, & of course of an infinitely better speech than Horace Mann will ever make."

Two weeks later, Mann was involved in the Drayton case and — although Sumner was one of those who had urged him to take it — Sumner was writing again about that maiden speech. "I think you are the hardest taskmaster since Pharaoh," Mann cheerfully replied. "I came into class here when the other members of it had read the book half thro', so I had all the back lessons to make up." But not even the new metaphor silenced Sumner.

In June, Mann began to prepare the speech, having found the occasion for which he waited. He said nothing to the impatient Sumner but confided his plans to Mary. "I must begin, these three days, to lay out the foundations of a speech on the grounds of admitting new territory to the Union. This is the great question. All Oregon is now to be provided with a new territorial government & if we obtain New Mexico & Upper California, provision must be made for them. Shall they be permitted to hold slaves in those territories or shall they not? This is the greatest question of the age. Several speeches have already been delivered on it in the House & it is now under regular debate in the Senate. I mean to prepare myself as well as I can. . . . I need a month to study it. I do not intend to speak very soon."

This letter was written on the sixth of June and on the thirtieth Mary received a short, desponding note. "Well, Dearest, I have made my speech. All first speeches are listened to, so mine was." Mann felt that he had "made out so poorly" that he must now "write out" the speech and send a long manuscript to the papers, to save his reputation.

Mann's cold reception should not have surprised him. He advocated that slavery should be prohibited in the new territories. His connection with the Drayton, Sayres case was well known — and the House had a pro-slavery majority. But for twelve years, although Mann had sometimes spoken on education to small audiences, they had always been responsive ones. It was difficult to have his best effects received with scorn and his well-planned arguments rejected before they were completed. It would be hard for anyone and it was particularly hard for Horace Mann to receive condemnation when he felt he deserved praise.

Then the news from home began to arrive and it was all the more acceptable since Mann had labeled his speech a failure. Sumner's letter was prompt. "I am truly happy in all that I hear and see in regard to your speech. The papers speak of it, una voce. . . . You now have a vantage ground which I pray you use for the cause of Freedom. . . . It will gladden thousands of hearts throughout the country."

Sophia Hawthorne's reactions, relayed through Mary, were gratifying, though expressed in thoroughly feminine terms. "First let me tell you about Mr. Mann's speech. It is the theme of all conversation. . . . One day I met Mrs. Augustus Peabody and Augusta in the street in a chariot. Mrs. Peabody extended her hand as I approached the chariot, — after a few words . . . she began to exclaim about the speech. 'It is very great,' she said, 'it is superb, magnificent, — it is wise, it is moderate, — its logic unsurpassed.'" Mrs. Augustus Peabody's father, Judge Putnam, had liked Mann's speech too, but Sophia could not remember whether he had said it "equalled Webster" or "surpassed" him! And Judge White stopped Sophia on the street in Salem to say, " 'Well, I have been reading your brother-in-law's speech — I may say it is the best speech I ever read.' "

"I was much amused," said Horace Mann, returning Sophia's letter to Mary.

In the fall of 1848, when the conventions and elections for the coming term were held, the effect of Mann's course in Washington was clearly seen. A Whig convention was held in Dedham, that county seat where Mann began his political career, and he was unanimously nominated. The Free-Soilers also unanimously nominated him, and in November he was elected. Now Horace Mann was no longer filling the place of another — he was Representative in Congress on his own. This is not to say that life in Congress would be peaceful. Already, there were "Cotton Whigs" and "Conscience Whigs" and Mann had friends on both sides. The dissension soon split the Whig party wide open and Mann's friends fought over him like dogs quarreling over a bone!

"The anti-Taylor movement promises to sweep over New England like a hurricane," wrote Sumner, who was a "Conscience Whig" if there ever was one and who demanded that Mann come out against Taylor at once. But the Mills brothers, bankers, wanted to see Mann supporting General Zachary Taylor. Mann wisely minded his own business and kept his own counsel but when Taylor was elected, Mann wrote to Whig friends: "If the administration becomes the instrument in carrying out the principles of freedom in the territories, it is a better administration than any other we could have, for General Taylor, if he will do this, is all the better for being a southern man. He may do without civil commotion, what a northern man could not do." Mann never missed a chance to speak out against militarism and in favor of peace, so that Taylor's military background was no recommendation for the Presidency and yet, Mann thought, "it may enable him to do without blood, what a man of peace must shed blood to accomplish." It seemed to Mann as though the Whig party might as well get together, their consciences reasonably clear and their cotton cloth still rolling from the looms.

While it was gratifying to be returned to Congress, Mann was not happy in Washington. "It is not a life at all congenial to me," he told Mary. "The great question of freedom or slavery is the only one that would keep me here." And on January 15 of the new year 1849, he wrote, "Dearest, Seven weeks from today will be the 5th of March; the new President will be inaugurated, school will break up & all the boys can go home. It looks longer in prospect than it will in retrospect. Yesterday, I enquired for a little boy named Benjy, or some such name, whom I used to know, but whom I had not heard of for some time. Today you tell me a long story about him." In each letter to Mary, Mann included a special message to his children and many of these carefully block-printed postscripts Mary cut out and pasted into a scrapbook so that each child had a little book of his father's letters from which to learn to read.

Faithfully, Mary wrote, recounting all the children's doings. When Horace was five, his father received news certain to please. Little Horace had begun Latin! *Ad rivum eundem, Lupus et Agnus venerant,* read Horace and then he was allowed to enjoy Aesop's fable of the wolf and the lamb in English. Before long he could tell the story either way. It must have been a fairly exciting household, linguistically speaking, for both Horace and Georgie spoke German with their nursemaid while Benjy's first words were in French, or so his mother fondly believed!

"If Georgie & Horace will write Papa a French letter every week," their father promised, "Mama may get them any good & proper thing they want, if it do not cost more than a dollar for each."

In spite of his long absences, Mann took pains to supervise his children's education. They were not to read stories of military exploits, lest they grow up warlike. The boys were to hear nothing of religion while they were little because they might suffer from fear of an avenging Jehovah as their father had done. But in this Mary took matters in her own hands and explained to Horace about his loving Father in Heaven. Mann walked the floor in agony, it was said, but when he saw how radiantly happy was his little son's faith in God, he "wept tears of joy."

There was one other taboo which Mary was not successful in observing, but this was because she reckoned without her redoubtable sister Elizabeth. The Mann children were to hear no fairy tales but were to be taught the wonders of natural science instead. Their father greatly admired Professor Silliman of Yale who made the Deluge seem but a puddle and extended the seven days of crea-

Elizabeth Palmer Peabody

The mother of Mary Peabody Mann, from Sophia Peabody
Hawthorne's sketchbook.

Three Sons of Horace Mann
Benjy, Horace Jr., Georgie.

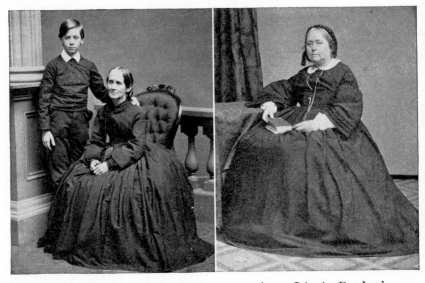

Mary Mann and Benjy

From a family album belonging
to Horace Mann, 3rd.

Aunt Lizzie Peabody

As she appears in Horace
Mann, 3rd's little album.

tion to the long ages of geology. The little boys were to be brought up on Silliman and Agassiz instead of Grimm and Mother Goose. But one day Aunt Elizabeth [1] arrived in West Newton to find little Benjy in tears "over some mishap." Taking him on her lap, she began to sing, "Hey diddle-diddle, the cat and the fiddle, the cow jumped over the moon!" Little Benjy stopped crying to listen in astonishment.

"No, no, Auntie, it couldn't," Benjy exclaimed. He could not have been over four but he knew the neighbor's cows could not jump the fence his father had built — and if pressed, he probably could have told the moon's distance from the earth! But he was smiling now in pure delight. "Tell it again, Auntie," he whispered. It is to be feared that Benjy and his Aunt Elizabeth entered into a conspiracy whereby she told him marvelous tales of giants, princes and pumpkins. What witchery this Salem side of his family seemed to have! In all probability, Mary failed to report this subversive activity of Elizabeth's.

Long before the seven weeks were up, Mary began preparing the beloved house for the return of her husband. Carpets were taken up and beaten, windows polished, curtains washed, ironed and starched. Mann's niece Rebecca Pennell was now in charge of the model school at the West Newton normal school, and she lived with her Aunt Mary and the children. Mary had handed over the best room in the house — her own. But now Rebecca must make do with the little bedroom at the top of the stairs.

"Before I write you again," Mann told Mary on March 3, 1849, "the question of freedom or slavery in the Territories will be settled." The bill "for defraying all expenses of the civil government for the current year" had to come up before Congress could adjourn, and the "slave party & those who act with it" had tacked on a proviso that all new territories should be admitted to the Union "without any restrictions as to slavery."

It is to be feared that Mary paid less attention to the critical situation for Free Soil than to the fact that the adjournment of Congress might be delayed. "Dearest, best beloved," she wrote, "the near approach of the hour of your return, (near only when compared with the long night of your absence) — makes the interval seem unendurable. We count the days and hours, I assure you. Whatever I am doing, the recollection of the fact, — ah — I must needs say of the hope, thrills every nerve and makes music in every fibre as on a harp of a thousand strings. I think, *again* that noble head and nobler heart will rest on my bosom and love it too! Dearest, I love you too much. The dream of my youth is fulfilled — I love and am loved."

Fortunately, Horace Mann was not the only member of Congress anxious to go home. Sessions continued two days and three nights and on the fifth of March Mann wrote, "Well, dearest, I am just up & breakfasted. I am safe & the Republic is safe. We commenced our session yesterday morning at eleven & adjourned this morning at seven. It was a tumultuous night, but it was fought bravely & the victory is ours. . . . At last, at about 2 o'clock this morning we succeeded in attaching an amendment to the proviso which virtually took the *slavery* out of it. It was then sent to the Senate; & there, after 2 or 3 hours hard fighting, they yielded. There were two regular fist-fights in the House, — in one of which blood flowed freely, & one in the Senate."

Now the little boys were admonished again and again and they promised to be good and not to bother dear Papa. They took to watching for train smoke far down the valley and listening for the whistle with its drifting, minor notes which sent shivers down their spine. Their excitement mounted to fever heat when the train stopped at the station below their hill and they watched to see if a tall "clerical-looking gentleman with white hair" would come striding up the road.

Alas, when the long-looked-for dear Papa arrived, the little boys forgot all their promises. Horace Mann, who had abolished "the rod" in the common schools, must have been sorely tempted to put them over his knee. "When papa comes home, they behave *awfully*," Mary told their Aunt Rebecca. "He perfectly bewitches them. They go to bed not only willingly but gladly when he is not here, but when he is, they wish to stay with him. They ride upon him, wish to get into his rocking chair or be on the sofa by him, they wish to go with him, to play hard with him — they are excited to the last degree and he thinks they are very lawless."

These "lawless" boys were five, four, and a little over a year at this time — but their father was fifty-three. He had neither the experience nor the detached attitude to give him the serenity of a grandfather, while he also lacked the youthful exuberance that makes the

oung father more than a match for his children. There were three
veeks of "the worst possible weather" just after Mann got home.
he little boys could not go outdoors to play and their father took
o his bed with "no lungs, no stomach, no brains, or only as foes &
ot as allies."

Spring weather came, Mann recovered his "vital currents," but
e was called back to Washington for one of the Drayton trials.
he little boys had calmed down, the garden which Mann loved so
nuch was springing into life, his apple trees budding. Mary spoke
or her husband as well as for herself when she wrote him: "Every-
hing has stopped growing today, and the sun does not give any
ieat, but only cold light because my heart is cold and sad. Perhaps
oon I shall forget myself again and remember only you, and then
t will be all warm and joyful and my mother nature will let her
lowers bloom and her grass grow because you *are* and you are
nine."

Somehow, Mann worked in "a lecturing tramp" of ten days or so,
'as we must have bread and butter." The tour paid for more than
read and butter — for white paint for "the summer house and the
wing" and, in June, for one of those rare vacations for "Mr. Mann
nd family." They stayed at the Catskill Mountain House and their
iill was fifteen dollars.

In August 1849 Mann received a letter from an old friend, Jared
parks. They had first met at Mrs. Clarke's boardinghouse, and
parks had been a member of the State Board of Education, where
ie was ever Mann's ally against all enemy attacks beginning with
Fred Packard and ending with Matthew Hale Smith. Mann must
iave thought something new had developed on the educational
ront. But Jared Sparks was now President of Harvard and his letter
ead: "The Diploma will be found at the Bookstore of Messers Little
ind Brown, Boston. Please to inform me if it comes safely to your
iand." Horace Mann had received the degree of LL.D. from
Harvard.

When Mann returned to Washington for the winter season, Mary
lecided to rent her house to a Miss Quimby who would take teachers
from the nearby West Newton normal school to board. Mary re-
erved the smallest possible space for herself, turning over all the
other rooms to be rented either to teachers or to pupils. "Today I

moved back into the nursery," Mary told her husband, "and le
the beloved chamber, consecrated anew by your divine presenc
— in Rebecca's keeping again — who has set her house in order an
planted herself there in the holy places." By December, Mary
house was full of strangers and she realized that she must suffe
a great deal of discomfort. Cyrus Peirce was again ill and the Rev
erend Eben S. Stearns had taken his place at the normal schoo
and had taken Horace Mann's study for his bedroom. Mary did nc
like him — but it would have been almost impossible for her to lik
anyone who sat at her husband's desk. Little Horace grieved for h
own room and all the children were puzzled and unhappy whe
Miss Quimby forbade them to play in the living room lest the
leave toys about. "I stay upstairs most of the time," Mary wrot
"except when I go out under the sky. I can think my own thought
— it is my kingdom — I can fill the sky with my love and the fre
winds fan my conceptions into glorious proportions." At the en
of this letter of December 28, 1849, Mary betrayed her lonelines
"Why don't you write me any love letters?" she said.

If Horace Mann could have read over his love letters to Charlott
and hers to him, it would have grieved him to see how the role
had been reversed with his second marriage. Now it was he wh
was passionately loved and he was now the absent one for whor
a heart was hungry. But his days were so occupied that he had t
snatch whatever moment offered, often writing to Mary from h
desk in the House, a background ill suited to lovemaking. He alway
wrote affectionately — he could not help it if he left her unsatisfie
as once he had been. His postscripts to his little boys warmed thei
mother's heart in any case. Horace was to "make Georgie a goo
boy" by setting a perfect example. Georgie, who had just begu
to print, was told, "Please do not hold your pen so tight in you
little fingers. The pen is not a mouse that will run away." These wer
terms to make a little boy smile — and remember. Often the brothe
shared a letter. "Dear Horace & Georgie, I saw some poor littl
boys who had no Mama to take care of them & I said, how good m
little boys ought to be to their Mama."

As the year 1849 drew to a close, the House of Representative
chose a speaker. The usual conflict developed over the slavery ques
tion with a Southern pro-slavery candidate, a Free-Soil candidat
and Mr. Winthrop of Massachusetts, representing the Whigs. Man

voted for Winthrop, and his State Street or Cotton Whig friends were delighted. It would be Mann for Whig governor of Massachusetts, Loring jubilantly declared, and it must have been hard for Mann not to picture how different life would be if his home in West Newton were a governor's "mansion" instead of a normal school boarding- and rooming-house. But he knew he never could and never would make the compromises necessary to remain in Cotton Whig favor. "I shrink from the praise you say I receive in certain quarters," he wrote with devastating honesty. "I have voted for Mr. Winthrop & in that way fulfilled the hopes of the Whigs. He was their first choice; he is only my second or third."

While the Cotton Whigs were busy praising him, Mann's Conscience Whig friends were accusing him of "office-seeking." To them he replied with equal frankness, "My Free Soil principles are as firm as ever, I shall make the freedom of the territories the cardinal question, the question paramount to all others." But to a question put to him to test him, he replied, "There might be circumstances in which I would vote for a slaveholder"! Here was honesty which Mann said he supposed would lose him "a hundred votes."

On February 15, 1850, Mr. Mann of Massachusetts addressed the House of Representatives on the subject of slavery in the territories. It was the strongest, most effective speech Mann had so far made in Congress and it marked his repudiation of Cotton Whigs and Conscience Whigs alike and his allegiance to the new party. "The term 'Free Soiler' is perpetually used upon this floor," he began, "as a term of ignominy and reproach; yet I maintain that in its original and legitimate use as denoting the advocates of the doctrine that all our territorial possessions should be consecrated to freedom, there is no language that can supply a more honorable appellation. It expresses a determination on the part of its disciples to keep free the territory that is now free; to stand upon its frontiers as the cherubim stood at the gates of Paradise with a flaming sword . . . to keep the sin of slavery from crossing its borders." Mann spoke impressively of the "Wilmot Proviso," which said that "neither slavery nor involuntary servitude shall ever exist in any part of said territory [New Mexico]." He did not touch upon the problem of the slaves then lawfully held in Southern states. He simply begged

Congress not to let slavery increase. This was not "abolition."

The people back home had little idea of the vast extent of the new territories. Already, Mann pointed out, there were more slaves in the United States than there had been colonists at the time of the revolution. And now slave territory could become vastly larger than free territory. It was time to make a stand. Let the new territories choose for themselves, was the idea of many Whigs, but Mann feared that "slaveholders will go (into the territories) and exercise an influence in favor of slavery . . . so that slavery will ultimately be established through present neglect." Five years later that "influence" Mann feared became civil strife in Kansas, with nights made terrible by the burning of homesteads and fellow countrymen shooting each other at sight.

But in this fatal year of 1850, Daniel Webster made his "Seventh of March" speech. History has remembered great lines from that speech. "I wish to speak today, not as a Massachusetts man, not as a Northern man, but as an American. . . . I speak for the preservation of the Union." These words were worth the immortality accorded them, but Webster also said other things and Horace Mann was there and heard him. "If the infernal Fanatics and Abolitionists ever get the power in their hands they will override the Constitution," Webster said; "they will set the Supreme Court at defiance, change and make laws to suit themselves." The South was right and the North wrong as to "the return of persons bound to service who have escaped into the free States," Webster told the South, and out of this came the "Fugitive Slave Law" — which would be like a match tossed into a powder keg.

"I have the most intense fears that all is lost," Mann confided to Mary. "Since Mr. Webster's desertion, the cement has set the wrong way. It was a bid for the Presidency, as I think." This letter was written April 9 and Mann was more astute than some of his contemporaries, for it took most of them much longer to discover that Webster's oratory was designed to cover up a deal whereby, if the South got their Fugitive Slave Law, the Northern textile men could have the *promise* of a tariff. Webster's bid for the Presidency followed in due course.

When he was a lawyer, Mann had admired Webster, although it is doubtful if he ever went so far as to wear a blue coat with brass buttons in imitation of the great man — as many of his friends did. Mann had watched Webster walk along the streets of Boston followed by admiring crowds, as though he had been a king. The heavy, dark face was handsome then, not flushed and fleshy with excessive meat and drink as now; the great shoulders were carried well and the outthrust lower lip seemed properly aggressive rather than arrogant. Watching Webster deteriorate had been like watching an idol crumble. Probably Mann did not believe it when Bancroft (who was a Democrat) said that bankers and merchants in Boston gave Webster "sixty or seventy thousand dollars" when he went to England in 1840 and that, once there, Baring Brothers had given him a thousand pounds to sell out his banker friends by giving it as his opinion that the United States should assume responsibility for the debts of the individual states. But ten years had passed, and Webster had grown wealthier than even such a celebrated lawyer could hope to be. He had spent more than he made no matter how his income mounted, and stories of his deals with New York bankers made his early efforts in Boston seem penny ante.

Horace Mann fought Webster now with the zeal of a knight against a Saracen. And Mann's best weapons were Webster's own speeches made before his about-face of the Seventh of March — which Mann used with devastating effect to show that Webster had favored Free Soil, had championed freedom, once upon a time before he thought the Presidency would be his if he turned coat. Mann's letters appeared in Free-Soil papers while Whig-dominated papers refused to print them. Mann was violently attacked in the Whig papers, which refused to print his replies, while Sumner wrote that "Webster men" were saying that " 'Horace Mann is a formidable antagonist.' "

All during the summer, Mann wrote, spoke and campaigned with fervor, not so much for his own election to Congress but for Free Soil. There were many who said that he was too bitter an antagonist, but in a letter to Benjamin Seaver (soon to become Mayor of Boston) Mann expressed his personal point of view. "Let us look charitably upon differences of opinion, except in cases where there is high evidence of bad motive." [2]

Mann felt that he had all the evidence against Webster. "In point of pungency, truthfulness and force," Sumner said, Mann's letters and speeches "strike a very hard blow."

For the most part, Mann attacked Webster and his policies in long words, with classic allusions and with dignity. But at least twice he could not help making fun of the great statesman, and this caused Webster's jutting eyebrows to meet in blackest anger, his throat to swell within the high wrappings of his black cravat. One day Webster came into the House of Representatives in Washington and, seeing three empty seats, took one of them. What must have been his horror when he discovered that he was seated next to the place, on the far left of the Speaker, which belonged to Horace Mann! "I came in soon," Mann gleefully told, "and in order to get to my seat, had to pass right by him so near that he drew up his feet to let me pass." Of course Webster used his favorite weapon, the "cut direct."

The Representative sitting in front of Mann turned around and whispered loudly, asking if Mann "knew the gentleman" on his left.

"I told him," Mann recounted, "that I believed it was a gentleman from New Hampshire, in attendance here, seeking some office!" The would-be President of the United States was not likely to forget this jibe.

Mann's next joke carried appalling results. Webster was "out upon him" in a speech at Newburyport "in very savage style." Mann read Webster's attack, column after column of it, in the Whig papers; and he noted that Webster had misused a quotation in Latin from Cicero. Mann made fun of Webster's Latin and instantly the press was full of letters defending — not Webster's turncoat tactics but his "Latinity." Mann's old friend, schoolmaster George Barrell Emerson, did not even bother to look the passage up but assumed that Mann must be wrong. Professor Felton was violent in his denunciation of Mann. And Sumner, who had checked the passage beforehand at Mann's request and knew that Mann was right, now refused to come out in defense of Mann because Felton was his dear friend!

As a matter of fact, the Cotton Whigs were not all of them without Conscience and Mann had been so right in his opposition to Webster's politics that they were very uncomfortable. They wanted less said about Free Soil and the Fugitive Slave Law and Mann's jeering provided the perfect red herring. Webster's morals, both public and private, might be doubtful but he was intensely proud of his Latin and all his friends leaped into print to say that it was above reproach. Then, to the rage and dismay of all proper Whigs,

Mann proved to be right, even in his "Latinity." Emerson took a look
at his Cicero. And Felton, Professor of Greek at Harvard, "got very
much the worst of it" at the hands of Dr. Beck, Harvard Professor
of Latin! But Mann's friends who wrote him of this triumph were
cast down just the same. They were sure he had lost his seat in
Congress — for it is possible to be right at the wrong time! [3]

Back home, Mann's friends were reading his letters to the papers
and watching his campaign with mingled hopes and fears. Mary
wrote him all the news — but home news came first. Dating her
letter *May 31, 1850*, "We have had a very happy day gardening,"
Mary said, "and rounded off this evening by the visit of the Searles,
who came to announce the presentation of two rabbits, just arrived
into this wicked world and to appear here in about three weeks.
The children were wild with joy to see the boys — Benjy as well as
the rest."

Miss Lucy Searle was a friend of Mary's from Brookline days and
the two boys were relatives of hers she was bringing up after the
death of both their parents. Arthur, the older boy, became a professor of astronomy at Harvard, writing books on astronomy and
verse in Latin and in English. He "received his education in private
schools," and Mary Mann had a hand in that, for he came to live
with her in West Newton for a time while she taught him along
with her own children. But Arthur was about seven years older than
Horace, Jr., and Mary had certain misgivings because of Arthur's
advanced knowledge of the world's good and evil, which considerably surpassed anything little Horace had encountered.

The Searles, young and old, were all back in Brookline now and
there was much visiting back and forth. This time, while the children played together, Miss Searle held forth to Mary on Mary's
favorite subject of conversation — Horace Mann. "She says her
brother, who was an old-fashioned Whig, was so wrought upon by
your letters," Mary told her husband, "that he proposed to have a
letter of thanks written you. . . . Lucy said she had heard great
rejoicings over Mr. Webster's Newburyport letter, because it seemed
to place the game in your hands and gave you such a good opportunity to come out in full."

"It seems it is Mr. Ticknor who wrote the articles in the *Daily*,
defending Webster, and then the attacks upon you," Mary went on.

"Miss Hooker attended an anti-slavery meeting in Boston yesterday and says she did not know there could be such doings. There were six police officers present to keep the peace and such speeches! They handled Mr. Webster without mittens and then eulogized you to the skies. William Channing spoke then, and told them they were doing more harm than good — upon which Mrs. Abby Kelley Foster jumped up and said who did he mean — and he replied 'Thou art the man' at which she was very much incensed." There must have been laughter also, for Abigail Kelley Foster was a militant abolitionist who had given up teaching for the lecture platform in defiance of the current prejudice against women speaking in public. She had been "denounced by the clergy as a menace to public morals" and it would be the same clergy who denounced Horace Mann.

Mary knew that her husband would smile over her lively picture of the abolitionist meeting. She knew also that he loved peace, yet was so often the center of storm. "I do not like to have you talked about and handled in such a way," she said. "It makes me feel worse than any of the strifes you have had — but I like your position, and think you may do a great work for freedom in it. In common phrase I should exclaim, 'Heaven help you and guide you aright' — but I am rather disposed to feel that your precious life has been a preparation for this emergency, and that without that, Heaven would not help you for all your crying for aid. I believe I have no worldly ambitions for you, nor do I desire to see you rise . . . but if you set the world right in this crisis, shall I not be proud of you! . . . I know of no one else who stands above party or prejudice, or passion on this subject. What a position Mr. Webster has put himself into! He cannot redeem himself now.

"Peace be to your poor brain! How I wish I could comb the outside of it tonight." And Mary ended her letter with one more of those home details which meant so much to Horace Mann — as much even as her praise of him and confidence in his work. "I have set Mr. Porter to digging a trench on the lower side of our road, for there is no use in doing anything to the border without it. I have been measuring out the border with line and plummet, and staking it out for him. I hope to get all the violets in, in a few days."

Mann was nominated for Congress at the Free-Soil Convention of 1850, as all his friends knew he would be. But it was generally assumed that he would not be the Whig candidate as well because of his opposition to Webster. Then the Whig machine got a terrible scare. Horace Mann came within three votes of being nominated on their first ballot! A recess for luncheon was hastily called and urgent consultations were held at tavern tables till the delegates were able to understand their duty to the Webster faction. Mr. Mann lost only two votes but the machine coraled enough scattering votes to nominate a Mr. Walley of Roxbury.

Mann was utterly cast down. "I, who before was in some respects very popular, have become unpopular," he said; and he was so certain that the Whig candidate would be elected that he refused to go down to the village on election night to get the returns. Rebecca went down the long hill and returned to announce joyfully that her uncle was elected. But Mann refused to listen to her, reminding her that the returns had not all come "over the telegraph." Rebecca went to bed, her bright balloon of joy all deflated.

Next morning she was walking sadly down the hill toward the town when she met the village omnibus on its way up the steep road. The driver waved his hat and shouted to her — Horace Mann elected! There was no doubt about it this time. Rebecca turned and ran madly back up the hill to be first to tell the news. But when she got there she was too out of breath and excited to speak!

CHAPTER TWENTY-FOUR
Men from Antioch

THE YEAR 1850 was a fairly prosperous one for Horace Mann. In addition to the eight dollars a day paid to Congressmen, he received seven hundred and fifty dollars from Massachusetts for editing the tenth school report. Then there was income to be derived from lectures and certain small pickings from writing. Mann was able to buy fifteen shares of Boston and Worcester railroad stock and have something left. Accordingly, he wrote Edmond Clap, a friend in Boston. Mr. Clap was to buy "a gold watch of about a hundred dollars' value — a lady's watch." And Mann wrote a note which Mr. Clap was to carry to the lady.

"Dearest," said the note which Mary Mann kept all her life in its little white envelope, "I have just received my pay from the State for the Revised edition of the Tenth Report. You have helped me so much thro' all my labors, that I cannot let the occasion go by without leaving a memorial of it in your hands . . .

"Please accept the accompanying watch as a remembrance from me of the assistance you have always so cheerfully given me. To this at least, you would be entitled even without that relation between us which makes gold worthless."

Mary was taken completely by surprise. "Dearest, beloved," she replied, "who should appear tonight, smiling thro' this northeasterly storm — so smiling that I immediately knew there must be something special in his pocket or his heart — so smiling that I immediately accused him of having seen *you* — but our dear friend Edmond! A golden watch in a tortoise case for *me*, and a note far more valuable than the watch or any weight of gold, because of the dear intent of giving me pleasure! But you should not thank me for services which paid themselves a hundred-fold in the rendering. . . . Even the tables over which we groaned in spirit together . . . how much happiness has been instilled into me . . . when the fact of your bringing them to me was the best compliment to my love and friendship. I will never look upon the watch without remembering to rejoice that those exhausting labors are at an end. It will be a watch that not only keeps time but keeps joy."

Extra sums of money continued to find their way to Horace Mann's pocket — as a result of his enormous capacity for work. Back in 1849, he had delivered a lecture to the Boston Mercantile Library Association called "A Few Thoughts for Young Men." It was popular and was published by Ticknor and Fields — the publishers of Nathaniel Hawthorne, Mann's distinguished brother-in-law. In March 1850 Mann met James T. Fields in Washington, "with a lady just made his wife." Mr. Fields said that "Hawthorne's book is *great*" — and he was right for this was *The Scarlet Letter!* But Mann was understandably more interested in hearing how his own book was doing. "Fields tells me they have sold 6000 copies of my Lecture to Young men — but that 2000 copies of such a production is considered a very large sale," Mann reported. He was also working on a series of arithmetic textbooks, and in 1850 the first volume appeared. Mary sent a copy to her sister Sophia's children — a gift by no means popular with them!

It was a great satisfaction to Mann to win a stiff contest against Webster forces but he looked forward to the coming long term in Congress with misgiving. It seemed to him that there was little he could do in the cause of Free Soil when speeches in Congress were made by men "too drunk to articulate" and where "fist-fights" and "challenges to duels" took the place of reasoned argument. "I might as well have been at home," Mann wrote to Mary, and he let his mind play with miraculous means of reaching West Newton. "I go for some new invention that will carry a man a hundred miles a minute," he said. "I do not see why there should not be an air-tight tube . . . so that we could have the air as an impeller, & be driven with the speed of forty hurricanes. But I have not got this thing perfectly matured in my mind yet."

Since Mann had no time to invent the airplane, the next best thing would be to send for Mary and the children. To be sure, Mary did not share all of Mann's enthusiasm for railroads — for she had twice been in trains which were derailed. "When we came to that same curve," she told of her second experience a short time previously, "off jumped the engine and up bounced the car and there we were stuck fast in the mud. No one was hurt. Horace's head was slightly bumped but even the engineer, who fell off head first, was not at all injured!" Mary would always be a little nervous while on a train and anxious for her husband's safety while he was on his many journeys. But she promised to introduce herself to the conductor who would take care of her and the children. Mr. Mann knew conductors and engineers by name on all the partially completed railroads between Boston and Washington.

A trip to Europe would have been simpler; but once on the way, Mary and the boys enjoyed the journey. Their train stayed on the track to New Haven; their steamer from there kept off the rocks, although "detained a long time by fog." They were all on deck and eager for new sights as their vessel reached New York with its forests of masts that fringed an island covered with low buildings. Four or five church steeples pointed an upward finger among green trees. Their boat was so late that they had missed their connection and "could not go in the cars."

"We went from the New York boat to the Philadelphia boat," Mary said, "only riding round an hour or two in the interval and in Broadway, what should we see but Tom Thumb's carriage, ponies, coachman and footman mounted upon a cart and trundling through the street behind Barnum's band, by way of advertising the evening's entertainment. . . . It is the silver mounted carriage presented by Queen Victoria and it is just large enough for a well-sized *cat* to sit comfortably in. . . . The boys enjoyed the spectacle immensely."

Horace Mann was in Philadelphia awaiting his family. He would take them the rest of the way to Washington but meanwhile they visited "Lucretia Mott and her husband," prominent Quaker abolitionists whom Mr. Mann had recently met in Washington. "Philadelphians wanted to give Mr. Mann a public reception," Mary said — but Mann refused to be lionized. He went instead to visit the new water system and to learn more of this marvel — pure water for a whole city!

Instead of attending large social gatherings, Mann preferred the informal evenings at the Motts' house where, among others, he "met a highly educated gentleman . . . a gentleman of property residing fifteen miles from Philadelphia on his estate — but a *colored man*." Because of the new Fugitive Slave Law, this man's young children were "afraid to walk away from the house for fear of kidnappers." It was Mary Mann who reported the evening's conversations. "Fugitive slaves resort" to this colored man, she said, "and he arms them with revolvers and bowie knives and sends them north. . . . All the Quakers . . . are opposed to his arming. . . . They all argued all around very ably and very beautifully. Mrs. Mott's voice and expression are as melodious as an octave flute. They called my husband 'Horace' and me 'Mary' and it seemed to bring us very near. There is something very lovely in a Quaker social circle."

The Mann family continued their journey to Washington with "a long wait in Baltimore" and were at last established, by December 2, 1850, in "three rooms and a privilege in the parlor." Mann could "write all by himself mornings" in the parlor and there was a "spacious garden" where the children could play without disturbing him. The boardinghouse was "at the end of a street with only a wide ravine and hills beyond," yet it was "not five minutes' walk from the capitol and Pennsylvania Avenue, — the Broadway of Washington," Mary said. She was delighted with everything except that she was not sure her husband enjoyed absolute perfection. "Our quiet situation cuts my husband off from society and he has no *rocking chair!* He can recline on the bed which will answer for a sofa, but the comfortable loll in the rocking chair, he will have to dispense with."

As the old year ended and the year 1851 began, there was "a powder of snow" in Washington, but soon the warm weather the Mann family longed for "brought fresh shoots on the rose bushes that cover the summer houses on the Capitol grounds," Mary said. If the Manns were "cut off from society," they corrected this by making calls; and Mary told of Dr. Bailey, that courageous editor who had refused to take his presses and flee the city when the mob surrounded his home and his office during the Drayton-Sayres excitement.

"The pleasantest place we go is to Dr. Bailey's, editor of the *Era*," said Mary. "Grace Greenwood and one or two other ladies are spending the winter there, and Mrs. Bailey is a very fine woman.

On Saturday nights they have a Free-Soil gathering and Mrs. B. has invited me to come and help preside over the refreshments to which the guests are invited in the dining room after they have talked politics till they are tired." The Ohio Congressman, Joshua Reed Giddings, who had worked hard for the liberation of Drayton and Sayres, was often at these Saturday night parties — "a broad-shouldered man with a grey head" who spoke enthusiastically to the Manns about his home state.

Terrible as the Fugitive Slave Law was, Horace Mann thought it was better not to attempt to amend it lest "men's minds would get reconciled to it by degrees." He saw hope in the fact that "people are filled with such a horror of such a summary law that the public mind is kept alive to the subject and people resist as a matter of conscience." Or so said Mary, writing to her sister Sophia, who saw existing conditions in a much more rosy light.

In the spring of 1851, Horace Mann was back in Boston when a "Anti-Fugitive Slave Law convention" was held at the Tremont Temple — Faneuil Hall having been denied them. He was elected president and addressed a packed auditorium. The Cotton Whig *Transcript* came out against Mann's speech with heavy sarcasm. Garrison's *Liberator* did not like Mann's speech either, and this was a disappointment. Mann was growing weary of the role of politician with its impossible requirement that he please everybody. But the Fugitive Slave Law was now in full operation. Once more, Horace Mann tried to bring it to the light and to make perfectly clear to all — whatever their party affiliation — that Daniel Webster was responsible for this law.

First victim of the slave hunters in Boston [1] was Shadrach, who was rescued by his Negro friends. But the fugitive Sims had just been taken and was now in prison and this meeting was in angry protest. Long after Mann's words were forgotten, his friends would remember the patience, tact and generalship he showed in keeping order.

On April 3, 1851, Thomas Sims had been seized on Richmond Street, Boston, by "police disguised as city watchmen" and "on the lying pretext of theft." Sims struggled but was overpowered and thrust into a waiting carriage and carried into the courthouse yard. Only then did he realize what had happened. "The kidnapers!" he shouted, and word was carried to Theodore Parker.

Next morning chains were found "drawn entirely around the courthouse," so that "the judges from Judge Lemuel Shaw down, had to crawl under." Theodore Parker rounded up lawyers for Sims's defense. He sent for a sea captain by the name of Austin Bearse, a member of the newly organized and more or less secret "Vigilance Committee."

Bearse himself told the story of what happened next. He went down to the docks and had a look at the vessels tied up there. He spotted the *Acorn*, whose owners "were having a little house built on deck." " 'That's the place we're going to put Sims in to take him to Savannah,' " a workman told Captain Bearse. Parker and his friends thought they could raise the money and Bearse looked for a vessel to follow the *Acorn* out of the harbor and rescue Sims. But there was no time to buy the boat, and Bearse could not have brought off his rescue for Sims was swiftly convicted of being a runaway slave and a revenue cutter was ordered to escort the *Acorn*.

"The great Anti-Fugitive-Slave Law meeting, which sat in Tremont Temple when Sims was kept in durance vile in the chained court-house of Boston, should have marched in solid order . . . to the Boston Bastille," said Garrison. "Horace Mann should have led the rescue."

But Mann could only do what he believed to be right. "Republics have been delivered over to anarchy and thence to despotism; and because they would not obey their own laws, they have been held in bondage to the law of tyrants," he had written. This he believed. He would labor to abolish a wicked law but not to break it.

In March 1852 Mary and the children were again in Washington, but now Mary was as lonely for her husband as she had so often been back in West Newton. "There is no use, certainly, in imagining you in danger, or in feeling solitary when you are absent," she wrote. "But so it is. When you are gone, the pleasantest places seem deserted and the pleasantest people 'sounding brass and tinkling cymbal.' The same spell is over all nature that rules my dreams when I dream that I am not your wife, and that you are gone and I shall never see you more. The impression was made upon my brain, perhaps, at the time when I did not know but it might be so in reality, — when I thought I never should be your wife and fancied I could be happy if I were only sure of your everlasting friendship."

Mann had gone on an extended lecture tour. "I do not see that they are doing anything in Congress that needs my help," he told Mary. "If you were not there, I should have no objection to being away." And Mann told Cyrus Peirce how affairs in Congress had been going. "A politician does not sneeze without reference to the next Presidency. The greatest interests & the worst passions are *assayed* for this end & the value determined accordingly. The next Congress will doubtless be the most corrupt & the most corrupting one ever witnessed in this country."

Mann thought that only one Whig had a chance of winning the Presidency and that would be General Scott — but that a democrat would unite the country and Sam Houston was his choice. "I believe the man whom the public irreverently call 'old Sam Houston, alias Old San Jacinto,' to be a man of incomparably more character, honesty & resolution than any other of the democratic candidates."

The decision to go lecturing was taken rather suddenly and Mann explained it to Howe. "I am itinerating & lecturing 'to order' on Education, Temperance etc. The truth is that I need several hundred dollars of interest money . . . so I took the method of 'raising the wind' by selling some of my own wind. I get the best of the bargain in two ways, because I obtain 'material aid,' for less than a 'song,' that is for a *speech* only; & then I have always found that it helps my dyspepsia to deliver Lyceum lectures. It cures flatulence by getting the wind off my stomach."

Mann started on his tour under a considerable handicap — and he made fun of himself on this point also. He had just had all his teeth taken out by the famous Dr. Morton of Boston who was visiting Washington and using the new discovery — ether! But Dr. Morton sent Mann's set of false teeth to him by express, and they did not arrive in New York in time for his first speech. "Well, dearest, here I am with my toothless jaws," Mann told his wife. "I made a sort of Irish gibberish of it last night, but I had a grand audience & they didn't know I ever spoke any better." About a month later, while still on tour, Mann added to the story. "In tumbling over an old file of Oswego papers just now . . . I found a letter from its correspondent in New York, giving an account of the Temperance Banquet, in which Gen. Houston & I figured rather more conspicuously than any body else. I am described as a tall, stern man, *about*

60, with long white hair, tho' not bald, & having an imperfection in my articulation owing to the loss of my front teeth! Front teeth indeed! If I have lost only my front teeth, what shall be said of a man who lost *all* his teeth! It says I tried to be witty & then relates some of my *quips;* but rather regrets them, as I am so old that I ought to be thinking of my grave. Is this the way history is made up?

"I had a pretty good audience last night, tho' it did storm, & they laughed quite heartily at my 'wit' forgetting how old I am."

Whatever lecture was ordered, Mann gave. He spoke on education, he gave his advice to young men, and his Temperance lecture was powerful and popular with the earnest churchgoing descendants of Puritans. A Virginian heard in his home state a "street lecturer" reading Horace Mann's " 'Letter to the Worcester Temperance convention' to a large crowd he had collected." Here was fame indeed and Mann was amused. He was now beginning to use a new lecture which would be published as a sort of companion piece to his "Thoughts for a Young Man," and would be equally popular. "A Few Thoughts on the Powers and Duties of Women" it was called.

There were two people Mann must have had in mind when he wrote part of his lecture on women — his sister Lydia Mann [2] and his sister-in-law, Elizabeth Peabody. Lizzie was now visiting Mary in Washington, selling "Bem's Historical Charts" and teaching her little nephews their history as they colored the squares on the chart she had given them. "What a blessing in the circle of the families to which she belongs, is the unmarried sister," Mann told his audiences — and there would be rustling of Sunday black silks as a large number of his hearers looked pleased although a little self-conscious. California gold lured many a fine young man to the far West, while others, traveling westward in search of land, saw new faces and forgot old promises to return. There was an unmarried sister in nearly every home. "She watches by the aged father or mother with a vestal's fidelity when her brothers and sisters abandon the old homestead for Cupid or cupidity," Mann said, and there was appreciative laughter at his play on words.

Mann's audiences were delighted when he described the adored maiden aunt . . . "for childrens' dresses does she not know all the styles; for their learning has she not seen the sagest books; and for their health has she not the newest cure-alls by heart? And oh for romping and roistering groups of the nursery, does she not carry all the toy-shops of France and China in her pocket? Who, of all the household, can help paying homage to such a divinity, even though it sometimes seems as if she would kill us all with kindness!"

It was a new stand which Mann took when he declared that there was "no conceivable reason" why a woman shall have "less occupation than a man, and receive but half his remuneration for equal services." And Mann believed that the "law of nature" summoned woman "to the highest posts of honor and glory" — namely teaching. "The artist's work is but surface work," said Horace Mann. "The teacher's work is heart-work — yea in the very core of the heart. . . . As a teacher of schools, how she shames the wisdom of the lawgiver and the retribution of the judge, by saving what they sacrifice and redeeming what they destroy!"

His "Woman lecture" was going very well, Mann told Mary. He was content with his tour for he was rapidly collecting the necessary funds for his family. Albany offered fifty dollars for one lecture, Rochester paid sixty and small towns along the way gave twenty-five.

Mann settled himself comfortably in the train for an all-day ride from Albany to Syracuse. Snow swirled outside the grimy train windows but within, the red plush seats had a cheerful air and the iron stove gave out blasts of heat. Cinders leaked in along the edges of the windows and lay in black piles on the sill. Sooner or later, Mann would get one in his eye in spite of his spectacles. But he loved trains and everything about them. How right he had been to press for the building of railroads in his younger days! The hours went by and he had plenty of time to think. The date was February 25, he remembered. Next day he wrote a letter.

"What do you think I thought of as I was riding all alone in the cars yesterday?" Mann asked his little son Horace. "I was thinking of you and I remembered that you were eight years old that day.

"Now you are eight years old, you must begin all new, & be a better boy & a more learned boy, & then you will be a happier boy." To begin "all new" — that was Horace Mann's own formula for obtaining happiness. Horace and Georgie were to get out the map and trace their father's travels. Although he did not realize it, Horace Mann was bound on a momentous journey — and he would soon "begin all new" himself, at the age of fifty-six.

Almost invariably, it was to Mary that Mann turned first to speak his thoughts. On March 9, 1852, Mann was at Lima, New York, having traveled eighteen miles by wagon over "a plank road" from Rochester. "In this place, a new college has been established, for both sexes indiscriminately," Mann said. "A man came to see me this morning, who is one of a company engaged in getting up a similar college, tho' perhaps of a somewhat less sectarian stamp, at Yellow Springs in Ohio. It is to be for both sexes, is well endowed, & will pay their President from $2500 to $3000 a year. How would you like to go & be the wife of its President?"

Three days later, Mann wrote to Howe. He wrote for advice and until the following May he was "deliberating," but the letter shows that his mind was already made up and Antioch had cast its spell.[3] "You refer so often to my being in a certain governor's chair instead of my own rocking-chair, that if I knew the genuineness of your friendship less well, I should think you meant to tickle my love of approbation," Mann told Howe. "The whole philosophy of the matter can be summed up in a very few words. I have no desire to be in any political office, *per se*. I would never be in one, but, as I am now, as the representative of a principle; or to do some special service as I hoped to do in Congress. I would not, therefore, consent to be a candidate in Massachusetts, at the present time except on the Temperance platform — I mean the Maine Law. But would not that be fatal to anybody? Would the coalition take it up? I doubt it & this ends the subject.

"The Free Will Baptists are erecting buildings for a college at Yellow Springs. They have liberal endowment & aim high. I have been applied to, to navigate that ship. What do you think of it?"

Howe thought very little of the idea and said so. Why would not Mann run for Governor of Massachusetts on the Free-Soil ticket — that should be cause enough even for such a crusader as he! As for Mann's chances — had he not beaten the Whig candidate for Congress? Howe was sure that the Free-Soilers, the Abolitionists and the Conscience Whigs could forget their quarrels and be made to see that Horace Mann represented the cause they all held in common. In the end, Mann agreed to the Free-Soil nomination.

At Blooming Grove, New York, Mann met "Mr. Austin Craig, a New Jersey man by birth," and an ardent young minister beginning his pastorate in a poor, scattered, very rural community. Tall, slender and blond, Craig looked like a young saint of the early church and he drew Horace Mann to him as a saint drew converts. Mann tried to tell Mary what Austin Craig was like.

"He is now about 28 years of age & a most extraordinary young man. He was led to write to me to come here, having seen my 'Thoughts for a Young Man.' He devotes himself very much to the young. He is very earnest & sincere. . . . His introductory remarks this morning, & his sermon, were exceedingly beautiful in spirit & in manner, — all based on Phrenology & full of the most delightful religious spirit." So Mann and Craig talked long into the night and discussed the heads of all great men of their era — meanwhile admiring each other's high foreheads. The young minister was thrilled to hear that Mann really knew George Combe, the phrenologist, personally, and he listened eagerly to Mann's stories of traveling with Combe. "Aside from Howe & Downer, I hardly know such a lover of the true," Mann said of Craig. "He is more simple than Howe & far more literary than Downer, — & yet so young!"

Austin Craig wrote to Mann in behalf of Antioch. He quoted figures. The agents who had been soliciting money "have secured $100,000 as a permanent fund for the support of the instructors, together with $30,000 for the erection of buildings. Much more, it is supposed, may be obtained." [4] This was a great deal of money but Horace Mann was much more interested in another point Craig brought out. Antioch was not "Free Will Baptist" as he had supposed, but "Christian" — the denomination which Austin Craig represented.

Mann had heard little or nothing of the "Christian" denomination but Craig loved to define his views. "The Bible is our rule to the exclusion of all creeds, covenants, disciplines and articles of faith ever prepared by uninspired men and imposed upon the church." This, Horace Mann felt, was exactly the kind of religion he had been searching for. He had helped to build the Unitarian church in West Newton and he paid them twenty dollars a quarter for his family pew. But even Unitarian liberality as to creed was not broad enough for him. Austin Craig said further, "Christian character is our only test of fellowship and communion, to the exclusion of all the shibboleths of party, and tests of bigotry ever urged upon the humble follower of Christ." [5] And Mann felt as though he had seen the Holy Spirit descending like a dove. What could he not do for future generations by becoming president of a college sponsoring this kind of teaching! The members of the Christian denomination decided to name the new college "Antioch" in honor of "the place where men were first called Christian," and this seemed to Mann a happy omen.

It was not long before he was thinking of Austin Craig as an ideal teacher for Antioch. But first he wrote to his niece Rebecca. "If your uncle will be President of a Male & Female College, will you be Professoress of the same?"

In November 1852 Mann dutifully ran for Governor of Massachusetts on the Free-Soil ticket. He campaigned ardently — not so much for himself, but for Free Soil. And he came in third in the race. No one had a majority and the choice was thrown into the legislature with Mann needing only two thousand more votes to become one of the two names put up for legislature decision. But he had no regrets. Horace Mann had accepted the presidency of Antioch.[6]

CHAPTER TWENTY-FIVE

Risk of a New Enterprise

ANTIOCH, as Horace Mann saw it in his dream, was to be larger than Harvard — even as Ohio was larger than Massachusetts. Mann was beginning his life "all new" and he supposed he would have an entirely free hand in selecting the faculty for an entirely new college.

Nothing but the best would do for Antioch and therefore Mann chose his niece Rebecca to be "Professoress" first of all. Was she not the "Jewell" of Lexington normal school? Mann was convinced that Rebecca could have had no better schooling and he was indignant when "female teachers" were sent to the Cherokees from Mt. Holyoke Seminary. "I wonder what wicked deed the Cherokee people have done, that teachers should be sent to them from Mt. Holyoke & you kept away," he wrote Rebecca, who had wanted the job. But he added (still in playful vein), "What a missionary spirit did flare up in you when you proposed to go!" Rebecca had not been popular at the normal school the last year, her Aunt Mary said — but her Uncle Horace never considered for a moment that it might have been the girl's own fault.

Although no teacher on earth could equal Rebecca in her uncle's eyes, her brother Calvin came close to it. Calvin's professor of "electricity and magnetism" at Colby considered the boy "first in his class in sheer intellect," with "gentleness of manners without the least approach to effeminacy." If Calvin's cousin Thomas did not exactly go along with these sentiments, it was of no consequence to Uncle Horace. Later, Mann would recommend another niece, Eliza Pennell Blake, "a lovely creature, & I have no doubt of her success." (Her husband, Gardiner Blake, was to work on the college accounts, which would drive him into a "brain fever"!) Mann also spoke a good word for Rebecca Wilmarth, granddaughter of his mother's brother — and properly normal school-educated. A niece, Charlotte Mann, would go to Antioch — but as a student, not a teacher!

It was a shock to Mann to discover that he was not going to appoint the entire faculty of Antioch after all. Who, then, had the right? he wanted to know. Mann had heard vaguely that people were subscribing to "scholarships" of a hundred dollars which entitled them to send a student to Antioch. The financial pitfalls implicit in the plan escaped him but he wanted to know if each "scholarship owner" was "entitled to a vote in choosing the faculty & also in dismissing them. Suppose you have 12 or 1800 entitled to vote," Mann said. "Disaffected students might disaffect their patrons (enmities are more active than friendships, most people will go further to satisfy a grudge than to reward a merit) — the Malcontents" would assemble and vote, "while the *Contents* would remain at home . . ."

Mann spoke from bitter experience and his gift of prophecy was upon him although he knew it not. He was writing to the Reverend Mr. Eli Fay, idealistic leader in the Christian denomination and destined to be his friend in need. "The trustees alone employ the faculty," replied Mr. Fay — thereby setting Mann's fears at rest while disappointing his hopes.

In the next paragraph, Fay disappointed Mann still further. "Your suggestion with regard to a 'female Professor' though new, meets with universal approbation and we have a number who are admirably qualified for such a station. Our friends, no doubt, will be glad of your counsel in the appointment of our Faculty, but we think a majority of the Professors should be solicited from our own people, as the college is the fruit of our munificence . . ."

Still envisioning Antioch as very large, it did not occur to Mann that in the eyes of Yellow springs, and the Christian denomination as well, he and his nieces and nephew and all their in-laws would seem not merely a "majority" but an invasion of Easterners.

Mann wrote out a course of study for Antioch, included his list of teachers and awaited results. "I shall not think of going, unless I can have the arrangements to my mind," he said. "If they are made so, then perhaps I may risk a new enterprise even at my time of life."

The "risk of a new enterprise" — there was both the danger and the lure. Like his ancestor, the Reverend Samuel, Horace Mann longed to strike out along a new trace, and at last a letter dated September 20, 1852, brought the news he wanted to hear.

DEAR AND HONORED SIR,

This is to notify you that the conditions (which you proposed to our corresponding committee) on which you would accept the Presidency of Antioch College, are complide [*sic*] with, and that at a meeting of the sub-committee held at the College Office at Yellow Springs, Green Co., O. Sept. 15th 1852, you was legally chosen by sd Committee, to fill the Presidential Chair in Antioch College; also that Mr. and Miss Pennell (of whom you spoke in your letter to our corresponding committee) were then, and there, duly elected members of the College Faculty. . . .

Spelling, punctuation and grammar Mann mentally corrected and proceeded to read the postscript which contained, as so often, some of the most important news.

P.S. The rest of the faculty is composed of Rev. Thomas Holmes of Portsmouth, N.H. Rev. W. H. Doherty [1] of Rochester N.Y. and Mr. Ira W. Allen of Albany N.Y. Rev. Arther [*sic*] S. McKenney of Crawfordsville Ia. was chosen teacher in the primary department.

For a moment, Mr. Mann must have wished he had accepted the offer of the presidency of Girard College which was made to him some time previously. He would not have been happy in a college where religion was barred, but what was he to do with all these reverend gentlemen? Instead of "renouncing all creeds but the Bible" as a pamphlet on Antioch promised, some of these men were as orthodox as any of Mann's old enemies in the days of his school secretaryship.

Mr. Fay wrote further news. After choosing a faculty that was anything but liberal in theology, the trustees expressed ideas about the courses of study and how to teach them. But Mr. Fay held off any action. Speaking for himself and almost no one else, he told Mann, "We thought it hardly right to take the Mann without his 'Plan.' "

Mann heard with deep disappointment that Austin Craig had been approached to become a teacher at Antioch but had declined. He wrote Craig expressing his regret. "I do not expect . . . to remain connected with the institution for many years," he said. He already pictured Austin Craig as taking his place as President.

On November 4, 1852, Mann called the first faculty meeting of Antioch to take place at his home in West Newton. How Mary worked, to see that curtains were crisp and fresh in bedrooms — that there was plenty of food in the larder, for six guests stayed "two whole days and parts of the preceding and following days." The Reverend Mr. Holmes was there, and Ira Allen, Calvin Pennell and his wife, and Mr. Fay. Mr. Merrifield, architect of Antioch, was present part of the time. Rebecca Pennell was of course the Manns' permanent guest.

The meeting was "harmonious," Mann said — it was even "unanimous." The faculty were "all teetotallers: all anti-tobacco men; all anti-slavery men; a majority of us believed in Phrenology; all anti-emulation men, that is all against any system of rewards and prizes designed to withdraw the mind from a comparison of itself with a standard of excellence, and to substitute a rival for that standard. We agreed entirely as to religious and chapel exercises . . ." It was all so perfect that only Horace Mann with his great-hearted confidence in human nature could have believed that such harmony really existed or would continue.

By December, Mann was in Toledo on a lecture tour and on his way to visit Yellow Springs. As always, everything Middle Western rejoiced his heart. "Dunkirk is a marvellous looking place," he wrote.[2] "It looks as tho' all the railroads in the world might have terminated or begun there." Mann became more lyrical over railroads than over the beauties of nature as he watched "the single track begin to ramify and spread, like nerves over an organ of sensation, and then diverge and multiply till acres and acres are covered with a net-work of them."

In Pittsburgh, Mann's lectures were heavily attended and he was urged to stop over and give his "Thoughts for a Young Man." He could not, because he was due in Cincinnati. It startled but delighted Horace Mann to find his lectures advertised "on fences & posts & even on the pavements, in great sheets not less than twenty inches by two feet, — not only as 'Horace Mann, President of Antioch' but, what was entirely new to me, as 'the distinguished orator of the West.'" And on a Ohio River "steamboat," Mann was recognized and spoken to by a perfect stranger. How could he help liking the Middle West, where he found himself unexpectedly famous and where people were so friendly!

In Cincinnati, where Mann lectured to "a tremendous house," he also had an important interview. "I found at the 'Burnet House' where I stop, Judge Mills, as they call him, who is the man who gave the land — 20 acres, for Antioch, & $10 or $12,000. He is the right sort of man, has got his head cleared of all the old cob-webs. He offered to go out with me to Yellow Springs tomorrow, & I have had a good talk with him today & he talks capitally."

It was raining when Judge Mills and Horace Mann stepped off the train at Yellow Springs — into a sea of mud. Yet so "capitally" did Mills talk and so vivid was Mann's imagination, so predisposed his mind, that he could see just how beautiful everything would be, come spring.

Mann was too weary that night to write very much to Mary, but he told her of the miraculous ravine that cut through the rolling fields just below the college. Here the "Yellow Spring" flowed full and ceaselessly, "a hundred gallons a minute," out over ledges; and here were the gaunt, half-deserted buildings of the once fashionable resort — "now old and tumble-down-y" Horace Mann said. Judge Mills was engaged in forming a company to buy up the property, which he declared would be cheap at a hundred thousand dollars. Mann was suitably impressed. But the "rocky sides, little cascades & something in the way of cliffs" delighted him with their odd, unexpected beauty. He loved the "glen" even though he smiled a little to hear one of the men with him describe it as " 'Alpine,' meaning from fifty to a hundred feet high" where the banks rose sharpest from the bed of the stream. Since contrast is so important an ingredient of effect — why "Alpine" those cliffs really were!

"You know the position of the College buildings, facing east, with a gentle slope down to the railroad, which is the eastern boundary of the grounds," Mann reminded Mary. This railroad, running so close to the college, instead of being regarded as an eyesore, was considered an ornament and was the particular pride of Judge Mills. It was his personal triumph, for plans had been made by the "Little Miami Railroad" to by-pass Yellow Springs and go from Xenia to join the "Mad River" line at Springfield by way of Clifton — a neighboring town.

Mills had gone East and raised $500,000 — the first Eastern money loaned to a Western road, with Josiah Quincy, Jr., among the investors. Then back came the victorious Judge Mills, riding his horse into town and bearing the great news that he had won the railroad for Yellow Springs. Mills was like a conqueror of old in the eyes of his fellow townspeople, and surely, as they remembered it, his horse was white and the railroad contract he carried he waved aloft like a banner! Disappointed citizens of Clifton brought suit in vain. They had no champion like Judge Mills.[3]

"The cars will not be whizzing by all day," Mann told Mary, lest she be disappointed. He was right, for this was a single track with an "up train" and a "down train" only. "Judge Mills is capable of wielding an immense amount of influence," Mann said — and again he was right.

The main building of Antioch was in process of construction and Mann was assured that dormitories would be ready before the college opened. What struck him now was the welter of mud and the stumps of great trees where a beautiful tree-shaded campus ought to be. He spoke of the pity that such fine trees were gone. Judge Mills was surprised. In pioneer country, the clearing of land is an achievement involving tremendous labor and not a cause for regret. But he rallied quickly and said that there was a "forest" on part of his own six hundred acres which he might make into a public park.

"Yellow Springs . . . is a beautiful place," wrote Horace Mann, and he had yet to see it all flowering in spring! "What thoughts rush into the mind, when one surveys the scenes of anticipated labors, or looks upon those of the past — not thoughts, for they are molten into feelings, & by expansion, swell & dilate the bosom. . . ."[4] He returned now, not to his home in West Newton but to Washington, where he awaited the end of his final term in Congress. He had long since written a letter to his constituents, thanking them for their support but saying that he would be a candidate no longer. His heart was in Ohio and to Mary he wrote of plans for their new home.

"Will it not be best to have my library the South-West corner room, on the first floor, because that overlooks the college buildings

& grounds & will give me a chance to oversee what may be going on? & then our parlor behind it, which will be a beautiful room for sunsets & for new moons tho' not for full ones and sunrises." Horace sketched a floor plan and asked Mary to improve upon it.

One of Mann's cherished hopes was to have his house in Ohio resemble the beloved West Newton home which he had built. It was a blow to hear that "Rebecca begs that the new home shall be in better proportion, for she says she suffers every day when she looks at this." Rebecca wanted a piazza "on the other side" — and in the end, the president's house in Antioch had a piazza all the way around.[5] The president's house was well-proportioned, square, high-studded and Victorian of the best phase. Rebecca drew Mann's plans all over again but for once her uncle was sharp with her. He was having things his way and the plans he drew himself were what he wanted.

Mary's letters to her husband, although full of happy thoughts of their new life, carried nevertheless a note of sadness in the early part of 1853. Her mother, that valiant soul whom Mann had found in the shop in West Street studying German, was now very ill in West Newton. She suffered greatly from a tumor in the throat and her daughters could not wish to see her life prolonged. "I have just returned from my evening visit to Mother," Mary wrote. "She grows weaker, but coughs less. I hope she has some pleasant musings in her long silences — it seems very hard for her to call herself from afar for any communication. I go with longing to attend her steps to the threshold of that home whither she is slowly tending, and leave her with regret that her steps are stayed." And the next day, Mary wrote, "Mother expired gently and peacefully in my arms this evening."

"She always smiled upon you," Mary told her husband, "for the sight of you gave her delight and the sound of your voice was music in her ears." It was a long time before Mann received this letter for he was returning to Washington from his lecture tour and was snowbound in the train for five hours at one point in his journey. As soon as he could, he wrote words of comfort to Mary but her loneliness could not be lessened by anything short of his presence. She began to think with increasing eagerness of their life together in Antioch where she hoped they would be separated almost never.

Howe made one last attempt to dissuade Mann from leaving

Massachusetts. But Mann replied, "I find my mind, within the last few months, to have taken an entirely new tack. The rudder has been put hard up. . . . My associations are all clustered round a new nucleus, — new prospects, new labors, new dangers, — & new devices to avoid them."

Now that the decision to leave was final, West Newton people began to call on Mary Mann to say good-by. She had not realized that she had so many friends and she was touched — but no more turned aside from the great adventure than was her husband. "I have been hindered all evening from writing to you," she said, and she begrudged the time when friends "invade the hour that I wish to be talking to you, for I like to take it leisurely, and hold my pen suspended, and think about you as long as I please. It is the only time when I seem to possess you while you are so far away. I wish I could make you feel the warmth of my love nearer and dearer than written words can do — I long to feel myself in your arms again and say you are mine and hear you say *yes*. We live all the time in reference to you — to improve all that is possible while you are gone — to be good for your sake . . . but we all have moments when the recollection of you does not soften but sharpens the pain of absence. 'When we go to Ohio, Papa will live at home,' is a favorite saying of Benjy's."

There was one more ordeal of controversy which Mann had to endure before he left Massachusetts. Just before his term in Congress was over, Wendell Phillips attacked him for not being sufficiently ardent in the cause of antislavery! Mann was both angry and hurt. A series of letters by Mann and Phillips appeared in the *Liberator*, and the *Liberator* was outrageously unfair, editorializing in favor of Phillips in every issue. Theodore Parker tried to make Mann and Phillips see that they were really both of them on the same side. "What a good man you are," Mann said to Parker. "I'm sure nobody would be damned if you were at the head of the universe" — but Mann could not forgive Phillips's "personalities, & those mainly outright falsehoods."

Edward Loring, Mann's "glorious Neddy" of Litchfield days, was now on the pro-slavery side in the fierce argument that was separating friend from friend in Boston. Loring and Mann were no longer speaking but Loring wrote a last letter. "You were overheated toward your adversaries," Loring said, "and you could be unjust to them. But I knew you to be overheated toward your friends and that you were as excessive in affection as in opposition, that this fervor which would boil either way was temperament and left honor, truth and nobleness unscorched, unsullied and most lovable." It was perhaps the most accurate description of Mann that any friend ever gave him and he kept the letter even if he could no longer travel Ned's road. It was Commissioner Edward Greely Loring who, three years later, ordered the fugitive Anthony Burns to be taken from the jail in Boston and returned to his master.

In June 1853 Mann wrote to Judge Mills to know how the buildings were progressing at Antioch. "I can well appreciate your anxiety," the Judge replied and he assured Mann that all was well. In the "female dormitory" the plastering was finished — the foundations for the "male dormitory" were laid. And the president's house? "Materials being already procured, it will be only a question of labor as to its speedy erection." Mills wrote in glowing terms of what went on in the town of Yellow Springs. "New buildings are being erected, streets opened and graded. . . . None visit the locality but to admire it, and all express astonishment at the magnitude and costliness of its chief attraction, Antioch College." Mann's prophetic spirit slept and the "costliness" of Antioch raised no misgivings in his mind.

Early in the autumn of 1853, Mary packed all her worldly goods. The dear house on the hill was put up for sale but she gave it never a backward look — she was no Lot's wife. The three little boys were alive to the great adventure, in their separate ways. Dark-haired Horace, now nine, kept his intense excitement bottled up inside him except for sudden bursts of misplaced enthusiasm which exasperated his equally nervous father. Georgie, blond as his father had once been, approached the experience with a certain calm confidence of which his father approved. He was not yet eight, well along in his Latin declensions. And Benjy, just a little over five, was his usual prankish self — allowed to be a baby much longer than either of his brothers had been. He was always in his father's good graces it seemed and he was sometimes the object of his brothers' jealousy on this account.

The first letter with a Yellow Springs heading was written by Mary Mann to her father. She loved him dearly. He had comforted her in her loneliness and she remembered how she and her father used to sing together and how the children soon learned to join in. The "lost sweetness" came back into her father's voice as he sang a lullaby to little Benjy. And Dr. Peabody had insisted that the baby's milk be kept cool — a new-fangled idea for which he built a new-fangled contraption, a refrigerator. His three little grandsons, who followed him around adoringly, learned much from watching his skillful hands at work. Mary knew that her father's health was failing. "Remember the remedies with which I used to cure you," she wrote. Best of all remedies was the knowledge her letters brought that he was not forgotten.

Since the Mann family arrived in Ohio in September, there was no mud when they stepped off the train at Yellow Springs. But neither was there any exuberant Judge Mills to make all things beautiful with his fluent optimism. A "relative" — perhaps Calvin Pennell — met them with a wagon. The flat "table-land" with its stumps of trees seemed utterly desolate to Mary, but her husband told her that here was freedom, not desolation; and a future all untouched, all theirs to make glorious.

And suddenly, there it was — many-towered Antioch [6] rising from the plain! It was more Gothic than the Goths. Higher rose the towers than any Goth could have carried them unless he used red brick — and higher still they seemed in contrast with the level farm land. Antioch was extravagant, impractical — yet marvelously, incurably romantic! [7] A farm boy, finding himself the happy possessor of a tower room, would hear the clash of knightly arms as he walked, dreaming, to his classes. He might walk as though stepping over plowed ground but he held his head a little higher and his spirit was wrapped in the white mantle of Galahad. The boys (Clay Badger [8] from Honeoye Falls for example) would say of the tall, erect President Mann, with his white hair and fiery glance, "He was like a Prince."

CHAPTER TWENTY-SIX

The Happy Years

INAUGURATION DAY at Antioch was October 5, 1853.[1] Since the college buildings were far from completed, few invitations were sent out but the fame of Antioch had spread far and wide so that three thousand people streamed into Yellow Springs. They came in carriages and carioles — in farm wagons with provisions for whole families and quilts to cover them at night. Most of these people were experienced veterans of religious camp-meetings where they had gathered after the crops were in to listen to a revivalist, to sing rousing hymns and get "full of glory." They had come to Yellow Springs to fill themselves with a new kind of glory — education — and Mr. Mann would not disappoint them. Mann often referred humorously to his "preachments" with poundings upon the pulpit cushions to the glory of education. He faced three thousand willing converts.

Magnificent as Antioch's new chapel was, it could not possibly accommodate all the visitors; but at nine-thirty in the morning, when the crowd gathered before Antioch's attenuated towers, they found a "temporary platform" built "over" the "grand entrance" from which "Mr. Phillips,[2] the prime agent, addressed the multitude." But first, Elder Phillips presented "three splendid Bibles" which Horace Mann accepted in behalf of Antioch.

What a contrast these two men made upon the platform! If Horace Mann, erect and elegant in his long black coat, looked like a prince to his students, then John Phillips looked like a giant out of another fairy tale. He was huge, swarthy, careless of his appearance. He had a great bull-bellowing voice and "his intonations were peculiarly his own." Ohio was his love and he had been campaigning for at least a year to bring Antioch to Ohio — as a bright star in her crown which she deserved for every reason from the cost of living — ("I can buy eggs enough in Spring in southern Ohio for 4 cents a dozen to sink a steamboat," John said) to the low death rate, "about one half per cent lower than New York."

The desire to help young people who had no money to acquire an education, which inspired Horace Mann, moved John Phillips as well. In spite of poverty, Phillips had struggled through three years at an academy, but this was all the education he had the means to acquire. He was now a self-taught minister in the Christian denomination, having been a carpenter until he experienced conversion and the call to preach. When the inspiration came, he climbed into his old wagon, took his wife along, and set out westward from New York state. Phillips obeyed apostolic injunction, carrying with him "neither gold nor silver . . . nor scrip for the journey," but his wife, perhaps unaware that as many as two coats were forbidden an apostle, brought along a small bundle of warm clothes. Each day they drove from morning until nightfall, when they stopped at some farmhouse along the way. Kindly people took them in, fed and cared for Brother John, his wife and his weary horse. If the spirit moved Brother John, he might remain a month, preaching and organizing a church — or he might journey on next day.

John Phillips had been a "Millerite," preaching world cataclysm. But when, on August 11, 1843, the world failed to come to an end, Brother John was reconciled to putting up with it a little longer. He turned to other enthusiasms, and Antioch with its ideal of higher education for boys and girls alike, and at the lowest possible cost, appealed to him almost as much as seeing "the world cleansed by fire" and becoming a saint. He was now known as "Antioch John."

Mann was greatly attracted to "Antioch John" — a person in many ways his opposite but sharing certain ideas. Phillips was a phrenologist. "Talk about benevolence," he would say, "why this bump on the head of God Almighty is larger than a thousand mountains." Mann smiled at the similes of this fellow phrenologist, and enjoyed Phillips's exaggerations about Antioch, sure that everyone took them with a grain of salt. "The great Antioch telescope," Phillips declared, "will be placed on such a high tower that we can see Lake Erie and the people in the streets of New Orleans." It seems likely that Phillips got to believing his own tall tales and certainly plenty of other people did. He sold sixty-five thousand dollars' worth of scholarships to Antioch, saying, "These very scholarships which I offer you today for one hundred dollars will, in less than two years, be worth two hundred dollars and cannot be obtained." All Phillips asked was six dollars in cash as his commission. The signed promise to pay he sent to Antioch and his enthusiastic contributors went to bed feeling rich — having just made two hundred dollars for a six-dollar outlay!

John Phillips was not now soliciting scholarships — he was asking for outright gifts to Antioch. With perfect timing born of long experience in preaching repentance and persuading the unregenerate to come forward and receive salvation, Preacher Phillips urged his listeners "to ascend the steps of the platform and place their contributions upon the table." All were to come, "from $500.00 men down to three-cent men." Antioch John was swayed by his typically fantastic optimism if he thought he saw any five-hundred-dollar men in the crowd gathered among the stumps of trees, building debris and trodden earth before him. But men climbed the steps, a long line of them, each laying upon the table a silver dollar or a quarter — their contributions representing in many cases at least five hundred dollars' worth of hard labor. "Six hundred dollars was taken immediately" and Mrs. Horace Mann, for one, knew that this was a splendid offering.

But as is usual with such affairs, the program was running behind schedule. The "band from Springfield" was "an hour or two late" and other speakers "were cut off." The governor of the state and his wealthy friends who had arrived by train, Judge Mills and the other trustees, filed into the chapel to sit upon the platform with the new faculty, their wives, the new president's wife — and Horace Mann. Soon the "beautiful and spacious chapel was filled to overflowing — seats, aisles, galleries and platform," said Mary Mann, writing about it all to her father, back home in the East.

During the past few weeks, workmen had put in every day including Sundays so that the chapel, in the main building, should be ready for use. The great wooden vault sprang high and aspiring overhead until the apex of the arches disappeared into the shadows and the men and women of Ohio, their eyes accustomed to level horizons, felt a lift of the spirit as they gazed aloft. The Middle Ages had come to the Middle West — by way of Tennyson and the

Gothic revival, and by means of fresh-cut lumber and red brick. People stared at the faculty and whispered about the strangers from the East — almost as curious a spectacle as towered Antioch itself. They speculated about the pale and interesting Miss Pennell and wondered if she were a "new woman" such as one read about in the papers who actually made speeches in public! She was something new in education certainly — a "professoress." Mrs. Mann, the president's wife, looked sensible enough and even pretty if she had not been so thin. One elderly farmer in the audience decided to ask her how old she was and how many children she had.

But when Horace Mann began to speak all else was forgotten. He stood excessively erect as though expressing the uprightness of his life and in his black coat he looked taller than his five feet eleven and a quarter. Thick, white hair and dark, almost bushy eyebrows combined to make him striking so that heads turned to look at him in any gathering. But it was the fire in his deep-set eyes, the humor as well as the firmness in his large mouth that made Mann's face unforgettable — that made him "magnetic."

In the East, the age of the sermon was over and the age of oratory well under way, but in the West the pulpit still held the lead with oratory just coming into its own. Mann gave his listeners the perfect combination of entertainment and uplift as he read from a manuscript a "Dedicatory and Inaugural Address" of approximately four thousand words — most of them long ones. He pointed out that "no epidemic prevailed in the garden of Eden" and proposed the theory that diphtheria, typhoid and tuberculosis, which were filling the churchyards of his era, were the result of such sins as "polygamy, the basest harlotry and drunkenness."

Watching the effect of her husband's speech upon the crowded audience, Mary said, "I shall not soon forget the sea of eager upturned faces which met my view from the platform. . . . They have a way here of groaning out 'Amen' . . . when they like anything. It issued from their lungs in various keys and with various gradations of fervor as he went on and when we came out many persons accosted him and expressed their gratification."

"Eight or ten babies" brought into the chapel by their mothers began to howl lustily long before the inaugural address was over. The Grand Marshal asked that they be taken outside and some mothers, red-faced and unhappy, went up the aisle. Others, doubtless remembering that Horace Mann advocated a woman's right to equal education, decided to assert this right and remain. "It was at first amusing, but became not a little provoking," Mary said. But Horace Mann had spoken under difficulties before.

On the platform and sprinkled liberally in the audience were the "million-dollar farmers," so-called because of successful land deals — first along the canals and now along the railroads where country towns were turning into cities overnight. Farm land became city real estate with rocket speed and although sky-rocketing fortunes would also come down to earth in a trail of smoking sparks — that time had not yet come. Mann looked over the million-dollar farmers with but one thought in mind — how much money would they give to Antioch? He had no quarrel with wealth — far from it. He often said that if he had money he would know just what to do with it. He would give it to the cause of education!

Those who stirred Mann's heart in the audience were the less prosperous farmers, occupying a whole row of seats with their children in stair-step array from the boy and girl of college age all the way to the infant in arms. How well Mann knew their life! All during his oration, certain faces appealed to him, certain eyes lighted. These were the people he had come to help with his priceless gift of education. And then there were the old people — the pioneers who had settled this new land just as Mann's forebears had settled the wilderness out Wrentham way. Mann loved and understood such people, for if he had not, he would not have been standing on that platform in the chapel of half-built Antioch.

"One old man asked him how old he was" when the address was over, Mary said. Mann was fifty-seven and had no objection to saying so. Surely he had years ahead and time for a new career — for pioneering.

"Well, good-by, Horace," said the old fellow.

A speech by Judge Mills had been planned as part of the program because Judge Mills was the one to unloosen the purse strings of those million-dollar farmers. But the other speeches had all taken too long and now the return train came snorting and puffing along the single track, its bell clanging, its smokestack belching live coals! It was a stirring picture everyone rushed to see. Letterheads and pamphlets with pictures of Antioch had been appearing for some time with each picture a different flight of fancy on the part of the artist. Sometimes the main building had a massive Gothic entrance complete with arrow-slits and battlements. This medieval portal remained in architectural dreamland forever, as did the ornamental fountain in full spate. But the train, always in the foreground in all the pictures, was real enough, with its bell-shaped smokestack, box-like cars — and ladies with parasols, gentlemen in high hats, ascending and descending. They were all ascending now (angels and others) with their funds intact, but Horace Mann was not dismayed. Large contributions would surely arrive by the next mail, he felt sure — and so Judge Mills assured him.

In these varying pictures of Antioch[3] there were always two dormitories, "male" and "female," flanking the main building, sometimes shown as if connected by a handsome arched colonnade — destined to remain in architectural never-never land along with the ornamental cypresses and shrubbery. North Hall was the "female" — easily distinguishable. In the middle of its south wall there was a door on every floor which led by narrow passageways to a five-sided brick building. Antioch had as yet no water system — no "bathing room with a pump" such as had graced the Mann house in West Newton, so this brick building was an enormous privy. The "male" dormitory had a separate outhouse.[4]

Neither dormitory had a furnace but each boasted sixteen chimneys. "Trustworthy boys" would be allowed to bring firewood to the girls' dormitory (as well as their own) and boys and girls alike were prone to let their stoves get so hot that floors and partitions were soon scorched and charred. It was a miracle that both male and female dormitories did not become raging brick furnaces some winter night, but the oak was newly cut and planks were thick.[5] In any case, stoves were not all in place by Inauguration Day. As Mary Mann wrote her father, "the man who sets stoves struck that day — 'No,' said he, 'I been lotting on hearing that ere speech today, and I aren't going to set stoves for nobody.'"

In the one partly finished dormitory, the dining room was framed but not floored. Boards were laid over the joists and tables were made of saw-horses and more boards, so that two hundred dinner guests could be accommodated. And then, on the afternoon of In-auguration, the improvised tables were "swept and the examination papers laid upon them." Meals and examinations alternated for three days.

The examinations[6] were difficult because Mr. Mann was determined that Antioch standards should be the equal of Harvard's. Mann knew that Oberlin had conferred college degrees on women since 1841 but he was apt to suggest that the wind had been tempered to Oberlin's ewe lambs and the women's courses made easy. This was by no means true, but Mann felt that he was really pioneering when he decreed that his women students should take exactly the same courses as the men. There were still plenty of people who believed that women were mentally inferior to men and would break down in health if taught mathematics or the sciences. Antioch was going to show the world! But Mann's hopes were dampened by the results of the examinations. "Many of these great *women* cannot read intelligibly!" he exclaimed. "The profundity of their ignorance" was shocking. The men fared no better. Some of them were already ministers — but Antioch's entrance examinations were far beyond them.

Fortunately, it had been part of the plan to have a preparatory school. "Our college is in fact a school," Mann acknowledged when examinations were over. "Only eight were found qualified . . . though some with conditions, to form a freshman class." A total of two hundred and twelve were listed in the first catalogue as attending Antioch the first term.

But Mann wrote cheerfully to Cyrus Peirce and succeeded in raising his own spirits. It was disappointing to turn his back on Massachusetts where he had been the authority on education; to give up Washington, disillusioned though he might be with politics — and find himself head of a prep-school. But he wrote: "The molding of minds is about the noblest work that man or angel can do. I ought to be content to fill even a subordinate sphere in such work. I have a course of lectures, mainly Physiology . . . and I have constant opportunities to say a word that may serve to shape opinions and character."

Listed in the Freshman class of 1853–1854 was Henry Clay Badger,[7] a tall young man with a small mustache and hollow cheeks. It would have pleased him to know that, in his graduating class picture, he resembled Edgar Allan Poe — long dark hair, poetic melancholy and all. Badger wrote poetry on all collegiate occasions and joined the Adelphian Union — a college society similar to the

"United Brothers" at Brown, to which Horace Mann had belonged, save that at Antioch the emphasis was less on debate and more on "literary" effort. Badger kept a diary in the most approved soul-searching, Alcott style.

He wished to write "a full and candid record of his thoughts," Clay Badger said. He wrestled with his "sins" and spoke of his "vices," his "intemperance" and his "yielding to temptation." Alas for the reader of Clay Badger's journal who might hope for scandalous revelations — Clay was "intemperate" in the matter of maple sugar and crackers, while his "vice" was chocolate cupcakes such as those served by Mrs. Mann at the President's house at teatime! Clay "yielded to temptation" and took two.

Much of Clay's diary was devoted to the praise of a classmate, Ada Shepard, to whom, by April, 1856, he was engaged. He was "thrilled with the sweetest of sensations at the angelic look of my dear Ada in the Pres's class" — he never tired of describing her "soul-filled eyes." But love did not blind young Badger to all else. He was associated for the first time in his life with a truly great, internationally famous man and he was keenly aware of it. Badger later became a minister and a writer, with Antioch a favorite theme. Allowing for youthful enthusiasm and hero-worship, he already wrote well and he painted a picture of Horace Mann as he appeared to a student.

"Horace Mann sits over there in the corner," Clay Badger wrote one Sunday evening, dating his diary entry May 17, 1857. "Fifty years hence, men will ask, Who saw him? Who walked with him? And was he such a man as he demanded that others should be? We do not realize our privilege that we walk under his eye and with his cheer. I suppose that there have come upon earth, among all mankind, not a hundred such as he."

Clay described President Mann's way of teaching — a familiar pattern now but at that time startlingly new and original. "Special lessons" were assigned to "special pupils," giving each some question "to pursue at leisure" and upon which to "prepare a paper to be read to the whole class." Agriculture, canals, railroads, the cotton gin — all came under discussion instead of the theories and abstractions formerly exclusively taught in colleges. Clay Badger tried to put down on paper exactly what it was he found so exciting about studying under Horace Mann. It was "the impetus with which his mind smote our minds." Mann "kindled a heat of enthusiasm."

In the Eastern colleges, student discipline left a great deal to be desired. The disorders at Harvard under President Kirkland were over but not forgotten. At Dartmouth a perpetual poker game went on in an upper room and when the students emptied one of their beer kegs they kicked it down long flights of iron-bound stairs till it burst through a lecture-room door at the bottom.[8] The professor who was lecturing hardly raised an eyebrow. Town and gown riots were commonplace at most Eastern colleges. But Horace Mann was determined that Antioch should be finer in every way than any Eastern college — Antioch must set an example for good behavior first of all. As the second college year opened, Mann said that there was "a much larger number of students and not one fourth the cases of discipline." The students were "a most exemplary set of young people" and there was "obedience without punishment, order without espionage, great diligence without any trace of an artificial system of emulation . . ."

There were thirty-one rules in the list of "Laws and Regulations," and later five more were added. Students were "prohibited from using tobacco on the college premises." This sounds unduly severe, but Mr. Mann was not thinking in terms of the modern, ever-present cigarette — as yet unheard-of. He was talking about chewing tobacco, and the nation-wide habit of spitting tobacco juice upon the floor of no matter what room! It was not easy to make young people see that this was a nasty trick, especially when some of them had begun to chew tobacco at the age of twelve and when they were accustomed to see the minister in the pulpit pause between "thirdly" and "fourthly" in his sermon for an accurate shot at the spittoon! It was a tribute to Mann's persuasiveness that by the end of the first year all but three students had given up tobacco. These three were expelled but not for the "use of tobacco" — for drunkenness. After tobacco, "fire-arms and liquor," in that order, were forbidden at Antioch.

Mann had advocated co-educational high schools and normal schools back in Massachusetts and the fierce arguments of the opposition still rang in his ears. He was determined to make co-education succeed at Antioch and the only way to do it, in his era, was to see that no breath of scandal touched his Antioch students. "Young Gentlemen and Ladies are not allowed to take walks or rides together unless accompanied by one of the teachers," Mann ruled. The beautiful glen, just across the railroad from the college, would be sure to attract the students but "in order to give the respective sexes opportunities of visiting the Glen, they will have the privilege to do so (of course with the owner's permission) on alternate days only: the young Gentlemen may visit it on the odd days of each month; the young Ladies on the even days."

Rules like these were hard for Ohio young people to understand. They represented the parlor-politeness of the East, and it was pure common sense and a desire to save money that brought a girl to Mr. Mann to explain that her brother-in-law had made a wagon-trek to visit her and it would be all right, wouldn't it, if he slept on the floor of her room?

Horace Mann was amused at such a primitive sense of the proprieties and he explained gently — loving his students all the more for being so innocent and unspoiled.

To a correspondent asking advice about starting a similar college, Mann wrote, "The advantages of a joint education are *very great*. The dangers of it are *terrible*. I have seen enough of young men to satisfy me, that in our present state of society there is not any great majority who would not yield to the temptation of ruining a girl if he could. The girls are far more pure but are they safe? We never have had here the happening of one of those events *mildly called accidents* but it is only because of our constant, sleepless vigilance." Mann never ceased to be fearful lest his young men and maidens should tread not only the paths of the Glen together but the Primrose Path as well!

For explaining and enforcing the thirty-one and more rules of conduct and for much of the teaching, Mann depended on his niece, Rebecca Pennell. During the first year, for example, students were "divided into twenty-nine classes of which Rebecca, being the most accomplished teacher, takes seven, besides having them by platoons at odd hours to teach them how to study their lessons," Mann said.

"We must take care that she is not quite spoiled," warned Rebecca's Aunt Mary Mann, not once but often. "Rebecca is more influenced by you than anyone," Mary told her husband, "and will do that which she thinks in her innermost mind will make you approve and admire her most." [9]

Mary's warnings about Rebecca's increasing egotism went unheeded but Mann was certain of his influence over her, and therefore it was a shock to him when Rebecca announced that she planned to marry the Reverend Austin Scannell Dean — a man whom her uncle disliked and distrusted! Dean was assistant treasurer of Antioch, agent for collecting Antioch funds, and he had a finger in several other pies from time to time: a boardinghouse for students, the printing and sale of Mann's Inaugural Address, a bookstore. "Have you any doubts whatever of Mr. Dean's perfect veracity and reliableness?" Dr. Henry Bellows, prominent trustee, had queried. Doubts were nebulous until Mann asked Mr. Dean for his accounts as agent and assistant treasurer.

Mr. Mann tried to take the most generous view he could of the Reverend Mr. Dean, but it was undeniable that Dean had collected varying commissions as agent for Antioch — some of them large ones. Dean's accounts were in a muddle, with receipts and disbursements which refused to balance. A faulty memory seemed to be Mr. Dean's only explanation for this state of affairs. However you looked at it, Antioch seemed to come out at the little end of the horn — and this was the man Rebecca wanted to marry! There must have been bitter scenes between two high-tempered people, Rebecca Pennell and her uncle. Trying to make peace between them, Mary explained that niece Rebecca could be happy only with a husband she could dominate. Mann agreed that Dean was weak but Mary's argument made him all the more distressed. Mary never forgave Rebecca for hurting Horace Mann as deeply as she did — and Mary had forgiven much throughout the years, where Rebecca was concerned.

Rebecca's wedding took place at six in the morning of June 16, 1855.[10] The bride wore a "brown and white plaid silk dress" and a bonnet of white straw with white watered ribbons and "a most beautiful wreathe of white and pink flowers inside." She had trimmed it herself and her pupil, Ada Shepard, described it and also "had the honor and pleasure of helping Miss P. dress . . . and of packing and unpacking her carpet bag several times."

"Mrs. Mann gave us a beautiful breakfast, at which they placed me beside the bride," Ada went on. "She was lively and cheerful as ever, while Mr. Dean, on the contrary, was much agitated all the time, apparently."

Ada Shepard had one more observation to make. "I never saw

more distress pictured on anyone's face than on Mr. Mann's during the sacrificial ceremony. He feels her loss more than any other person."

First years at Antioch were nevertheless happy ones. One morning Mann looked in the mirror and told Mary that he was getting fat! She laughed because he could never be anything but long and lean. There was a change in Mann, however, which Mary's loving eyes were quick to note. His face had lost much of the drawn look, result of sleepless nights when his brain was on fire in behalf of common schools. He was less tense than he had been in the days in Washington when he fought not only for Drayton and Sayres "but for the whole colored race."

Some of Mann's hardest battles were still to come, but Mary Mann saw now his "happy looks, his buoyant, hopeful, radiant smile" — she heard "his voice of unutterable tenderness."

CHAPTER TWENTY-SEVEN

Antioch "Saved"

IN THE beginning, Mann paid little attention to the state of Antioch's finances. Assured and reassured by Judge Mills, he thought it was only an oversight when his salary was unpaid and he devoted himself to creating the ideal college. Everything he had done or tried to do and everything he had learned while creating the Massachusetts public school system was to become a part of the new dream: co-education, teaching of the sciences, building of body as well as of mind — the highest moral code.[1] Antioch was to be free of religious and racial prejudice, an original and daring conception for that day and age. But Mann's whole life had prepared him for the task, and he saw victory within his grasp.[2]

When Mann awoke to Antioch's financial situation,[3] it was as though the crew of a ship had failed until too late to notify the captain of a dangerous fire in the hold. Once alerted, Mann took charge with every ounce of energy at his command. He organized help from every possible source, and one of his first and most valued allies was the Reverend Henry Whitney Bellows. Born in Boston, Dr. Bellows went to Harvard College and Harvard Divinity School, but New England was too small to hold him. He was only twenty-four years old when he was called to the First Unitarian Church of New York City and this was the pulpit he held now, at the age of forty, when Horace Mann crossed his path. Bellows was a born organiser and would, in the course of his life, help found the Century Club, the Union League Club and the Harvard Club of New York. He had a remarkable talent for raising money and when he visited Antioch in 1854, Horace Mann enlisted this talent in behalf of the college.

"My heart and hand have all been busy with your concerns since we parted," Bellows wrote Mann on Feb. 7, 1854. "They have had the almost undivided possession of my soul. Mr. Dean will probably have told you of my efforts to rouse our New York public to the claims of Antioch. Last Sunday a subscription of about $10,000 was made in my church — another of about $8,000 in Brooklyn — next Sunday another I hope will be made to complete the $25,000." Dr. Bellows was off for Boston, where he hoped to raise $100,000, "by stepping up our whole Unitarian community to the effort."

The money, when raised, would be placed in the hands of trustees in New York, with Francis A. Palmer of the Broadway Savings Bank heading this group. "Our cherished institution," Mr. Palmer called Antioch, and he worked manfully for the good cause. But, being a banker, the first thing he wanted was to look at Antioch's books: Judge Mills, who had been treasurer, was to come to New York. Mr. Palmer overlooked the fact that Judge Mills was a big man in Yellow Springs and would not like taking orders. Moreover, the books were not ready for inspection.

It appears from a letter written to Mann on April 23, 1855, that Palmer went to Yellow Springs. Palmer wrote, "The best that I could make out in the short time I was examining was that while he [Mills] was Treasurer, he received $776.25 more than he produced vouchers for and he said he could not tell anything about it." Naturally many questions were asked, blame passed back and forth. It was finally determined that, in 1855, Antioch's debt was eighty thousand dollars. Mr. Palmer became Treasurer of Antioch for the years 1855–1856, with Gardiner Blake as his assistant. Blake was married to Eliza Pennell, who along with her sister Rebecca graduated from Father Peirce's Lexington normal school. Eliza taught in Antioch's preparatory school.

During practically every college vacation, Mann lectured and attended "Institutes" to spread the gospel of education throughout Ohio and Illinois. In November, 1855, he set out Eastward, to earn money by lecturing — since his salary, even if paid, would not support his family. The verbally and all too vaguely offered three thousand [4] a year became two thousand "and use of a dwelling" by order of a "Sub-Committee Trustees" meeting, Sept. 17, 1852, and the two thousand would go down to fifteen hundred before long — when and if paid. But to be short of funds was not new to Mann, and he wrote his little boys to get out their maps and find Cleveland, Erie, Buffalo, Syracuse, Little Falls and Albany. The assignment was easy for they had learned much geography by following "dear Papa" on his lecture tours ever since they could remember.

"I wish you to apply to Mr. Blake for my salary for this term," Mann wrote to Mary, perfectly confident that funds raised by Dr. Bellows and others must have reached Antioch by now. "Tell him I want it and that you need it, or some of it, and don't let him put you off, if you can help it."

Mary was to direct her reply to Boston, but when Mann got her letter the news was not good. Poor Gardiner Blake was ill of a "brain fever" caused by his difficulties with Antioch's finances! Unpaid professors were resigning and spreading tales of trouble at Antioch.

Mann went to New York to rally Antioch's forces, and on January 31, 1856, he wrote his "Dearest" telling her what he hoped was good news for the whole New Year:

"I have just come from the meeting, wh. has adjourned & have only time to say that

Antioch is safe.

Everything has been mutually & satisfactorily adjusted. All parties have acted most nobly and generously."

No matter how bleak his personal financial outlook, Mann always tried to look on the bright side for Mary's sake. There was no use urging economy, for Mary saved every possible cent. In those days before bakeries and laundries were common and before kitchens were built like a scientist's laboratory, a servant was a necessity. But Mary could hire one for a dollar and a half a week and she had brought Catherine Kelly with her from West Newton, "a perfect treasure in the house." Catherine not only could cope with housework but make "pantaloons for boys as well as any tailor," Mary said, figuring a saving here that almost paid Catherine's wages!

The vegetable garden was another source, if not of revenue, at least of saving, which delighted Mary's thrifty soul. During their first winter at Antioch, Mann planned his garden. It was to be "150 feet one way and 200 the other" and he wrote to his old friend Sam Downer for seeds and stock from the Downer estate in Dorchester, Massachusetts. Sam was one of the founders of the Massachusetts

Horticultural Society and the "Downer Cherry" which he developed was named in his honor. He had sent generous gifts of fruit trees and strawberry vines for Horace Mann's West Newton garden but Mann wrote in an attempt to forestall further generosity. "I tell you *poz* I will not have anything unless I can pay for it," Mann said. By Kasson's Railroad and Steamboat Merchandize Dispatch came blackberries, raspberries, twelve pear trees — a Beurré, a Buffum, a Dix, a Bartlett — Mann was to see which variety flourished the best in Ohio. Never were there more reasonable prices and in spite of Mann's stipulation there were gifts as well — red currant cuttings and quince roots which Mr. Mann must try "at the West," just as a favor.

Mann wrote joyfully to Downer. He had been exhausted by his work in the college followed by a lecture tour in the spring vacation. "But I have my garden now and I mean to recruit." Mann's garden was always his antidote for discouragement and nervous tension. With each miracle of life springing from dormant root and seed he renewed his faith in the future.

Mary was as nervous and high-strung as her husband, as she freely admitted. But for his sake, she forced herself to be the calm member of the family in times of crisis. There were moments, however, when this calm deserted her — as for example when Mann's garden "with all its valuable stock was twice ruined by cattle because no one could be prevailed upon to build a fence around it." The loss loomed large economically and psychologically, and Mary spoke angry words. The twice-ruined garden seemed symbolic of the odds against her husband and Mary begged Mann to leave Antioch.

The school months of 1856 had been particularly trying, for the trustees of the New York fund had decided to keep it intact until Antioch's debts were paid and then invest in "a sound institution." They were firmly convinced that these debts must be paid "at the West" and to this end Mann arranged a meeting in Buffalo "to settle definitely what was to be our fates." A new genius at raising money had come into the picture along with Dr. Bellows. This was Dr. Rufus Phineas Stebbins, first President of Meadville Theological Seminary — a school supported by Christians and Unitarians.

"We held a small meeting, but of very devoted men," Mann told his friend Theodore Parker. "We have severally agreed to be responsible for the amounts of money which, with the $25,000 which

Dr. Stebbins has become responsible for, will pay the debts of Antioch College. About a dozen of us in and around Yellow Springs have
become responsible for $30,000." But in his letter to Parker, Horace
Mann added one last revealing sentence. "Please do not tell Howe
that I have become bound for any more money, for if you do, he
will write me another amico-damnifico letter." Dr. Howe not only
urged Mann to stop contributing his slender means to Antioch, but
constantly begged Mann to consider his pioneer work done and to
leave.

Alternating hopes and fears for Antioch were indeed difficult for
a person of Mann's temperament to bear. He understood this himself,
and sometimes he had that rare gift of being able to see himself
clearly. "It is the tendency of all of our blood to enter into any work
too intensely," Horace Mann said. "Hence we are all inclined to
make too serious matters of small ones; & when matters are really
serious, they absorb & incite & stimulate us, to a degree which our
organization is not fitted to bear. We have a tendency to extremes.
I have felt this & have contended against it as well as I could."

Mann knew that Mary, in spite of the calm she managed to sum-
mon for his sake, was equally high-strung. To Dr. Howe he confided
one of the purposes of the lecturing tour undertaken at the end of
1855. "One of my cherished hopes in coming east on this tour was
to get some money . . . to treat my wife to a little journey for
health and recreation next summer."

In June, 1856, Mary and the three boys set out on this trip her husband had earned for her. In the first of her daily letters, Mary spoke
appreciatively of "this pretty boat," but she was already a little
homesick and she knew that a family can be a burden upon a man.
"I hope your solitude will be as profound as you wish," Mary wrote
— wanting to be contradicted.

It did Mary's loving heart good to receive a letter from her husband written even before she reached New York and speaking as if
her absence from home had been already long. "Should the boys
come back full-grown into manhood, & you gray & tottering &
decrepit, it would hardly seem much longer." And "Ever & aye
yours, yrs, yrs," Mann signed himself.

Gardiner Blake and his wife Eliza Pennell Blake were back in their
home in Brooklyn now, and Mary Mann's first stop was to visit them.

"It seems half a year since I was in Yellow Springs," Mary wrote. "Such a succession of sights and people have bewildered me. I was never meant to live in cities." The children had enjoyed a wonderful 4th of July, "firing crackers and a little cannon from morning till night with the interlude of going over to Barnum's museum in the afternoon where they saw many strange sights. In the evening, they saw from the top of the house, thousands of rockets, roman candles etc., from N.Y. and Brooklyn. I believe they were for once satisfied with fireworks."

There had been time, during the two-day visit, for Mary to talk over the situation at Antioch with the Blakes. Eliza had taught in the preparatory school right from the beginning and Gardiner's recent struggle with Antioch's accounts made their opinion worth listening to. "The more I think of it, my dear husband," Mary wrote, "the more I hope you will not stay where you are much longer." Mr. Palmer "did not speak encouragingly about money," and certain faculty members who had been dismissed for incompetence were doing Antioch all the harm they could by claiming that religious persecution went on there!

Mary went on to say that Rebecca Pennell Dean should also leave Antioch. Rebecca had confided to her sister Eliza that she "should be most unhappy not to have children and feared if she waited much longer it would not be well for her and perhaps she should lose her chance — but she did not like to leave and give up helping her uncle.

"Now do make it easy for Rebecca to leave and let her *live* and be something else besides a teacher," Mary begged her husband. "She is truly worn out by it, as you were by your twelve years secretary-ship and needs a change as much as you did for recovery of mind and body." Here was wise advice, both for Horace Mann and for Rebecca — but Mary knew it would be unpalatable to both of them. It was easier to put things on paper than to say them, sometimes.

Mary's next stop was at Perth Amboy, New Jersey, where her sister Elizabeth Peabody was teaching at Eagleswood School. This school was connected with an experiment in co-operative living similar to Brook Farm, and the community was sponsored by Marcus Spring, wealthy abolitionist. The school was headed by Quaker abolitionists, Theodore Weld and his wife, the former Angelina Grimké. It was a strange, delightful, thoroughly unorthodox sort of school, where Elizabeth Peabody found herself properly appreciated. She had brought her father, Dr. Peabody, to live with her at Eagleswood and here old Dr. Peabody died and was buried. Mary, who loved and understood her father, grieved over his death and wanted to visit his grave.

Mary described Eagleswood and people there for the benefit of her husband. "Mrs. Weld and her sister, Miss Grimké, dress wholly in the Bloomer fashion," Mary said, "and with their gray hair and attenuated forms [it] does make them look ridiculously — but they are perfect fanatics on the subject and seem to think it is the only way in which they can assert their personal liberty." Eventually the Bloomer costume would invade Yellow Springs but Mr. Mann was not going to be very happy about it!

"I am now engaged upon my cookery book," Mary told her husband. "If you do not think it will disgrace your good name when you come to see it, I will print and be a *great author*."

Christianity in the Kitchen, a Physiological Cook Book was Mary's title and on the title page she quoted, "There's death in the pot." But right underneath, and before the would-be purchaser should put the book down in terror, she set Scripture against Shakespeare with "In that day, every pot in Jerusalem, and in Judah should be holiness unto the Lord of Hosts." Mary's thesis was that by avoiding such evils as alcohol and oyster suppers, death would be cheated, while "rice [for example] is very wholesome . . . and even when mixed with rich ingredients, tends to neutralize their deleterious qualities" — so that the faithful housewife expressed true Christianity as she served rice pudding — and other foods of which Mary approved. In spite of the serious note, it was nevertheless a most delightful cook book that Mary wrote — with its recipes for sponge cake, for instance — with "the weight of ten eggs in sugar, of six in flour, and a little salt."

On went Mary Mann, to visit her husband's former sister-in-law, Mary Messer in Providence — to Salem to see old friends. Meanwhile that "solitude" Mann was supposed to crave was short-lived. Detroit was the heading on his letter of July 20, 1856, and he spoke of driving to Springfield, Ohio, at 4 in the morning the previous day, "to take the early train of cars for Sandusky." Rebecca, her husband Mr. Dean, Miss Wilmarth and "little Lizzie" were with him and they were all bound for a Great Lakes holiday. The boat from Sandusky to Detroit "had not the slightest motion but the forward one" and Mann rejoiced in being able to sleep well after so many nights when nervous tension had broken his rest.

On Sunday, Mann and his whole party did the unheard-of thing — they stayed home from church. Again Mann slept and "after dinner, Rebecca combed my head until I lost myself when I went to my room and nature would not be satisfied until I slept again."

After Rebecca returned from her European honeymoon, her Uncle Horace had tried hard to be reconciled to her husband. But it was good news when the Reverend Mr. Dean decided "to go on to Port Huron tomorrow" and Rebecca thought she would "stay here tomorrow and then take the boat to Mackinaw on Tuesday. . . . I think I will stay too," Mann told Mary. "I want to take the change gradually."

It was all of it just what Mary wanted to hear — but she would have liked to be the one to comb her husband's hair until he slept. When she heard that her letters "had better be directed to Yellow Springs" and Mann's nephew Calvin could forward them, the distance seemed to widen. Mary had gone "home" on a visit, but she found that her home was in Ohio — or wherever else her husband might be.

By the middle of August, 1856, Mary was on her way back to Yellow Springs and her heart was gladdened by a letter from her husband. "I miss you *dreffully*," Horace said, using the children's language. "I am rejoiced that you conclude never to run away from me again, but perhaps it will turn out like sailors' vows made during a storm."

It was time to think of Antioch's first Commencement in the spring of 1857. The first diplomas were being made in New York and Mann's good friend Dr. Bellows was designing them. "I am in favor of something more showy than our Cantabrigian style," Dr. Bellows wrote. The diplomas were to be in English rather than Latin but "if we come down to the vernacular, we must throw it into a wilderness of flourish and make it as illegible as Latin or Greek if nothing more!" The engraving would not be on copper or steel "but on *Stone* which I find equally handsome and full *half* cheaper. The whole thing, with fifty copies on vellum and the Stone as our property, will cost about a hundred dollars."

They were not going to need all fifty diplomas the first year. The college catalogue listed sixteen seniors, four of them "ladies." But on the platform in the chapel at graduation were the lady seniors, of whom there were but three: Ada Shepard, Achsah Waite and Mahala Jay. Every senior was to take part in the ceremonies and they had been rehearsing together in the Glen — with a faculty member of course — no breaking of rules!

" 'Tis but a part we see and not the whole," proclaimed Mahala, prettiest of the girls, at least as they appeared in their class picture. Achsah read of "Poetry and Religion," while Ada set forth the theory that "All Success is Partial Failure." Ada wore her "shower of golden curls" [5] in the manner of Elizabeth Barrett Browning, whom she would soon meet face to face while traveling with the Hawthornes in Italy as their children's governess. Before coming to Antioch, Ada had been to the normal school at West Newton, where she worked with fanatical zeal to please Father Peirce. The Manns were sending their best-qualified graduate to Una, Rose and Julian. And Ada, on her part, was to study modern languages so as to teach them at Antioch when she should return and marry her fiancé, Clay Badger.

"Do not tell Mr. Mann," Rebecca had urged when she had been entrusted with the secret of Ada's engagement. Uncle Horace would not like the idea to get abroad that Antioch was a sort of matrimonial agency! But it was all right on this happy day — graduates could be engaged!

Most of the senior gentlemen were distinguished for their splendid whiskers. Mustaches, sideburns — what had they not achieved, all the way to full beards without waiting for General Grant to set the style! "Life" was the subject Clay Badger tackled singlehanded with a poem. Eli Jay discussed "The Mission of Learning" while the reputation of Antioch as a seat of higher learning was upheld by Charles K. Robinson of Flint, Michigan, who gave his address the title, "Homo Sum, Humani Nihil A Me Alienum Puto."

Horace Mann prepared his first Baccalaureate with all the ardor of Clay Badger with his poem on "Life" or Ada with her philosophy. "I laid down the great doctrine that the power of knowledge ought never to be added to the power of vice," Mann said. And he amended with a new clause the ancient form with which he conferred the

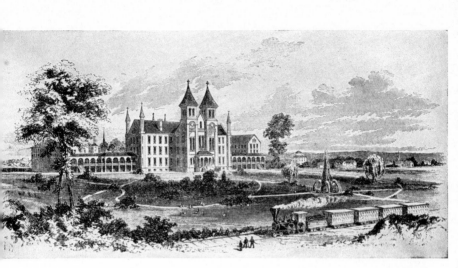

As it never was — with arcades, portico and fountain all complete.

As it is — except that no photograph quite does it justice.

Antioch College

Antioch's First Graduating Class

LEFT TO RIGHT (*standing*): Asa M. Weston, Newell Tibbetts, A. Adaline Shepard, Charles F. Childs, Frank S. Curtis, Phineas H. Clemons, Roderick D. Yeoman, Henry Clay Badger; (*sitting*): Achsah E. Waite, Nathan Fellows, Charles K. Robinson, Roswell G. Horr, Mahala Jay, Eli Jay, John Burns Weston.

degrees. ". . . In further consideration also of the reputable character which you have here maintained and the exemplary life you have here led . . ." It was a solemn little band of young people who went out into a troubled world.

The true pioneer never rests on his laurels but plunges forward to grapple with new difficulties. And Horace Mann, the pioneer reformer, was only happy when plunging ahead with new ideas too big for one person to see accepted in one lifetime. As his early ancestor, the Reverend Samuel Man set out upon the Wrentham Road with ax, with armor and with his Bible, so Horace Mann now set out by way of the new western railroads with his ideas of public education, of low-cost college for both boys and girls — and with his new idea that higher education must be linked with integrity. On Dec. 29, 1856, a convention of delegates from Ohio colleges had met in Columbus. Mann was there, active on the committee concerned with "conduct of students." He explained about his beloved little class of exemplary students and his success in making them feel that he was no enemy of theirs to be tricked and cheated with infringments of rules, but like a loving father to whom they should come with all their problems. A further development of this relationship was the promise on the part of the students to tell Mr. Mann if a fellow classmate were straying.

The delegates assembled at Columbus passed resolutions with many a "whereas" — but coming to the following conclusion: "That in just proportion as the students of any institution will co-operate with its government in maintaining order and good morals, just in the same proportion should the government of such institution become more lenient and parental, substituting private expostulation for public censure and healing counsel for wounding punishments." Student self-government lay just ahead in Mann's prophetic mind.

To his own students, Mann put his case persuasively. "If one student sees another just stepping into deceitful waters where he will probably be drowned, or proceeding along a path which has a pitfall in its track or a precipice at its end, is it not the impulse of friendship to shout his danger in his ear? Or if I am nearer than he, or can for any reason more probably rescue the imperilled from his danger, ought he not to shout to me? But the student just entering the outer verge of a whirlpool of temptation . . . is in direr peril than any danger of drowning or of pitfall or of precipice, because the spiritual life is more precious than the bodily. . . . If a student will allow me to co-operate with him to save a fellow-student from death, why not from calamities worse than death? He who saves one's character is a greater benefactor than he who saves life. Who then, is the true friend — he who supplies the immunity which a bad student desires, or the saving warning which he needs?" The argument was a long one but Antioch's graduating class saw things Horace Mann's way. They deserved the new clause in the presentation of their degrees for they had tried hard to lead an "exemplary life."

The greatest obstacle to Mann's new reform was the old conception of the students' code of honor whereby the talebearer was cut off forever from his fellow students' good graces. But Mann felt that it should be easy to discard this immature conception. At Litchfield Law School students had informed upon each other and no hard feelings! Of course, at Litchfield much greater latitude was allowed the student before he was considered to have transgressed seriously, and the future lawyers felt little hesitation in playing witness since sooner or later each would take part in a defense. The thing to do was to take Litchfield as a step in the right direction but to advance to a higher standard of conduct — with the story of the Spartan boy with the fox in his bosom forgotten forever.

After Antioch's first graduation, Mann went again to Mackinac Island, this time with Mary and the boys. "The climate, the air etc. perform the promise made last year," he wrote, "and as the family are all with me, I enjoy it vastly more than I did last year. I never breathed such air before and this must be some that was clear out of Eden and did not get cursed. I sleep every night under sheet, blanket and coverlit, and no day is too warm for smart walking or vigorous bowling. The children are crazy with animal spirits and eat in such a way as to demonstrate the epigastric paradox that quantity contained may be greater than the container." At last Mann had time to play with his children, to get acquainted with them and to enjoy them. The happiness in Mary's eyes must also have been something "out of Eden."

It was fortunate that Mann had this happiest of vacations, for now his difficulties gathered about him thick and fast. First and always there was the matter of money. "I am in very close quarters as to money," he wrote to Sam Downer in this same letter in which he had just described the pleasures of Mackinac. "The breaking up of the college as it did, without paying me a cent on half a year's salary . . . has left me a sort of beggar." Mann's home in West Newton had been sold but the new owner was in arrears in a second payment of a thousand dollars which Mann had counted on. There was "general indebtedness" to Mann from various sources, but such doubtful assets were of little use in supporting a family.

The year 1858 began with an invitation to Horace Mann to become President of the "State University of Iowa." But the previous September had brought more students to Antioch and Mann was certain that his beloved, his ideal college had weathered her worst storm. He refused the invitation. By May 1858 Mann learned that he had been "elected President of North Western Christian University," and he refused this position also — this time because Antioch was again in a precarious condition and he could not think of leaving her in time of trouble. With every opportunity Mann refused, Mary must have wept bitter tears. It was not wealth — neither was it security she cared about, nor high honors. It was her husband's constant state of tension that worried her. What if he should fall ill!

CHAPTER TWENTY-EIGHT

Final Victory

IT IS natural to speak of the horns of a dilemma and to think in terms of two equally difficult problems. At Antioch, Horace Mann's dilemma was three-pronged. The financial problem overshadowed all others, but religious controversy had begun, such as vexed Mann's days in Massachusetts — and a storm over Mann's code of honor was brewing.

He summed up the financial situation in 1856 in a letter to George Combe in Scotland — that old friend to whom Mann told so much. "Our college is most prosperous in all respects but want of money. By great want of wisdom, if not by something worse, we were involved in great debts at the very outset; and the books and papers were in such a condition that our embarrassment was not known. Revelation after revelation first startled, then astonished, then overwhelmed us. As time revealed deeper and deeper difficulties, the fair-weather friends of the institution, one after another, dropped off, or were turned into antagonists and maligners."

When gifts are to be withheld and pledges repudiated, it is but human nature for men to seek excuses. Almost from the beginning there had been some hostility to Mann because of his liberal religious views and here was the excuse favored above all others. Religious controversy always gathered around Horace Mann like clouds around a mountain peak.

Almost as soon as they reached Antioch, the Mann family joined the local Christian church — which should have settled everything. Mann was not asked to "accept baptism" or subscribe to a creed, but simply to make a statement of belief. This he did with pleasure, saying that he "believed the whole duty of man consisted in knowing and doing the will of God" — but he "entered an official caveat against the idea that belonging to any visible church organization was essential to salvation." In support of this, Mann quoted "the case of Cornelius the Centurion," which should have been well received because by implication he called himself a Philistine and the story of the Centurion took place near Antioch of old, "where men were first called Christians."

Mann was "unanimously voted in" to the church as were Mary Mann and his niece Rebecca — but without a statement on their part. There would be no flouting the advice of the Apostle Paul concerning women's speaking in the synagogue. Mary spoke reassuringly in letters to friends back East, however. In some Christian denomination churches there was ceremonial washing of feet but not at Yellow Springs.

There could be no difference of opinion between himself and his new church, Mann felt sure. And then with that "impetus" and "hot enthusiasm," at once his greatest asset and worst failing, Horace Mann set about making over the church he had just joined. It would have exasperated him to be told, but he behaved exactly like his sister-in-law, Elizabeth Peabody! The church needed money — very well, they must charge rent for pews, with each family paying for as good a seat as they could afford, as Mann and his father and forefathers before him had done! But to the Christians at Yellow Springs this was like letting the money-changers into the temple. Seats in their house of God had always been and always would be free to rich and poor alike.

The young minister, Elder Derostus Ladley, was but a year settled in Yellow Springs and already greatly beloved. But he was ill and again Horace Mann, the still more recent arrival, had just the solution. The church must call Austin Craig, that inspired, Christlike young man from Blooming Grove, New York, whom Mann dearly loved. Ladley must retire for the sake of his health. Mann was astonished when this suggestion was misunderstood and when friends of Elder Ladley thought his departure was being hastened. Hardest blow of all for Mann was Craig's wise refusal to leave his parish at Blooming Grove for a church that was hardly more than lukewarm in his favor.

An anti-Mann faction easily formed within the town because of these misunderstandings in the church. As financial difficulties mounted, an anti-Mann faction was easy to foster among Westerners generally — or among those who were seeking an excuse to withhold help for Antioch. Much of this objection to Mann on religious grounds simmered under cover, with the two reverend gentlemen of the faculty, Doherty and Holmes, making things difficult for their president in a righteous sort of way almost impossible to handle. Professor Ira Allen was militantly pro Christian-denomination. By the end of 1857, the faculty was well rid of these incumbents, but Mann was no better off, because of the gossip their departure occasioned. And then Elder Orin J. Waite[1] of the Christian Church did Mann the great favor of asking him some honest, point-blank questions instead of speaking against him behind his back.

Waite's first question was, as Mann put it, "whether there has been any opposition, open or secret, direct or indirect, on the part of myself or the Faculty against Mr. Doherty or Prof. Allen on account of their supposed religious views." Mann registered a "decided negative." And in the matter of Holmes, "tho' I advised Prof. Holmes to go abroad and study for the duties of his chair, yet I did it with the utmost friendly feelings."

Mann felt that he could best answer all the rest of Elder Waite's questions "by a general statement of Religious views." Mann must have spent a great deal of time and thought upon this part of his long letter, as he tried to tell of his belief in "God's Holy Spirit . . . pervading every part of the moral universe in the same manner as His omnipotent power pervades all space." It was the philosophy of a lifetime that Mann tried to set down on paper. "The manner in which I have often expressed myself is this: We are to imitate the painter or sculptor, who seeks first to become acquainted with the most perfect model and then he strives to copy or transfer that model, feature by feature . . . to his marble or his canvas — so we, having decided to love God . . . should strive to grow up in the likeness of God and Christ, eradicating something here, supplying something there, moulding, shaping, conforming, until it may be said without blasphemy that man is in the image of God." Mann was proud of his beliefs and glad of the opportunity to express them. But when he was through, he restated that principle upon which his first speech in the Massachusetts legislature was based so many years ago — the principle of religious freedom.

". . . I have now, my dear sir, attempted to answer not only you inquiries but your inquiring mind. . . . But having now endeavored to reply, I have something to say on my own account.

"I think no man or body of men has a right to propound such questions to me. My *life* belongs to the world and I hold myself at all times answerable to it for my *conduct;* but my opinions are between God and myself, and except so far as I wish to avow them, are sacred and inviolable. . . . I am not in quest of any political office. I have a duty to perform in maintaining the inviolability of religious opinions and if I yield to the 'question' I set the example by which many may be coerced into yielding."

With this letter, Mann won a stanch friend and fellow warrior. Elder Waite showed the letter everywhere, to people he met on trains, to people in the street. He wrote a long reply and many other letters to Horace Mann which it must have been heartening to receive.

Waite's unlettered style was in sharp contrast to Mann's highly educated and occasionally too legal language, but Elder Waite could speak his thoughts. "I have written twenty letters and sent them broadcast. . . . My heart and hand are with you day and night. . . . I will *back you;* so will the mass of our people. The great heart of the [Christian] denomination is sound and if it can get the truth it will abide by it."

As Antioch's second commencement approached, Mann was aware of all his problems except one. Surely there was no student behavior problem for his boys and girls were still exemplary. He wrote to George Combe,[2] boasting like a proud parent! "And we really have the most sober, diligent and exemplary institution in the country. We passed through this last term, and are more than half through the present; and I have not had occasion to make a single entry of any misdemeanor in our record-book, — not a case for serious discipline.

"There has been no rowdyism in the village, no nocturnal rambles, making night hideous. . . . It is now almost five years since I came here, and as yet I have had no 'practical joke' and no 'college prank' . . . played upon me, — not a single instance."

No one needed to tell Horace Mann that pride always goes before a fall — he must have been brought up on the proverb. Parental pride such as he felt for his students is the most sensitive of all and made the blow doubly severe when, just at commencement time in 1858, a paper appeared, written by three or four students and circulated among students and commencement guests. The *Probe*, the paper was called, and it satirized the college. One article, "Our Graduating Class," was amusing and harmlessly collegiate as it told, among other things, of seniors raiding juniors' rooms in search of stolen stovewood. But in a vein by no means friendly to President Mann was another article entitled "Soliloquy of an Injured Junioress," done in spelling to indicate a Boston accent. There were only two junior girls, one of whom was the President's niece, Charlotte. The injured junioress was made to speak of "Bosting" as that "ne plus ultra city" and to say, "I don't know why it is, but it seems to me that I have not been fully appreciated. But how could I expect it, for the President is the only person in the institution who can comprehend my abilities."

This was humor that cut altogether too close to the truth about Mann's pride in his family of nieces and nephews. The editors promised to publish "Remarks of the Prex on Receiving the First number of the *Probe*," which would be "like the bristling back of a porcupine, for every word will be a dagger." It was foretold by the young editors that they would be condemned in chapel and that the pages of Mann's indictment would flash with epigrams like the jeweled "breastplate of a Queen." Mann's oratory was so universally praised that this sarcasm must have been a shock, but what really hurt him was to hear that his words were like daggers. He knew that his tongue was sometimes too sharp and he was sensitive about it.

Less excusable and seriously damaging to the reputation of Antioch were allusions in the *Probe* to a supposed house of ill fame in Yellow Springs and the alleged visits there of drunken and disorderly students. College humor was one thing, but this article alone would have made the *Probe* the "scurrilous sheet" Mann called it, and its editors deserving the punishment they got — expulsion.

In every college and in every era, student humor gets out of bounds from time to time. But here was the first serious test for Horace Mann's new "Code of Honor," to which much publicity had been given. According to the code, the culprits should have confessed authorship of the *Probe* at once, or, failing that, their classmates should have denounced them. Nothing of the sort happened and this nearly broke Mann's heart. Students refused to answer questions. They preferred suspension to betraying their comrades and here was the story of the Spartan boy all over again. The culprits were finally discovered and brought to account, but they refused to leave Antioch! As their room rent was overdue, the college treasurer evicted them, tossing some of their belongings out the window. The students brought suit against the treasurer and the president of Antioch and the whole thing got into the papers.

"Don't be alarmed if you hear great reverberations about us," Mann wrote his friends. "We expelled four of the boys engaged in the *Probe* and suspended two." When the case came to court, "the jury, thinking the Treasurer had been a little hasty and had injured some of the furniture a little, bro't damages against him — 6¼ cents, but acquitted me."

Plenty of people believed that college students were incapable of exercising authority over themselves and each other as Mann was teaching them to do. It was hard to see a cherished ideal held up to ridicule — but the *Probe* affair was soon forgotten.

Trouble in the faculty was less easy to dispose of. The little world of Antioch was drawn close together by the common occupation of teaching. The faculty were all intellectuals in varying degrees, and as such they preferred each other's society to any other, — even when they reacted upon one another like opposing chemicals in a test tube. There was Mr. Zachos, principal of the preparatory school, "a Greek of fine Oriental temperament." He had "jet black hair" and was "small, lithe and graceful . . . wore a diamond and carried in his white hand a . . . black cane." But he was no more temperamental than Mr. Sobieski, who graced the faculty for a time and who was said to be "a Prince who, if Poland were free, would have first claim to the throne." In Ada Shepard's opinion, he was "always in a state" and she was glad when he left. Faculty members came and went but each was a prima donna in one way or another. Most avid of the limelight was the President's niece Rebecca, whose "elevation" to a higher position "lashed her vanity into a passion."

In his search for a catalyst for this foaming test-tube society, Mann thought not once but many times of his friend Austin Craig. In 1855, Mann persuaded Craig to fill temporarily the place of Professor Holmes, gone to Europe in search of health (and knowledge). Mann hoped fervently that the Reverend Professor Holmes would find almost any other place more healthful than Yellow Springs and that Austin Craig would remain permanently. But it was not to be and Craig returned to his parish at Blooming Grove. He reckoned without Mann's inability to recognize defeat, however, for in 1857, when Professor Doherty departed, Mann sent for Craig again.

"Now my dear friend, we have a chance for a College such as never was known before," Mann wrote to Austin Craig. "I feel God-authorized to say you must come and work with us and when my mantle falls off, take it upon your shoulders. I see no alternative but this. Blooming Grove is but the tiniest islet to the vastest continent, compared to this."

Craig was to say "Yes, with the Lord and Antioch!" And Craig was again persuaded. Tall, blond and gentle, he was a person "of transparent goodness." A student said of him that "he conversed like an archangel" and others spoke of him as "even-tempered, kind, tender, unassuming." Austin Craig lived in the President's household, where he had often come as a guest. At Mann's request, he taught the three boys a happy, confident religious faith such as had been so sadly lacking in Mann's childhood. When Austin Craig fell ill, Mary Mann cared for him as though he had been an elder son. And Adelaide Churchill, a senior in 1858, a gifted and lovely girl, captured the heart of Austin Craig. They were married soon after her graduation.

But perhaps Mann spoke too often of Craig as his successor. In any case, jealousy among the faculty increased. The atmosphere was more than the sensitive young minister could endure, and once more he went back to Blooming Grove where he was so happy and content in his country parish. Mann's letter to Craig upon learning that Craig had left him would have been unforgivable but for the fact that Mann's nerves were so close to the breaking-point. "Amid the exhaustion of past efforts and the frightful labors that now stare me in the face . . . never speak to me of the *Practice* of Duty, but only of its theory . . . of Jesus Christ as a being whose life is to be *imitated* but only *to be talked about* . . ." Even as he wrote these bitter words, Mann knew he would repent them. "Were I to wait till tomorrow; — perhaps if I were to wait but for an hour, — my old love for you (and what man did I ever love so well) would come back." Mann's love for Austin Craig did return and hasty words were forgiven and forgotten. But Craig's wise decision to leave strengthened Mann's courageous determination to stay at Antioch.

For the sake of her husband's health, Mary "used some strong expression in relation to our position here." But "such suggestions made my husband nearly crazy," Mary confessed. "We were two keen, high-strung people who could not live calmly, — though we were both trying for it, always."

Horace Mann now stood alone facing a task that everyone told him was impossible. Yet how could he leave while the dream still possessed him? At this darkest moment came a ray of light and it was the result of a move made at the end of 1857 when "with hesitation and great regret," President Mann and members of the faculty "refused to work any longer" with Ira W. Allen. All the members of the faculty joined in this move with the exception of Mr. Doherty and this was the only way in which to dismiss a young man who had ingratiated himself with many of the trustees. The charge against Allen was talebearing. He had informed students of confidential faculty conferences — and he had told them lies! As though this were not enough, he had fostered factions within the faculty, and outside of Antioch he had spread stories to discredit Mr. Mann. Much of the evil that he did remained after his dismissal but he spent the ensuing year and a quarter compiling a book which he published at his own expense. *History of the Rise, Difficulties and Suspension of Antioch College* it was called — and as Antioch had never yet suspended operations, Allen's first lie was in his title. He peddled his book "through Ohio, New York and New England, representing himself as an abused and insulted man because he was not re-appointed to his chair." By coming out in the open with his series of false statements, Allen provided Horace Mann not only with a ray of light but with a whole sunrise of renewed hope.

At last, Mann had something tangible to work with. Long experience in the law had taught him how to call witnesses and gather evidence — all of which he would finally print in a "Reply" more devastating than any of his many replies to past enemies of his cherished public school system. Some of the evidence was appalling. Faculty members had been told by Allen that "Horace Mann was a sharp lawyer; that he would lie and deceive." Allen had said that "he knew strange things about Mr. Mann; and that if he were not careful, he [Allen] would get him removed from the Pres. chair; that Mr. Mann was afraid of him." Such accusation against Horace

Mann, whose blameless life and tremendous courage needed no
defense, proved only one thing — that Ira Allen must have been at
least temporarily of unsound mind!

As soon as the "Reply" was out letters began flooding in upon
Horace Mann. People who had been critical of Antioch and sus-
picious of its president wrote in to say that they had been mistaken.
People who had been friends all along wrote to encourage and
praise Horace Mann — and to assure him that the whole thing was
beneath his notice. "Fifty cents' worth of disappointed ambition, and
double-distilled love of revenge, tinctured with envy" was the way
Allen's book was described in one editorial.

Only one tragic scar remained. While preparing his "Reply,"
Mann had taken statements from his niece Rebecca's husband, Mr.
Dean — which proved that Allen's statements about Dean had been
untrue. Dean's percentage as agent for Antioch, for example, had
not been 16 per cent of all donations as Allen said, but "only 3 per
cent on a very large portion . . . 8 per cent on another portion and
on still another, 16 per cent." Mr. Dean had wished to put a statement of his own into the "Reply," something which exonerated
him still further, doubtless, but this was rejected. And Rebecca,
like an avenging fury, came to her uncle's study to demand the
reason. Mary Mann told a little about "that terrible night"[3] and
said that Rebecca "had a paralytic stroke in consequence of the
interview, in which" Mann "was obliged to tell" Rebecca "that
Mr. Fay and others would not consent to Mr. D's putting his statement into the book." Mann also refused to withdraw his own statement at Rebecca's request and Rebecca said that her uncle "sacrificed
justice to expediency." Only someone who was close to Horace
Mann could have thought of a way to hurt him so deeply. "Justice"
had ever been his great ideal and "expediency" the thing he most
despised.

Rebecca's "paralytic stroke" may have been a form of hysteria,
for she recovered in due course. But jealousy sometimes tortures
people who have the least cause to suffer from it, and Rebecca
seems to have been one of these unhappy souls. She always opposed
her Aunt Mary's teaching at Antioch — even as a substitute in beginning German, a subject in which Mary was well qualified. Rebecca could not bear to see students influenced by Mrs. Mann and
perhaps Clay Badger, with his fondness for chocolate cupcakes, was

too often at Mrs. Mann's tea table. In any case, Rebecca now gave him to understand that Mr. Mann was not pleased with him and that neither he nor his financée, Ada Shepard, would really be acceptable as Antioch professors. Rebecca Dean was brilliant and charming — and perhaps she never realized how often she told people just what her Uncle Horace would think and do. She could hardly have known how difficult it was for faculty members, in particular, to endure this high-priestess attitude of hers.

Clay Badger went to Horace Mann and was astonished to learn that Mann had no complaint against him. But Badger felt that his future at Antioch was still doubtful, and he wrote to his Ada (who was in Europe with the Hawthornes) since she must be told that her hopes of marriage in the near future had suddenly grown dim. Badger "sent his head and heart . . . weekly in quires of paper," to Ada, as Mrs. Hawthrone put it. And when Sophia Hawthorne found her children's governess in tears, she extracted the story.

In great excitement, Sophia wrote her sister Mary, not one but many letters, not dating any of them.[4] Rebecca Dean "and her husband will probably sap the foundations of things there [at Antioch] and become the cause of all good professors leaving the college so that Madame may reign supreme," Sophia said. She usually considered it wrong to utter so much as a word of criticism about anyone, but now she said much that she had kept to herself through the years while observing Mann's niece as a member of Mary's household. "I want you to beware of her and not trust her too much — and look about you when she asserts anything. . . . She is . . . ambitious. . . . Alas me! . . . I always mistrusted her. With great reluctance I tell you this out of love and justice to you — just as I would guard you from any other evil. . . . Under what a spell you seem to have been to have pleaded for her to Mr. Mann — and to have left your bed to please her! Do you not see that she casts her nets around you! . . . Her accomplishments and intellect only make her the more dangerous. . . . I hope you know I must be a disinterested person in this matter, dear Mary, for Rebecca has always been very flattering to me and mine."

Mary read part of these letters to her husband, "suppressing some of the worst expressions . . . which I thought unjustly severe," she said. "We both laughed at Sophia's fear that I was the victim of

Rebecca's arts." But when difficulties within the faculty arose, and Mann's feeling of tension increased, it became "very painful for him to see R. and he shook his head whenever" Mary "told him she was in the house."

With the passing of the year 1858, some of the storms over Antioch reached their climax and diminished. People stopped talking about the expelled editors of the *Probe*, and whether or not Mann was too stern a disciplinarian. Hereafter, Western college graduates going East for further work would be shocked to see monitors patrolling the aisles during examinations. Mann's ideal — the college student on his honor — had begun to be realized.

There was far less talk of Mann as a sort of misguided missionary, persecuting faculty members of the Christian denomination and trying to make Unitarians out of his students. Mann's letter to Waite and Waite's rallying of forces had taken care of that. While it would be laughable to call the faculty one happy family — now that Doherty, Holmes and Allen were gone — there was more peace and good will than ever before. Eliza Blake and her husband were back in Brooklyn and Mann had found a position for his nephew Calvin Pennell as principal of the high school in St. Louis. Calvin must have used tact to an unusual degree while at Antioch, for he was never a storm center. "There goes the cornerstone of the college," his uncle said when he left — but it must be admitted that Antioch's first president was better off with fewer close relatives on the faculty to furnish an excuse for jealousy.

The ever-present financial cloud hung over Antioch as it does over most colleges. In spite of heroic efforts, Antioch's debt in 1858 was eighty-three thousand dollars. New York friends pledged thirty thousand but there was a string to the offer. New England must raise twenty-seven thousand dollars to pay the Connecticut Life Insurance Company's mortgage on Antioch. Old Josiah Quincy, now ex-President of Harvard, once more backed his friend Horace Mann and circulated a subscription paper. And then there was the "Reyburn claim" of twenty thousand dollars, which New York and New England friends of Antioch insisted must be paid in Ohio. Horace Mann said himself that he was now a "Buckeye," and he tried to raise this fund. On July 10, 1858, he wrote his friend Downer, telling how he fared. Mann knew that his letter would not please Sam Downer, who had tried to keep him clear of financial deep waters for many years.

"I suppose you will call me a fool," Mann began. "It was absolutely necessary to raise $21,000 by subscription, or else the college was remedilessly lost. We got all its friends to be present at Commencement, whom we could prevail upon to come, helping to make a strong rally. But those most bound to step into the breach shrunk & skulked & would do nothing. The thing looked irretrievable. I then did what I suppose you will blame me for; but it really was a question whether this one liberal Institution in the midst of a world of intolerance . . . should be sacrificed or I should be. I chose the latter.

"In consequence of which, it is necessary for me to raise five thousand dollars by the first of August, next." Downer had charge of Mann's finances in the East. "There is the thousand dollars that Littlefield owes me," Mann reminded him — this was on the West Newton property. "There are the Capen securities, there are the Orono bonds. Out of some or all of them, I must raise the money."

Good old Downer [5] replied to his letter in characteristic style. "I rec. yours of 10th inst. which was decidedly a damper, but we all have our hobbys & I hope you may get satisfaction from the gratification of yours, but you are like to spoil mine. Mine was to put your property as far as possible safe, for income & principals for your Independence as old age advances. The income had come & I hoped slowly to save the principal." Downer then listed Mann's assets. "Capen's note — $6218.00." This represented loans made by Mann to support Capen's publishing firm for the sake of the Common School Library and Journal. "Littlefield notes — $5500.00." This was the value of the West Newton property. "Orono Bonds — 4700.00" — these were made over to Mann by the state in payment of debts in connection with public school publications. Downer gave sound reasons why it would be difficult to liquidate any of these holdings. Nahum Capen, for example, was now Postmaster and able to pay interest on the mortgage Mann held on his property. But the value of the principal would be "more doubtful, depending on the value of R. Estate & management when notes mature," and the notes therefore were now "totally unsaleable at any price." So the list went, with poor Downer most reluctant to abandon his hobby of protecting Mann's interest. In the end, Mann managed to pay his pledge. He had a second mortgage on an Ohio farm which was not in Downer's careful hands.

Josiah Quincy's subscription paper was not filled — despite the weight of his honored name. Stebbins, who had promised great things in his money-raising campaign, quit cold. And the Reyburn claim was not paid.

That drop in the bucket, Mann's five thousand dollars, was swallowed up in Antioch's sea of debt, and the college was declared bankrupt, "just like any railroad or Bank or Manufacturing Company" as Mann put it. On April 20th, 1859, Antioch was put up at auction and sold to the highest bidder — Mr. F. A. Palmer, the New York banker who had worked so hard for the college during past years. Mr. Palmer then made over his purchase "to those friends of the Institution representing the collected funds." Antioch was completely reorganized, and Palmer promised to assume payment of debts, "provided friends of the new institution should endeavor to remunerate him as far as possible for his loss."

Antioch's first friend from Yellow Springs was a friend no more. Judge Mills attempted to have the sale of the college annulled. He had given the college twenty thousand dollars in cash, but "in laying out the town to be built around the college, he had also expended large sums of money. . . . He sold lots on credit and put too much faith in the value of paper." When Antioch was bankrupt, so was Judge Mills, and finally "real estate and personal estate, household furniture, plate, all were sold for the benefit of his creditors." Mills had been one of the signers of the "Reyburn note" whereby money had been raised to pay Antioch's running expenses, building debt and so on. In one of his last letters to Horace Mann, Judge Mills wrote: "The more I reflect upon the proposition that the original signers to the Reyburn note provide for it themselves, the more monstrous it appears — nine out of the eleven being already crushed to insolvency."

But if one friend was lost, another came forward. "Mr. Birch of Yellow Springs deeded to Mr. Palmer a thousand acres of land" to help liquidate the college debt of about eighteen thousand dollars. Erastus Mitchell Birch was the foremost friend of the new Antioch and his son Hugh was always to remember Horace Mann. He would recall Mann's magnetic personality and the transforming smile with which Mann greeted a little boy, tagging along beside his father.

Hugh Taylor Birch would eventually become a still greater friend to Antioch.

Everyone could now see that Horace Mann had won the victory and that Antioch was saved — even though it might need saving again from time to time! Mann's mood of despondency lifted and he felt able to accomplish all things. Joyfully, he wrote to his friend Dr. Howe — but the letter was mostly about Horace, Junior, and Mann had no success at all in concealing parental pride. "I am afraid we seized upon your kind invitation for a visit from one of our boys with too much avidity. But Horace has been pining to visit mechanics' and artisans' shops and see the process by which things are made . . . and I am afraid we accepted your invitation more for his benefit than for yours.

"You will see that just now he has the croak in his voice belonging to the transition stage. He is a tremendous eater . . . I am afraid you will think him constrained and awkward — and though I would rather see him as he is than tending to Dandyism, I would like to have his manners softened and refined . . ."

On the 3rd of August, 1859, Dr. Howe wrote to Theodore Parker. "I had Horace Mann Jr. with me two weeks — a worthy chip of the old block." Howe was "counting on Mann's being here in a few days."

Soon after young Horace, Jr.'s, arrival in the East he was taken seriously ill. His mother had given up a projected trip East but there was talk of sending for her. Mary could not leave, however, for she was ill herself. Long before she was well, her second boy, George, had the illness, and then it was Benjy's turn to lie, thin and feverish, in one of the square upper chambers in the president's house at Yellow Springs.

Afterwards, Mary blamed herself bitterly for leaving her husband "unwatched" while he fought his last battle for Antioch, won his final victory — and then wrote his last Baccalaureate at white heat without having so much as time to look over the manuscript before he delivered his address.

CHAPTER TWENTY-NINE

Think Shame to Die...

STANDING for the last time under the Gothic vault in the chapel at Antioch, Horace Mann made his greatest speech all unrehearsed and straight from his heart. Mann looked through life into eternity and found immortality of the soul as completely provable as any case he had ever argued in court. "God's laws abide forever and we abide forever under them," he said. The law still shone for him in all the glory with which his youthful ardor had endowed it. "How shall we obtain happiness, how avoid misery?" Mann knew the answer. "By obeying the law of God."

Looking back upon his own life, Mann said to his seniors, "When I think, after the experience of one life, — what I could do and would do . . . more and better than I have ever done for the cause of humanity, of temperance, of peace; for breaking the rod of the oppressor; for the higher education of the world and especially for the higher education of the best part of it — woman: when I think of these things, I feel the Phoenix-spirit glowing within me . . . I yearn for another warfare in behalf of the right . . . I would enlist for another fifty years' campaign, and fight it out for the glory of God and the welfare of man."

The last Baccalaureate ended with Mann's greatest words: "Be ashamed to die until you have won some victory for humanity."

"How did he look?" asked Mary Mann, who had been too ill to leave the house.

"*Too* happy, but very tired," she was told.

After the college dinner, great numbers of people flocked to the president's house and stayed till late at night. Next day, Mann felt ill but there was a committee meeting he must attend — and another the following day. And now at last the college year had ended, duties were over for a while.

Mann wandered alone at night from parlor to dining room, from study to kitchen. He would not go to bed for he could not sleep and had not slept since commencement. There was nothing he could eat except some fruit juices from a jar of Mary's preserving which he found in the pantry. The heat was intense. If only it would rain! But there had been no rain for weeks — his garden was drying up and wells were low. What water there was failed to quench his thirst, it was so brackish-tasting.

When Mann finally knew that he was ill, "loving and devoted students watched over him and his sick children all the nights of many days," Mary said. Mary was so ill herself that for the first time during her married life her household was without her guiding hand. What happened she could only learn from others but bitterly she blamed herself because she had not been constantly by her husband's side to protect him and care for him — perhaps prevent his illness.[1]

What exactly was the nature of Mann's illness?[2] In Yellow Springs, the word went around that it was the dread "milk sick," or milk sickness. Although no one then knew the cause, this illness came from drinking the milk or eating the milk products or the meat of cattle poisoned by grazing on white snakeroot. Ordinarily, cattle will not touch white snakeroot. But there had been a prolonged drought and at such times cattle could be driven by hunger to feed on this unpalatable herb. Milk sickness in cattle and in human beings was almost invariably fatal. In the East, the papers carried news of Horace Mann's illness — calling it typhoid. The symptoms of both typhoid and milk sickness are very similar. But in milk sickness, death comes swiftly preceded by coma. The patient does not linger more than a few days and there is no lucid period of farewell.

Mann had been ill since the end of June and it was now August 1. "All the arts of medicine seemed unavailing" and a doctor from Cleveland arrived "the evening before the last day."

Told for the first time of her husband's serious condition, Mary summoned strength to go downstairs and the doctor asked to see

her alone. He told her that "the symptoms were very bad" but
Mary "would not look in the face of the possibility of losing" her
husband. She asked what to do, "what changes to watch for," and
was told that pain would be a good sign.

Mary sat beside her husband to watch till daybreak and to "give
him the last remedy" if the coldness in his hands increased. "But
he soon found I was there and insisted on my going to bed," Mary
said. "I pled hard, and only wish I had told him what Dr. Pulte said
and begged him to let me stay with him. But he was in such a tender
state that I did not dare to and he longed so for rest that when
he said I kept him awake and that *he* could not sleep if *I* did not, I
complied."

It was for her own sake that Mary was sent way — she knew that.
But it was hard to see Sally Birch take her place, even though Sally
was a much-loved and trusted student who promised to call Mrs.
Mann "if any change took place."

Mary went to her husband "just before dawn." There was no
hopeful sign — no improved circulation. She gave him the final
medicine and Mann begged for perfect quiet. "No noise, no whisper,
no footfall, no face."

When the doctor came in, it was decided that Mann should be
told his condition. He "looked a little animated" and asked how long
he had to live. "Three hours," they told him.

"I do not feel as if it could be so," Mann exclaimed and he asked
Mary to take down messages. "Tell Elizabeth I love her dearly and
make her a beautiful present for me — let it cost a hundred dollars."

"I will tell her gladly, for she has loved you dearly," Mary said.
And Mann remembered that he had been "displeased" with Elizabeth
Peabody once or twice but "he repeated that he loved her still."

"I will place you by the side of Charlotte," Mary whispered.

But Horace Mann smiled and said, "If you will promise to lie
down there too. I must lie by you." These words Mary Mann
cherished all the rest of her much longer life. She kept her promise.
But the few moments in which she could speak privately with her
husband were over now. Rebecca arrived.

Owing to the bitterness between them, Rebecca had not seen her
uncle for some time and Mary left them alone together while she
went for the children. "You have been to me, sister, friend, counsellor," she heard her husband say to Rebecca, although this was not

the way Rebecca recorded his words. Later, Mary received a sheet of notepaper with her husband's last words to his niece in Rebecca's handwriting: "You have been to me the loveliest, dearest, gentlest, tenderest, faithfulest daughter, sister, friend, almost wife." After Mary had time to think calmly, she realized that this was Rebecca's final and most cruel exaggeration dictated by a burning desire to be first and to yield first place to no one. Mary brought in the children, Georgie and Benjy — Horace, who had been sent for from the East, had not arrived. The children "wept convulsively" and after "sweet recommendations" from their father that they look to their mother for guidance, she took them upstairs and tried to comfort and quiet them.

"Oh my beautiful plan for the College!" Mann exclaimed, and he "asked for those students who had not yet left Yellow Springs." Mary returned and as the students gathered, his hand which she held grew hot and "wonderful was the sight of him, lately so pale and languid, now so animated. His voice was even stronger than his ordinary voice."

A group gathered around "the low couch near the window" where Mann lay. "He took each student by the hand, spoke his name" and urged him to live according to Antioch's highest ideals. "Or if a student had learned little," Mann urged him to "begin now to pattern his life upon the life of Christ and to live according to divine law."

"The grandeur of his life lifted him without a break to the order of eternity," said one young student who was there.

But, "I doubt if each can remember all that he said," Mary thought, "so great was the excitement of feeling, so wonderful the sight of him." Could this animation be the hopeful sign the doctor had talked about? Mary prayed for a miracle. Three hours went by.

"I feel as if I could sleep now, if all is quiet," Mann said. And Mary tried to clear the room but she was powerless. "Other people began to come, some of whom I had never seen."

"I can sleep now, if there is no noise," Mann said again. And to Mary, "Sing to me, if you have the heart."

"Yes," she said, and in her soft, sweet voice she sang "something without words."

Horace Mann had defied death, the King of Terrors, in a fearless deathbed scene that would become legendary. He had given his last words of counsel to friends, students, even to strangers. And now, said Mary, "they robbed me of my husband and my right to him in his last moments."

The dread coldness invaded Mann's hands again as Mary tried in vain "to warm them in her bosom." She "searched his face for one look of recognition" — but he turned away and she heard the breath catch in his throat. "I could never tell him of my love again or hear him tell me his . . ."

The college bell tolled when Horace Mann was gone. They draped the chapel in black and when, on the night of August 4, they laid him in the college grounds, rain fell upon the open grave. "I did not go to the college when they carried him there," Mary wrote. "I could not." It would be a long time before Mary Mann could forget her bitterness. "If he had not been vivid with life, buoyant with hope, rejoicing in victory, brave against any odds, running over with power, I should be more easily resigned," she said. But the time would come when she could rejoice because Horace Mann was all these things — forever.

Back in Boston, Dr. Samuel Gridley Howe wrote Theodore Parker that he was expecting his dear friend Horace Mann for a visit any day. Word came that Mann had been ill of "an ordinary attack of typhoid fever" [3] but was recovering rapidly. Howe opened his sealed letter to add dreadful news — Horace Mann was dead!

Elizabeth Peabody went with Horace, Junior, to Yellow Springs "as quickly as steam could carry us" — but Mann "was in his grave." Young Horace rushed weeping into his mother's arms and she comforted him. Yet Mary Mann shed no tears. She went silently about the business of breaking up her home and leaving for the East — for "Wayside" in Concord, which Sophia Hawthorne had offered her as temporary shelter.

True to her promise, Mary brought her husband to lie beside Charlotte, his beloved first wife. This second burial was a ceremony she could attend, for she had begun to believe again the beautiful words she had ordered carved upon her husband's monument in North Burying Ground, Providence: "This mortal shall put on immortality."

Mary educated her boys, wrote of her husband's life, and once more formed a teaching partnership with her sister Elizabeth — this time helping to establish the first free kindergartens in America. Bitterness against those who had made her husband's path difficult faded from Mary's mind. She remembered many true friends in Yellow Springs, and still loved Ohio, where once she had thought to live all her declining years with her husband "on our beautiful farm." To renew faith and to forget bitterness — Mary Mann had strength of soul for these things. But loneliness remained. When Sophia lovingly begged Mary to cease grieving, she replied, "But my darling, if your husband should die you would wish to be very sure that he was near. . . . You would cry aloud as I do sometimes, 'Where are you in the universe!' And no echo even would tell you where."

Long years later, Mary wrote to Adelia Gates, a dear friend in Yellow Springs. "My children saved me. George, a little boy then, clung to my side and never left me till one day I remember his saying, 'There, she has smiled.' "

Mann's friends in Boston were shocked by his sudden death, and some of them must have felt that they had failed him in those last years. Dr. Samuel Gridley Howe, who had done everything in his power for Mann always, was moved to action. A few years previously, a statue of Daniel Webster had been placed before the Massachusetts State House and Howe was so incensed he humorously suggested that Mann's friends get ropes and pull the statue down and dump it in the Frog Pond. But now was the time to correct Boston's mistake in a more practical manner.

Howe circulated a petition and raised money for a bronze statue of Horace Mann to be placed opposite that of Webster. Thousands of school children contributed their pennies to the fund. School children were massed upon the State House lawn and sang together as the statue was unveiled, and their great benefactor stood forth — all bright and glorious reflecting the sunlight. Webster's statue had grown dark and tarnished, Dr. Howe observed — but Horace Mann shone like an archangel.

Children troop down city streets or they gather at country crossroads waiting for the school bus — all over these United States. Large or small, famous or unknown — it is still a HORACE MANN SCHOOL which thousands attend. Or if a school has not this magic name graven in granite over the door, then somewhere a vivid face smiles down upon the children from a photograph on the wall — or a plaque with a fine profile bears the words: BE ASHAMED TO DIE UNTIL YOU HAVE WON SOME VICTORY FOR HUMANITY.

Not in the United States alone, but in many lands, children in free schools are Horace Mann's living memorial. Mann's words have been translated into many languages and devoted teachers have taught rising generations "to obey their own laws" or "be held in bondage to the law of tyrants." It is a hard lesson, not always understood, but those who teach and those who listen are winning their victory for humanity. They are the living proof that Horace Mann's whole life was victory.

Notes

The Mann Family — Afterwards

MARY MANN bought a home for herself, her sister Elizabeth, and the boys in Concord. The house is still standing, Number 7 Sudbury Road, just across from the Concord Public Library. Mary's boys went to Frank Sanborn's famous school, just cross-lots from their house, and when they were ready for Harvard their mother sold the Concord house and bought one in Cambridge at 29 Follen Street. The story of her subsequent years has already been told in *The Peabody Sisters of Salem*.

YOUNG HORACE MANN became a botanist. The little boy who learned somewhat reluctantly about *Lupus et Agnus* grew up to handle botanical Latin as though it were his native tongue, publishing a *Catalogue of the phaenogamous plants of the United States east of the Mississippi, and of vascular cryptogamous plants of North America, north of Mexico.* (Prof. Benjamin Carroll Tharp of the University of Texas tells me that, in plain English, young Horace was talking about ferns, ground pine and horsetail!) Young Horace Mann visited Hawaii and in 1866 he published *Revision of the genus Schiedea, and of Hawaiian Rutaceae* which he followed with *Enumeration of Hawaiian Plants.* (And this, Dr. Tharp says, had to do with pinks and members of the orange family.)

As already noted, young Horace took a botanical trip westward with Thoreau in 1861 — Thoreau then being ill with tuberculosis. I do not know how long it was before Horace was known to have tuberculosis. Many remedies were tried in vain, and Mrs. James H. Woods writes me that she once lived in Mary Mann's Cambridge house and that there was a window of blue glass, which had been installed in the hope that the sunlight passing through this glass would have a therapeutic value. Mary Mann's hopes seem pathetically futile — but are not the sun's rays still divided for the alleged benefit of mankind, by means of various sunlamps?

Young Horace died November 11, 1868, aged twenty-four. Horace Mann 3rd has recently sent me an account of this young great-uncle's death, written by George Mann:

"A few minutes before 8 P.M. Horace coughed a little harder than usual, and mother spoke to him. . . . She went out a minute and returned to find him . . . gasping for breath. She called me, who tried to raise him a little but he gasped five or six times, at intervals of a few seconds, and ceased to breathe.

"He had been comfortable all day. After his pain was driven out this morning he said he almost wished he had it to drive out again, it felt so deliciously. He wanted mother to be with him all the time, kept repeating how comfortable he was and wanted to continue just as he was. He enjoyed the day, it seemed, as much as any one [day] in his life."

Miss Elizabeth Hoxie sent me a clipping from a Washington paper at the time of BENJAMIN MANN's death in 1925. He too was a botanist, but was also at one time President of the "Kolumbia Esperanto-Asocio." Perhaps his acquaintance from the cradle with French, German and Latin led him to hope that one language might do for all mankind someday! He "left one-fourth of his estate to the American Association for the Advancement of Science to study the causes of poverty in Massachusetts" and "three-eighths of the estate was left to the Massachusetts Historical Society to care for the works of Horace Mann and Elizabeth Peabody . . . and for research into the genealogy of the Mann and Peabody families. A bequest went also to the Peabody House in Boston."

GEORGE MANN, the middle son, became Principal of the High School in Jamaica Plain — taking up the profession which would have pleased his father best. His only son and the only representative of the third generation was named Horace Mann. As the years went by, George Mann called daily upon his mother and his Aunt Elizabeth, two aging ladies living together bound by deep affection — and enjoying as much peace and harmony as their strong personalities would permit.

A letter by Elizabeth Peabody to Miss Lewis of Yellow Springs was brought to my attention through the kindness of Miss Louette Thompson while I visited Yellow Springs. It is the only account of Mary Mann's death that I have seen. The date is March 27 — without the year, which was 1887.

MY DEAR MISS LEWIS:

Your letter to Mary and me arrived this morning, & was brought and read to me by my nephew; but Mary is no longer *here!* She ascended into heaven the 11th of February, after weeks of pain & weakness of body that made those that loved her rejoice that she had not to draw another breath on this scene of things, that she so ardently desired to be freed from . . .

It seems that Mary suffered severely from rheumatism and five days before her death, after finishing a letter to her son Benjamin, she said that she could never write another letter, "for her fingers were so stiff." But the next day came a letter from an old friend telling of family tragedy.

" 'I will answer that letter,' " Mary said, "and immediately got up out of the chair she had been sitting in — without help — not having been able to do so for more than a fortnight. . . . She went into her own chamber that opens out of mine," Elizabeth told, "sat down at the table — and wrote a long letter with flying pen — sealed and stamped it and gave it to me for the post office. I said, 'Aren't I to see this letter?'

" 'No,' said she, 'there is a secret of hers alluded to in it that I have no right to tell you' " — so Mary Mann was her independent self to the very end of her life, and Elizabeth the loving but all too interested sister must still occasionally be put in her place!

"I tell you this," Elizabeth went on, "to prove to you how completely she was herself (an eternal self) . . . That was the last letter she wrote and I am going to write my friend to send me a copy of what in the letter was not strictly private." So if Mary was herself to the end, so was Elizabeth — with the last word!

Chapter Notes

The purpose of these notes is to add material impossible to include in the text without breaking the current of the story. Questions have occurred to me while reading letters and diaries, and when the answers I have been able to find proved interesting I have placed them here in the Notes, so that readers may share my pleasure.

There are instances where my facts drawn from letters and diaries differ from printed sources. Wherever this seems to me to be of any interest I have indicated in the notes my reasons for such disagreement. But this is not a textbook, and the sort of notes proper to textbooks would be out of place in this biography, which attempts to bring to life a man who was not only important to his country's development but also a human being. I include no bibliography but I enjoy paying my just debts of gratitude to authors whose books I have used and I also mention books on my subject or my period which I think others might enjoy.

CHAPTER ONE: *Mr. Mann of Dedham*

1. Receipted bills among the Mann papers at the Dedham Historical Society provide details for the young lawyer's wardrobe. In February, 1828, Horace Mann paid Ruth Thymes of Dedham "$.25" for "putting buttons on a Gt. Coat" and "$.25" for "altering the silk in the skirts of Gt. Coat." Mann owned a plaid cloak but in November, 1826, this was already so faded that he paid Ruth Thymes $2.50 for "Turning" it and $.63 for adding a "Fur Collar and Hooks." It would seem that the greatcoat was the newer garment and therefore more suitable to wear on opening day in January at the State House.

On January 27, 1829, Mann paid $40.00 to C. Golderman for "1 Super Black coat and pantaloons" and this essential outfit for a rising young lawyer was made to last a long time with "Black Frock Coat and pantaloons" frequently listed for small repairs by Ruth Thymes.

For summer clothes, the village dressmaker would have to do her best. In July, 1827, Mann had Ruth Thymes make him "a pr. white pantaloons" and a "white Marseilles vest." She charged $3.75 for each. Mann bought a hat for $8.00, an extravagance, doubtless. But he traded in his old hat for a dollar.

2. Mention of Mann's unusually erect posture is made by Dr. Samuel Gridley Howe, in criticism of the Stebbins statue of Horace Mann in front of the State House in Boston.

In the course of my search for an accurate description of Horace Mann, I wrote the Department of State asking if a Horace Mann passport were on file. H. B. Shipley, Chief of the Passport Division, very kindly replied. Passport No. 1281 was issued on April 25, 1843, to Horace Mann. The description is as follows: "Age 46; stature, 5 ft. 11¼ in.; forehead, high; eyes, grey; nose, large; chin, long; hair, grey; complexion, light; face, long." This passport was issued for Mann's wedding journey after his second marriage and I had hoped to find a description of Mary Peabody Mann. But in 1843 a married woman had no passport, and Mary's only identification consisted in the phrase, "Accompanied by his lady."

In Mary Mann's opinion, Mann's eyes were not gray. Writing to her husband on May 10, 1848, shortly after the birth of their third son, Benjamin, Mary said:

"We were talking about Benjy's eyes this morning and I said to Horace, 'They are the color of those beautiful violets.'

"'And so are papa's eyes, mama, aren't they?' — Did I not tell you so?"

3. The Codfish witticism and mention of the mills along the Merrimack is from the *Rhode Island and Providence Gazette*, Jan. 9, 1829.

4. *Dorothea Dix: Forgotten Samaritan,* by Helen Marshall, is a most interesting book with chapters dealing with the care of the insane which combine with Mann's reports to give a picture of his first crusade.

5. Horace Mann's proposal of marriage is the first letter in a series made available to me by Mrs. Manning A. Williams and Mr. Sydney Williams — as I have mentioned in my Acknowledgments.

CHAPTER TWO: *Wrentham Road*

1. Material for this chapter was supplied by Mr. Horace Mann, 3rd, and comes also from an unpublished monograph on file in the Seymour Morris Reading Room at the New England Historic Genealogical Society, Boston: "The Reverend Samuel Man, A.B. (1647–1719), compiled for Chauncey Devereux Stillman by Winifred Lovering Holman, S.B." The Reverend Samuel's letter to his children is there quoted in full. The names of his eleven children are there recorded, and it is interesting

to note that the six sons all lived to maturity, married, and spread abroad the name of Man — later spelled Mann.

2. The story of the burning of Wrentham is from *A History of the Town of Wrentham* by Mortimer Blake. This history is valuable, since it was published only twenty years after the death of Horace Mann; but, like most town histories, it is laudatory to an astonishing degree, full of folk tales which add charm but must be taken with a grain of salt. I have used dates found in Miss Holman's recent and painstaking study.

CHAPTER THREE: *King of Terrors*

1. "Miss R. Pennell says, that in her childhood she used to see Rev. Dr. Emmons, an old Orthodox minister, dressed in antique style, with his hair powdered and in a queue, a three-cornered hat, knee-breeches etc. He looked so much unlike everybody else, that it never occurred to her that he was a man, but some other sort of contrivance." So wrote Nathaniel Hawthorne in his *American Notebooks* (edited by Randall Stewart).

2. I own a volume of the Reverend Dr. Emmons's sermons, published in 1796, and I have examined an almost endless number of Emmons's sermons which were subsequently published. In the opinion of many people I interviewed in Franklin, Dr. Emmons's sermons still exist in manuscript, but I traced them as far as the Reverend Jacob Ide, his son-in-law, who edited the long series of volumes. It would appear that after Mr. Ide's death most of the manuscripts were destroyed, but a few have found their way to the library at Congregational House, Boston. From these I learned that Emmons dated a sermon the first time he delivered it and again each time the sermon was repeated. The printed sermons are cut, softened, edited and undated. I quote from a manuscript dated as in text.

3. Bennett Cerf in his column "The Cerfboard," *This Week Magazine*, July 29, 1951, says there are now 33 towns named Franklin. My figure is from *A History of Franklin* and represents the number in Mann's time.

4. The story of the drowning of Stephen Mann was told me by Mrs. Harry F. Saunders. Mrs. Saunders is related to the Mann family and the story was well known to her father and his contemporaries. Family letters also touch upon the subject; but the disgrace was keenly felt, especially by Mann's sister Lydia and their mother, and nothing was openly mentioned.

CHAPTER FOUR: *Tuition Twenty Dollars*

1. I visited Franklin in the hope of finding school records giving the name of Horace Mann's first teachers. Boyish essays written around 1811 and kept, perhaps by a proud and loving mother, indicate that young

Horace met somewhere along the line an unusually fine teacher able to bring out the boy's natural gifts. But school records were not kept in Franklin at that time and although every effort was made to help me, at the school office, the town hall and the library, I found little beyond the names of three teachers: John W. Richardson, Joel Daniels and Hiram Knap.

The town was poor and always in difficulty over raising money enough to keep bridges over their many small creeks. Money was raised in curious ways, as for example "A fine for Profane Swearing — $1.00."

2. The manuscript for "The County Justice" and other early manuscripts are at the Massachusetts Historical Society, as is a copy of the will of Thomas Mann. The beautiful manuscript notebook on mathematics is at the Horace Mann Library, Antioch College, Yellow Springs, Ohio.

3. "Master Barrett" is referred to in various printed sources as Samuel, John and Thomas! Mrs. Harry F. Saunders tells me that Master Thomas Barrett held classes in an upper room in the Daniel Fisher house, which was about a mile from Horace Mann's house in the direction of City Mills.

4. E. I. F. Williams states in his biography, *Horace Mann, Educational Statesman,* that Mann "betook himself, first, to the Williams Academy in the town of Wrentham." But in the John Hay Library, at Brown University, there is a letter written by Horace Mann to Nahum Capen (publisher of the Common School Library), dated June 3, 1850, in which Mann says, "I never attended an academy." Mann was taking exception to statements made in a recent "biographical sketch."

5. Henry Barnard's "Biographical Sketch of Horace Mann, LL.D," published in the *American Journal of Education,* speaks of Mann as "having obtained a reluctant consent from his guardian to prepare for college." I found no record of Mann's having a legal guardian. His older brother Thomas was instructed in his father's will to pay bequests but in the few letters that still exist Thomas expressed nothing but pride and satisfaction in his brother Horace's ambitions.

6. William Angell, for whom Angell Street was named, was one of Roger Williams's "Five Companions," founders of Providence. Mrs. Deborah Messer, wife of President Asa Messer, was descended from this family.

7. One source of material on early days at Brown University is *Memories of Brown,* edited by Robert Perkins Brown, Henry Robinson Palmer, Harry Lyman Koopman and Clarence Saunders Brigham. In this book, the chapter on Horace Mann is by Ira Moore Barton. A children's play has been written, based on the supposition that it was Mann who

broke into the chapel in order to deliver his oration. Little Charlotte pleads with her hardhearted father, Asa Messer, and induces him not to expel Horace. Unfortunately, Mann's letter to his sister Lydia explodes this plot.

President Messer and the Brown of 1819, by Merrill R. Patterson, in the Rhode Island Historical Society Collections, Vol. XXXIV (July, 1941), makes livelier reading; but the sarcastic remarks of a disgruntled student are not to be taken any more seriously than the eulogies older writers produced.

8. I wish to thank Miss Martha Mitchell of Providence, who, with the generous help of the staff of the Brown University libraries, obtained for me the minutes of the United Brothers.

CHAPTER FIVE: *Flute and Flageolet*

1. The preparation of this chapter has brought me a dividend of pleasure in visits to Litchfield, Connecticut, where the beauty and dignity of an earlier day lingers as it does in Salem, Concord, or Dedham.

The rooms of the Litchfield Historical Society in the Wolcott Library are well worth a visit. Rarely have I seen such choice examples of American art and craftsmanship so well displayed. Miss Charlotte Wiggin, Curator, was most helpful in locating for me records, manuscripts, and photographs.

The Tapping Reeve Mansion was restored in 1931 by a group of lawyers, including Chief Justice William Howard Taft. The "Office," which had been hauled away by cart and several yoke of oxen, has been rescued from falling into ruin and restored to its original position in the garden of the Reeve Mansion. Within the house, the Princeton Trustees restored the south wing; members of the Yale Corporation, the north room; and Harvard Alumni, a second-story room. Other donations helped to make this house worth a pilgrimage to Litchfield. It is now open to the public under the auspices of the Litchfield Historical Society. The hostess, Mrs. Clifford Turner, has been especially helpful to me and most patient with my many questions.

Litchfield Law School, according to the Dictionary of American Biography, was "the first — if we except the 'school,' or department, of law at the College of William and Mary."

Material for this chapter comes from the Mann papers in the Massachusetts Historical Society: *Litchfield, First American Law School*, by Burton S. Hill, *Michigan Alumnus*, May 27, 1950; *History of Litchfield, Connecticut, 1720–1920*, compiled for the Litchfield Historical Society by Alain C. White; *Chronicles of a Pioneer School from 1792 to 1833, Being the History of Miss Sarah Pierce and Her Litchfield School*, compiled by Emily Noyes Vanderpoel, edited by Elizabeth C. Barney Buel, A.B.; and *Litchfield Law School, 1774–1833, Biographical Catalogue of Students*, by Samuel H. Fisher.

2. The date *February 15, 1822* is at the head of Mann's letter to his sister Lydia describing his first trip to Litchfield. Further evidence is in *Litchfield Law School, 1774–1833, Biographical Catalogue of Students*, by Samuel H. Fisher (Yale University Press, 1946). Judge Fisher lives in Litchfield and I have been in correspondence with him. On page 8 of his catalogue he says: "The date at the right on the first line of each item is the date of entry of the student to the School as shown by his registration or by his notebook or from other evidence." Then:

"509. MANN, HORACE.   1822."

CHAPTER SIX: *Turbulent Dedham*

1. Dedham's earliest records give the name of the town as "Contentment." Mrs. Chester M. Pratt, one of the directors of the Dedham Historical Society, has given me the explanation from the records. When a "companie" of pioneers from Watertown petitioned the General Court of Massachusetts in behalf of their settlement, they asked to "distinguish our town by the name of 'Contentment' or otherwise what you shall please." At the same session of 1635, another town asked to be called "Concord." The General Court agreed to "Concord" but pleased otherwise when it came to "Contentment." Dedham was the name assigned. Perhaps "litigious and turbulent" Dedham could never have lived up to "Contentment" but Concord and Dedham are sister towns and their kinship is apparent to one who loves them both.

2. Alden's hotel was later the Norfolk Hotel, but in Mann's letters it was familiarly referred to as "Alden's." Receipted bills at the Dedham Historical Society show that on Feb. 17, 1827, Mann paid Alden $5.00 for board for ten days and $17.00 for the use of horse and sleigh on five occasions.

3. Different printed sources give differing dates for Mann's first Fourth of July oration and for his subsequent speeches contributing to his political success. Mann himself was vague about these dates in later years — quite understandably. With the help of my assistant, Mrs. Richard H. Lee, I have located Mr. Mann upon each of a series of Independence days. This was done through Mann's letters to his sister Lydia written from Dedham, from accounts in the Dedham *Village Register and Norfolk County Advertiser;* from the *Memoirs of John Quincy Adams*, edited by Charles Francis Adams, and from *The Works of John Quincy Adams*.

4. When Mary Peabody Mann prepared her biography of her husband, she wrote to Catherine Haven Hilliard for information concerning

Mann's years in Dedham. The story of Mann's social life is from Mrs. Hilliard's letter in reply, Feb. 13, 1860. Catherine's brother Sam married Lydia Sears, close friend of Elizabeth Peabody, who extracted from them the story of Mann and the Haven sisters. Elizabeth, with her love of a romantic tale, wrote it all to Mary, who was in Cuba.

5. It has been stated that Horace Mann was for twelve years a member of the Dedham School Committee. Mann was a resident of Dedham for a little more than nine years, and school records are not available for 1823 through 1832.

6. With the help of maps, old and new, and the kind assistance of personnel at Wrentham and Franklin town halls, my husband and I were able to locate the site of the Eagle Manufacturing Company and the City Manufacturing Company. One rainy autumn day, we visited Pearl Lake, traced the old spillway and discovered huge foundation stones now overgrown with grass and underbrush. Mist hung over the lake, and as we followed the track of an old road hidden under fallen leaves it took very little imagination to recreate the scene of this ill-fated enterprise. We spent a long day at the Dedham Courthouse searching out the documents giving details of purchase and sale, debt, mortgage and foreclosure. I am deeply indebted to my husband, Carey E. Tharp, for his interpretation of the mass of figures collected from these documents.

CHAPTER SEVEN: *Dearest Miss Charlotte*

1. I am indebted to Senator Richard H. Lee of Newton, Massachusetts, for an explanation of the Blandford case in layman's language. Material on this case is from Mann papers at the Massachusetts Historical Society and from periodicals at the library of the Unitarian Society, Boston.

2. *The Memorial History of Boston,* edited by Justin Winsor, gives a description of the Quincy Railroad and so does Bowen's *Picture of Boston.*

3. While preparing her biography of her husband, Mary Peabody Mann read Mann's letters to Charlotte Messer and hers in return. "His most intimate letters of that period . . . cannot be published," Mary Mann decided (*Life of Horace Mann,* page 37). But to her sister Sophia, Mary wrote (Concord, October 18, 1859): "I have been reading, as I told you, all their early and late correspondence and I love to dwell upon that picture of human felicity. . . . His letters are so characteristic of him, that I see him in every line — hers are sweet and loving too, but it is the calm flow of a gentle river instead of the rush of the cataract that one feels in his." These letters were kept in a small box in Mann's desk in West Newton; they were carried to Yellow Springs, came back East

to Concord and were at last given to Caroline Messer Williams, Charlotte's younger sister. I have spoken in the Acknowledgments of the kindness of the Williams family and others in connection with my use of them.

4. Mann's notes on the breach of promise case are in the Dedham Historical Society. Results of the case were found in the vaults of the Dedham Courthouse after patient and diligent search on the part of Mrs. Richard H. Lee and members of the courthouse staff.

CHAPTER EIGHT: *A Fine Gold Ring*

1. Sometime shortly before 1853, John Livingston of the New York Bar decided to include Horace Mann in his *Portraits of Eminent Americans Now Living*. For his material, Livingston usually approached a friend of his intended subject who in turn extorted a letter of reminiscences from the — shall I say *victim!* In Mann's case, the friend may have been Austin Craig, since a few lines from the "letter from a friend" which Livingston quotes can be found in the Mann–Craig correspondence.

Horace Mann's sister Lydia took violent exception to a contemporary biography for overstressing Mann's early poverty. She did not mind the excessively pious tone, however, and Mann himself — although he protested occasionally — allowed his contemporaries to speak of him as they pleased.

I quote a few items from the receipted bills among the Horace Mann papers at the Dedham Historical Society to show that Horace Mann was not the dreariest reformer of them all. He in no way resembled that cartoon figure, the teetotaler, but was temperate in the true sense of the word.

MR. HORACE MANN DR.   BOSTON, *Jan 2 1828*
TO THE EXCHANGE COFFEE HOUSE
5 bots Port $10.00
Washing $1.69
2 tickets for Theatre $2.00
Cards .75
10½ Weeks board at $1.00 per week
Fire and Lights $9.00

It was on January 27, 1829, that Mr. Mann paid for "1 super Black Coat and Pantaloons $40.00." In October of that same year the plaid cloak which Ruth Thymes had turned seems finally to have worn out, for Mann bought a new one for $22.00 — but whether plaid or not, the bill does not say.

2. The house which Horace Mann found for his bride in Dedham has been torn down, but Miss Elizabeth Humphreys, Curator of the Ded-

ham Historical Society, remembers it well and described it for me, finding also an early drawing of Church Green with the church still standing and a corner of Mann's house visible.

3. A letter by Sophia Peabody to her sister Elizabeth gives the following thoroughly baffling description of Charlotte. Charlotte "was about as tall as Eliza Dwight or Sarah Sullivan — with much the same complexion and form as Sarah Sullivan's — very soft and very sweet, with dark eyes and arched brows, if my memory serves me right. She had such a formed face as Sarah Sullivan's, I am very sure."

Josiah Quincy 2nd in *Figures of the Past* describes the William Sullivan family, of whom Sarah was the fourth child, born in 1810. "How that pew (at King's Chapel) used fairly to blossom with the large and lovely family. . . . There was a noble poise about them all." Perhaps somewhere there is a portrait of Sarah Sullivan, twin sister, almost, to Charlotte Messer — at least according to Sophia!

CHAPTER NINE: *Major Mann*

1. Horace Mann's name appears, in the records at the Massachusetts Adjutant General's office, as Judge Advocate of the First Division of Massachusetts Militia from July 13, 1831 to February 3rd, 1843. He held the rank of major but resigned because of "health and engagements." There is no record that he was paid for his services. Albert E. Sargent, Military Archivist, has kindly supplied this information.

2. The *Boston Patriot and Mercantile Advertiser* for February 12, 1830, lists the members of the House of Representatives by occupations as follows: Farmers, 207; Merchants, 126; Lawyers, 60; Mechanics, 44; Manufacturers, 25; Clergymen, 11; Gentlemen, 10; Deputy Sheriffs, 4.

CHAPTER TEN: *A Light upon Earth*

1. There is a tradition in Dedham that Charlotte Messer Mann died in childbirth. In papers placed by the late Miss Abbey Guild in the Dedham Historical Society, Miss Guild recalled that (many years previously) Horace Mann's first wife had died "leaving one child" who was "carried across Church Square" to neighbors "to be nursed." The child was thought to have died after a few weeks or even months. However, a careful search of volumes of vital statistics both by me and by Dr. Worthington, President of the Dedham Historical Society, fails to show any record of such a child — and Dedham records were unusually well kept.

2. It is not now possible to determine the cause of Charlotte's death but almost every allusion to her illness seems to point to tuberculosis, or possibly cancer. It was a common belief that child-bearing strengthened young women of "delicate constitution" but Edward Loring's oblique

references to his own wife's improvement in health are the only intimations I have found that Charlotte might have hoped for a child. Mann's series of descriptions in his diary of Charlotte's death are so detailed that it seems almost impossible for him not to have mentioned a child if child there ever was. There are said to be certain Peabody sisters' letters which I would not be able to obtain permission to see, however, and I am aware that they could contain the proof I seek.

CHAPTER ELEVEN: Somerset Court

1. Found among receipted bills in the Horace Mann papers in the Dedham Historical Society is one from Joel E. Richards headed, "Dedham, August 2, 1832." It is as poignantly tragic today as on that date: "Mahogany Coffin and Trimmings for his wife 25.00. To moving corpse to Providence 12.00." And there is one more sad memorial in a bill paid to Freeman Fisher of Dedham: "One hundred and fifty three dollars and 13/00 in full for ten and a half months Rent of house ending August 15, 1832 ($153.13)."

2. Mann wrote his sister Lydia, August 18, 1832, about the disposition of Charlotte's effects. On November 11, 1832, Lydia wrote her brother that she was making a chain for him of Charlotte's hair. "I am fearful, very fearful, it will not equal your anticipation." These are among the Mann letters at Massachusetts Historical Society.

3. Mary Peabody's description of Mrs. Clarke's boardinghouse is from a letter to Sophia dated February 17, 1833 — also the description of Elizabeth "bright as a diamond." The description of Mary by Sophia is from a letter written February 3, 1851. These manuscripts are in the Henry W. and Albert A. Berg Collection, New York Public Library.

4. Mary Peabody's letter telling of Mr. Mann's sudden departure from Mrs. Clarke's is the property of Nathaniel Hawthorne's granddaughter, Mrs. Beatrix Hawthorne Smyth, and I quote with her kind permission. Readers of *The Peabody Sisters of Salem* will recognize a few letters now quoted again but more fully where they concern Horace Mann. For the most part, Mr. Horace Mann, 3rd, and Mrs. Smyth have provided hitherto unpublished manuscripts for use in this book.

CHAPTER TWELVE: The Honorable Horace Mann

1. Letters from Louisville, Kentucky, and a deposition by Thomas Mann, are at the Massachusetts Historical Society.

2. Mrs. William Ellery Channing referred to Mary Peabody's voice, saying that "its low tones were like a summer evening." In *The 100th Anniversary of the North Church, Salem* Dr. Peabody is mentioned as singing tenor in the choir while "Mrs. Horace Mann sang soprano." She

was still Mary Peabody, of course, and in her early letters she spoke of her father as choosing and arranging the church music. She probably sang whatever part he chose for her.

3. "Estimate of Horace Mann, a Journal of Remembrance" is a manuscript notebook from the Mann collection at the Massachusetts Historical Society. Other details of Mary Peabody's early love for Horace Mann are drawn from miscellaneous unsorted papers in this same collection.

A letter from Mary Peabody Mann to her sister, Sophia Hawthorne, headed CONCORD, *October 5, 1859* mentions "those years when I loved him as one unapproachable by human affection . . . I could have seen him happy with another without ever letting him know my pain in it — so truly and disinterestedly did I love him." This I quote with the kind permission of Mr. Horace Mann, 3rd.

4. Elizabeth Peabody's political campaign for Mann is from the Cuba journal. After Horace Mann withdrew from the Convent Case because of ill health, the newspapers continue mention of a Mr. Mann. This was S. H. Mann, a lawyer from Lowell appointed to represent the rioters.

CHAPTER THIRTEEN: *To Present to the People*

1. From "Institutional Care of the Insane in the United States and Canada," by Henry M. Hurd, Vol. I (Baltimore, 1916), I learn that "the first state institution exclusively for the pauper insane was at Worcester, Massachusetts."

2. I have referred to *Portraits of Eminent Americans Now Living,* by John Livingston, as containing a biographical sketch of Horace Mann not entirely devoid of errors. Let me now do Mr. Livingston justice by saying that his account of Mann's work in codifying the laws is very good. Livingston, being a lawyer himself, understood Mann's legal achievements.

3. The discovery that the Alcotts had been reading Elizabeth Peabody's private correspondence is from a group of unclassified letters at the Massachusetts Historical Society, not available when I was collecting material for *The Peabody Sisters of Salem.* Mary's reply to Elizabeth is among these papers, and after telling Elizabeth to ask Mr. Mann's advice, she proceeds to tell what that advice is sure to be! "I suspect he would agree with me & say it was only justice [a favorite word of Mann's!] & the respect you owe yourself & the cause of truth, to free yourself from any participation in the course or the consequences of Mr. A's mistaken views. . . . I think you are mistaken by sacrificing your own comfort for his convenience — perhaps to *lose* his records would do him good."

Mary was right, of course. But Lizzie did not lose *Conversations on the Gospels.* This book, designed to follow *Record of a School* (many copies of which had been burned in a warehouse fire) was even more ill-fated. It touched off the controversy that ruined Temple School.

CHAPTER FOURTEEN: *Let the Next Generation Be My Client*

1. Horace Mann's first diary is one of the most illuminating of the many documents among the Mann papers at the Massachusetts Historical Society. It begins in 1837 and ends in 1843, and I have used it in all the chapters dealing with these years. It has been suggested that Mann devoted himself to the education crusade from a sense of guilt, assuming that Charlotte died in childbirth. This seems to me a sentimental idea not borne out by the diary or letters. Whether Charlotte died in childbirth or not (and she certainly died of other causes as well), Mann later wrote that he was never particularly "philogenitive." In my opinion, Mann's early struggles to get an education inspired him to help the next generation. He believed and often said that a democracy such as ours could not long continue without an educated voting public, and he fought for his ideals with passion — but not with a sense of guilt.

CHAPTER FIFTEEN: *Lost . . . Two Golden Hours*

1. It is amusing to hear Horace Mann's aphorism "Lost . . . two golden hours . . ." used as part of the commercial on the radio program sponsored by the Longine Symphonette. In *Three Generations*, by Maud Howe Elliott (Boston, 1923), Mrs. Elliott writes: ". . . Some malicious governess taught me a bitter adage, which to this day I repeat, as a penitent plies the scourge on his lacerated back: 'Lost, one golden hour. . . .'" Little Maud, aged three, never dreamed that it was her father's close friend Horace Mann who wrote the "bitter adage."

2. Mann's hasty letter to Packard is in the Massachusetts Historical Society. The best account of this and all the other religious controversies is *Horace Mann and Religion in the Massachusetts Public Schools*, by Raymond B. Culver. Mr. Culver has carefully reread the letters used by Mary Peabody Mann in her biography of her husband — restoring deleted names and passages. These letters are in the Massachusetts Historical Society where I myself have read them, disagreeing only occasionally with Mr. Culver's interpretation of Mann's handwriting!

3. While preparing this book, I visited Framingham Normal School (direct descendant of Lexington Normal) and I want to thank Dr. Martin F. O'Connor, President, Miss Corinne Hall, Head of the Economics Department, and Miss Cora Morse, distinguished alumna, for their help in providing me with books and pamphlets and for the opportunity to meet students and see the school. During the delightful luncheon, cooked and served by students in the Home Economics Department, and during

my tour of the school, I thought constantly of how proud Horace Mann
would be if he could see the growth of that seed planted at Lexington.

4. Quotations from normal school diaries are from *The First State
Normal School in America: The Journals of Cyrus Peirce and Mary
Swift, with an introduction by Arthur O. Norton.* I have already expressed my gratitude to Dr. Norton personally and his book was most
useful. The story of Mary Swift's life is from this same source.

CHAPTER SIXTEEN: *Political Madmen*

1. Horace Mann's sister Lydia was born in 1798 and died in 1888, long
outliving her famous brother. There was a particular bond of affection
between them and Mann's early letters to Lydia are among his best. The
only picture I have been able to find of Miss Lydia Bishop Mann shows
her in later life, a handsome old lady. In the same box of family pictures,
sent me by Mr. Horace Mann 3rd, I found a photograph marked
"Grandma Mann." This was obviously made from another picture and
shows brush strokes. Mrs. Charles W. Harrington recognized this picture
as "the Mother of Horace Mann," and believed a portrait once existed.
I learn that this picture appears otherwise identified, in an album, but I
have accepted this family evidence.

2. During my first visit to Franklin, I was told that a certain resident
"knew all about Horace Mann." I lost no time in calling on Mr. Matthew
J. Van Leeuwen, a delightful old gentleman who operates a nursery garden and greenhouse. Mr. Van Leeuwen told how he became interested in
Horace Mann. It was about 1906 as he recalled, when two foreign gentlemen arrived in Franklin bearing a large memorial wreath! They were
from Brazil and they were looking for the birthplace of Horace Mann
in order to place their wreath upon the door. "Old man Leonard was
cabdriver, then," Mr. Van Leeuwen recalled. "But he was in a quandary
for he'd been driving these gentlemen all over town. He'd been stopping
and asking people who Horace Mann was!

" 'Who, the piano-tuner?' somebody said. Or, 'You mean the printer?' "

The cabdriver and his passengers finally wound up at the office of Carl
B. Johnson, where Mr. Van Leeuwen happened to be sitting — passing the
time of day. Here the foreign visitors were able to make their errand
clear but they were told that the house where Horace Mann, the educator, was born had been torn down and no marker showed the site.
Mr. Van Leeuwen could not recall what became of the memorial wreath.

The earnestness of these foreign visitors impressed Mr. Van Leeuwen,
however, and he got to reading everything he could find about Horace
Mann. He himself came from Holland at an early age and he had had
almost no opportunity for education such as he saw the Franklin boys

and girls enjoying. How could Franklin forget such a citizen as Horace Mann! Van Leeuwen persuaded the local Grange to set aside "Horace Mann Day" and have it celebrated in the schools. Next he raised money for a monument to be placed on the site of Mann's birthplace, and it was a great occasion for him when the great-granddaughters of Horace Mann came to Franklin to unveil the granite stone with its inscription. Franklin's new school was named for Horace Mann now. And Mr. Van Leeuwen brought out many boxes of clippings concerning Horace Mann which he had collected during the years. He intends to bequeath them to the local library, he told me, as we sat together on the lawn beside his garden. Horace Mann would have loved Matthew J. Van Leeuwen!

3. By means of records in the County Court House in Dedham, my husband and I were able to locate the house which Horace Mann bought for his sister Rebecca Pennell. We drove along the road to Wrentham and called upon the present occupants, who explained that they had built over the house completely. Just as we were leaving, however, we were told that the house next door was exactly like the Mann house but had never been remodeled! I stopped and made a rough sketch of this house — which I describe.

4. After Horace Mann's death, Mary Peabody Mann wrote to a nephew of George Combe asking for her husband's letters to be used in the biography she was preparing. Combe's nephew refused to part with them but allowed Sophia Peabody Hawthorne, who was then in Europe, to copy them. He underlined all passages which he considered unsuitable for publication; Sophia dutifully underlined her copies, and Mary agreed to delete. These copies are now at the Massachusetts Historical Society and the underlined passages make the best reading. There is nothing indiscreet in them, of course. They are the human touches. Disregarding the prohibition of this long-dead nephew, I have replaced these passages in Horace Mann's letters wherever they add interest.

CHAPTER SEVENTEEN: *The Auspicious Years*

1. The political history of Massachusetts and of Boston in particular is complicated but fascinating. I have consulted many sources, but faithful to my promise not to include boring bibliographies, I will mention only those which I consider really worth reading. *Boston's Immigrants, 1790–1865*, by Oscar Handlin, is a splendid study. It combines a high degree of scholarship with readability. *Personal Recollections*, by Robert S. Rantoul, gives an excellent contemporary picture. *Civilized America*, by Thomas Colley Grattan, who was British Consul in Boston in Governor Everett's time, gives an outsider's viewpoint which must have been infuriating when written but which is now merely amusing.

CHAPTER EIGHTEEN: *On Earth No Other Treasure*

1. Correspondence between Mary Peabody and Mary Jane Quincy was among the papers recently discovered and sent me by Mr. Horace Mann, 3rd. These letters are now in the Berg Collection at the New York Public Library.

The Articulate Sisters, edited by M. A. DeWolfe Howe from letters and diaries, gives a delightful picture of the Quincy family.

2. The Hotel Albion was on the northeast corner of Beacon and Tremont Streets. Photographs at the Bostonian Society, taken after Horace Mann's time, show a building with bay windows and wrought-iron balconies. *The Boston Evening Transcript* of January 4, 1888, printed what might be called an obituary of the old hotel as follows: "The work of demolition (of the Albion) began yesterday. The location as a residence was first utilized by James Penn, an elder of the First Church. Succeeding him was James Russell Lowell Jr., founder of the Lowell Institute. . . . Mr. Lowell's immediate successor was the founder of a famous family here, Samuel Eliot, a leading dry goods merchant, the grandfather of President Eliot of Harvard College. It then had delightful garden surroundings, its own garden extending back to what is now known as the Congregational House. . . .

"The Eliots were the last family to occupy the site, and then came the Albion, changing the aspect of the neighborhood materially, and became the abode of many prominent people who preferred hotel to home life. Major Barton was its most celebrated keeper. . . ."

In *The Saturday Club*, by Edward Waldo Emerson, I find: "First meetings of the Saturday Club were at the Albion . . . a bachelors' hotel."

CHAPTER NINETEEN: *Accompanied by His Lady*

1. See Note 2, Chapter One.

2. This second of Horace Mann's diaries was sewed together with the pages out of order toward the end. The manuscript is in the Massachusetts Historical Society Mann papers, and may be a copy of rough notes taken from time to time and discarded. I have omitted mention of a side trip to Ireland.

3. Julia Ward Howe wrote to her sister Louisa of this trip to Europe, and I quote from *Julia Ward Howe* by Laura E. Richards and Maud Howe Elliott assisted by Frances Howe Hall. Mrs. Mann "wears a monstrous sunbonnet; he [Mr. Mann] lies down in his overcoat. . . ." In the hope of being able to fill out this quotation, which is deleted as I have shown, and to search for other references to Horace Mann, I spent a

few days with Miss Rosalind Richards, granddaughter of Julia Ward Howe. I was unable to locate this particular letter but I wish to thank Miss Richards for her gracious hospitality and kind permission to examine letters.

4. "Elsler" was the ballet dancer who charmed the heart out of Emerson in Boston in 1841. Emerson spelled her name "Elssler." In *Memories of a Hostess*, by M. A. DeWolfe Howe, I find "Ellsler." So I think Mr. Mann is entitled to a third variation.

5. I quote from Mary Peabody's letter to Sophia Hawthorne with the kind permission of Mrs. Beatrix Hawthorne Smyth, to whom the letter belongs.

6. This most human of Horace Mann's diaries was afterwards used for a collection of pressed flowers by Horace Jr. One of these flowers is labeled as follows:

Pulsatella nuttaliana
Redwing Bluff
Redwing
Minn.

June 24, 1861 (Journey with Mr. Thoreau)

This was the journey undertaken in the last year of Thoreau's life when Thoreau's friends had persuaded him to seek a dryer climate in the hope of his regaining his health. Thoreau died of tuberculosis and so, subsequently, did "the young naturalist, Horace Mann" — referred to thus on page 436, in *Thoreau*, by Henry Seidel Canby. Tuberculosis was not then known to be infectious, of course; but the diary which contains the record of the birth of Horace Mann, Junior, contains also flowers collected by him on a journey which may have led to his death. It is in the Houghton Library, Harvard College, Cambridge, Mass.

CHAPTER TWENTY: *Owls in the Sun*

1. Horace Mann's letters to the Reverend Edmund Burke Willson were placed in a letter book which was recently found by his granddaughter, Mrs. Amey Willson Hart, and I quote them with her kind permission. Mrs. Hart's letters have given me the chance to give a sort of case history showing Mann's methods.

2. Bills for the building of Mann's house and developing his property are in the Dedham Historical Society. Guided by early maps of West Newton, and with the kind assistance of Mr. A. Harold Wooster of the Newton Free Library, I visited the site of Horace Mann's house. It is no wonder that he lost his heart to the wooded acres on the hill.

3. Quotations from Sarmiento are from a letter from Sarmiento to

Mary Mann, 1865 from *A Sarmiento Anthology*, edited by Allison Williams Bunkley, and from a biographical sketch by Mrs. Horace Mann in *Life in the Argentine Republic* . . . I want to thank Mrs. Alice Houston Luiggi who, while preparing a book of her own, generously helped me with Sarmiento material.

4. Through the kindness of Mrs. Luiggi, I have recently received reprints from *The Hispanic American Historical Review*, Vol. II No. 2, (May 1952), containing her article called "Some Letters of Sarmiento and Mary Mann, 1865–1876." These are letters written after Horace Mann's death and deal mainly with Mary Mann's efforts to find well-qualified American teachers willing to go to South America. I found Mrs. Luiggi's footnotes particularly useful and from them I gleaned the story of the language mix-up.

5. Mrs. Charles W. Harrington, granddaughter of Thomas Mann, tells me of his success, and of the beauty of his bride, which daguerreotypes attest to. There was a daughter named Mary Peabody Mann, much beloved by her great-aunt for whom she was named; she planned to be a teacher but died in her senior year at Wellesley College.

CHAPTER TWENTY-ONE: *Mann of Massachusetts*

1. The Capen correspondence, which is followed by the Fowle correspondence, is voluminous and complicated. Mann finally received money due him in the form of bonds issued by the town of Orono, Maine. His correspondence with Samuel Downer, who advised him on financial matters, is full of references to the Orono bonds. Mann would not have accepted them if he had had a choice but in the end they were among the best of his investments.

2. The passage from the *Common School Journal* concerning the fate of republics is buried deep in other material, and I have never seen it quoted, although many less striking passages appear often. In this case and in the case of Horace Mann orations, I have decided to cut passages without the usual marks indicating deletions. I have done this for the sake of the appearance on the page and the reader's convenience. No passage has been altered as to meaning, of course.

CHAPTER TWENTY-TWO: *Turning Point*

1. The story of the escape and capture of the slaves is from *Personal Memoirs of Daniel Drayton: 1855*. The subsequent fate of some of the fugitives is from *Key to Uncle Tom's Cabin* by Mrs. Harriet Beecher Stowe. The *Liberator* for December 30, 1853, tells of Drayton's visit to Boston: "His constitution is wholly broken down by his imprisonment. . . . He came on here a few weeks since, hoping to spend some time in

Massachusetts in travelling, and selling his narrative (which has just been published) and thus do something for his own support. . . . He is entirely destitute." The book was advertised in 1854 "Price 25 cts., or 38 cts., in cloth . . . for sale by Bela Marshal, 25 Cornhill."

2. Captain Drayton is buried in the Rural Cemetery, Bedford, Mass. There is no record of his having lived there, so perhaps death overtook him on his travels. Mr. William H. Tripp, Curator of the Old Dartmouth Historical Society and Whaling Museum of New Bedford, has kindly searched the records for me.

3. Material on the trial was sent from the National Archives and Records Service, Washington, D.C., through the kindness of Charles L. Stewart.

4. English had been allowed to escape but to everyone's annoyance he managed to get captured again. There were 74 slaves and 2 white men in jail.

CHAPTER TWENTY-THREE: *Free Soil, Question of the Age*

1. I am indebted to Miss Elizabeth Hoxie for the story of little Benjamin and his Aunt Elizabeth Peabody. Miss Hoxie's grandparents were once at Brook Farm. They knew Miss Peabody well and loved her dearly even when she tried to take a firm hand in their affairs, as evidenced by a letter from Miss Lizzie which Miss Hoxie sent me. Miss Hoxie remembers Benjamin Mann and says that he remained true to science, his Aunt Lizzie notwithstanding, earning for himself the nickname of "Bug" because of his study of entomology.

2. This line is from a letter from Horace Mann to Benjamin Seaver, dated August 2, 1850. The letter was most kindly given me by Mayor Seaver's great-grandson, Charles B. Blanchard.

3. "Gentleman of Property and Standing: Compromise sentiment in Boston in 1850," by David Van Tassel, in the *New England Quarterly*, Vol. XXII, No. 3 (Sept. 1950), gives an excellent detailed picture of the political situation at this time.

CHAPTER TWENTY-FOUR: *Men from Antioch*

1. There were three famous fugitive cases in Boston: that of Shadrach (February, 1851), who escaped, that of Thomas Sims (April, 1851), and that of Anthony Burns (May, 1854). The Burns case is the better known, but Mann was in Antioch when those dramatic events occurred. He wrote anxiously to his friends Downer and Howe, fearing for their safety. The account of the Sims case is from *Reminiscences of Fugitive-Slave Law Days in Boston*, by Austin Bearse.

2. Nieces and nephews were growing up and Miss Lydia, at about

this time, longed for "an opportunity to relieve much suffering and do much good." She proposed to follow in the footsteps of Dorothea Dix, whom she greatly admired. "I intend to take a look within those dreadful walls, next week," she wrote her brother. But Horace Mann told his sister that he felt she was too tender-hearted to become a prison visitor and urged her to teach little children, telling her that she could "help to restrain vice" best by "preparing the rising generation to do right."

In 1850, through her friendship with Mary Messer, Miss Lydia became "Associate Matron and Teacher" at the Providence Association "for the benefit of colored children." The work was difficult, the hours endless and the first year Miss Lydia received eighty-three dollars for her services! Nevertheless, in October, 1855, she again felt she was not doing enough good in the world. She resigned to "engage in missionary work in our city," according to the Association's annual report.

But the orphanage could not survive without Miss Lydia and with the new year, 1856, she agreed to return. She became Matron in 1868 and continued in this capacity until 1871, when she retired at the age of seventy-three. Annual reports of the institution at the Rhode Island Historical Society in Providence contain great praise of Miss Lydia Mann and are also enlivened by letters from Negro orphans for whom homes were found. They wrote to tell their dear Miss Mann of success in farming, carpentry, dressmaking — of prizes received in Bible School.

Recently, an article appearing in the *Norwich Connecticut Bulletin* for February 13, 1951, has been brought to my attention. "Recollections of Bean Hill Set Down by William T. Case" is the title and I quote in part. "The next house around the corner and facing Town Street and the Green was owned and occupied by Charles Williams. He was an intelligent, brazen, out-spoken man. . . . His house was a noted place for meetings of the spiritualists, his wife being a prominent medium. After the death of his wife, by whom he had a daughter, he employed as his housekeeper, the sister of Horace Mann, the celebrated college president. She was also a noted spiritualist. Under the influence of Miss Mann, Williams imprisoned his daughter who was then ten or twelve years old, in the attic. She was kept there a long time without sufficient food, she was severely beaten by her father and the housekeeper. . . ." The story goes on to say that the child jumped out of a window and escaped, was cared for by neighbors, and that a crowd of angry townspeople attacked Williams's house. "While the mob was in pursuit of Williams, his housekeeper escaped. She went to Massachusetts and was never heard of in this section again. . . ." Williams was arrested and sent to prison.

It has been difficult to determine the date of these events, since they are mentioned merely as things remembered by an old man. But I am indebted to Norwich, Connecticut, friends who make it clear that no sister of Horace Mann could have been involved.

Mr. Raymond B. Case of Norwich writes: "My father was born in 1856. . . . Father [Samuel Bailey Case] was one of the lads who rescued Eunice Williams and often told me of the story." Horace Mann had only two sisters, the elder of whom, Rebecca Mann Pennell, died in 1850 — before this eyewitness, Samuel B. Case, was born.

Mrs. Albert Hunt Chase, genealogist, of 1 Sachem Road, Norwich, Connecticut, has kindly consulted town records for me and finds that a guardian was appointed for Eunice H. Williams 29 April, 1867. This must have been very shortly after the arrest of Charles Williams. At that time Miss Lydia B. Mann, only living sister of Horace Mann, was at the Negro orphanage in Providence.

3. In the spring of 1951, I had the pleasure of seeing Antioch for the first time and I shall see it in my mind's eye as forever beautiful. It was a wonderful experience for me, a stranger, to be the guest of President and Mrs. Douglas McGregor and to find warm hospitality awaiting me in their home. I wish to thank everyone at Antioch whose kindness made my stay both fruitful and happy.

4. Letters quoted in this chapter are in the Mann papers, Massachusetts Historical Society of Boston.

5. Material concerning Austin Craig was most kindly furnished by Mrs. Adelaide Craig Snyder, who has sent me books and clippings concerning her father, Austin Craig, President of Antioch after Mann's death, and her mother, the former Adelaide Churchill, who graduated at Antioch's second commencement. The statement of "Christian denomination" beliefs is from *Life and Letters of Austin Craig*, by W. S. Harwood.

6. At Oberlin, during the early years, women "kept silence in public and had their papers read aloud in class by the men students," according to Harlan Hatcher, in *The Buckeye Country: a Pageant of Ohio*. Antioch had the first woman professor, in the person of Rebecca Pennell.

CHAPTER TWENTY-FIVE: *Risk of a New Enterprise*

1. Mr. Doherty wrote Mann, objecting to Mann's proposed course of study. (Dec. 19, 1852; Mann Papers, Mass. Hist. Soc., Boston.)

2. Mann to Mary (Dec. 21, 1852; Mann Papers).

3. The story of the bringing of the railroad to Yellow Springs is from accounts in the newspapers written at the time of Judge Mills's death. New England's innumerable branch railroad lines testify to the fact that this struggle for "the cars" was universal.

4. Mann to Downer (Feb. 13, 1852; Mann Papers).

5. Judging from photographs, Horace Mann's house at Antioch was a gracious, dignified Victorian mansion. That it was a "woman killer," as mentioned in *Pioneering Days at Antioch*, by Lucy Griscom Morgan, I can well imagine — for stud was high and stairs must have been steep and long. This house was burned and the college library stands in its place.

6. Not all of Antioch's towers were finished when Mary Mann arrived.

7. Antioch Hall still stands today and still contrasts sharply with its surroundings — new buildings in the most modern manner. The old Hall is romantic still, defying fashion but having style and appeal all its own. The brick has mellowed and ivy adorns it. And the ivy itself is now old enough to have acquired conflicting traditions! There are those who believe it was brought to Antioch by Sophia Hawthorne, sister of Mrs. Mann. Mary Mann did indeed invite her sister and her sister's famous husband not only to come to Ohio but to settle there. But Horace Mann died while the Hawthornes were still in Europe and I am quite certain that Sophia never went to Yellow Springs. The other tradition about the ivy is fully as interesting, in any case. A Miss Renwick of New York, the original of Burns's "Blue-Eyed Lassie," visited Melrose Abbey in Sir Walter Scott's time and he gave her a cutting of his ivy. She gave some to Washington Irving and it flourished at Irving's place, "Sunnyside," on the Hudson. Miss Altoona Holstein Johnson brought ivy from Irving's home and gave it to Dr. Hill, President of Antioch, after Dr. Craig's brief tenure. Dr. Hill was to plant the ivy at Antioch in memory of Irving.

8. In the Antioch catalogue for 1853–1854 Clay Badger is listed as living at "No. 65 G.H." (Gentlemen's Hall). While a senior (Catalogue, 1856–1857) Clay lived in Antioch Hall, Number 28. He had a "tower room" entered through the chapel and the bell rope came down through it.

CHAPTER TWENTY-SIX: *The Happy Years*

1. The description of Inauguration at Antioch is from a letter by Mary Mann to her father, Dr. Nathaniel Peabody, October 8, 1853, a copy of which has been very kindly loaned me from the Antiochiana file, Horace Mann Library, Antioch. This and other letters were the gift of Mr. Horace Mann, grandson of Horace Mann.

2. I am indebted to Professor James Holly Hanford for the use of his notes on John Phillips, a colorful character we both admire.

3. Pictures of a dreamland Antioch also include a delightful Greek Revival building with a four-columned portico and a low, squat tower. It is somewhat in the style of the home of Judge Mills which is still standing in Yellow Springs.

4. The description of the "female" dormitory is from *Pioneering Days*

at Antioch by Lucy Griscom Morgan, a delightful, all too brief account of Antioch's rebirth under the inspired guidance of her husband.

5. This unhappy prophecy was written before the fire of 1953.

6. I have found *Horace Mann at Antioch* by Joy Elmer Morgan to be one of the best sources of information concerning Mann's Antioch years. This and letters in the Antioch library form the basis for these chapters.

7. Quotations from Clay Badger are from his manuscript diary so kindly loaned me by Mrs. Joseph O. Edwards (the former Adeline Badger, daughter of Clay and Ada Shepard Badger).

8. This state of affairs at Dartmouth was described to me by my father, who graduated there in 1888.

9. This quotation concerning Mann's niece Rebecca is from a letter written by Mary to her husband (Dec. 6, 1852; Mann Papers, Mass. Hist. Soc., Boston).

10. The description of Rebecca's wedding is from the Edwards papers mentioned above.

CHAPTER TWENTY-SEVEN: *Antioch "Saved"*

1. The greater part of the material for these final chapters comes from the Horace Mann Library at Antioch College, Yellow Springs, Ohio. Letters from Mary Mann to her family and friends back home, describing Antioch's early years, have been presented to the college by Horace Mann, 3rd, her grandson. In addition, there are more than two hundred manuscript letters to and from Horace Mann together with pictures, pamphlets and periodicals, preserved under the guidance of Miss Bessie L. Totten, Curator of Antiochiana. I am deeply grateful to Mr. Paul Bixler, head of the Horace Mann Library, and to Miss Totten for their unfailing kindness during my stay at Yellow Springs. I also want to thank Mr. and Mrs. Douglas Crown, Antioch students, for their assistance in copying material for me.

2. "Mustard Seed," an article on Horace Mann by Paul Bixler in the *American Scholar* (1938, Vol. 7), was of particular interest for its summary of Mann's achievement at Antioch.

3. From "Antioch's First President," an article signed "D. H." in *Antioch Notes* for April, 1936, come figures on Antioch's indebtedness. Miss Totten supplies the information that the author of this article was Dorothy Hall, assistant to former President Henderson of Antioch. I have used some of Miss Hall's figures in this and other chapters. They are in round numbers and you can find almost as many different totals as there are letters on the subject. Mr. Mann was angry with Miss Peabody when he heard that she had exaggerated Antioch's debt as she went about so-

liciting funds for the college as well as for her many other good causes.

4. The figure of $3000 is from the letter from Horace Mann to his wife. It represents optimism on both sides.

5. I am indebted to Miss Totten for finding this description of Ada Shepard in *The Making of a Schoolmistress*, an autobiography by Irene Hardy. Ada was "tall, slender and very fair with a shower of golden curls," Miss Hardy writes.

CHAPTER TWENTY-EIGHT: *Final Victory*

1. Waite's interesting letters and Mann's statement of religious faith are at the Horace Mann Library at Antioch.

2. Mann's letter to George Combe about the exemplary students was the last in a long correspondence, for Combe died in 1858.

3. Quotations are from a very long letter to Ada Shepard after her marriage to Clay Badger and after Mann's death. Mary Mann had written reproachfully to Badger after Mann's death, accusing him of disloyalty. Badger produced files of correspondence (which may have been destroyed) and cleared himself. In writing to Ada whom she had always loved, Mary Mann spoke a final word concerning her sixteen years of married life and the relationship between herself and her husband's niece, Rebecca. "I was no match for her wiles, & when my indignation is aroused I speak very plainly. We had had experience before, & she was more afraid of strait (sic) forward bluntness than of anything else. I have written her since & told her that she must not say she sacrificed herself for her Uncle, or that he never wished her to be married to anyone, for those two things I always denied & with explanations & should continue to do so. . . ." This letter is at the Massachusetts Historical Society.

4. Mary Mann collected all of Sophia's letters concerning Rebecca and placed them in one envelope labeled "Badger papers." They were extremely confidential and it would seem that she tucked them safely away. Although Sophia's letters were not dated, the year could not be earlier than 1858 when Ada Shepard entered the Hawthorne household. These letters are now in the Berg Collection, New York Public Library.

5. I have punctuated Downer a trifle. He wrote many remarkable letters and I wish I could quote more — spelling, punctuation and all. Papers in a miscellaneous unsorted file at the Massachusetts Historical Society show that Mann had been investing in Ohio farm mortgages — but just how much money he made or lost I do not know. Mann died without a will. In 1862, the inventory of his estate on file among the Suffolk County Probate Records gives a list of assets almost identical to the one Downer sent. The total was $16,367.14. Downer did well!

CHAPTER TWENTY-NINE: *Think Shame to Die* . . .

1. I have quoted from countless letters written by Horace Mann. Now I am happy to quote one written by his grandson, Horace Mann, the third of that name. "I was delighted this morning to receive your letter of the 6th and to learn that you have 'set your heart' on writing the life of Horace Mann."

Mr. Mann had been looking through a storeroom at his home. "During my search I looked into a big wooden box. On top of it was an old shoe box, marked on one end, in my mother's handwriting, 'Feathers and ribbons.' When I picked it up, I said, 'Feathers and ribbons, my aunt!' I looked inside . . . and it was jammed with old letters. I have now read nine tenths of them. Night after night, since I began, I have dreamt that you, armed with a rolling pin, were hovering over me and intoning, 'Why, when I particularly asked you if you could not find any more old family letters, didn't you make a real search?' *Hinc illae lachrimae.* But if you will only stick to your guns I think a few of the letters may give you some interesting side lights on my grandfather."

My friend, the present Mr. Mann, writes with his grandfather's humorous touch — but I do not belabor with rolling pins a person who has been so unfailingly kind, helpful and encouraging! I only thank Mr. Mann for helping me to correct an error. It was from these letters that I learned for the first time that Mary Mann had been by her husband's side during that terrible deathbed scene. All the letters Mary Mann wrote describing her husband's death she put aside and they did not reach the Massachusetts Historical Society with the Benjamin Mann papers. I have since found one letter from Mary Mann to her sister-in-law Lydia Mann, at the Massachusetts Historical Society in a folder I have referred to as unsorted — not previously available. I had not realized that Mary's words to her niece Rebecca (October 2, 1859), "the privation of all I most desired in those last hours of which I was robbed," and similar expressions in other available letters, were figurative rather than literal. *The Peabody Sisters of Salem* was then in print, but as soon as possible, some corrections were made and I now wish again to express my gratitude to Mr. Mann for looking once more in his attic — so that I could rewrite the scene.

2. I am indebted to William A. Drayton, Chief of the Division of Dendrology and Range Forage Investigation, United States Department of Agriculture, for his thoughtful answers to my queries concerning "milk sickness." My information in this chapter is from his letter and a pamphlet written by him, *Stock-poisoning Plants of the Eastern Seaboard* and from *Diseases Transmitted from Animals to Men* by Thomas G.

Hill. Further help was given by the staff of the Library, Metropolitan Life Insurance Company, New York City. It is not possible to diagnose Horace Mann's fatal illness now, but in my opinion his last remarkably lucid hours rule out milk sickness — which ends in a coma, generally.

3. The symptoms of typhoid are similar to those of milk sickness. It was customary to give champagne and this was tried in Mann's case, but caused distress. Mann turned his face to the wall. "Give me the Allen-thrust," he said, referring of course to Ira Allen's treacherous treatment.

Typhoid was not unknown in Yellow Springs, for Ira Allen in his diary (April 4, 1850) wrote "Taken sick with what I called a slight cold but which proved to be typhoid fever of the slow variety." The Allen diary is at the Horace Mann Library, Antioch College. If Allen could be proved to have been what is now called a "typhoid carrier," then indeed truth would be stranger than fiction! It is not necessary to go so far for a source of possible infection, however. Regular wells had failed and the Mann family were using water from an unknown source, possibly polluted. On August 4, 1859, Mary Mann wrote her sister Sophia, "Six weeks ago Benjy was seized with a typhoid fever."

Whether he had milk sickness or typhoid, Mann's resistance was low and Mary was right when she felt that overwork and anxiety played their part in cutting short his life.

Acknowledgments

Before beginning this biography, I wrote to HORACE MANN, grandson of the great educator, to ask him if he planned to use his family letters for a similar purpose. Mr. Mann replied that he had "considered the matter seriously for some time," but he felt that he would be "handicapped by being a grandson." With generosity typical of his famous grandfather, Mr. Mann has helped me in every possible way. I wish to express my heartfelt thanks.

I am also deeply indebted to MRS. MANNING A. WILLIAMS and MR. SYDNEY M. WILLIAMS for the use of their unpublished letters of Horace Mann and his first wife, Charlotte Messer Mann. "A small trunk filled with letters," wrote Mrs. Williams, came to her late husband and his cousin through the sister of Charlotte, Caroline Messer Williams. In making these letters available to me, the Williams family have opened an entirely new phase of Horace Mann's life. They have made it possible for me to present, not only Mann the educator, but Mann when he was young, successful in law and politics, ambitious — and in love. My thanks go also to Dr. Arthur O. Norton, formerly Professor of Education at Wellesley College and lecturer in the Harvard Graduate School of Education. Mr. Sydney Williams had, some time ago, given his friend Dr. Norton the use of the Mann–Messer letters. Dr. Norton graciously loaned me his photostats of these letters, which ill-health had prevented him from using. He also gave me the benefit of his comments and notations — a gift beyond price.

I wish to thank MRS. LEILA HARRINGTON, great-granddaughter of Horace Mann's brother Thomas, for family photographs, books, clippings and much interesting information about Mann's nieces and nephews.

MRS. HENRY SNYDER, daughter of Austin Craig, has most kindly furnished me with books, clippings and excerpts from the diary of this young friend of Mann's Antioch days. I am grateful to Mrs. Joseph O. Edwards for the use of the Antioch diary of Henry Clay Badger and letters of Ada Shepard — her grandparents. Mrs. Harry F. Saunders, a connection of the Mann family and a native of Franklin, supplied me with interesting and valuable details concerning Mann's early life, as did Miss Margaretta Sullivan of the public library in Dedham, her native town. Miss Elizabeth Hoxie was most helpful in contributing information, since her grandparents were friends of Miss Elizabeth Peabody.

The bulk of the Horace Mann letters and diaries, as indicated in my notes, are in the Massachusetts Historical Society. The Mann Collection, bequeathed to the Society by Benjamin Mann, Horace Mann's youngest son, contains letters from the Peabody sisters, from Sumner, Howe, Governor Edward Everett — all Mann's associates. Raymond B. Culver, author of *Horace Mann and Religion in Massachusetts*, estimates that Mann wrote an average of thirty letters a day in 1838. During Mann's twelve years as Secretary of the Massachusetts Board of Education, the number of letters he wrote and received rises to the astronomical. The mere handling of this material is hard labor, yet the Director and Staff at the Massachusetts Historical Society have been cordial and unfailingly helpful during all the many months when I daily darkened their doors!

Antioch College has, I think, the second largest collection of Horace Mann letters, pamphlets and information. I want to thank President Douglas McGregor for his kind co-operation. Professor Holly Hanford was more than generous in allowing me the use of an unpublished manuscript concerning Mann and also most valuable notes. This scholar's gift of time and critical judgment I appreciate greatly. I also wish to thank Mr. Paul Bixler, Director of the Horace Mann Library at Antioch, and Miss Bessie L. Totten, Curator, Antiochiana, who knows Antioch's history through long and careful study and who put in uncounted extra hours to answer my questions.

I want to thank Mr. Bruce Bigelow, vice president of Brown University. Miss Marion E. Brown, in charge of Special Collections at the Library of Brown University, has been most helpful in placing Mann material at my disposal and in suggesting fields of further investigation.

At the Dedham Historical Society are folders of Mann's legal papers. I want to thank Mrs. Chester M. Pratt, prominent member of the Society, Dr. Arthur M. Worthington, president, and Miss Elizabeth Humphreys, curator of the Dedham Historical Society; also Mr. William E. Everett and members of the staff of the Dedham Courthouse, and Senator and Mrs. Richard Lee, who led me through the mazes of Mr. Mann's legal notes!

As in the past, the New York Public Library was an invaluable source of information. I wish to thank DR. JOHN GORDAN, Curator of the Henry W. and Albert A. Berg Collection, AND HIS STAFF for their kindness in making acquisitions, both new and old, quickly available. MR. IVOR AVELINO of the American History room was most helpful and co-operative.

I am most grateful to MISS ROSAMOND RICHARDS for permission to read the letters of Horace Mann to Dr. Samuel Gridley Howe. DR. HAROLD BOWDITCH has assisted me with explanations of medical references found in letters.

Other sources of material, some of which are further mentioned in the Notes, are the Massachusetts State Library, the Congregational House Library, and the Unitarian Association Library; the New York Historical Society; and the Boston Public Library (both of the latter especially valuable for files of contemporary newspapers); the Boston Athenæum; the New England Historic Genealogical Society; the Bostonian Society; the Houghton Library of Harvard University; the Framingham Normal School Library; the Litchfield Public Library and the Litchfield Historical Society of Litchfield, Connecticut; the Columbia University Library; the Ferguson Library, Stamford, Connecticut; the University of Rochester Library; the Library of Congress and National Archives, Washington, D.C.

The list is so long that I have not space to mention by name all those whose kindnesses have made this book possible, but some further acknowledgments occur in the Notes. Many, also, are the friends of *The Peabody Sisters of Salem* who have written helpful letters telling of family connections with Mr. Mann. They have shed much light on my subject and I wish I could name them all.

Index

mal schools, 164–167; enemies become friends, 167; sells old family homestead, 168; buys home for widowed sister, 169; first vacation, 171; admires Middle West, 172; builds Normal Schools, 174–176; Fourth of July oration in Boston, 177, 178; sees much of Mary Peabody in Boston, 182–185; marriage to Mary, 186–189; European honeymoon, 190–192; visits schools, 191, 194, 195, 198; admires British railroads, 192; visits prisons, 193; goes to a German fair, 195; amusing difficulties with German language, 196, 197; visits Leyden, 197; glad to turn homeward, 198; writes "Seventh Report," 198; first son born, 199; attitude toward child, 200; birth of a second son, 201; fights for religious freedom in the schools, 205–207; new home in West Newton, 210–215; resumes politics, 216; in Washington, 218; anxious about Mary's expected child, 219–221; a third son, 221; writes final school report, 222; sounds a warning concerning the fate of Republics, 223; takes antislavery stand, 227; defends Drayton and Sayres, slavery case, 230–234; maiden speech in Congress, 235, 236; is praised in Boston, 236; elected to Congress, 237; a father to his boys, 238–242; lectures, 241, 256–259; LL.D. from Harvard, 241; ardent for Free Soil, 243–246; challenges Webster, 246–249; buys a gift for Mary, 250; final legislative term in Washington, 246, 265; meets men from Antioch, 259; runs for Gov. of Mass., 261; accepts Presidency of Antioch, 261; plans ideal college, 264, 265; first faculty meeting, 265; goes West, 265–269; final Mass. controversy, 269, 270; arrives Ohio, 271; inaugural, 274–276; organizes college, 278; teaching described, 279; discovers Antioch's financial predicament, 284, 296, 304, 306; attempts remedies, 285–288, 306, 307–309; first commencement, 291–293;

frames "code of honor," 292–294; offered Presidency Iowa State, refuses Northwestern, 295; joins church in Yellow Springs, 296, 297; religious controversy, 298; states right to private religious belief, 299; difficulty with students, 300, 301; trouble among faculty, 301–306; personal finances, 307; sees ultimate victory, 309; plans trip to Boston, 309; last Baccalaureate, 310; last illness, 311–313; death, 314; memorial statue, 315; Horace Mann schools, 315; namesake, 318; biography of, by Mary Mann, 327

Mann, Horace, Jr., 212, 219, 238, 242, 247, 252, 258, 270, 309, 313, 314, 317, 318, 322, 336

Mann, Horace, 3rd, 318, 322, 331, 335, 341, 342, 344

Mann, Lydia (sister of Horace Mann), 20, 25, 28, 33, 34, 37, 42, 44, 46, 47, 51, 53, 54, 73, 78, 81, 93, 96, 125, 157, 168, 189, 214, 219, 220, 257, 323, 325, 326, 328, 330, 333, 338–340, 344

Mann, Mrs. Mary Peabody (second Mrs. Horace Mann), 169, 209, 214, 227, 229–232, 235, 237, 262, 266; meets Horace Mann, 101; her beauty, 103–105; attempts to cheer Horace Mann, 106–109; falls in love, 112–114; goes to Cuba, 114–116; receives letters from Horace Mann, 117, 119, 121; hears of Mann's attentions to her sister, 124, 126; asks if Elizabeth loves Horace Mann, 127; returns to Salem, 128; starts a school, 130, 132; her "sisterly" friendship, 134; hopes deferred, 138; describes Mann's Salem speech, 142; writes for the *Common School Journal*, 158; sees Mann in Boston, 178–182; her Boston school, 183, 184; happiness in helping Horace Mann, 185; engaged to marry, 186–188; wedding and journey, 189–195; expects a child, 196, 197; helps her husband with 7th Annual Report, 198; her first son is born, 199; as a mother, 200; her second son, 201; her primer, 204; describes new home, 211;